Germaine Dulac

Women and Film History International

Series Editors
Kay Armatage, Jane M. Gaines, and Christine Gledhill

A new generation of motion picture historians is rediscovering the vital and diverse contributions of women to world film history whether as producers, actors, or spectators. Taking advantage of new print material and moving picture archival discoveries as well as the benefits of digital access and storage, this series investigates the significance of gender in the cinema.

A list of books in the series appears at the end of this book.

Germaine Dulac

A Cinema of Sensations

Tami Williams

University of Illinois Press
Urbana, Chicago, and Springfield

Manufactured in the United States of America
1 2 3 4 5 C P 5 4 3 2 1
∞ This book is printed on acid-free paper.

Library of Congress Cataloging-in-Publication Data
Williams, Tami, 1970–
Germaine Dulac: a cinema of sensations / Tami Williams.
pages cm. — (Women and film history international)
Includes bibliographical references and index.
ISBN 978-0-252-03847-1 (cloth: alk. paper)
ISBN 978-0-252-07997-9 (pbk.: alk. paper)
ISBN 978-0-252-09636-5 (ebook)
1. Dulac, Germaine, 1882–1942—Criticism and interpretation.
I. Title.
PN1998.3.D745W66 2014
791.4302'33092—dc23 [B] 2014003225

For Valerie, Janet & Doris

Contents

Acknowledgments

Many film scholars, teachers, archivists, editors, and research institutions made this project possible. My first thanks go to Dulac scholars Sandy Flitterman-Lewis, and Prosper Hillairet, who led me to discover the filmmaker and her rich oeuvre, and to Rodolphe Lussiana of the Cinémathèque française and Christian Lebrat, director of Éditions Paris expérimental, who first gave me the opportunity to view and publish on these films in France. My inspiring undergraduate film studies mentors, Edward Branigan, Mary Desjardins, Janet Walker, Mark Williams, and Charles Wolfe, set me on this path at UC-Santa Barbara; and the brilliant Carlo Ginzburg, Peter Wollen, Dudley Andrew, and Yuri Tsivian, helped shape my archival research methodology during my doctoral studies and graduate coursework at UCLA, the University of Iowa, and USC. I could not have accomplished this project without the dedicated personal mentorship, archival guidance, and attentive manuscript readings of my UCLA doctoral chair, Janet Bergstrom, and the faithful support of my committee members, Stephen Mamber, Patricia Harter, and the sadly missed Teshome Gabriel. All of these amazing scholars and mentors continue to inspire me to cast my own research broadly across media, and across national and disciplinary boundaries. My deep gratitude goes to my discerning readers Peter Dreyer, Alison McKee, and Charles O'Brien, my generous, talented, and indefatigable copyeditor Deborah Oliver, my enthusiastic and steadfast editors Joan Catapano, Daniel Nassett, and Jennifer Clark, and the University of Illinois Press for their faith in this book. Thanks also to Kay Armatage, Jane M. Gaines, and Christine Gledhill, who created the Women and Film History International series, in which I am honored to have this book included.

Several years of research in France and an in-depth examination of archival materials were made possible with support from the following sources: Charles F. Scott, Charles Boyer Paris research fellowship, UCLA Graduate Division Dissertation Fellowship, UCLA Center for Modern and Contemporary Studies Paris Program Fellowship, and UCLA Center for the Study of Women Travel Award. Generous support from the University of Wisconsin–Milwaukee Center for 21st Century Studies and the UW-Milwaukee Center for International Education provided me with time and resources necessary to complete final revisions.

I am indebted to personnel from several research institutions in Paris, including the magnificent archive staff of the Bibliothèque du film (BiFi), Nadine Teneze, Valdo Kneubhüler, Delphine Warin, Karine Mauduit, Régis Robert, and Marc Vernet, who welcomed me, made me feel at home, and helped me navigate the vast Dulac archive, the Fonds Germaine Dulac (FGD) held at the Bibliothèque du film (BiFi) of La Cinémathèque française. I am also thankful for the hospitality of Frédéric Lacépéde at L'Office universitaire de recherche socialiste (OURS); the attentive guidance of Noëlle Giret, and Emmanuelle Toulet, formerly of the Département des arts du spectacle of the Bibliothèque nationale de France (BNF-ASP; and the accommodating staff of the Bibliothèque de la Ville de Paris and the Bibliothèque Marguerite Durand (women's library). While the attentiveness and resourcefulness of the archivists and librarians I worked with is too great to detail here, I will just cite the example of Alain Carou (BNF), who waded through the stands of the *bouquinistes* (used book and record sellers) so that we might experience Dulac's musical films with their original gramophone recordings.

My heartfelt thanks also goes to Francophone research scholars and friends Bernard Bastide, Christophe Gauthier, Valérie Vignaux, Laura Vichi, Pascal Manuel Heu, Gilles Delluc, Marie-Ange L'Herbier, Luce Vigo, and the late Alain Virmaux, for generously sharing key correspondence and documents from Dulac's work with Baroncelli, the cine-clubs, Benoît-Lévy, Stork, Vuillermoz, Delluc, L'Herbier, Vigo, and Artaud, respectively. I am also grateful to Tangui Perron, Ester Carla di Miro, Richard Armin for sharing their insights on Dulac's work with the SFIO, Richter, Hillel-Erlanger. I am especially beholden to Jean-Michel Mareau, who shared invaluable stories about the life of his aunt, Marie-Anne Colson-Malleville (née Mareau). Yet, none of my work (film viewings or publications) would have been possible without the immeasurable kindness and generosity of the assiduous guardians of what Dulac calls "the future film archive of history": Yann Beauvais and Christophe Bichon at Light Cone Film, dear friends Eric LeRoy (Archives françaises du film du Centre national du cinéma et de l'image animée), Agnès Berthola (Gaumont-Pathé Archives), and again Rodolphe Lussiana (Cinémathèque française). I also want to express my sincere thanks to Bryony Dixon (British Film Institute), Gabrielle Claes (Cinémathèque Royale de Belgique), Serge Bromberg (Lobster Films), and Catherine Cormon and Marleen Labijt (EYE Film Instituut Nederland), for their amiable assistance in making hard to see films accessible. I am particularly grateful for the warm hospitality of five dazzling and inspiring women, Karola Gramman, Heide Schlüpmann (Kinothek Asta Nielsen, Frankfurt), Irina Leimbacher (formerly of the Pacific Film Archive, Berkeley), Maria Komninos (Greek Film Archive), and Peggy Parsons (National Gallery of Art, Washington, DC), who graciously invited me to present films, and to engage in open, dynamic, and fertile discussions over the course of several Dulac retrospectives and workshops from 2002–7. Marie Dupeyron (Musée d'Orsay), Laurence Schifano (Université Paris X-Nanterre), and Guy Borlée, Gianluca Farinelli, and Mariann Lewinsky Sträuli (Cineteca Bologna) provided generous personal, and institutional support for the organization of the 2005 Dulac Integral Retrospective and Conference "Germaine Dulac, au-delà des impressions" (Germaine Dulac, beyond impressions) in Paris and the 2006 and 2014 Dulac Retrospectives at Cinema Ritrovato in Bologna.

Finally, this book could not have come to fruition without the love and inspiration of my extraordinary grandparents, Charles B. and Doris Cook Williams, and my chic nana, Janet Fee, each of whom told me many animated stories about the 1920s and '30s; my wonderful parents, Valerie and Brandon Williams; my trusty siblings, Jason and Misty; my witty Scottish auntie Angela; my Uncle Brian; and cousins Darren and Kenny Fee, all of whom over the years provided me with transportation to the airport, hot meals, and bottomless cups of tea. Dear friends Julie Cristiano, Jenny Lefcourt, Erdal Paksoy, Ichiro Irie, Thomas Gauthron, Hunter Keeter, Susan Kerns, and Ramsey Finger, the baristas of Colective and Roast, and silent cinema colleagues Richard Abel, Mark Cooper, Laurent Guido, Sarah Keller, Tom Gunning, Charlie Musser, Maud Nelissen, and Shelley Stamp helped cheer me on at various stages of this project. In Milwaukee, the J-Jos (Jennifer Johung and Jennifer Jordan), Winson Chu, Stewart Ikeda, Aims McGuinness, and Anika Wilson, and from afar Martin Lefebvre, inspired and pushed me through the final process. Last but not least, I want to thank Liam Callanan, Lorilee Flores, and Kathy Kilkenny of the UWM English Department, and my fabulous colleagues and friends Gilberto Blasini, Elena Gorfinkel, Tasha Oren, Andrew Martin, and Patrice Petro of the Media, Cinema and Digital Studies Program at UW-Milwaukee. *Merci.*

Notes to the Reader

This book is based in large part on original documents in the Fonds Germaine Dulac (FGD) held at the Bibliothèque du film (BiFi) of La Cinémathèque française. These and other archival and bibliographic abbreviations are listed at the beginning of the notes section. Dates attributed to films in the text refer to the earliest verifiable screenings.

I refer to Germaine Dulac as "Dulac" and to her husband, Albert Dulac, as "Albert" throughout the book.

All English translations are my own unless otherwise indicated.

For updates, supplementary information, and extended discussion, visit http://www.tamiwilliams.com.

Germaine Dulac

Introduction

Germaine Dulac (1882–1942) played a founding role in the evolution of the cinema both as art and social practice. History has overlooked her importance as a pioneer of the 1920s French avant-garde, and as an innovator of a modern cinema. Over the course of her film career (1915–42), Dulac directed more than thirty fiction films, many marking new cinematic tendencies, from impressionist to abstract. She made an equivalent number of newsreels and several documentaries, whose discreet, unobtrusive approach to filming daily life had an important impact on the evolution of nonfiction filmmaking in France. Moreover, she developed and promoted her modernizing vision of the medium across hundreds of public presentations and articles.

One of the principal limitations of Dulac studies to date has been the tendency of scholars to approach her work through the single lens of contemporary feminist theory, which grew out of the desire to theorize a feminist aesthetic and to develop a new feminist film practice in the wake of the U.S. women's movement and the disciplinary emergence of feminist film criticism in the 1970s. An alternative, critical historiography that is archive based allows us to examine Dulac's work on its own terms and to use contemporary feminist theory as a tool for interrogating primary and secondary sources. This approach facilitates a comprehensive reconstruction and evaluation of Dulac's conception of cinema within her unique historical context and in terms of the specific sociopolitical and artistic influences that shaped it.

A careful study of Dulac's life and work establishes the importance of her voice in the diffusion and legitimization of French film and film culture, as evidenced through her prolific writings and lectures. She also played a prominent role in several key cultural organizations such as the Société des auteurs de films (SAF, Society of Film Authors), the Fédération française des ciné-clubs (FFCC, French Federation of Cine-Clubs), the International Council of Women (ICW), the International Educational Cinematographic Institute (IECI), and the League of Nations' International Committee for Intellectual Cooperation (ICIC), among others.

Despite Dulac's foundational role in developing cinema as an art form and as a social tool, our knowledge of the *cinéaste* was long limited to short biographical overviews and (principally psychoanalytic) textual readings of a couple of her fiction films most readily accessible in the United States, specifically the impressionist *The Smiling Madame Beudet* (1923) and surrealist *The Seashell and the Clergyman* (1927). These films are not without interest, as Sandy Flitterman-Lewis has shown in *To Desire Differently: Feminism and the French Cinema*. However, the isolated consideration of and limited discourse on these two films, which also are not definitive of Dulac's larger body of work, has inherently obscured the historical specificity of her approach, as well as her broader contributions to cinema and feminism.[1]

An extensive historical study of Dulac's work was not possible until the opening of her personal archives, the Fonds Germaine Dulac (FGD) at the Bibliothèque du film (BiFi, film library) in Paris in 1996. Drawing principally on the FGD and related collections, I examine Dulac's work and its role as a bellwether of twentieth-century social and cultural transformation, and as work that moves with and against the shifting sociopolitical tides that marked this transformative period in French history.

The Fonds Germaine Dulac, entrusted to the Cinémathèque française by the filmmaker's partner Marie-Anne Colson-Malleville (1892–1971), includes material from 1829 to 1964 and comprises over forty storage boxes containing over five thousand original documents. These range from production notes, scripts, photographs, and press clippings to conference papers, manuscripts, course materials, and legal files, to personal and professional correspondence. One of the most striking pieces of the collection is an unpublished thirteen-chapter manuscript outlining Dulac's unique approach to cinema as a transcendent form of "visual music" and as a potent tool for social transformation. The title of its introduction, "Qu'est-ce que le cinéma?," and its socioaesthetic line of inquiry—echoing Dulac's critical writings, from her first film article, "Mise-en-scène" (1917), to her 1930s texts on the newsreel's potential as "pure cinema"—prefigure in certain respects those of aesthetic realist film theorist André Bazin's renowned four-volume treatise of the same name (1958–62).[2]

Other important resources for this study include the extensive collection of fan magazines and trade journals relating to the 1920s ciné-club movement and the 1930s International Institute of Educational Cinema, all held at the BiFi; production files, publicity brochures and press clippings from the Bibliothèque nationale de France, Département des arts du spectacle (BNF-ASP), as well as correspondence and publications related to the Section française de l'internationale ouvrière (SFIO, French Section of the Workers' International), film cooperatives, and workers' unions with which she was affiliated, held at the l'Office universitaire de recherche socialiste (OURS, University Office of Socialist Research) in Paris. Film sources crucial to this project include Light Cone, the Cinémathèque française, Gaumont Pathé Archives, Archives françaises du film–Centre national du cinéma et de l'image animée (CNC-Paris, French Film Archives, National Center of Cinema); the British Film Institute (London); the EYE Film Instituut Nederland (Amsterdam); and the Cinémathèque royale de Belgique (CRB, Brussels). Twenty-five Dulac films, an enactment of her first theater play, a live gramophone film program, and a selection of newsreels formed the basis for the 2005 Musée d'Orsay retrospective and conference, and the resulting anthology, "Germaine Dulac, au-delà des impressions" (Germaine Dulac: beyond impressions).[3]

Making extensive use of these paper collections, archival prints, and untranslated secondary sources, this critical feminist historiography retraces, recontextualizes, and reevaluates Dulac's life and cinema, within the context of early twentieth-century France. While this book explores Dulac's commercial and avant-garde, narrative and nonnarrative, fiction and nonfiction films, it also interrogates and invites a rethinking of these categories with respect to her work. Spanning the length of Dulac's life, it is divided into six chapters or three major periodized sections comprising two chapters each, and presented chronologically. Each section corresponds to major shifts in her life and career, which coincide with Dulac's early years from the Belle Époque through the Great War (1882–1918), cinema's late silent era and the principal years of the French cinematic avant-gardes (1919–29), and the sound era through the beginning of the French Occupation (1930–42).

The two chapters in part I of this book present a critical, socioculturally inflected biography of Dulac's early years. Drawing on personal records, memoirs, and correspondence, part I examines Dulac's family background and her encounters with certain people, events, and tendencies during France's Belle Époque, as they later impacted her political and aesthetic views and the many alternatives and choices that shaped her film career. These include the influence of moderate socialism on her views of class, gender, sexuality, and national politics, and the impact of nineteenth-century symbolist and naturalist tendencies on her inventive rhetorical and representational strategies as they contributed to her filmmaking and activism. An overview of her early life and career beginnings, chapter 1 also examines Dulac's "women's portraits" and theater reviews for the feminist weekly *La Française* (1906–13), her first stage production, *L'Emprise* (1907), and her early political activities and nonfiction writings as a pacifist and feminist from 1906 to 1913, the years immediately preceding the Great War. Chapter 2 looks at Dulac's wartime activism and literary writings, as well as the debut of her film career—from her first activities as a film producer for Pathé (*La Lumière du cœur*, 1916) to her first directorial efforts (*Sœurs ennemies* to *Le Bonheur des autres*, 1917–18)—and assesses the historical significance of her incursion into and negotiated course within the French film industry as a female artist and entrepreneur.

Aside from Charles Ford's short chronicle of Dulac's career, and Flitterman-Lewis's biographical overview based on Ford's account, there is no detailed study of Dulac's work prior to the 1920s.[4] A close examination of archival sources documenting her early personal and professional activities provides insight into her humanist egalitarianism, and universalism, and her strong belief in the emancipatory potential of art, as well as her early rhetorical strategies.

Part II considers Dulac's corporate, artistic, and pedagogical initiatives of the 1920s, and comprises a historical overview and several intertextual analyses of her commercial and avant-garde, narrative fiction or impressionist films, and traces the evolution of Dulac's cinematic approach as it evolved from figuration to abstraction (*La Cigarette* to *Princesse Mandane*, 1919–28). It also looks at her surrealist film *La Coquille et le clergyman* and her abstract shorts (1929) in relation to her ideal of a "pure cinema." It examines the vast array of narrative and formal techniques, from intertextuality to a highly cinematic and sociopolitical use of space and time (interior vs. exterior, notions of scale, contrasting volumes; duration, repetition; movement, rhythm), that Dulac used to elaborate her vision of the struggle between the traditional and modern, and the concerns that faced the "New (modern) Man" and the "New Woman" in the morally and economically constraining environment that followed the First World War.

Chapter 3 focuses on several of Dulac's early narrative impressionist films, and her ideal of cinema as a spatiotemporally complex "universe of symbols"—one in which meaning is created through an intertextual network of figurative associations, such as pictorial and rhythmic gesture. Dulac's "integral" approach, based on life, movement, and rhythm, exemplified in a surviving extract of what is considered the first impressionist film, *La Fête espagnole* (1920), is used in a particularly innovative and feminist manner in one of her earliest extant films, *La Belle Dame sans merci* (1921). Dulac's use of dance as a discursive metaphor disrupts a heteronormative, monogamous, linear narrative structure, creating a queer subtext (at times manifested forthright as text) in her later films, both commercial and avant-garde.

Chapter 4 explores Dulac's gradual shift from scenic naturalism and pictorial symbolism to the use of film-specific technical effects, and a choreography and montage-based notion of "rhythm within and between the images" in her feminist classic *La Souriante Madame Beudet* (1923), her subversive short *L'Invitation au voyage* (1927), and in a new restoration of her riot-provoking first surrealist film *La Coquille et le clergyman* (1927). It also analyzes in-depth her lesser known *La Folie des vaillants* (1925), which among her narrative films comes closest to fulfilling her ideals of a "visual symphony" and a "pure cinema" free from the conventions of literature and theater. These conceptions, which are echoed in the title of her 1925 lecture "Les arts contre le cinéma" (The arts against the cinema), find their ultimate demonstration in her three pure or abstract films released in 1929, to which the final part of the chapter is devoted.[5] These films, *Disque 957*, *Étude cinégraphique sur une arabesque* (also released under the title *Arabesque*), and *Thèmes et variations*, are examined within the context of her filmography and writings, and particularly in relation to dance, a motif that allows her to move inventively and harmoniously from figuration to abstraction.

A crucial but largely ignored period of Dulac's career as a nonfiction filmmaker (1930–42) is addressed in part III. Chapter 5 traces Dulac's transition to nonfiction filmmaking in the early 1930s, in her work as founding director of one of the most important newsreel companies of the period (France-Actualités-Gaumont, 1932–35). It explores the aesthetic and social dimensions of her conception of the newsreel and its capacity for objectivity, and its ability to reveal reality and inner meanings beyond that which is visible with the human eye. This chapter also considers Dulac's socially and politically engaged nonfiction films and projects of the Popular Front, at the dawn of another war, including her unique newsreel-based, pacifist documentary feature, *Le Cinéma au service de l'histoire* (1935), which investigates cinema's role as an actor within history. Finally, chapter 6 traces the evolution of Dulac's socialist humanist politics under the Popular Front, through her activism and syndicalism or labor union work within the context of the vast cultural movement of Mai '36, to a rather controversial shift that led to her complex political position under the Vichy regime.

By examining Dulac's cinematic approach, as it develops within a radically evolving sociocultural climate, this book seeks to provide a more comprehensive understanding than has been available to date of the work of this prolific and groundbreaking woman activist and filmmaker, recontextualizing its apparent contradictions in order to reestablish its originality, its coherence, and its place in film history.

PART I

Figure 1. Germaine Dulac. (ca. 1923). Rights reserved. Collection Cinémathèque française.

Chapter 1

"How I Become a Film Director"

Dulac's Early Life and Pre-Filmmaking Career

> Pierre de Coulevain [nom de plume of Jeanne Philomène Laperche] observes that our life, since childhood, is filled with desires, aspirations, facts, and encounters that, despite their disparate appearance, are very closely related. . . . and that all lead us, sooner or later, to our destiny, to the real role we must play, and for which we are truly created. . . . Looking back I now realize that everything, all of my joys and dominant tastes, fit together to form this art. . . . that all my trials, all my projects and experiments, were part of an unconscious apprenticeship, and that the directing career to which I am devoted is the true response to my desires, the synthesis of my faculties.
>
> —Germaine Dulac, "Comment je suis devenue 'metteur en scène' cinématographique" (1924)

Belle Époque Paris (1890–1914), where Dulac came of age, was the epicenter of all that was modern in art, science, and social politics. These developments ranged from the renovation of the literary, plastic, and performance arts (poetry, novel, theater, painting, haute-couture, pantomime, and dance), to the elaboration of grand scientific theories (Marie Curie on radioactivity, De Vries on genetic mutation, Rutherford on atomic structure) and revolutionary technological advances (electric lights, phonographs, horseless carriages, airplanes, and moving pictures). They also entailed a fundamental modernization of social attitudes, and research disciplines (political science, sociology), including a positivist (and counter-positivist) turn in philosophy (Nietzsche on human creativity, Henri Bergson on vitalism, duration, and perception), as well as the secularization of women's education under the Third Republic.

In the 1924 *Ève* magazine interview quoted in the chapter epigraph, Dulac aphoristically depicts her youth in this dynamic environment as the foundation for her film career.[1] While this path may not have been as inevitable as she suggests, a study of her early life reveals many of the key persons, events, and tendencies that shaped her unique approach to filmmaking. While Dulac's diverse film career may appear disjointed or incoherent at first glance, read in context it proves to be both fluid and complex, and a mark of her extraordinary ability to move both with and against the currents of her time. Original sources, from private and public archives, indicate a great deal about her early life, from her struggle for emancipation and the affirmation of her feminism and homosexuality, and her first creative and professional activities to how she came to create a cinema that was at once visually engaging and politically effective.

"Entirely Parisian": Family Origins as Model and Counterpoint

Central to understanding Dulac is an appreciation of her family background and social standing, as well as her influential relationship with and marriage (1905–22) to Albert Dulac. Her family was both the source of her exposure to the arts, and their modernist promise, as well as the conservative and traditionalist backdrop against which her nascent activist politics emerged. While scholars have rightly highlighted her privileged social status, Dulac's tumultuous childhood also shaped her self-reliant personality and the independent social ideals that set her apart among young women of her milieu.[2]

Pierre Maurice Saisset-Schneider (1849–1921) and Madeleine Claire Waymel (1863–1918) married in 1881. Their first of two children, Germaine Dulac was born Charlotte Élisabeth Germaine Saisset-Schneider on November 17, 1882, in Amiens, in the Somme department of Picardy, in northern France (coincidentally, near modernist fantasy and sci-fi writer Jules Verne). During her childhood, her father, a brigadier general, was stationed in various parts of rural France, from Normandy to the Haute-Loire. During her late teenage years, Dulac's parents were effectively absent. After the early passing of Dulac's six-month-old sister, Françoise Adelaide Gabrielle, in 1885, her mother was diagnosed with chronic depression, and spent extended periods at a sanatorium from 1898 until her death in 1918 at age fifty-five.[3] While prior accounts suggest that Dulac's parents passed away at the turn of the century, leading her to seek out a new life in Paris, archival records indicate that they lived through World War I and suggest that she distanced herself from them during her adult years.

With the instability of her home environment, Dulac spent much of her childhood in Paris with her Franco-Polish paternal grandmother, Jeanne Catherine Elisabeth Schneider (1817–1901), who had a tremendous impact on her early artistic development. Not surprisingly, Dulac later referred to her birth in Amiens as "completely accidental" and considered herself "entirely Parisian" in terms of her origins and education.[4] During her late teenage years (ca. 1897–1902), she stayed in a Catholic boarding school in the rural town of St. Étienne (near Lyon, central France), returning to her grandmother's city apartment near the Opéra Garnier with increasing frequency. This transition from rural to metropolitan, a dichotomy that reemerged with her future husband Albert, an agricultural engineer, and inspired the representation of urban modernity and rustic provinciality in her work, would have a major impact on her intellectual development, as well as the emergence of her progressive political and aesthetic ideals.

The Schneider Legacy

Dulac's grandmother, Jeanne Schneider, who essentially raised her, was a woman of great culture and aristocratic privilege—the daughter of a Polish countess, Catherine Zawelska (ca. 1795–1832), and Lieutenant-General Antoine Schneider (1779–1847), a Napoleonic colonel (and *chevalier de l'empire*, or "imperial knight").[5] The Schneider family had a foothold both in the nation's government and in its most important industrial enterprises.[6] Jeanne's father, Antoine Schneider, and Dulac's not-so-distant great-grandfather, was the national defense secretary (ca. 1839) under the July Monarchy of Louis-Philippe I (1830–48). He was also a key player in the founding of one of France's most powerful corporations, the Creusot metallurgical empire, owned and administered by his first cousin Eugéne Schneider (1805–1875), whose exploitation of the poor Antoine later condemned.[7] This industry's dynastic financial subsidiaries extended from the first national railway system (over which founder Antoine Schneider presided as of 1838) to its first nuclear (and electric) power industry (overseen by Dulac's cousin and future supervisor at Gaumont-Franco-Films-Aubert, Charles Schneider, until 1960).[8] These subsidiaries included the leading French arms and weapons enterprise, which had no fewer than twenty thousand employees on the eve of World War I, and which after this human cataclysm became a world leader in its domain.[9]

Despite her initiation to the Schneider family's imposing upper-bourgeois and industrial capitalist milieu, whose values (religious education, bourgeois marriage, wartime profiteering) Dulac later would condemn in her literary projects (e.g., novel "Denise Serpe," 1915) and films (e.g., *La Souriante Madame Beudet*, 1923; *Antoinette Sabrier*, 1926; *Le Cinéma au service de l'histoire*, 1935), the future filmmaker affiliated herself with the burgeoning Section française de l'internationale ouvrière (SFIO, founded in 1905 and the basis for today's Partie socialiste, PS), and several associated feminist, humanist and universalist organizations in the mid-1900s. Her progressive politics, radically oppositional in the face of her family's heritage, were most influenced by her uncle (Virgile) Raymond Saisset-Schneider (1844–1926), who lived with Dulac's grandmother from the early 1890s until her death at age eighty-four in 1901.

Early on, Dulac's "Oncle Raymond," a staunch socialist close to many of the party's founding members, took his niece to illustrious events at the Elysée presidential palace, introducing her to artists, intellectuals, and statesmen, including her future husband, Albert Dulac, in 1904. He also served as a role model for her progressive stance on politics, religion, and art education, providing the radical edge that would offset conservative predispositions. An executive member of the Conseil d'état (France's highest ruling court), and the Department of Education and Fine Arts (later the Ministry of Public Instruction and Fine Arts) under cultural luminary Jules Ferry, Saisset-Schneider helped carry out some of the widest ranging and most enduring educational reforms in modern-day France (such as access to secondary education for girls), while helping to establish other major public liberties (freedom of press, assembly, and unionization), for which Dulac would become a staunch advocate. Close to the future Socialist minister, Marcel Sembat, with whom he drafted the reforms leading to the separation of church and state in 1905, Dulac's uncle no doubt influenced her adoption of a strong anticlerical stance. Sembat, a lifelong friend who devoted much of his political efforts to bringing art to the masses and who sponsored major art salons, would be an important ally for her in the 1910s, as would future prime minister Léon Blum and ministers of education Yvon Delbos and Jean Zay. Thus, while Dulac's family heritage served in part as a counter-model for her politics, it also gave her access to considerable financial means and to a powerful support network for her social and cultural reform efforts.

Early Exposure to the Arts

Above all, Dulac's family background influenced her unique career in cinema by exposing her to new schools of thought, the latest in painting and opera, as well as emergent technologies including amateur photography (1888) and cinema (1895). Belle Époque Paris was the center for a diverse reevaluation and reconfiguration of suggestive forms that galvanized the world of modern art through a variety of approaches. Among other things, this Parisian renaissance brought about new pictorial models (from symbolism to abstraction), exhilarating new dance forms (Loïe Fuller, Isadora Duncan), innovative musical compositions (Éric Satie, Claude Debussy), and widespread theatrical renovation through naturalist (André Antoine) and symbolist mise-en-scène (Aurélien Lugné-Poë, Maurice Maeterlinck). The influence of these newly emerging trends in the arts and the new representational possibilities they offered can be seen in Dulac's eclectic poems, creative drawings, lively essays, and correspondence from the late 1890s and early 1900s.[10]

In 1904, a year in which the influence of her religious education remained robust, she expressed a deep admiration for the classical and religious works (painted panels, illuminations, tapestries, needlework, and stained glass) that she viewed at the Exposition des primitifs held at Paris's Pavillon de Marsan that spring.[11] These medieval works were known for their masterful use of light to link beauty and divinity, estheticism and the sacred—a conception that would have bearing on the spiritual and mystical components of Dulac's artistic sensibility, later articulated in films such as *Vénus Victrix* (1917), *Malencontre* (1920), and *Le Diable dans la ville* (1924). Similarly, the future filmmaker noted her affinity for the works of Pablo Picasso's blue period (Paris, 1901–4), which employed monochromatic color to portray themes of poverty and social injustice, a technique that would characterize her own approach to art and social representation.[12] At times, Dulac's work can be seen to take the form of a stylistic dualism that juxtaposes or combines a dramatic, often symbolist representation of psychic life, and a social, often realist depiction of domestic life. These early painterly influences anticipate her symbolist exploration of natural settings and lighting sources, as well as monochromatic tones (for instance, the use of sun-drenched yellow in the tinted *La Fête espagnole*, 1920; bitter wintry whites enveloping a bleak château in *Malencontre*, 1920; an array of suburban greys in *La Souriante Madame Beudet*, 1923).

Dulac also attended by chance, at an age that forbade her the music hall, the spectacles of U.S. dancer Loïe Fuller, whose multicolored, luminescent projections on her mobile and transparent veils stunned the Parisian crowds and prefigure the filmmaker's conception of visual music. "Could light provoke emotion? Ignite our sensibilities?" she asked.[13] In subsequent years, she followed the modern dance performances of Ida Rubinstein and Isadora Duncan, the latter of whom conceived of her choreographic art as a "nature-inspired" manifestation of the human psyche and spirit, and thus as a liberating social tool. Dulac also frequented the opera and attended on several occasions impressionist composer Claude Debussy's groundbreaking five-act opera, *Pelléas et Mélisande*, based on Flemish dramatist Maurice Maeterlinck's 1893 symbolist play, which premiered at Paris's Opéra comique in April 1902. Notably, Debussy's pioneering work employed layers of sound (atonal music, orchestral tone-color) and silence to express the ineffable or elements of human consciousness or soul that are beyond language—essentially transforming Maeterlinck's "theater of silence" into a "music of silence." These terms would anticipate Dulac's ideal of cinema as visual music, alternately as a "music of silence" or a "music for the eyes."[14] Her predilection for visual primacy and her aversion to cinematic ventriloquism and intertitles fit hand in glove with her investment in an impressionist signifying system. Alongside these diverse cross-medial tendencies, from the painterly to the operatic, Dulac's engagement with musical composition, photography, and early cinema would also leave their mark on her unique artistic and social vision.

A Passion for Music

Dulac described music as her earliest and most profound love. Struck by its ability to stimulate the imagination and allow for a reinvention of the self, she would view it as an ideal thematic, visual and structural model for the creation of an artistic and socially effective cinema in the 1920s and 1930s. "More than elsewhere," she explained in her 1924 *Ève* magazine interview, she found in it "joys of a magnificent intensity."[15]

Dulac's grandmother Jeanne Schneider appears to have exercised the greatest influence on the early development of her musical sensibility: Dulac's companion and assistant Marie-Anne Colson-Malleville (1892–1971) asserted that "[Dulac] was very musical . . . raised by her grandmother who was very musical . . . she knew all of the operas by heart."[16] In this early era of liveness, and brief and limited recordings, Dulac also had a considerable music library that, according to Colson-Malleville, had been in the family since 1870.[17] Like many artists of her time (from the symbolist poet Stéphane Mallarmé to the pre-surrealist painter Odilon Redon), Dulac was influenced early on by Wagner's operas, especially the notion of visual equivalences (see especially *Gesamtkunstwerk* in "The Artwork of the Future," 1849), lending support to Theodore Adorno's assertion that cinema was born out of opera in the darkened theater of Bayreuth.[18] As Henri Fescourt, who worked with Dulac as a producer, wrote: "When she was very young, she drank insatiably from the fountain of *Parsifal* [. . .]; from the age of five, she was deeply moved by certain passages of *Tannhäuser*."[19] Certainly, the key romantic character types and symbols of these operas (the chivalrous male hero; the femme fatale; the swan motif in *Tannhäuser* and *Parsifal*, presented in Paris in 1914) can be found in her films (*La Cigarette, La Belle Dame sans merci*), as can the expression of deeply felt emotions and visceral sensations. However, it is the role of the leitmotif, which creates suggestive meaning through repetition, and Wagner's conception of symphonic orchestration as integral to drama that is most apparent in Dulac's work. In particular, she incorporated these elements into her models of cinematic impressionism and so-called integral (i.e., abstract) cinema, which operate as autonomous, indivisible signifying systems (see, e.g., chapter 4 on *L'Invitation au voyage*).

For Dulac, cinema operates through an associative rather than a narrative logic; like music for Wagner, it should not be conceived of in terms of numbers and recitatives, but instead as a network of interconnected scenes and interpenetrating motifs, which percolate into the consciousness of the masses. Crucial here and prefiguring Dulac's stylistic dualism is the interrelationship of the pragmatic (or realist) and the symbolist, which is the underlying structure of Wagner's *Parsifal*. That is, while certain elements (like the Wagnerian swan) are peripheral to the outer action (plot), they are crucial to the inner action (character psychology), a strategy that would become vital to Dulac's feminist approach to filmmaking. Moreover, unlike other composers of his time such as Verdi and even the younger Puccini, Wagner conceived of and scripted each element of the opera (sets, decor, lighting, written texts, composition, and conducting), an auteurist approach that Dulac shared. The figurative and esoteric aspects of Wagner's work (with its use of myths, symbols, and soul-states) also found echoes in Dulac's references to Hinduism and orientalism, with which she associated female liberty. Such references can be found in her collection of archival objects (i.e., a mandala, a tantra) and her films from

Vénus Victrix (1917), *La Cigarette* (1919), and *Malencontre* (1920) to *Antoinette Sabrier* (1927) and *Princesse Mandane* (1928).[20]

During her youth, Dulac, an avid Wagnerian, made a pilgrimage to the composer's residence and opera house, known as the Temple de Bayreuth, where many of his noncirculating works were performed, long before their twentieth-century release in France. The composer's dream of creating an opera where all people could see his work performed influenced Dulac's pedagogical view of cinema. Nonetheless, and in spite of Wagner's widespread influence on early twentieth-century French art and culture, Dulac like many of her compatriots (doubtless in response to aggrieved postwar Franco-German relations) would later downplay the role of Wagner, more overtly referencing Francophone artists such as Polish-born Romantic composer Frédéric Chopin (1810–1849) and his Wagner-influenced successor, impressionist Claude Debussy (1862–1918). Dulac spent long periods at her grandmother's flat (91, rue Taitbout) until 1905, situated directly across from the Square d'Orléans (80, rue Taitbout). The square was dedicated to Chopin and his longtime muse and companion, novelist Georges Sand (1804–1876) who lived there during the composer's most creative period (1842–47). Similarly, Dulac's next home (24, rue Chaptal, Paris 9th arrondissement, or district), where she lived through the 'teens with her husband Albert, and briefly with her first lover, Stasia de Napierkowska (stage name Stacia Napierkowska), neighbored the atelier of the painter Ary Scheffer (1795–1858), Hôtel Renan-Scheffer (16, rue Chaptal; today this is the Musée de la vie romantique), an important artistic and literary hub that gained renown after being frequented in the mid-nineteenth century by Chopin and Sand (along with Franz Liszt, Jean-Auguste-Dominique Ingres, and Eugène Delacroix, the last of whom painted a double portrait of the composer and the novelist in 1838).

This rich musical upbringing manifests itself across Dulac's film oeuvre, from her 1918 script for a film on the life of Chopin and Sand to her 1929 experimental shorts (*Thèmes et variations*, *Disque 957*, *Arabesque*), two of which propose a visual corollary for the sensuous sonorities of Chopin and Debussy through expressive forms in light and movement.[21] Chopin's intimate style also intersects with Dulac's treatment of characters and locations. Her interest in the more modernist composer Debussy—who, inspired by Pre-Raphaelitism and symbolist poetry, broke with traditional harmonic syntax, classic four-four rhythm, romantic melody, and bombastic orchestrations in favor of atmospheric tone color, rhythmic spontaneity, and imperceptible metrical pulse—exposed Dulac to more experimental forms, such as the short, fanciful musical arabesque. With its rising and falling notes that mirror individualized and rhyming forms and movements found in nature itself (e.g., *Deux Arabesques*, 1888–91; and "Clair de Lune," 1892–93, which Dulac played), this paradigmatic form figures prominently as a visual and structural analogy in her films and reinforces her own modernist style.[22]

Discovering the Mechanical Image: Photography to Early Cinema

During this same period (1900s–1910s), Dulac explored certain visual corollaries for music in photography and cinema. This period would prove crucial to her feminist film aesthetic, as subsequently evidenced in her colorful journalistic portraits of women and her vibrant figure drawings capturing the dynamic arabesques of Napierkowska (1891–1945), eternalized later in Francis Picabia's paintings of the celebrated Franco-Polish dancer (e.g., *Catch as Catch Can*, 1913).

In her 1924 *Ève* magazine interview, Dulac retrospectively emphasized her early and lifelong predilection for photography (over dolls, perhaps a veiled reference to her feminism), and its uniquely expressive ability to capture nuances of light.[23] In a 1923 article for the popular fan magazine *Mon Ciné*, she nostalgically recounted the purchase of her first still camera—a privilege then reserved for the well-to-do—using her childhood savings:[24]

> When I was a child, I spent my time photographing everything I saw. My greatest childhood joy, which marked my little life and thrilled me in a way that I still remember today, was the purchase of my first camera at Gaumont. [. . .] I was ten then [1893] and wanted to shop by myself for what I considered to be the most precious of treasures. I thought I possessed all the happiness in the world, in carrying over my heart a little black box, which I knew could capture the mystery of light, the blaze of the sun, the shadows and the gestures; or everything in life, whose expressivity already enchanted me.[25]

As an adolescent in turn-of-the-century Paris, Dulac also had a vantage point with regard to the new invention of motion pictures. Dulac was twelve years old when Auguste and Louis Lumière exhibited their camera and organized the first public film projection in the basement of the Grand Café in December 1895, on the Boulevard des Capucines (one of the four east-west running *grands boulevards*) a few blocks southwest of her grandmother's flat; she recalls, "More than any other attraction, that one left its mark."[26]

A few years later, in the early 1900s, Dulac witnessed illusionist Georges Méliès's early efforts at the Théâtre Robert Houdin, a couple of blocks southeast of rue Taitbout. In his book *Cinéma 1900*, René Jeanne described the hustle and bustle of this neighborhood in which passersby, "nose in the air" and "dumbstruck," stopped to see Méliès's enigmatic trailers featuring men and women dressed *en travesti* or "incarnating *déesses*, nymphs and fairies."[27] Although in the 1920s and 1930s Dulac paid frequent tribute to the Lumières' mechanical invention that "captured life in movement," she considered Méliès to be the first to understand the new medium's unique capacity to express through his technical effects the spiritual (or that which at times eludes photographic realism): "Wasn't Méliès an avant-garde director, in his time, substituting the cinematographic spirit for the photographic?" she asked.[28] Yet, despite frequent eulogies to these pioneers, Dulac claimed that initially she did not like the cinema. This position was shared with many others among the upper class, who generally dismissed the new medium as a passing fairground attraction. In her interview for the popular journal, *Cinémonde*, provocatively titled, "Madame Germaine Dulac did not like the cinema!" she avowed, "while attending . . . Gaumont-Palace in 1908, I thought it was disgraceful that an excellent symphony orchestra, whose musical performance I had gone to listen to, would be heard in a movie theater."[29]

In light of her appreciation for the established arts, Dulac's early retrospective emphasis on the primacy of music was not surprising. In the same interview, Dulac credited her discovery of a visual corollary to music's transcendent quality as a key turning point in her development: "One day, by chance, I *looked* at the film. I remember very well, it was a reel entitled: *The Battle of Waterloo*. I saw reflections of light on a pond: in an instant, the silent art had conquered me."[30]

Dulac's emphasis on photography, and on the filming of natural elements, corresponded to her ideal of a "pure" cinema based on movement and rhythm found in "life itself." To this end, her references to luminous forms, like those of Loïe Fuller's dances, highlighted the abstract and spiritual aspects central to her vision: that is, a cinema that did not simply reflect life, but one that like music opened out onto a world of imagination, reverie, and transcendance. These early experiences also had implications for Dulac's conception of a socially engaged cinema, one that drew from her class origins and religious education, as well as her exposure to new philosophical ideas during this period.

A New Social Consciousness

Dulac's early life and her connection to the cultural life of Paris not only laid the foundation for her aesthetics but also helped shape her social consciousness and awareness. Her independent disposition and progressive character blossomed during the first years of her adult life, particularly from 1901 to 1906, when she began her career as a feminist journalist. Following the death of her grandmother in 1901, Dulac underwent a major emotional crisis that ignited her artistic and social ambitions, and helped set her on her future career path. The traditional religious education she received (1898–1902), which was designed to indoctrinate women with social norms based on religious morals, awakened Dulac to certain philanthropic and pedagogical ambitions, but it also fueled her desire for emancipation and independence.

During this period we see the development of Dulac's social consciousness and a desire to help emancipate the less fortunate (poor), the disenfranchised (working class, women), and the misguided (bourgeoisie). In the spring of 1904, Dulac had a transformative experience while attending *Le Fils de l'étoile* (The son of the star), an opera by Camille Erlanger (husband of her future lover and film partner, Irène Hillel-Erlanger) at a middle-class theater (l'Opéra comique). Unable to obtain tickets to the Comédie-Française as planned, she was enthralled by the venue's mixed-class audience, which had donned brightly colored hats and was singing "La Marseillaise," yet was dismayed by what she saw as their enthusiastic and mindless diversion. "Du pain et des jeux" (bread and circuses, from the Latin *panem et circenses*), she conceded, is all people need. Dulac explained that she had found her calling to gain a better understanding of people of distinct social backgrounds and to help emancipate them through art.[31]

Her marriage a year later to Albert Dulac, a humanist and universalist close to the social democrats (French Marxist socialists who would join the SFIO), also proved influential, orienting away from a religious and conservative family background, and bolstering her progressive politics and humanist values (linked to the nobility, but not to the capitalist bourgeoisie). Alongside certain universal values of tolerance and social equality, Albert instilled in her the notion of constructing a progressive, more modern world through social action (in contrast to purely political ideals), via feminist and pacifist organizations, trade unions and, most importantly for Dulac, the mass medium of cinema. During these years, Dulac was exposed to a wealth of new ideas that led her to make unconventional choices and, eventually, to forge a career in domains that were relatively atypical for women. It also led Dulac to assume greater confidence in her personal desires as exemplified by her emerging awareness of her homosexuality. This period would be vital in shaping her view of the cinema as a tool for social change.

Religious Education and a Crisis of Independence

Dulac's religious education constituted an important step in the development of her social consciousness, and above all, of her feminist convictions and pedagogical ambitions regarding gender politics. As historian Cécile Dauphin reminds us, "Catholic moral codes, which taught resignation and chastity, carried the seeds of contestation."[32] In the fall of 1898, at age fifteen, Dulac began a lengthy stay (1898–1902) at the Visitation de Sainte Marie de Bel-Air or the historic Visitandine Pensionnat, a Roman Catholic boarding school in St. Étienne (central France); the reputable girls' school may have been chosen by Dulac's mother, who, unlike her father and grandmother, was a devout Catholic.[33] Letters that Dulac received between December 1900 and June 1904 from Sister Marie-Lucie Saignol, while staying at her grandmother and uncle's home in Paris, detail the evolution of her social politics during her early adult years (ages eighteen to twenty-one).[34] The letters provide insight into Dulac's transformation as she shifted from pious faithfulness and an apparent aspiration to enter sisterhood to a desire to explore the world outside the convent, as it laid the foundation for subsequent developments in her artistic and philosophical life.

Like most late-nineteenth-century girls' schools (whether religious or secular), the Visitandines' convent was principally designed to turn out dutiful wives and mothers.[35] As Françoise Mayeur notes, subjects such as philosophy, Latin, and Greek, while central to the curriculum for boys, were not taught to young women for fear of creating *femmes savantes*, or "learned women."[36] As such, the education of most young women was largely literary. Yet, unlike secular schools (founded under the 1881 Camille Sée law), Catholic institutions, like the one Dulac attended, considered novels to be dangerous gateways to new worlds and nonconformist ideas, and subjected the curriculum to more rigid controls.[37] Dulac's regimen then consisted almost exclusively of religious and censored literature (such as the bowdlerized version of *Quo Vadis*) which she came to reject and protest.[38]

Dulac's frequent trips to Paris and Dinan (Normandy) around the time of her grandmother's death (1901) coincided with a greater interest in secular readings, and a more resolute assertion of her autonomy, or what Sister Saignol referred to as both a "moral crisis" and a "crisis of independence." In the summer of 1902, after expressing her ennui with the rural town of Dinan and her disillusionment with the idea of a religious life, Dulac abandoned the convent and moved to Paris. In January 1903, Saignol wrote to Dulac, "In this stay of several years at St. Étienne, God has been very good to you . . . this long (too long) stay away from St. Étienne, has prepared you for a permanent departure." In a subsequent letter she admonishes Dulac for her decision: "[How is it possible that] your will has become a fortress so impenetrable that nothing can reduce it to submission: neither reason, nor prayer, nor affection."[39]

A long letter from Saignol in August 1903, referring to Dulac's "violent crisis of revolt," decries Dulac's desire for emancipation: "You dream of independence and liberty, and your age, character and situation increase this thirst. I understand that obedience is difficult for you, but, my poor Germaine, how can you escape it? It's the law, the law for all, and especially women."[40] Subsequent correspondence indicated Dulac's emerging view of gender in particular as a mere social construction. In June 1904, after meeting her future fiancé, Albert, who soon introduced her to the philosophical writings of René Descartes, her desire for independence found a new source of inspiration. By the summer of 1904, Sister Saignol wrote in a final letter to Dulac: "you have chosen to find the truth on your own through doubt. [. . .] I want to believe in your complete sincerity in the pursuit of truth. [. . .] However, I am surprised that you do not see the obvious falsity of the principles of which you say you approve: 'I am a product, and not a personal being [. . .], a product!'"[41]

Dulac's pronouncement, quite progressive for its time, showed her heightened awareness of her own gendered identity as a construction, shaped by her family background, education, and social mores. It also anticipates her distinctly antiessentialist approach to feminism. In this same letter to Dulac, Saignol acknowledged a grain of truth in Dulac's newfound ideal: "I admit that our roots are somewhat responsible for our tendencies; social milieu and above all one's education influences these tendencies in such or such a way, yes, no doubt . . ." A final pronouncement by Saignol indirectly affirms gender (if not sexuality) as a central aspect of Dulac's budding social consciousness: "What do you mean, when you say that in your new orientation, you feel more like a woman? You mean more independent, no doubt."[42]

Dulac's relationship and lengthy correspondence with Sister Saignol (too voluminous to be parsed here) recontextualizes and reconfigures Dulac's little known proximity and resistance to the French Catholic tradition, a facet that proves interesting in the larger trajectory of Dulac's life. This close relationship had an important bearing on her development. It even inspired her early draft of a novel with semiautobiographical overtones titled "Denise Serpe" (1908–1915), the story of a nun who leaves the convent to become a theater actress, abandoning a religious life to enter the arts, much as its author had done.

In addition, toward the end of her life, in the period leading up to World War II and the Occupation, Dulac elaborated a strikingly similar, yet ideologically inverse feature-length film script (1938–41). In this project, she recounted the life of the ultramodern stage actress Ève Lavallière (1866–1929), who first popularized the cropped "Joan of Arc" haircut, yet who, unlike Dulac's earlier protagonist, Denise Serpe, eventually took an opposite path, giving up a successful theatrical career to become a nun. This decision to write a biopic on Lavallière's transition from "belle dame" to "modern Magdalene" could be seen to reflect a growing conservatism in late 1930s France, if not a conservative turn at the end of the filmmaker's own life (taken up in more detail in chapter 6), or perhaps a strategy to move ahead with a complex project, in the face of the Vichy ideology.

In the years following her departure from the convent, Dulac adopted a firm anticlerical stance, a posture that had gained force with the left and the Women's Progress movement following the Dreyfus Affair (1894–99), and which had led to the secularization of schools in 1905, considered one of the most "turbulent" and "passionate" issues to face the church and state during the Third Republic (1871–1940).[43] Yet, she seemed to maintain her belief in a higher power, while also entertaining a variety of mystical notions and superstitions, frequenting chiromancers and graphologists (at least as early as 1905, and as late as 1938), and exploring spiritual ideas and concepts, often related to Hinduism, in her films and writings on the cinema (*Âmes de fous*, *Malencontre*, *La Mort du soleil*).[44] (One amusing superstition she carried into her film career was to never begin a project on a Tuesday.)

Albert Dulac

Just as Dulac had begun to break away from the influence of the convent and to forge a place for herself in Parisian society, she met her future fiancé Albert (b. Marie Louis Albert Dulac, 1877), who facilitated her transition between these two worlds. Their relationship in and out of marriage would be complex—cool, often conducted at a distance, but marked by mutual respect, mentoring, and shared political and intellectual explorations, despite their many divergences—different temperaments, fondness for city versus country, and her evolving sense of her own sexuality. Despite several break-ups over the course of a seventeen-year marriage, intellectually and politically complementary, they would become devoted life and work partners. Initially, perhaps a replacement mentor for Saignol, he provided a link between the religious, social, and artistic influences in her life and was a catalyst by encouraging her to explore and realize her desires and ambitions.

Anxious to gain independence from her parents and the convent, Dulac met Albert while attending a gala event with her uncle at the Elysée Palace in June 1904. Her parents had rejected prior suitors, but Albert, born into an independently wealthy family of Catholic stock (or what Michel Winock calls the good bourgeoisie), much to her pleasure gained immediate acceptance, and they were married the following spring.[45] Dulac saw Albert as a modern-day renaissance man and his broad culture and decidedly liberal Catholic education, which encouraged freethinking, progressive politics, and social activism, made him a valuable companion for her during this formative period. His diverse artistic interests (music, painting, literature, theater), his strong humanist values, as well as his experience in economics and politics had a great influence on her career. Further, his letters to her over the years (1904–22) offer rare insight into the early sociopolitical underpinnings of her work as a filmmaker and activist.

Before attending the Grignon School of Agriculture, Albert received his secondary education under the distinguished prior Henri Didon (1840–1900), popular orator and theologian of the Dominican order, trained by Catholic liberal and editor of *L'Ére Nouvelle* (The new era), Henri Lacordaire (1802–1861). A founder of the modern-day Olympics (1896), Didon was known for his progressive and universalist values, his efforts to reconcile Christian principles with the philosophical tenets of modern society, as well as his advocacy of the church as a place for social action.[46] These intellectual, philosophical, and political ideals, broadly disseminated through numerous lectures and published texts, left their mark on his disciple Albert, and indirectly on Germaine Dulac.[47]

Dulac frequently praised her husband's intellect and free spirit, and described him as "a man of action merged with a dreamer and a thinker," "a man of science, as well as an artist," of "uncommon intelligence, [and] extraordinarily inspirational ideas."[48] Like his mentor, who was devoted to theology, philosophy, and poetry, Albert was an active player in local politics, a contributor to key literary journals, a novelist and author of several plays, aside from being a well-published agronomist.[49] Significantly, Dulac particularly admired his egalitarianism. She wrote: "I really like this type of man who is very cold, not very gallant, who treats woman as an equal and not a feeble being to whom one should humble oneself and for whom constant care must be shown. I've truly met my ideal, and this is a rarity in life."[50]

From an intellectual perspective, Albert's broad knowledge of literature and philosophy was perhaps most influential on Dulac's early development.[51] He introduced her to the work of Dostoevsky, Marx, Spinoza, Bergson, and most notably, during this early period, the work of Friedrich Nietzsche (1844–1900), and its call for a general transvaluation or transmutation of established values. In September 1904, following Dulac's reading of Nietzsche's philosophical novel *Thus Spoke Zarathustra* (1885), Albert wrote, "You are right to read Nietzsche and when you say that you associate me with this reading that you like to do in a flower garden . . . I see how well you have come to know me. For no philosopher, no poet has helped me as much as Nietzsche to build my own worldview, by extending or elucidating the reflections, convictions, and ideas that are dearest to me and that perhaps represent me best. I will never forget the day when you told me that you understood and loved Zarathustra." And yet, Albert added, "I know that you do not entirely embrace [Nietzsche]. For he differs from you . . ."[52] If Dulac had reservations about Nietzsche's *Zarathustra*, known for its positivistic declarations on the death of god and religion, his ideals of self-determination and liberation from established values accorded perfectly with her emerging aspirations of feminism, sexual liberation, and social activism.

Perhaps most important for Dulac was Nietzsche's conception of a *morale créatrice*, or moral creativity, based on sensation and concretized through will and action. Crucially, the notion of sensation, which Albert refers to as the "source of emotional life," the "very foundation of the harmony of things" in its "communion with infinity," would be a cornerstone of Dulac's conception of cinema.[53] In keeping with Nietzsche (and Didon), and foregrounding Dulac's view of cinema as a social tool, Albert emphasized the ultimate importance of the oeuvre: "But beyond this *sensory* world, *reason* and *will* operate. Like knowledge, sensation, you see, is only a means. The aim is the work" (emphasis added).[54] Albert's subsequent letter bore out his intellectual influence on her: "you tell me that you are growing with what I write you . . . Your . . . letters fill me with proud delight!" Dulac was also aware of the work of philosopher Henri Bergson (1859–1941), considered by many to embody the "spirit of the era." During the war, Albert would ask her to send him Bergson's discussion of French philosophy from *La Revue de Paris*.[55] Bergson's placement of the image and intuition (versus rationalism) at the center of knowing, and his ontology derived from duration as indivisible, finds echoes in Dulac's own preoccupations with the experiential image, integral duration, and active perception.

If Albert influenced Dulac's philosophical thought, he had an impact on her left-wing political and economic views, as well. In contrast to the industrial aristocracy and liberal capitalism of Dulac's heritage, Albert's defense and promotion of collectives and labor unions finds echoes in her associative work in the immediate years and in turn her activities with ciné-clubs and nonprofit organizations later on. Albert's commitment to the working class also left its mark on the soon-to-be feminist activist and future filmmaker. In August 1904, during a stay in the fishing village Port-en-Bessin (Calvados, Normandy), Albert wrote to Dulac expressing his compassion for the "laborious life of [its] humble people."[56] At a time when France's population was still 80 percent rural, Albert supported small farmers and cultivators by promoting agricultural cooperatives and price regulation for essential foodstuffs.[57]

While Dulac soon followed a similar path, she focused her efforts and actions on the needs of women workers, first in the country, but soon after in Paris. In late 1905, at the sprightly age of twenty-two, during her stay with Albert at his fifteen-room château in historic Bayeux (Normandy), she engaged in her first activities in defense of women's labor conditions.[58] In an article titled "L'Industrie au foyer. Les dentellières" (Industry at home: the lacemakers), she spoke out against the economic conditions threatening the rural and almost exclusively female industry of embroidery and lace making, and argued for the establishment of cooperatives, a cause she would carry with her as an artist and activist in the film industry.[59]

While today needlework invokes essentialist conceptions of women's labor, at the turn of the twentieth century, this independent sector of rural commerce was, for Dulac, one of the few occupations that allowed women to set aside domestic chores, to participate in a creative and collective activity, and, above all, to earn their own salaries. In view of women's progress, and more radically in her films of the 1920s, Dulac would later represent domestic needlework as a constraining and oppressive activity (*La Belle Dame sans merci*

[1921], *L'Invitation au voyage* [1927]), and would highlight more liberating forms of women's work in domains such as art and science (*La Mort du soleil* [1921], *Âme d'artiste* [1925]). This shift was no doubt precipitated by her work for the women's progress movement, which upon her return to Paris in mid-1906 provided a propitious environment for the development of her activism for the feminist cause.

The Women's Progress Movement

Dulac's earliest sociopolitical engagement in the arts began with her work as an activist, journalist, and theater critic for the association and journal *La Française* from 1906 to 1913.[60] These activities must be considered within the broader context of what was known in turn-of-the-century France as the Mouvement du progrès féminin (women's progress movement). The discourse of the late-eighteenth-century Enlightenment, and its values of reason, progress, self-fulfillment, and education, had laid the foundations for democratic and egalitarian ideas, and to a large extent for both the socialist and feminist movements. While the Napoleonic Code of 1804 placed women in a situation of civil incapacity and dependence with respect to their fathers and then their husbands, late-nineteenth-century France saw the rise of an entirely new social consciousness. In the 1880s and 1890s, as the writings of Karl Marx, August Bebel, and Friedrich Engels began to gain influence in France, these questions were often seen as part of the same social oppression.[61] While men were organizing themselves around issues of class, women began to do the same with respect to gender. In fin-de-siècle France, the women's question, or the "social utility of woman's emancipation," emerged as a subject of broad public discourse.[62]

According to the historian Anne-Marie Käppeli, two broad feminist tendencies could be distinguished: an essentialist "dualist" current, which, founded on the notion of *l'éternel féminin* (or womankind), stressed sexual difference, women's cultural capital, and maternity issues; and an antiessentialist "egalitarian" current, which emphasized individuality, the irrationality of the double standard, and women's right to political equality and suffrage. In keeping with her broader humanist and universalist views, Dulac adhered to the antiessentialist current, which situated its activism within the broader struggle to create a republican (nonmonarchical, anti-empire, social democratic) and egalitarian society.[63] Yet, while men tended to seek resolution of these issues through their governments, women, like Dulac, who were excluded from voting and political office, coordinated their efforts by creating their own structures in the form of feminist associations and alliances for social causes.

The Women's Association

Shortly after her definitive return to Paris in mid-1906, at age twenty-three, and, as letters show, after an initial romantic disconnect from her no-less-cherished husband, Dulac became involved with *La Française*, an association of "female-initiated social action" launched by Jane Misme in October 1906, and eventually serving as a platform for a journal of the same title.[64] (Albert may have provided Dulac's connection to Misme, who had worked for its precursor *La Fronde*, a feminist supplement to *L'Action Quotidienne*, for which he had written.) During the first season of a seven-year venture faithfully and enduringly championed by her husband, Dulac gave several lectures alongside Misme, which not only attested to her early prominence in this milieu that would carry over to her film activism, but also shed light on her feminist stance. The first of these presentations, "L'Influence des femmes dans l'évolution de la langue française" (The influence of women on the evolution of the French language), took place on March 25, 1907, at the first and still extant Alliance française (186, boulevard de St. Germain).[65] In her lecture, Dulac traced the contributions of women writers, from the twelfth-century *fabliaux* and letters of Héloïse to the nineteenth century novels of Madame de Staël and Georges Sand.[66] She not only extolled the significance of these authors' contributions for the emancipation of women, but also referred more generally to the importance of women as "agents of progress in the diverse manifestations of human activity," that is, as integral constituents of a larger struggle for social progress. Dulac declared: "No social progress can occur without all social elements contributing their part. [. . .] We must hope that one day women will understand that without them nothing great can be done, not only in the elaboration of language, which is already meritorious work, but also in the constitution of the superior conscience that [Ernest] Renan has called the goal of humanity."[67]

Dulac's second lecture, "La Tâche internationale de la femme française" (The international task of the French woman), presented at the Alliance française on July 15, 1907, adopted a more ambitious and militant tone, calling women to action through association.[68] The salon had been a place for women's activism in the nineteenth century, but the implementation of what became known in France as the *loi d'association de 1 juillet 1901* (association law of

July 1, 1901), following the misconduct of religious congregations during the Dreyfus Affair, facilitated the formation and diversification of nonprofit alliances and coalitions (while offering government oversight) and provided the women's movement with an official, legally recognized public identity.[69] Dulac promoted the association not only as a means of resistance to the "parliamentary machine" but also as a "veritable instrument of social relations" and, as such, a "great national force."[70] For the young activist, it was a woman's role and responsibility to participate both in the fight for emancipation and for broader sociopolitical progress, struggles she considered to be integrally connected. Noting that women's "influence on social life, in general, and on international relations, in particular, is no longer carried out in the salons [. . .] and, that on the other hand, it is unacceptable that half of humanity continues to be written off," she proclaimed, "if women want to keep their place in society, they must either enter into existing associations, or create them according to their own spirit."[71]

Dulac viewed the feminist movement as necessarily international, a Marxist conception rooted in its links to the mid-nineteenth-century workers' movement that anticipated her activism in the 1930s for the International Council of Women (ICW, United States, 1888) and the League of Nations. In an effort to assist Dulac with her presentation, Albert had jotted down quotations from Marx and Engels's *Communist Manifesto* (1848): "[M]odern industrial labor . . . has stripped [the worker] of any trace of national character. Law, morality, religion, are . . . bourgeois prejudices, behind which lurk just as many bourgeois interests. . . . Working men have no country. . . . The united action of the leading civilized countries, at least, is one of the primary conditions for the emancipation of the proletariat."[72]

While Dulac clearly adhered to the antibourgeois and anticlerical tenor of this passage, in her July lecture on the international task of women she appropriated the latter part of this extract, in particular, calling "united action" by women "in different civilized countries . . . one of the foremost conditions for the amelioration of their status."[73] Yet, in her internationalism, she did not subscribe entirely to the communist view.

Drawing on the lessons of mid-nineteenth-century history, Dulac noted how the efforts of radical women—such as Saint-Simonite Jeanne Deroin (1805–1894), who founded an international workers' federation; and Fourierist Flora Tristan (1803–1844), who sparked the creation of l'Unité universelle (Universal Unity) with her treatise *L'Union ouvrière* (The worker's union)—had been repressed following the 1848 revolutionary uprising, after which men played "the principal, if not unique role."[74] Crucially, for Dulac, the "less revolutionary ambitions" of the International Council of, and the actions of the Conseil national des femmes françaises (CNFF, National Council of French Women, 1901), in which she participated, "seemed better adapted to the era."[75] Indicative of her belief in the need to reassure in order to convince, this strategy of casting progressive ideas in more agreeable terms, common among moderate feminists, would be crucial to her critical writings and films.

Inseparable from Dulac's internationalism was her support of the pacifist cause. In her July lecture, she enumerated various emergent women's associations, including Marya Chéliga's Alliance universelle des femmes pour la paix par l'éducation (1896, 1899, Universal Alliance of Women for Peace and Education), Sylvie Flammarion and Séverine's Association de la paix et du désarmement par les femmes (1899, Women's Association for Peace and Disarmament)—over which Dulac would preside—and the Alliance universelle pour la vote des femmes (1904, Universal Alliance for Women's Suffrage).[76] Dulac's adherence to Chéliga's alliance at the time of the 1907 Women's Peace March in Paris, announced her lifelong commitment to education, and educational cinema, as a means of working toward international understanding and the pacifist ideal. Her position at the beginning of World War I was moderately pacifist, but the violence of the conflict eventually reinforced it, prompting her engagement as vice president of Flammarion's newly named Comité du désarmement moral par les femmes (Women's Committee for Moral Disarmament) in the 1920s and '30s, and anticipating her humanist and universalist approach to filmmaking, as well as her activism in groups like the League of Nations' Committee for International Understanding in the 1930s. As she concluded in the lecture, "I am just happy to have contributed to showing you the field of action available to women able to understand that they are perhaps better situated than many others to prepare, through an enlightened practice of international relations, the future era of peace."[77] This moderate pacifist position would stay with her throughout her career.

For Dulac, art and culture and, later, cinema should serve this larger political goal of international comprehension and cooperation. In her July 1907 lecture at the Alliance française—whose mission was to facilitate cultural exchanges between France and other nations—she announced Jane Misme's recent creation of an International Salon, attended by prominent members of the Paris arts scene.[78] During her early years as vice president of the Italian section at *La Française*, Dulac, assisted by Albert, promoted cultural exchanges through a long series of biweekly international matinees featuring modern women artists such as dancer Carlotta Zambelli, composer Juliette Toutain-Grün, and concert pianist Anne Vila, each of whom she had written about in the association's journal.[79] Of the political and social role of the arts, Dulac avowed, "Understanding other peoples through their literature, art, and customs broadens our intelligence, improves it, and even teaches us to see flaws [in ourselves] that we would not see without this comparison. [. . .] through contact with a civilization different from ours, we learn new things."[80] This international perspective, which anticipated her vision of the new mass medium of cinema, in light of its potential as an art, and later of the newsreel, as means for greater communication and understanding, saw its first concrete development in her work as a journalist and theater critic for the women's press.

The Feminist Press

Dulac's coming of age coincided with the innovation and development of the feminist press. She was only fifteen when Marguerite Durand founded the republican, Dreyfusard feminist newspaper *La Fronde* (The catapult/rebellion) in December 1897, the first daily written, edited, and distributed exclusively by women, including Dulac's future collaborator Jane Misme.[81] Its declared ambition was to "impose *La Fronde* in the journalistic world and have men read it," and it attracted a diverse readership (male and female) through its juxtaposition of general interest topics (political, financial, and literary) and progressive women's issues (access to higher education, equal pay for equal work, and freedom of choice regarding maternity).[82] With its unique hiring policy, the social consciousness that it engendered, and its flair for presenting women's issues in a nonthreatening way, *La Fronde* paved the way for women's journalism in early-twentieth-century France.[83]

Dulac did not actually write for *La Fronde* until its brief reappearance, in 1926, after a several-year hiatus, when it ran her weekly film column titled "Le Cinéma est un art nouveau" (Cinema is a new art).[84] However, *La Fronde* would indirectly contribute to her longer association with the publication *La Française.*

When *La Fronde* ceased publication in March 1905,[85] the former "Frondiste," theater critic Jane Misme, was quick to take up the reins or fill the void, founding one of the most successful and enduring feminist journals under the Third Republic, *La Française* (1906–34).[86] The first issue of the four-page, large-format, "documentary, critical and reformative" Sunday weekly appeared on October 21, 1906.[87] Contrary to its predecessor, *La Française* declared that it "[did] not at all exclude men from its collaboration," but it forbade itself any political or religious polemics and devoted itself to "the situation and role of women in France and abroad."[88]

Dulac wrote her first article for the new weekly on December 23, 1906, at age twenty-four, inaugurating, with her biographical portrait of the celebrated *comédienne* Réjane, a seven-year collaboration with the journal (1906–13).[89] During these years, Dulac quickly distinguished herself through her militant lectures for the association, and she developed and refined this mode of address through literary portraits (1906–8) and theatrical criticism (1908–13).

Women's Portraits

Between December 23, 1906, and October 4, 1908, under the signature Germaine Albert-Dulac, the future filmmaker animated a lively front-page column in *La Française* called "Figures d'autrefois et d'aujourd'hui" (Figures of past and present), which initially featured both a female subject and a male subject (the latter composed by former *frondeuse*, or female frondiste, Paule Lauribar). Dulac wrote at least thirty-five editorials for this section, which by mid-1907 would be devoted exclusively to women.[90] Significantly, the column's title announced its subversive design. Taken literally, its reference to "figures" of the past and present (which can be interpreted as "representations") also connoted the rapidly changing gender roles in turn-of-the-century France, implicitly affirming the existence of the traditional woman, while announcing the emergence of the *nouvelle femme*, or new woman.

Amid debates on the nature and identity of woman, the *nouvelle femme*, who was forging new educational and professional opportunities, represented a major threat to conventional gender roles.[91] Many feared that women, embarking on new careers, would be unable to fulfill their tasks as wives and mothers. As Mary Louise Roberts has noted, women professionals who challenged the conventional domestic limits established for women during this period were often depicted as *hommasses*, "mannish types, who scorned marriage and children in order to pursue a career."[92] Women's participation in the new mass media (women's journalism) allowed them to counter and correct these negative stereotypes by projecting and disseminating their own images of female identity.[93]

Dulac's articles constituted precisely this form of participation. Her principal subjects included women from a variety of artistic domains (literature, music, dance and theater), as well as from less conventional occupations such as public education, medicine, science, and (like Dulac herself) the groundbreaking field of women's journalism.[94] As Wendy Dozoretz has suggested, Dulac's portraits, based on live interviews with her subjects, come across, at least initially, as "glowing tributes."[95] When examined more closely, however, they also can be seen as a radical critique of the way women's identity was produced in turn-of-the-century French culture.

New Strategies

At the end of the nineteenth century, a new journalism had emerged. This modern discursive trend, which gave birth to reportage, emphasized observation, information, and narration via eyewitness accounts of public life.[96] It is perhaps in light of this development, and the fact that illustrated newspapers were relatively uncommon in France during this period, that Dulac's portraits often began with a vivid account of the figure's physique, gestures, and home or workspace before describing her talents, activities, and experiences.[97] By today's standards, Dulac's representations may seem to have a rather frivolous or whimsical style, conforming to the notions of fantasy associated with women's literature of the period, but her intricate descriptions gave her subjects a presence and lent her account a firm attachment to "reality."[98] This strategy also anticipated the detailed visual descriptions and meticulous elaboration of characters and atmosphere that characterize Dulac's narrative and nonnarrative films.

Highlighting the contradictions between the traditional woman as she has been represented, and her more modern attributes, for instance, Dulac frequently juxtaposed conventionally feminine qualities—such as charm, grace, beauty, caring, and devotion—with less established traits, such as will, intelligence, force, independence, and action. One of her first articles, a portrait of the illustrious novelist Countess (Anna) Mathieu de Noailles (author of *Le Cœur innombrable*, 1901), detailed the discrepancy between her subject's delicate appearance and gracious gestures, and her intellect and inner strength (which she characterized as supremely Nietzschean).[99] Citing one of de Noailles's novels, Dulac wrote:

> One wonders how this infinitely attractive, adorably frail woman can handle a heart, which "so strongly weighs at times." How her small hand which abandons itself graciously [. . .] can hold a pen so *heavy with thoughts* [. . .]; but one is fascinated [. . .] by her large, bright, feverish eyes, as if

> thirsting for visions, and the *strong spirit* that emanates from such a delicate beauty. [. . .] Madame de Noailles does not dream, she feels [. . .] always inspired by truths, *strong sensations*. [. . .] Regrets come [. . .], but she violently pushes them away, as hindrances to her flight. She's a Nietzschean in all her greatness. (emphasis added)[100]

Dulac not only couched modern female qualities (intellect, strength, action) and activities (writing, social activism, medical work) within a conventional framework, but, without being dogmatic, she also reassured readers that they would not have any negative repercussions on the woman's traditional duties. Of the novelist and playwright Marguerite Rolland, whose first play was premiering at the Théâtre des arts, Dulac wrote, "She can be cited as an example of the ideal type of the modern intelligent woman, who, *without neglecting any of her attractiveness and her traditional duties*, seeks to embellish them with the charm of her spirit. It's supremely coquettish" (emphasis added).[101] Dulac's reassuring tactics accorded perfectly with the journal's policy, which, "always moderate and respectable," was more devoted "to the demonstration by fact and actions than to discussions of doctrine."

The journal expressly sought to give "woman her true place in the organization of society; [and] to men and to children, a companion and mother worthy of her duties to them."[102] Yet, Dulac showed reluctance in affirming her subject's devotion to these traditional characteristics. In one case, she described novelist Colette Yver as "a charming young woman, not in the least bit pedantic, not at all intoxicated by her success, and who, *must we admit*, attaches more importance to caring for her husband and her home, than to caring for her novels" (my emphasis). Then, she closed with a feminist affirmation that inverted her initial assertion. While reassuring readers that her subject's intellect would not disturb social conventions and appearances, she affirmed, "She is a woman born of letters, without being so in her manners."[103] This is an odd juxtaposition, no doubt. Yet it is a strategy that avoids arousing widespread fears of female professionalization and virilization, some of which persist today.

While Dulac's praise for the self-sacrificing wife and mother and for the independent woman may seem contradictory, it aligned with the project of moderate feminists, who sought to reassure conservatives in order to convince. In the *mouvement du progrès féminin*, both figures had a role to play. As a former *frondeuse* and founding director of *La Française*, Jane Misme asserted, "The traditional woman and the new woman are in conflict and the whole world is rooting for them."[104] Roberts argues with respect to *La Fronde* and *les frondeuses* that the mixed identity of its journalists and the juxtaposition of conventional views of the traditional woman and the modern woman contested the line of separation between the two.[105] She further asserts that this blurring of boundaries, combined with the oscillation between male and female issues, rendered *La Fronde* "culturally illegible" and thus subversive.[106]

One can make a similar argument with respect to Dulac's women's portraits. By describing these figures through direct and attentive observation, the young journalist and future filmmaker constructed a new identity for these women, one that contradicted dominant male representations. Furthermore, by couching her descriptions within a conventional framework, and by emphasizing the inconsistencies and contradictions between the traditional and the modern, conventional and unconventional femininity, she not only rendered these figures less threatening, by reassuring her readers of the "social utility" of women's emancipation, but she also refused to create any single readable meaning, or any single reducible female identity.

New Identities, New Triumphs: Dulac's "Women of Action"

Through their variety, Dulac's portraits opened up a multiplicity of new identities for women, and contributed to her aim of enlarging the sphere of women's action, that later inspired and propelled her films. For example, her portrait of the enterprising humanitarian Madame Poilpot, who revived a girls' orphanage, prefigures the plight of her heroine in her postwar film *La Mort du soleil* (1921), who must choose between a medical career at an orphanage for sick children or attending to her husband and child.[107]

Dulac's work also exposed her to artists and movements that would inform her intermedial aesthetic. Indeed, her detailed descriptions of the recitals of performers, such as prima ballerina of L'Opéra de Paris, Carlotta Zambelli (1875–1968), and triumphant opera composer Juliette Toutain-Grün, who caused a stir as the first woman to win the Prix de Rome, anticipated her unique and expressive use of musical forms and dancerly arabesques in the development of her film style.[108] Of Toutain-Grün's controversial honor (previously held by Debussy and Erlanger), Dulac wrote, "It was discussed . . . as if merit should require a gender. Finally, Ms. Toutain-Grün won." Her portrait of celebrated novelist Judith Gautier (1845–1917, daughter of renowned Romantic novelist, travel and dance writer, and art critic Théophile Gautier), also accords with Dulac's extensive interest in the art and culture of the East, spurred on by the triumph of the itinerant, multidisciplinary collaborations of the Ballets russes as of 1909, as well as by its correspondences with a newly emerging, predominantly female consumerism.[109] Dulac employed themes, costumes, and decors inspired by orientalist fantasies of travel and female liberation in a number of her films (especially *La Belle Dame sans merci* [1927], *Âme d'artiste* [1925], *La Folie des vaillants* [1925], *Antoinette Sabrier* [1926], and *Princesse Mandane* [1928]).

Most decisively perhaps, her early contact with stage actress Suzanne Desprès (née Josephine Charlotte Bonvalet, 1875) and Desprès's husband, actor, director and promoter of the French Symbolist theater, Aurélien Lugné-Poë (née Aurélien Lugné, 1869–1940), who attended the association's International Salon in December 1906, directly informed Dulac's thematic choices, her modern acting style, and her symbolist approach to mise-en-scène as a means of expressing progressive social ideals.[110] In her November 1907 portrait of the actress, Dulac extolled Desprès's portrayal of feminist heroines in Lugné-Poë's productions of Norwegian playwright Henrik Ibsen's *Un ennemi du peuple* (*An Enemy of the People*), *Une Maison de poupée* (*A Doll's House*), *Hedda Gabbler*, *Solness le constructeur* (*The Master Builder*), and *Le Petit Eyolf* (*Little Eyolf*). Compensating for the modesty of Desprès, who ascribed her success to her husband, Dulac extolled her Ibsenian independence: "Yet, one could see that when she had to rely on herself alone, Madame Suzanne Desprès had already reached a milestone; and I watched her, energetic, industrious, honest and frank, rise up of her own strength, towards the artist dream that she herself had forged [. . .] proud, independent, like an Ibsenian heroine."[111] This momentous encounter spurred Dulac's summer 1908 trek across the Cap du Nord (Northern Cape) of Norway, referred to in her travel diary as "Ibsen's country," and eventually to write her own filmic adaptation of Ibsen's 1892 *Solness le constructeur*. Later she would pay Desprès the ultimate compliment by engaging her as an actress in her first film, *Les Sœurs ennemies* (The enemy sisters, 1916).[112]

These "women of action" (novelists, artists, and social advocates) proved to be crucial models for Dulac's own writing, filmmaking, and activism, providing her with a critical frame of reference for developing a feminist discursive strategy in the more constraining, industrial domain of cinema. However, before turning to the new medium, she pursued her feminist activism through yet another narrative and dramatic form, writing and directing her first theater play in 1907. In the years to come, Dulac's work as a promising playwright and theater critic at *La Française* exposed her to a wide variety of representational forms, providing a solid foundation for her film work.

Theater Projects

Between 1907 and late 1915, when she established her first film company, Dulac wrote more than a dozen theater projects, in a variety of genres that anticipate the diversity of her film oeuvre. Among these are a one-act comedy of manners, *Le Bonheur est chose légère* (Happiness is frivolous); a three-act fantasy, *Le Fantôme* (The phantom), based on a Norwegian legend; a four-act social parody titled *Les Pieuvres* (The octopuses);[113] and finally, an elaborate sixty-one-page, multiact class-conscious comedy, *Le Jardin magnifique* (The magnificent garden, 1911–14), which coincided with, and puts in perspective, the solid theatrical underpinnings of her first films.[114] Dulac's one-act feminist drama, *L'Emprise* (The hold, 1907), was her only play produced during her years at *La Française*, and as her earliest dramatic representation, it marked an important step for the future filmmaker.[115]

According to the program for the April 20, 1907 production at the Alliance française, *L'Emprise* was the feature attraction of a two-part matinee that opened with a performance by Juliette Toutain-Grün. Written in collaboration with Mlle V. Dutrey of *La Française*, it addresses the social constraints that the modern and forward-thinking woman faced in asserting herself in the public sphere, and specifically, in the domain of associative activism in which Dulac and her colleagues were involved. Despite sparse documentation of the production, its pragmatic script and its apparent one-time salon performance suggest a minimalist mise-en-scène.[116]

Evocative today of Dulac's feminist classic, *La Souriante Madame Beudet* (1923, *The Smiling Madame Beudet*), as well as of the filmmaker's own early struggles of conscience, *L'Emprise* is built around three characters: a young dissatisfied society-woman named Denise Merry; her bourgeois and conservative husband, Edmond, who holds a government administration post; and a more progressive family friend, Maurice Fosset, who acts as a sounding board for the expression of Denise's aspirations.[117] The play is structured around Denise's realization of her aspirations to live an intellectual life by contributing to the emancipation of other women. Denise, who wants to renounce her high-society soirées (seen as a mere support network for her husband's vocation) in favor of her own humanitarian and feminist activism, expresses her ambition, and in many ways that of the *mouvement du progrès féminin*, "to become someone, [. . .] to pour out one's thoughts and deliver them to the public, [. . .] to live an active, intellectual, impassioned life, [and] to improve oneself morally at each instant."[118]

Faced with her husband's incomprehension, Denise relates, one by one, the principal obstacles to women's progress during this period, namely, the institutions of religion, education, and marriage, impediments of real concern to partisans of the radical left and SFIO in the early 1900s. The issue of bourgeois marriage, which the heroine describes as "two blind wills working to constitute a family that itself will become a cog in a society that it doesn't understand," was particularly pertinent.[119] Following the laws ordaining the separation of church and state in 1905 and the secularization of schools in 1906, the socialist Léon Blum (a young administrator, alongside Dulac's uncle Saisset-Schneider, for the Conseil d'état (French Council of State), and future leader of the Popular Front Government, 1936–38, with whom Dulac would join forces) had launched a detailed attack on marriage's oppressive aspects in his pamphlet, *Du mariage* (On marriage, 1907).[120] The denouncement by Blum of these deep-rooted social conventions can be seen to prefigure how Dulac, as a moderate feminist, would resolve this controversial issue first in *L'Emprise*, and later through a more comprehensive approach in her films.

At a crucial moment, encouraged by Maurice's more progressive views, Denise, the heroine of *L'Emprise*, decides not only to act, but also to share her emancipatory experience with all: "I'll tell women that like them, I had lost faith in the fight; and that, each time that I surmounted my fears, when all I had left in me was pure willpower, I became emancipated." She declares her desire to "work for the women's cause, to give women a consciousness" like that she has gained. After these instances of exaltation, the play's denouement promises to be confrontational. Yet the work's title foretells its outcome: "l'emprise" literally means to have a hold on someone, just as Edmond constrains Denise. While the drama builds, preparing us for the moment when the heroine will express her desires to her husband, she abandons the idea out of fear. In the final moments of the play, when the husband asks, "What is wrong with her?" the friend responds with scornful regret, "She had a hallucination! . . . A simple hallucination."[121]

While *L'Emprise* reflects many of the contemporary issues raised in Dulac's lectures and portraits, its representational framework allowed Dulac to address them in a more precise way. On the one hand, Dulac was able to present and detail controversial issues with the same fervor and directness as in her lectures. On the other hand, by couching her ideas within the narrative and representational framework of theater, she granted them a degree of subtlety (characteristic of her women's portraits) that maintained their subversive character when read against the grain or considered in context. The play's ending, which acknowledges the limitations of the gender codes and class structures of the time, and the difficulties women faced in breaking out of their roles, doubtless reassured more conservative members of the audience. Yet a feminist message persisted. That is, with courage, women, including those of the upper class, could move beyond the constraints of established class and gender roles. Later, Dulac's work as a dramatic critic would expose her to a broad array of practices that would enable her to address her feminist concerns with greater subtlety and license in her films.

Theater Criticism or Reviews from "the Pond" (1908–1913)

In 1908, just one year after Dulac's first theatrical production, she took on *La Française*'s weekly theater column, previously penned by Jane Misme. On occasion, Dulac also wrote literary and dramatic reviews for other journals, including the theater weekly *La Rampe* (The footlights), to which her husband Albert also contributed. Dulac's fiery reviews, which vary in length from one to six columns, appeared on page two of the journal in a column titled "Le Théâtre ou les théâtres" (The theater and the theaters). For all of these dramatic reviews, Dulac used as her pseudonym a humorous and archaic variation on *du-lac* or "of the lake": G. De l'Estang (and later G. Delestang) meaning "of the pond."[122]

Between 1908 and 1913, Dulac reviewed more than 160 plays performed in Paris's most prestigious theaters—the classical Comédie-Française and Théâtre du Palais Royal, and the reformist, avant-garde Théâtre de l'Œuvre, founded by Lugné-Poë. She also looked at works at the Théâtre de l'Odéon, run by naturalist theater founder André Antoine (1906–14), which were considered the pinnacle of modern mise-en-scène.[123] These reviews typically addressed the narrative, acting, costumes, and decor, revealing Dulac's preferences and influences for certain types of mise-en-scène. However, unlike most other reviews at the time, they also tackled gender issues, revealing her developing interest in identifying innovative modes for their representation and expression.

A Feminist Critique

Assessing the conservative or progressive character of these works, ranging from light comedies to psychological dramas, Dulac used a degree of discretion similar to that found in her women's portraits. For instance, when reviewing

Sacha Guitry's *Un beau mariage* (A beautiful marriage), which premiered at the Théâtre de la renaissance, starring Alexandre Arquillère (who would play the husband in her 1923 *La Souriante Madame Beudet*), Dulac tactfully pointed to the author's "entertaining" yet "moralistic" treatment of a woman's refusal to marry. She chalked up Guitry's representation of the heroine's unconventional choice to "nothing other than an acknowledgment of a naïve and charming humanity."[124] Dulac asserted her feminism more readily, however, when considering more progressive works, such as that of French social dramatist Eugène Brieux, a disciple of Antoine's historic Théâtre libre (1887–94).[125]

Brieux's drama *Suzette* (Théâtre de vaudeville) addressed the rights of a divorced mother caught in a custody battle with her bourgeois mother-in-law for her child Suzette. In her five-column review, Dulac not only praised the play's treatment of women with regard to divorce and single motherhood, but also lauded its social relevance. Childless herself, she launched a frank, but judicious critique of the institution of marriage and the constraints of parenting:

> Too often women accept motherhood without realizing the duties they are engaging in. Sometimes it's better not to have children than to treat lightly the responsibility that they impose. Society today, in France, is based on the family. One must respect the law, as long as the evolution of moral standards has not [. . .] replaced it with other institutions. Those who have accepted, as they say, "to have souls in their care," have to recognize the needs of their time. Those who have remained free should work for the unconscious and profound transformations that will result in other laws.[126]

Diplomacy notwithstanding, echoing her early theatergoing experience and anticipating her commitment to film pedagogy, Dulac noted that a critic could gauge social change—in this case, women's progress—by examining audience reaction: "We can also measure the progress that our cause and our rights have had upon the minds of the public, since they always express themselves more or less in the plays that they applaud." Affirming the public's support for the divorced mother, who after much suffering wins her case, she writes, "Let's note . . . that the public applauded the dénouement . . . it admits to and approves of the fact that young sisters want to win their independence."[127] In the more industrial medium of film, this attention to audience response would prove crucial to Dulac's virtuoso manipulation of contradictory textual forces for viewers and censors, and manifests itself in various experimental shots of the audience in her film projects (e.g., the prologue to an early version of *La Souriante Madame Beudet*, an abstract shot in the opening scene of *Âme d'artiste*, and indeed inside jokes of sorts between the audience and certain protagonists in *Le Diable dans la ville*, *Princesse Mandane*, and other films).

Also elucidating here, Dulac assured her readers that her focus on the role of women was by no means restrictive: "Let's recognize that woman will remain the eternal puppet that makes theater enthusiasts laugh or cry. There is no drama, no comedy, without her. Whether effaced or triumphant, she is there. Consciously or unconsciously, her ill-fated and invigorating influence is exerted, ceding to the lives of others a repercussion of her own."[128]

Finally, for those unconvinced of the centrality of women's issues in theater, Dulac invoked writer Alexandre Dumas *fils* (1824–1895, author of *La Dame aux camélias*, aka *Camille*, 1848; *Le Fils naturel*, or *The Illegitimate Son*, 1858): "Celibacy, Marriage, Adultery: that is the tragic trilogy where the lives of women are debated; that is what we dramatic poets are eternally able to draw upon." Dulac saw these age-old stereotypes as a fertile ground for feminism, a place where women artists could "renew" dramatic themes, roles, and situations.[129] For Dulac, only feminism could expand the scope of female representation, and the theater (and later the cinema) should play a vital role in this process. In Dulac's films, this representational sphere would range from topics such as freedom to choose between work and family (*Mort du soleil*, 1921) to more controversial issues such as female sexuality (*Antoinette Sabrier*, 1927; *L'Invitation au voyage*, 1927; *Princesse Mandane*, 1928), which Dulac addressed in a review of Romain Coolus's *4 fois 7:28*, and which was just surfacing as a topic of public discussion during this period.[130]

Theatrical Renovation: Art and Technique

The title of Dulac's column, "Le Théâtre ou les théâtres," evokes the wide range of directorial approaches that emerged during a period of profound renovation in the Parisian theater circuit, artistic sensibilities, methods, and techniques that would have a considerable impact on her later projects. The modernization of twentieth-century French theater is largely credited to naturalist André Antoine (1858–1943), whose Parisian venues—the Théâtre libre (Free theater, 1887–94), the Théâtre Antoine (1897–1906), and the prestigious Théâtre de l'Odéon, where he directed (1906–14) and revitalized narration and mise-en-scène. For Antoine, influenced by Darwin, Nietzsche and Zola's *Naturalisme au théâtre* (1881), theater should reproduce an anatomical image of the reality of the struggle of daily life, a directive that acting, decor, and costume design should follow.[131] In this spirit (e.g., Nietzsche's *The Birth of Tragedy*, 1871), Antoine put forth a new positivist conception of the tragic that rejected destiny in favor of social determinism. Distributor-imposed notions of destiny notwithstanding, Dulac's films emphasize social causation, and a corresponding social realism that lays bare the relationship between character and environment (*Malencontre*, *La Belle Dame*, *Invitation au voyage*).

Yet, a second current, more influential for Dulac, as well as for future protagonists of cinematic impressionism, notably Louis Delluc and Marcel L'Herbier, was the theatrical symbolism of mystic Aurélien Lugné-Poë (1869–1940), and his associates Maurice Maeterlinck and Paul Claudel. Significantly, their respective muses, Suzanne Desprès, Georgette Leblanc, and Ève Francis, starred in key films for Dulac, L'Herbier, and Delluc, respectively. Francis, who married Delluc, played principal roles in the films of all three.

After an acting debut at Antoine's Théâtre libre (1888), Lugné-Poë, fascinated with spiritualism and the paranormal, founded the reformist and avant-garde Théâtre de l'Œuvre (1893). His work fit into a broader artistic trend that, as literary scholar Alain Viala put it, sought to "refine forms," "call on the imagination," and "to make [things] understood, without showing [them]."[132] Working with postimpressionist Nabi artists (Maurice Denis, Pierre Bonnard, and especially painter-printmaker Édouard Vuillard) with their emphasis on a purity of line, color and form, Lugné-Poë experimented with symbolist scenography, using low-lit, suggestive, painted, and synthetist decors to create an atmosphere that could capture and transmit the emotions or "inner life" of the artist. According to Lugné-Poë, a single, line-like figure (e.g., an old man seated beside his lamp) could evoke the "fullness of life experience" and the mysterious forces of the universe more powerfully than any action drama. Seeking to transport the spectator, not through physical movement, but through "stillness" (or "static theater") and narrative recitatives, his call for minimalist acting and decors, with the exception of atmospheric effects such as lighting, colored projections, music, and scents, would prove to be important to Dulac's work and her efforts to express the "ineffable," from her pre-impressionist *Les Sœurs ennemies* (1916) to her "pure" or abstract films (1929).[133]

The specter of Vuillard, and notably his work on Lugné-Poë's productions of Ibsen (e.g., *Solness le constructeur*), also merits consideration. His middle-class portraits, which play on spatial tensions—between surface placidity and deeper conflict, decorative impulse and affectionate observation (see Hilton Kramer,

The Age of the Avant-garde)—find echoes in Dulac's social aesthetics (*Belle Dame, Madame Beudet*). His combination of natural, abstract and geometric forms (e.g., *Une Partie de dames*, or *Game of Checkers*, 1906) prefigures the complex spatiality and play between two-dimensional geometric abstraction and cinematic depth of field in the 1920s (e.g., Dulac's *L'Invitation au voyage, La Coquille et le clergyman* [1927], *Princesse Mandane* [1928], *Arabesque* [1929]; Marcel L'Herbier's *Eldorado* [1921] and *L'Inhumaine* [1924]).

Dulac's exposure to these modern tendencies sheds light on her *stylistic dualism*, with its combination of realist representations of social conditions, and symbolist representations of psychic life. From her use of atmospheric effects, such as colored projections and visualized scents (lighted fountains, incense, exotic flowers) to conjure up the reveries of her heroines in her commercial films (*La Cigarette, La Belle Dame, Antoinette Sabrier*) to her avant-gardist call for a "visual symphony" or "pure cinema" that minimizes plot, décor, and acting (e.g., *La Folie des vaillants* [1925], *Invitation* [1927], and *Arabesque* [1929]), this period provides an important context for her aesthetic of "sensation" and "suggestion."

New Models, New Visions

Dulac also reviewed the work of many of the latest artists that Antoine and Lugné-Poë had brought to the Parisian scene, including talented national playwrights (e.g., Jarry, Claudel, Gide) and distinguished international authors (e.g., Strindberg and Tolstoy). Her reviews expose her particular interest in the psychological symbolism of Henri Bataille, Maurice Maeterlinck, and Fyodor Dostoevsky, each of whom she read, as well as in what she described as the "more direct" socialist realism of George Bernard Shaw, before fashioning her own film adaptations of Ibsen's *Solness le constructeur* and Maxim Gorky's *Radda* with her film *La Folie des vaillants*.[134] While the psychological character of Dulac's work has often been highlighted at the expense of the sociological, these two aspects actually go hand in hand.

Dulac's literary and dramatic criticism confirms her penchant for classic and foundational notions of scenic and historical realism, revived by Antoine. While her literary review of Karl Mantzius's *Molière. Les théâtres, le public et les comédiens de son temps* (Molière: the theaters, audience, and actors of his time, 1908) pays tribute to the playwright's "concern for truth . . . which should be ceaselessly copied from the live model," she panned Émile Moreau's play *Le Procès de Jeanne d'Arc* (The trial of Joan of Arc), starring Sarah Bernhardt, for its "fictionalization of known historical facts," anticipating her position years later as a founding member of the Coordination Committee for Jean Renoir's *La Marseillaise* (1938).[135]

Dulac's affinity for theatrical symbolism, considered both an extension of and poetic reaction to nineteenth-century naturalism, can be seen in her preference for the realist immediacy of Henri Bataille and Dario Nicodemi's symbolist works, which she says operated *directly "selon* la vie" (in accordance with life; emphasis added), over the more conventional works of playwrights Sam Benelli and Romain Coolus, written *indirectly* "d'*après* la vie" (based on life; emphasis added).[136] While Dulac, nonetheless, adapted Coolus, with her commercial, highly controversial, and censored Ève Francis vehicle, *Antoinette Sabrier*, Bataille and Nicodemi's works appear to have been more instrumental. Notably, this marks Dulac's first known reference to dramatic "impressionism." Comparing their theatrical symbolism to impressionist painting, she praised their "notation" and "superimposition" of sentiments and observed facts as a means of "interpreting abstract ideas," anticipating her own cinematic impressionism and abstraction in the 1920s. She noted a similar appreciation for the "poetry and truth of symbols" in Maeterlinck's fairy play *L'Oiseau bleu* (The blue bird, at Lugné-Poë's Théâtre de l'Œuvre, 1908) starring the avant-garde diva Georgette Leblanc.[137]

Like her early artistic interests, and her women's portraits, Dulac's work as a theater critic exposed her to a wide variety of sensibilities and provided her with a broad base for the development of her own unique style—from impressionism and abstraction in the 1920s to a direct, "pure cinema" approach to the newsreel in the 1930s—which she would use to promote her progressive social ideals.

In 1913, a year after meeting her paramour, the energetic young actress, pantomime artist and dancer Stasia de Napierkowska, and a year before the outbreak of war, Dulac left her responsibilities at *La Française* to devote herself to her own theatrical and literary projects. Her early creative, and intellectual influences, her mentoring by Albert, and her work as a journalist and dramatic critic had affirmed her engagement as an egalitarian and a reformist feminist, and introduced her to a wide variety of representational forms, refining the creative capacities and skills that would serve her as an activist and filmmaker for the years to come. While few traces survive of

Dulac's professional activities following her 1913 departure from *La Française*, correspondence with her early romantic and professional associates Napierkowska, and subsequently Hillel-Erlanger, as well as the almost-daily letters from her husband Albert during World War I, allow us to reconstruct her activities as a social activist and burgeoning filmmaker during this tumultuous and transformative period in French and world history.

Figure 2. Arabesque posture of Stasia de Napierkowska (stage/screen name: Stacia Napierkowska), star of *Dans L'Hellade/In Ancient Greece* (Charles Decroix, 1909, Film d'art), a "ballet pantomime" by Sacha Dezac. Courtesy of Fondazione Cineteca di Bologna.

Chapter 2

The Great War and Dulac's First Films

World War One was a "total war" that affected not just the life of combatants, volunteers, and conscripts, but also all aspects of the home front. In France, the war marked a fundamental rupture with the Belle Époque outlook of unchecked optimism about artistic creation, ever-expanding scientific and technological innovation, and universalist humanist progress.[1] A "psychological turning point . . . for modernism as a whole," it would have wide-ranging economic, political, and sociocultural repercussions, including a radical reorientation of the Women's Progress movement, along with profound transformations across the visual and performing arts.[2] With a preliminary separation from her husband, Albert, in 1913, and his successive mobilization to the front, the war also brought Dulac increased autonomy, exceptional access to a transitioning film industry, and the opportunity to refocus and refashion the means of her social and artistic intervention.[3] An account of Dulac's wartime experiences in this rapidly evolving environment helps us better understand the development of her oeuvre.[4]

Internationalist Pacifism and National Defense

When the Germans invaded France in early August 1914, the cataclysmic and irreversible impact of the Great War or "der(nière) des der(nière)s" (the war to end all wars) on soldiers and civilians alike became immediately apparent. Like a majority of feminists of her time, Dulac, faced with the reality and the magnitude of this cataclysm, found herself between two contradictory positions: her universalist, pacifist ideals, dating back to her early activities at *La Française* (notably her 1907 lecture on the international task of Frenchwomen), and the imminent concern for national defense, whose resonance in the government's call for *l'union sacrée* (sacred union, or a united front in the face of the aggressor) rekindled some of Dulac's early socialist ties.[5]

In the period immediately following the German invasion, Dulac's pacifist objections receded into the background as she devoted herself to a range of war-related activities from humanitarian assistance (medical care, food banks) to counterpropaganda (correspondence, articles, and films). From August 1914 through April 1915, she organized soup kitchens for war victims' families (on rue Cauchois in the heart of Montmartre), alongside Georgette Sembat, wife of cultural activist and socialist minister Marcel Sembat (with whom she had remained close since the anticlerical legislation with her uncle Raymond in 1905).[6] Yet, just one month after the hostilities began, Albert encouraged her to look beyond such efforts "You're right. The life of each and all, the fate of individuals and nations, poses moral problems and conflicts at each moment in these difficult times. [. . .] But seek out and listen to your instinct. You love Paris and the beautiful experience of its vibrating spirit. You feel a need to devote yourself and to be useful. But look further."[7] As the conflict raged, Dulac would turn toward more concrete intellectual and political activities, while also continuing to develop her creative projects. Her long-standing friendship with Sembat and several of his associates during this period (1912–19) also would intersect in auspicious ways with her new feminist and artistic orientations.

In the context of the call for a *union sacrée* (a patriotic prowar consensus), Marcel Sembat was one of only two socialist ministers (or state secretaries, along with Marxist Jules Guesde [1845–1922]) to serve in the national unity cabinet headed by rightwing prime ministers René Viviani (1914) and Aristide Briand (1915). An anticolonialist, as well as an arts education, and worker's movement activist, Sembat appears to have been an important mentor for Dulac, energizing and reinforcing her early intermedial, sociopolitical and pedagogical approach to the cinema and ciné-club activism.[8] Noteworthy are Sembat's passionate talks on contemporary art and literature (from fauvist and cubist painting to symbolist poetry), as well as his dinners and soirées, which Germaine and Albert Dulac had attended since before the war in the company of other artists and intellectuals (from Henri Matisse and Gustav Kahn to Anatole France). Sembat, also known for making art accessible to the people, as well as for having famously defended artistic freedom before the Assemblée nationale in 1912, played an instrumental role in the Salon d'automne (founded in 1903 by architect Frantz Jourdain, with painters

Matisse, Vuillard, and others).[9] Dulac remained in close contact with the Sembats after the war, personally inviting them to each of her film premieres, until the couple's fatal auto accident in 1922.

In the Sembat circle and close to Dulac were a number of intellectuals and artists of note. A friend and correspondent, Nobel Prize–winning novelist and poet Anatole France (1844–1924) was one of the first to publicly defend the cinema. Also important was the private salon of Fauvist painter and women's portraitist, Kees Van Dongen (1877–1968), frequented during the war by Dulac, actress Ève Francis, and dancer Djemil Anik, as well as esoteric novelist and poet Irène Hillel-Erlanger, all of whom would be early collaborators of the future filmmaker. Another figure, a lifelong friend of Albert, was poet and editor of the *Revue socialiste* (Socialist review), André Lebey (1877–1935).[10] Similarly, Yvon Delbos (1885–1956), future socialist deputy (1924), minister of education (1939–40), and editor of *Le Radical* (which superseded *La Fronde*), later accompanied Dulac to the Congrès du cinéma éducateur at the Cinémathèque de la ville de Paris (1926–28), and supported her 1920–30s film pedagogy efforts for the Fédération française des ciné-clubs, and the League of Nations' International Educational Cinematographic Institute (IECI, Rome, 1928–37). In 1927, Dulac dedicated one of her most important theoretical articles, "Les Esthétiques, les entraves, la cinégraphie intégrale" (1927), to Delbos, calling him an "ami du cinéma."[11] Finally, it was through this group that Dulac met and worked closely with the prolific feminist author, poet and dramaturge Jeanne Lapauze (née Loiseau, 1860–1921), a former Frondiste, whose novel *Justice de femme* (Women's justice), published under the pseudonym Daniel Lesueur, was adapted to film in 1917, and a brief partner in the creation of Dulac's film production company (fleetingly named La Parisienne) in April 1916.[12] Dulac also wrote an editorial for the prominent journal *La Renaissance Politique, Littéraire et Artistique,* created in 1913 by the author's husband, art curator Henry Lapauze. Founding director of the 1902 Palais des Beaux-arts de la Ville de Paris, an art museum housed in the Petit Palais, Henry Lapauze was also an early organizer of the 1925 Exposition Internationale des Arts Décoratifs et Industriels Modernes (a descendant of the Salon d'automne), where Dulac would lecture, screen films, and exhibit production innovations (e.g. *La Folie des vaillants*).[13] Dulac's early engagement with this entourage of politically progressive artists and intellectuals galvanized her activism both during and after the war.

Sisters in Arms: Citoyennes *and the* union sacrée

Dulac's proximity to this creative and politically engaged milieu went hand in hand with the reorientation of her feminist activism in support of the national cause. During the early stages of the war, Dulac contributed to the Belgian refugee program Aide aux femmes des combattants (Aid to Soldier's Wives) and to Daniel Lesueur's Office d'utilisation des femmes (Women's Use Office), an outgrowth of the Union française pour le suffrage des femmes (French women's suffrage union).[14] While historians have often evoked a "sacred union" of political parties and classes and rarely that of the sexes, at the height of the women's suffrage movement, as Françoise Thébaud notes, a majority of feminists opted to set aside their call for civil equality, along with pacifism, in order to support the imperiled nation.[15]

In the spring of 1915, as the war escalated, Dulac's efforts turned more overtly political, even militant, when she became secretary-general of the all-women's organization La Croisade des femmes françaises (CFF, Frenchwomen's crusade). According to an interview published in the *Gazette de Lausanne* (March 14, 1915), the group formed to counter the propaganda that Austrian and German aggressors were producing for neutral countries. For moderate feminists like Dulac and the CFF members, this participation in the war effort, in defense of the nation, appeared as a necessary step in gaining state recognition as *citoyennes*, just as the women's progress movement had been seen as essential to improving humanity. The organization's manifesto expounded upon what they saw as the importance of asserting the female political voice:

> The hour has come for the Frenchwoman to show everyone that she is not what jealousy abroad has published about her: "a doll without courage, without moral standards and without a heart." Unrestrainedly defamed, she must silence the libelers in showing herself to be worthy of our heroes. Her voice will rise to save this country from all of the trickery directed against it. For if cloaking oneself in proud silence has its greatness, tracking down all of the perfidious inventions of our enemies is even more opportune; it is the best way to preserve that which we hold as essential: the esteem and friendship of the neutral countries.[16]

For Dulac, the CFF would serve as both a vital counterweight to Austrian and German propaganda, as well as a powerful instrument for women's assertiveness in the war effort. In an interview with the *Gazette de Lausanne*, Dulac highlighted the organization's principal strategies: to distribute letters and to publish accounts of war events that would be as "objective" as possible, an idea that anticipates her proto cinema direct approach to newsreel filmmaking, as well as her 1935 pacifist, compilation documentary *Le Cinéma au service de l'histoire* (Cinema in the service of history). She declared,

> First of all [. . .], there will simply be correspondence. As you are aware the Austro-Germans have worked wonders in this area. They have flooded all of the neutral countries with a stream of tendentious letters. In the guise of commercial relations, they sent their correspondents pleas for the *Kultur*. The Louvain fires, the Belgian massacres, and the upheavals of Reims were represented as benign measures, rendered necessary by the viciousness of those invaded. We shall *reestablish the proportions* a bit while awaiting the judgment of history [. . .] we shall send summaries that are as *objective* and as *impartial* as possible of the real events to addresses our members identify as useful. (emphasis added)[17]

Dulac's statement affirmed her belief regarding German aggression and dishonesty toward the French and her conviction that women's authentic accounts of the war could serve truth and history. Significantly, along with lectures and conferences, the publication of pamphlets and illustrated post cards (a popular medium at the time), the group also turned to the cinema: "We even plan to have *films* that will reestablish the truth," thus illustrating the filmmaker's early investment in the medium's status and potential as visual and historical evidence. Appropriating the political term of union sacrée Dulac sought to extend its meaning to a new, women-initiated form of activism: "We have only one watchword, that which the head of state gave to parliament: sacred union" (emphasis added).[18]

Enemy Sisters: the International Culture of War

During the spring of 1915, Dulac also extended her efforts abroad. While maintaining her solidarity with the French national cause, and staying true to the internationalist and pacifist activism of her early days at *La Française*, she published two articles on Italian women's opinions that testify to her commitment to international feminism. In the first of these (published in Lapauze's *Renaissance Politique, Littéraire et Artistique*), Dulac interviewed the celebrated Neapolitan novelist Matilde Serao (1856–1927). Editor of the royalist daily *Il Giorno*, screenwriter of *La mia vita per la tua!* (My life for yours, Ghione, 1915), and one of first Italian intellectuals to write about cinema's impact on life and politics, Serao hoped to "dissipat[e] a misunderstanding" regarding the journal's "anti-French campaign."[19] In April 1915, less than two weeks before Italy secretly joined the Triple Entente (United Kingdom, France, and Russia) in alliance against Germany and its former allies, Dulac published a second related article, "L'Opinion féminine en Italie sur l'intervention italienne" (The opinion of Italian women on the Italian intervention), chronicling the diverse, but largely interventionist viewpoints of prominent Italian women, including that of Le Conseil nationale des femmes italiennes (Rome) president Dora Melegari.[20]

These articles affirm the complexity of an internationalist feminism that goes back to Dulac's early days at *La Française*. For example, Serao's Germanophile pronouncements notwithstanding, Dulac ended her first article with the author's equivocal, yet pacifist declaration: "Just tell my *ex-friends* the French . . . if you speak about me, that I am an enemy of the war, a friend of peace, and that I ardently hope for the end of this atrocious struggle" (original emphasis).[21]

However, Dulac's unconditional rejection of German aggression and her stalwart defense of the national position, would eventually come head to head with her internationalism, as evidenced by her attitude towards the International Women's Peace Conference in The Hague (Netherlands). In an article she published on May 1, 1915, as secretary-general of La Croisade, she promoted a national boycott of the peace conference to protest its inclusion of a German delegation and its decision to "prohibit a discussion of the responsibility of belligerent nations."[22] The ubiquity of the French boycott was emblematic of the temporary breakdown of the international women's movement (like the workers' movement) during the war. As Jane Misme had declared in *La Française* (November 19, 1914), "As long as the war continues, the wives of the enemy also will be enemies," a statement echoed in the title of Dulac's first film, *Les Sœurs ennemies* (The enemy sisters, 1917).[23]

At first glance, then, Dulac's solidarity with the *union sacrée* seems to contradict her pacifism, but it gains coherence when considered in context. If Dulac and her contemporaries became so invested in this devastating conflict, it was because they saw it as a matter of moral responsibility and obligation. Once hostilities erupted in August 1914, there was practically no alternate identity available for artists and intellectuals, except that of a radical pacifist or antidefensive position. The felt obligation to win the war, or to maintain French sovereignty, gave rise to an unprecedented and unconditional investment in the national cause, and it explains why a majority of artists and intellectuals, mobilized or not, were prepared to see the conflict through to its bitter end. Dulac's actions also were inscribed in this "culture of war," a phenomenon understood by modern French historians as the way in which contemporaries imagined and depicted the war through an ensemble of attitudes, practices, symbolic productions, and representations, both cause and consequence of this total investment in the national defense.[24]

Le Jardin magnifique: Romantic Pursuits and Creative Liberties

While the war brought moral obligations, it also created a momentary rupture from traditional social roles and offered an unprecedented experience of liberty and self-affirmation for many women. Female employment and professionalization, which had long been the object of public criticism, were now viewed as a manifestation of patriotism.[25] While at the height of the women's suffrage movement in 1914 feminists had felt obligated to put aside their egalitarian demands for the national cause, many began to see the war as a chance to access civil equality more quickly.[26] For Dulac, who belonged to a relatively privileged milieu, the war period provided a greater sense of self-reliance. In her husband's absence, and with a depleted labor pool in the film industry, she also was able to seize opportunities for the realization of her creative projects.

One of the most important influences on Dulac's subsequent creative activities was her liaison with the spirited and sultry twenty-one-year-old Franco-Polish actress and dancer, Stasia de Napierkowska (b. Renée Claire Angèle Élisabeth Napierkowski, stage name Stacia Napierkowska, 1891–1945). According to archival correspondence, the two first met on April 17, 1912, the day of a rare (almost total) "diamond necklace" solar eclipse, which interrupted the ordinary lives of 2 million admiring Parisians, just two days after the *Titanic* disappeared under the darkness of a new moon.[27] This chance meeting, and the newfound liberties that came with the war, would bring about a similarly spectacular eclipse for Dulac, who plunged more deeply into her creative activities, as well as a thrilling romantic relationship with someone who, having worked with leading directors Albert Capellani, Max Linder, and Ferdinand Zecca, would become her lead actress in several feature films.

Figure 3. Stacia Napierkowska, ca. 1910–12. George Grantham Bain Collection, Library of Congress, Prints & Photographs Division.

In the summer of 1913, shortly after Stasia's April arrest for indecency while performing a dance in New York, and as the unchained choreography of Stravinsky's *Le Sacre du printemps* (*The Rite of Spring*) for Diaghilev's Ballets russes provoked riots at Paris's Théâtre des Champs-Elysées, Dulac who had been working on several scripts since *L'Emprise* (1907), began to look more seriously at theatrical mise-en-scène. Over the course of the year, Napierkowska had been sending her various sketches of curved and spiral-like poses and movements (laying down, knees up, floating), provocatively labeled "tendrils," "trembling," and "spinning."[28] In July 1913, Dulac sketched a set for a project based on Oscar Wilde's provocative and lyrical French-language play, *Salomé* (dir. Maeterlinck), a role that she had seen Napierkowska perform in Strauss's controversial one-act opera a season prior.[29] In 1914, over the course of numerous stays with her at the Hotel Flora in Rome, from February to December, Dulac began attending the actress and dancer's film shoots for Film d'arte Italiana director Ugo Falena.[30] In the spring of 1914, Dulac announced her plans to produce her own stage plays in conjunction with her husband and Napierkowska."[31] During this period, Dulac had been developing several theatrical representations with Napierkowska set to play the lead, including her sixty-page three-act project, *Le Jardin magnifique* (The magnificent garden), a comedy of manners portraying class roles, and particularly those of the aristocracy, as unmasked by the war.[32] Drawing upon Dulac's experience as a journalist and critic at *La Française*, *Le Jardin magnifique* brings together her interest in the tension between surface placidity and deeper conflict, which she would seek to reveal through the more acute observation of the everyday gesture in her films.

In the spring of 1915, following *Le Jardin magnifique*, and her project for a liberatory novel on the nun-turned-actress, "Denise Serpe," Albert writing from the warfront, encouraged Dulac to set aside her associative and literary work, and to concentrate on her dramatic work: "I wanted to talk to you about your scripts, darling. I am happy to see you at last beginning a work. First, do not hesitate about the order: theater before the book."[33] However, owing to Napierkowska's continued activities at Film d'arte, and the actress's short-lived plans to create her own production company in Italy, Dulac's theatrical work was postponed.[34] Even as her theater projects stalled, her personal and professional relationship with Napierkowska and her exposure to the filmmaking milieu in Rome would prove decisive for the future cineaste. Years later Dulac declared, "It's alongside this beautiful artist Napierkowska, and thanks to her, that I learned the secrets of the cinegraphic art."[35]

Dulac's homosexuality, like her romantic relationships within and beyond her marriage, provides a fertile context for understanding the subtleties of her feminist aesthetic, rendered through a symbolist approach. Several letters from Napierkowska and Albert during this period suggest an openness in Dulac's marriage that would accommodate her on-and-off romance with Napierkowska from spring 1912 through early 1915, and her subsequent affairs with other women. Napierkowska writes to Dulac in April 1913, while on tour in Europe "The most beautiful day of my life is the one upon which I knew you, February 27, 1913. I am coming back!!!! I am crazy with joy."[36] After a dinner party at the Dulacs' home (24, rue Chaptal) in September 1913, Marcel Sembat refers similarly to "that little agile dancer, *la Napierkowska*, that Germaine is crazy about."[37]

Not surprisingly, perhaps, Dulac's marriage to Albert becomes increasingly strained during the prewar years, leading to a break-up in 1913. Several of Albert's letters reference a long, ambiguous, and even fraught romance while also testifying to a deeply sustaining friendship. Following a reference in 1906 to her "fear at opening her heart" and in 1910 to their amicable separation, a break-up letter from June 1913 seems more definitive:

> Germaine, I write this after three hours of reflection, in full consciousness of my thoughts and of my act. I want there to no longer be a question of love between us: there is no longer any love. I do not want to further damage the beautiful memory of our past. I want my freedom back and I want to give you back yours. I will do everything so that this separation gives you the greatest number of possibilities. I hope that you will allow me to show you for a long time still the great esteem that I have for your intelligence and your character and to stay very faithfully your best friend.—Albert[38]

In the period leading up to their legal separation in 1922, the two would maintain a strong amicable and professional bond and an enduring correspondence. In subsequent letters, Albert mentions the couple's unconventional conjugal situation and characterizes their encounter with Napierkowska as a source of liberation, making affectionate references to the latter and to the "trio" they now form, playfully signing these letters "Tim." (The nickname is perhaps a reference to Louis Feuillade's popular sixty-plus 1912–16 film serial featuring the character, and enfant terrible Bout-de-Zan, translated as Tiny Tim.) Barring further evidence, an additional March 29, 1915, letter referring to their marriage as a source of liberation raises the question of whether or not Albert himself was gay, and whether or not theirs might have been a marriage of convenience. He writes: "April is for us that of realizations. Ten years ago, the sixth liberated us [marriage April 6, 1905]. Three years ago, the seventeenth [April 17, 1912] we met Stasia. Two years ago her return from the U.S. [April 1914]." In fact, further correspondence suggests that he accepted and at times encouraged Dulac's romance not only with "Stasou," as he sometimes called her, but also with other women in the open relationship they maintained until their eventual separation after the war.[39] Of these women, seemingly of Jewish ethnicity, and around the time Dulac met her next partner Irène Hillel-Erlanger (as well as actress and dancer Ida Rubinstein), he queried, in a letter dated April 3, 1915, "Since we've been apart, how many haven't you known? When you feel inspired, I'd be curious to know what about them pleases you."[40] Her subsequent cohabitation with film programmer, realist songwriter and future documentary filmmaker Marie-Anne Colson-Malleville from 1922 (the year of her final separation from Albert) to 1942 further supports this.[41] Turning to Dulac's filmmaking, it seems reasonable to infer that her homosexuality (and perhaps that of Albert) contributed to the arguably subversive and queer aesthetics or the aesthetics of potentiality that her 1920s films display.

Voyages en kaléidoscope: *New Ventures, Preparing the Course*

In the spring of 1915, her projects with Napierkowska on hold, Dulac met Irène Hillel-Erlanger (née Berthe Rebecca Alice Irène Hillel-Manoach, 1878–1920), an unsparing observer and critic, with whom she developed an intense and impassioned affair, eclipsing her romance with Napierkowska, and with whom she would cofound her first film production company a year later.[42] Daughter of a prominent banker, and recently divorced from Opéra comique composer Camille Erlanger, Hillel-Erlanger had made a name of her own among creative circles as a regular contributor to Paris's most prestigious literary journals, including Paul Fort's *Vers et Prose* and André Gide's *Nouvelle Revue Française*. This was before publishing her fascinating esoteric *dispositif* novel, *Voyages en kaléidoscope* (1919), a work that evokes Bergson's 1908 proto-cinematic use of the phantasmagoric device to characterize the human experience in time, as a duration periodically shaken to provide new perspectives.[43] Hillel-Erlanger extends this motif, "think perhaps of Kaleido: Our Characters (it says) are the very same Structure and Substance of our condition."[44] As Richard Armin has pointed out, the poetess's dispositif, evoked by its Dada-inspired cover illustration, records, codes, compresses and stores our visions for posterity, and projects them back as "animated metaphors" or "kaleidosopic voyages," a vision that patently coincides with Dulac's view of newsreel cinema in particular (before digital media); as an archive of the unconscious gestures of our daily lives that makes us see anew.[45] Hillel-Erlanger's dispositif also accords with that of Dulac's contemporary, pacifist, banker, and founder of the Archives de la Planète and micro-cinematography lab Albert Kahn, as demonstrated by Paula Amad's groundbreaking study, *Counter-Archive*.[46] Aside from its Dadaist character that no doubt dislodged bourgeois sensibilities, Hillel-Erlanger's novel accords on several fronts with Dulac's humanistic vision of the new modern medium: not only as an apparatus for radical technological intervention into the human experience of space and time, one that links the individual and the collective, the subjective and the objective, the animate and the inanimate, but also as epitomized by Dulac's approach to the newsreel as a tool for greater human understanding. As Hillel-Erlanger writes, "individual and collective merge in a kind of transcendental and humorous physical chemistry," and, prefiguring Dulac's later position on the international newsreel, "HARMONY [IS] BORN THROUGH AN EXCHANGE OF IDEAS!"[47]

Hillel-Erlanger also frequented the city's most distinguished literary, artistic and political circles, and organized several important literary salons in the late teens, guest hosted by figures such as Jean Cocteau, Anna de Noailles, and founder of the Dada literary and art movement Tristan Tzara. It is in this context that Dulac came into contact with Louis Aragon, who founded and coedited with the poet Phillipe Soupault and André Breton the Dadaist journal *Littérature*, financed in large part by Hillel-Erlanger.[48] This early connection may help explain Dulac's future engagement as director of *La Coquille et le clergyman*, based on Antonin Artaud's script and financed by the Noailles family.

In the fall of that year, Dulac explored the economic feasibility of creating a film company that would draw on Hillel-Erlanger's talents as a writer, her own interest in mise-en-scène or directing, and Albert's literary and financial background.[49] As the Napoleonic code still restricted the financial transactions of married women (including opening a bank account), Albert's role as financial administrator of the film company was also a practical one. Yet he seemed to envision the enterprise as something to be carried out only after his liberation at war's end. In his war-worn words, Dulac's immediate task was simply to prepare the venture:

> Your role, which you understand perfectly, is to take care of everything currently within your power. Maintain your connections, and keep a circle of friends that is stimulating, understanding and reassuring; prepare the path that we must follow so that each of us, full of strength and youth [. . . .], will only have to rise when peace makes us free again; that is the great work. They are only preparations, momentary arrangements. Achievements will come later, all the better because of the path you have laid out, and the steps you have prepared. That role is yours.[50]

Despite Albert's tentativeness, in less than six months, by the spring of 1916 (with no end of the war in sight), Dulac was preparing to put her plans into action. Albert, who had hoped to play a more creative role, still gave his full support, while assuming the more symbolic position of chairman of the board and general manager.[51] Her choice to move ahead without his presence is in keeping with the profound shift in the social landscape for women during the war and with a more radical gendering of attitudes that would persist afterward.

Indeed, in 1916, the contrast between life on the battlefront and the home front was striking. In French, as in English, the literal terms that designate these two fronts—*l'avant* (the front), where men were, and *l'arrière* (the rear) or *l'intérieur* (inside), where women were—reminded the respective genders of their places in society. Yet the daily reality of the war was drastically different. It gave women increased liberty and mobility, and confined men to their trenches or outposts on the then-stabilized front. The hero of Henri Barbusse's celebrated naturalist novel *Le Feu* (which received the Prix Goncourt in 1916) expresses the general uneasiness that this contrast created: "There are two countries. I say, we are split into two foreign countries: notably, the [war front] out there where too many are miserable, and the home front here, where too many are happy."[52]

As the Great War continued, women were increasingly exercising their new independence, and taking advantage of the accompanying professional opportunities, in the absence of men, a realization that did not go unnoticed on the front. On April 18, 1916, Albert wrote, "You say that life is returning to normal at home. That is certainly the impression we have on the front, and increasingly so. Socially a situation that endures eventually finds a balance. One has to live and, inevitably, life adapts to its circumstances. The *poilus* [French soldiers, 1914–18] are adapting to the war; and little by little, civilians are learning to live without the *poilus*. Work, pleasure, everyone's social relations are organized without them."[53]

While Albert agreeably evoked the resumption of activity on the home front, he also pointed to the crisis that this was creating for the soldiers. He continued: "They feel it. Some already ask what will become of them upon their return. At first one kept a place for them. Then came the forgetting. More months will pass. Except in some hearts, their memory will be erased. They'll return. Will they not be intruders? [. . .] How will this multitude separated from the nation be assimilated again?"[54] This sense of detachment and extrication, which contributed to an emerging male identity crisis, did not go unacknowledged by Dulac, and it would later be reflected in her postwar films through the recurring tropes of male anguish, desolation and suicide (e.g., *La Cigarette*, 1919; *La Belle Dame sans merci*, 1921; *La Souriante Madame Beudet*, 1923; *Antoinette Sabrier*, 1927).

The prolonged absence of men from the home front and the workforce brought new job opportunities for women, even beyond the dominant wartime domains of agriculture and arms manufacturing (in which the Schneider family, *marchands de canons*, played a key role).[55] With most of its filmmakers, technicians, and actors mobilized, the French film industry (already in retreat after Pathé's departure from the MPPC Trust) slowed.[56] With the drop in national production, and the flood of films from the United States, Italy, and Scandinavia, the French motion-picture industry welcomed investors and was more open to engaging women as directors and, more particularly, as producers. While the work of female producer-directors during this period remains underdocumented, numerous women—including actresses Napierkowska and her 1915 costar in Feuillade's *Fantômas*, Musidora, with whom Dulac would work in 1922—established their own small production companies (as did Lois Weber and Alla Nazimova in the United States), however short-lived. The lack of documentation on the directorial careers of early women pioneers (excepting more recent efforts, notably by the projects of Women and Film History International) reflects the anxieties regarding shifting gender roles at the time.

In Dulac's case, in the spring of 1916, Albert endorsed her creation of a production company, not yet named but referring to it, even, as a contribution to national productivity, as the director herself would later. Within days of his legal authorization, Dulac and Hillel-Erlanger (whose privileged social situations rendered it possible) traveled to Marseille to discuss the details of the company's first venture.[57]

In April 1916, when the company's name was still La Parisienne, and before having settled on a script, Dulac decided that the first film would feature Ibsenian actress Suzanne Desprès, a choice that Albert considered "a masterstroke for the company."[58] She envisioned several possible projects, including Jules Renard's *Poil de carotte* (Carrot-top), in which Desprès had starred at the Théâtre de l'Œuvre, as well as Tolstoy's five-act play *Resurrection*. She also considered an untitled story that Albert described as "very cinematic" by Russian symbolist Maxim Gorky, whose story "Makar Chudra" she would later adapt with her "visual symphony," *La Folie des vaillants*, in 1925.[59] Yet, owing in part to copyright considerations, Dulac and Hillel-Erlanger almost exclusively directed their own scripts during the first few years of their company's existence.[60] Somewhat ironically, with the expansion of the postwar industry, Dulac would be forced to work for larger corporations, and to turn more frequently to film adaptations, broadly considered to be more reliable investments.

In May 1916, with the necessary authorizations from Albert to create a company, Dulac drew up a contract for the new enterprise, in association with Hillel-Erlanger and a third unnamed female collaborator (that appears to have been Mme Henry Lapauze, pseud. Daniel Lesueur), who did not stay with the company.[61] Dulac and Hillel-Erlanger's shared interests in astrology,

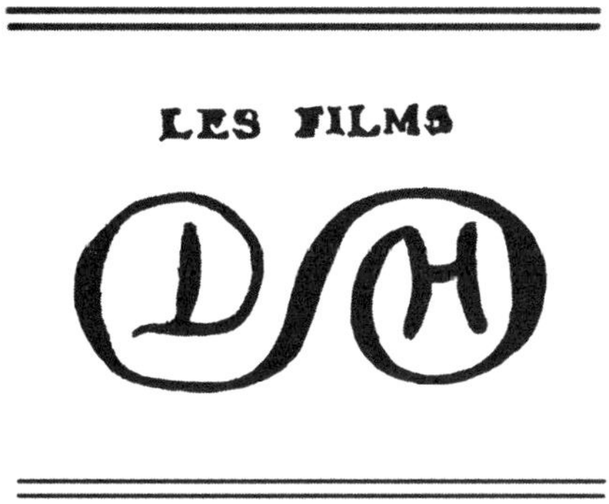

Figure 4. Les Films DH logo for Dulac Hillel-Erlanger films (1917). Rights reserved. Collection Cinémathèque française.

chiromancy, and Hinduism seem to have inspired the new establishment's numerous prospective names, and some of its most creative productions. As a letter from the Établissement Henri Lapauze indicates, the production outfit was initially to be named La Parisienne (April 1916). For this, Kees Van Dongen designed an art nouveau logo showing the heads of the three women, with their hair let down, mixing with and encircling the company's name. The name La Parisienne was followed by Astra Films (May 1916), Films Samothrace (June 1916), and the Hindu name, Krishna Films (June 1916), after which Albert joked, "I hope we shall soon celebrate the company's 100th name!" Dulac and Hillel-Erlanger then tried out Films Psyché (August 1916), and DELIA Films (October 1916), before joining their initials in the arabescally designed equanimic logo: Les Films DH.[62]

La Lumière du cœur: *Dulac's First Wartime Production*

Dulac's debut as a producer allowed her a certain degree of autonomy. In July 1916, before directing her first film projects, she financed a short film titled *La Lumière du cœur* (The light of the heart), directed by and starring Edmond Van Daële (produced under the company name Krishna Films and distributed by Pathé Consortium) as a means of increasing the nascent company's capital.[63] This wartime project, set in an arms manufacturing plant, also shows her determination to promote socially relevant works. During the first two years of the conflict, the industry was largely geared toward producing propagandistic films with patriotic themes connected to the war.[64] *La Lumière du cœur* (October 1916) is exceptional both in its pacifist topic of wartime mutilation and in its representation of the associated gender implications.

The film, currently considered lost, is summarized in a publicity brochure.[65] It is the story of Jean de Guersaut, engineer and director of an important explosives factory, and his young and beautiful fiancé, Sabine de Villepré. On the eve of their engagement dinner, Jean is blinded in an explosion provoked by a foreign spy in quest of the company's secret formula. He initially decides not to marry. Sabine, "wanting no other happiness than to be his light," elects to "sacrifice" herself for his love, however, and the two go on to marry, have children, and to live what is considered a happy life. That is, until one day, Sabine, while working alone in the explosives laboratory, is attacked by two strangers seeking the formula; she is left disfigured. Initially, this injury is of no importance to her, since Jean is destined to "forever keep her adorable image in his heart." The film reaches its turning point when a friend (who happens to be American) puts Jean in touch with an oculist who can restore his sight, and allow him to see his wife and children again. Of course, Jean is exalted by this prospect until, on the day of the operation, Sabine tells him of her injury, and her fear that he will be unable to bear the sight of her disfigurement. In a dramatic struggle of "two consciences," Jean saved long ago "from despair and death" by "the beautiful soul of Sabine," and given that "the beauty of her face will shine forever in his heart," refuses the operation, "preferring, to the light of the eyes, the light of the heart."[66]

Although sentimental heroics were prevalent in cultural representations during this period, the film's theme of wartime mutilation, present in literature, photos, and newsreels, was not common in French fiction films until after the war.[67] Abel Gance's later film *J'Accuse* (1919), which addresses loss of memory, reason, and eyesight, if not physical mutilation, has been considered a precursor in this domain.[68] *La Lumière du cœur*'s displacement of the theme onto a female character is more unusual. The heroine's actions and participation in the war effort, through her work in an explosives factory, is shown to contain elements of risk generally associated with men. Moreover, the representation of female heroism is also relatively uncommon during this period. Léonce Perret's war films (one of which shows a mother risking her life to neutralize a German spy) are one of very few exceptions.[69]

The treatment of blindness in *La Lumière du cœur* is also original. In the work of Perret and Gance, blindness functioned as a metaphor for the cataclysm of war, and the fact that things could never again be seen in the same way. Yet, in *La Lumière du cœur*, it also interrogates the notion that a woman's physical beauty is the measure of her value, relevant at the time, if not still today.[70] Notably, Dulac also employed the theme of mutilation in her abstract for a novel titled *Le Coup de feu* (Gunfire), a play on words with the expression *coup de foudre* (love at first sight).[71] This undated project, the story of a disabled ex-serviceman abandoned by his wife upon his return from the front, speaks to issues surrounding women's newfound liberty, questions of fidelity, along with questions of postwar masculine identity and displacement, which would be central themes in her films of the late 1910s and 1920s.

According to Richard Abel, as well as Georges Sadoul and Jean Mitry, during the latter years of the conflict, audiences grew weary of war subjects, and the industry called for more entertainment films.[72] Less categorical on this issue, film historian Laurent Véray argues that in 1917, production diversified, and the industry naturally turned to other subjects, including a new breed of films (e.g., Louis Feuillade's *Vendémiaire* and Gance's *J'Accuse*) that addressed war issues in a more sophisticated and realistic way, despite their attachment to certain simplistic, yet timeworn representational elements.[73] While Dulac's wartime films (1917–18) do not directly address the conflict, her two surviving postwar works written during this period, *La Cigarette* (script by Jacques de Baroncelli) and *La Fête espagnole* (script by Louis Delluc), contain themes that are strongly linked to its context. Both address masculinity, or male identity, seen to be in crisis by the culture at large. The latter film evoked wartime violence just as the notion of a crisis of masculinity was reaching its culmination point.[74] Men had returned from the war victorious. However, their distressing combat experiences, and the fact that women had proven their capacity to take on traditionally masculine roles at home, raised questions about men's place in a society that seemed to have gotten by without them. This crisis in male identity would become central to Dulac's critique of gender roles in her postwar films, particularly in relation to institutionalized inequalities such as bourgeois conceptions of marriage that reinforced traditional gender roles. Until then, however, Dulac's directorial projects centered on women and more immediately visible class divisions exacerbated by a relentless war.

Lost Films

All of Dulac's first directorial efforts undertaken during the war, regrettably, are thought to be lost. However, Dulac's scripts, production files, and correspondence tell us a great deal about the social issues and themes, narrative structures, and formal techniques she employed, and also provide a useful context for the study of her extant postwar films. These projects all appear to have been innovative, not only in their focus on women, often from diverse social backgrounds (working class, bourgeois, aristocratic), but also in their progressive approach to issues such as marriage, courtship, female companionship, motherhood, and career choice.

Between the summer of 1916 and the fall of 1918 (and prior to *La Cigarette* and *La Fête espagnole*, shot after the November 1918 armistice), Dulac produced and directed a remarkable six feature-length films, four of which were authored or coauthored by Irène Hillel-Erlanger, as well as a series of journalistic shorts.[75] These include the company's first production, *Les Sœurs ennemies* (DELIA Films, 1917), written in the summer of 1916 under Irène Hillel-Erlanger's nom de plume, Claude Lorrey, and Dulac's playful pseudonym, Dominique Dix; these names are followed by the pseudonyms Irène Hillel and Germaine de Sessey, respectively.[76] Dulac's next two films, *La Vraie Richesse* (True wealth), released as *Géo le mystérieux* (Géo the mysterious, 1917),[77] and *Vénus Victrix*, distributed as *Dans l'Ouragan de la vie* (In the hurricane of life, 1917), were written by Hillel-Erlanger.[78] The coauthored *Le Bonheur des autres* (The happiness of others, 1919), one of their first films promoted in the United States, was their final collaboration before the writer's untimely death from tuberculosis in 1920 at age forty-two.[79]

During this period, Dulac also wrote, directed, and produced a six-episode serial, *Âmes de fous* (Mad souls, 1918), starring Ève Francis, Paul Claudel's theatrical muse, released with a weekly novelization of the film in *Le Petit Journal*.[80] Then, for a series of popular *divertissements cinématographiques* (entertainment shorts), she also wrote, directed, and produced *Trois Pantins pour une poupée* (Three puppets for a doll, 1918), an intriguing commedia dell'arte–inspired "ballet-pantomime," a mode popularized by L'Opéra de Paris that made extensive use of dance and mime. This project dialogues with a more modernist turn during this period: first with Dulac's correspondent, pantomime innovator, and early cinema actor Georges Wague, and subsequently with Sergei Diaghilev's Ballet russes (1909–29). This modernized pantomimic form, which falls between the cracks of customary periodizations of early cinema (1895–1914) and the 1920s avant-garde (1919–29), carried the more abstract forms and provocative representations of gender of the emerging Impressionist movement. Set at a cross-dressing masked ball at which "a woman chooses the most loyal of four men" and featuring the archetypal performative commedia dell'arte characters (the independent and outspoken chambermaid, Columbine; the naïve Pierrot; the cynic Arlequin; and the duplicitous chameleon, Polichinelle), Dulac's *Trois Pantins* reversed gender expectations of the time and anticipated the mobility of social roles in her later films. It also prefigured a spectacular masked ball sequence featuring the same commedia dell'arte characters, lavishly cross-dressed, in her 1925 international melodrama, *Âme d'artiste* (An artist's soul, released in the UK as *The Heart of an Actress*).[81] After the war and Hillel Erlanger's premature passing, Dulac would write, direct, and produce three additional films under the DH name, including *Malencontre* (Misfortune, 1920), based on a novel by Guy Chantepleure, *La Belle Dame sans merci* (The beautiful woman without mercy, 1921), from an original idea by Hillel-Erlanger, and *Werther* (1922), an unfinished short, shot in Berlin, and based on Goethe's *Die Leiden des jungen Werthers* (*The Sorrows of Young Werther*). Of these three, only *La Belle Dame* survives.

The Dulac Hillel-Erlanger Collaborations

The early Hillel-Erlanger adaptations, like her novels, are highly autobiographical, and like certain of Dulac's later films, they are also satirical in tone. Albert Dulac, after reading Hillel-Erlanger's novel *La Chasse au bonheur* (The search for happiness, pseud. Claude Lorrey, 1913) remarked on this characteristic, as well as its mask of masculinity, giving perspective to Dulac's use of caricature and irony in their surviving collaborations (e.g., *Belle Dame*):

> I've finished reading the book I told you about yesterday. The subtlety of its deliberate sarcasm became clear to me in one or two chapters toward the end. It's only there that the author opens up. And we see that the irony of the first three-quarters of the work is simply a mask behind which a very beautiful sensibility hides. I'm afraid that women's literature is necessarily autobiographical. And I look forward to the book in which Claude Lorrey abandons her masculine disguise and unreservedly expresses her emotion. In fact, I expect a lot from that book, which, moreover, has perhaps [already] been written."[82]

One of the most predominant autobiographical aspects of Hillel-Erlanger's writings stems from her marriage to composer Camille Erlanger, who left her (and their son, Philippe Erlanger), for the famously beautiful cantatrice Marthe Chenal (see especially Erlanger's *Aphrodite*, 1908). While Chenal had offered to share Erlanger's favors in a "modern domestic arrangement," their divorce was finalized in 1912, after a protracted public celebrity-style scandal.[83] As Jacques Simonelli has noted, both of her novels (*La Chasse au bonheur*, 1913; and *Voyages en kaléidoscope*, 1919), and all of her film scripts (except *Géo le mystérieux*) feature a triangular relationship in which "a man hesitates (or is caught in a conflict) between two women, one of whom is a mother, or linked to a child."[84] Simonelli's description notwithstanding, the emphasis in these works, and in Dulac's films, is on the self-definition and self-realization of one or both of the female characters, in spite of the male protagonist (e.g., *Les Sœurs ennemies*, *Vénus Victrix*, *Géo le mystérieux*). Subsequent to her collaboration with Hillel-Erlanger, however, Dulac would go further, either by shifting the configuration to one woman and two men (*Antoinette Sabrier*, 1927) or by shifting the balance so that it is the woman who chooses (*Âme d'artiste*, 1925; *Princesse Mandane*, 1928).

As Simonelli has argued, the author also set up a "virgin-vamp" dichotomy, an opposition that would gain prevalence, particularly in cinema, with the emergence of the mythic figure of the newly liberated *garçonne* (flapper) in the 1920s. Simonelli defended this position by pointing out that, despite the obvious concern with women's emancipation, maternal issues remain important in these scripts. Furthermore, as is the case in the films *Vénus Victrix* (1917) and *La Belle Dame sans merci* (1921), the second woman is often either an actress or a dancer, emblematic of a more libertine femininity. Although, as Simonelli suggests, this virgin-vamp opposition is present, it differs from the Jazz Age flowering of this image in the sense that the nonmaternal figure is not vilified. Moreover, there is a transformation of the traditional role of motherhood, foundational for Dulac's later approaches to female emancipation.[85]

In the case of Dulac's *Les Sœurs ennemies*, where only a maternal figure exists, the archetype is called into question, and reconfigured outside of the conventional family structure.[86] *Les Sœurs ennemies* tells the story of two orphaned sisters (a theme related to the war): an elder sister (a typist), and the younger sister she raised, and whose sisterly bond is broken when the latter marries, ironically in order to care for her wealthy husband's motherless child. Embittered by this rupture, the older sister (Suzanne Desprès) attempts to sabotage her brother-in-law's business. Yet the narrative and visual design of the film compels the audience to identify and sympathize with her alienation, and the sisters' mutual affection in the face of what is portrayed as an undesirable new family configuration. Indeed, this depiction of closeness or alliance and reconciliation between the two female characters will be important to all subsequent DH collaborations, including that of the allied betrayed maternal figure and vamp archetype in Dulac's extant film *La Belle Dame sans merci*.

Figure 5. Suzanne Desprès as Lucile Aubry, and Marguerite Véry as Jeannine Aubry. *Les Sœurs ennemies*, 1917. Rights reserved. Collection Cinémathèque française.

Characteristics of Style

Production files, correspondence, and photographs indicate the dominant formal and stylistic influences and elements of Dulac's lost wartime films, particularly their realism and symbolism. While some early painterly, musical, and literary inspirations are evident, Dulac's early directorial choices were predominantly influenced by her relationship to theater. By 1915, she had moved beyond simply drawing theatrical sets (e.g., her 1913 sketch of decor for *Salomé*) and began to concretize her conceptions.[87] A June 1915 letter from Albert tells us that Dulac constructed a model theater set using a system of magnets.[88] In keeping with her evolving pedagogical aims, Dulac later created and exhibited a large-scale model of a film set (along with camera lenses she designed) at the 1924 exposition "L'Art dans le cinéma français," curated by Musée Galliera director Henri Clouzot. The vast retrospective and conference (featuring film luminaries Marcel L'Herbier, Jean Epstein, Dr. Jean Comandon, Léon Moussinac, Robert Mallet-Stevens, and Francis Jourdain) showcased the technical and artistic elements of cinema (cameras, objects, drawings, posters, and original manuscripts) alongside the fashion, furniture, and architecture of the latest art deco set designers (prefiguring the activities of the Cinémathèque française as Musée du Cinéma).[89]

In addition, Dulac's early works show an interest, not only in the theater as a representation of the world, but also in the world itself as a representation like theater. This self-reflexive notion of life as theater (popularized by the commedia dell'arte) anticipates Dulac's 1920s filmic explorations of life and art as social representation (via parody, caricature, gossip, etc.). In his letters to her, Albert often describes the events on the war front via references to the work of painters (e.g., the orientalist Eugène Fromentin) and writers (e.g., Edgar Allan Poe) of the romantic and symbolist era.[90] He also compared it to the violent spectacles of the Grand Guignol theater located on rue Chaptal, just across from their Paris home. In June 1915, after a nocturnal visit to a front-line battlefield, Albert compared the war's reality to the naturalistic horror of the theater: "I am still stunned, as if I'd really been to the Grand Guignol, a Grand Guignol that is neither pretend, nor cheap terror, but real horror, death with the smell of it." Of the "Dantean decor," he continued, "We depart from this illuminated theater as from a fairground stall, where the right to live is defended by a few obscure nurses, and we penetrate into the night again with the impression of escaping a simulation. Life is theater. Only death, which spreads its great wings over this fine night, is real."[91]

While Dulac's few extant writings of the early war period do not refer to this confrontation between art and life, representation and reality, many of her early films and production files contain self-reflexive references to the theater as world, or as a place of social representation anticipating the sophisticated *mise-en-abyme* of later films (e.g., backstage theater in *Âme d'Artiste*, and unreliable narration in *Diable dans la ville* [Devil in the city]). For example, in *Vénus Victrix* (1917), Dulac employed the theater milieu not only as the setting in which the drama of her principal characters is played out, but also as the representation of a world in which people of different walks of life confront one another. According to a publicity description of the film, "A large crowd draws back to create a space for the artists' exit at the Grand Theater. Men wearing tails and women in low-cut dresses mix with male and female workers in their Sunday best; it's a mixture of all worlds."[92] Similarly, according to a description by a *Ciné-Journal* critic, Dulac's sentimental comedy *Le Bonheur des autres*, starring Ethel Clayton, features "an unprecedented attraction—a night-time party in a Montmartre restaurant, shot with authentic personnel of a famous house, as well as a performance of *Hamlet*, seen from the wings of a grand theater."[93] Dulac would depict dance or theater within a film (and later, film within a film) in a number of her works of the 1920s, to create parallels and oppositions between dramatic and social representation (e.g., *La Belle Dame sans merci*, 1921; *La Souriante Madame Beudet*, 1923; *Gossette*, 1923; *Âme d'artiste*, 1925; *Antoinette Sabrier*, 1927; *Princesse Mandane*, 1928).

The theater also constituted an important stylistic frame of reference for Dulac's use of realist acting, outdoor settings, and authentic props and decor, traits that would later be associated with post–World War II film critic and theorist André Bazin (1918–1958). For instance, her first film, *Les Sœurs ennemies*, features two prominent naturalist and symbolist French theater actors. Suzanne Desprès, whom she knew from her associative and journalistic work at *La Française*, was distinguished for her realist acting in her husband Lugné-Poë's symbolist productions of Ibsen's work at the Théâtre de l'Œuvre. Dulac also hired Jacques Grétillat, a regular player at the Théâtre de l'Odéon under André Antoine, who had starred in Antoine's naturalist film *Les Frères corses* (The Corsican brothers, 1916), before going on to direct his own.[94] Dulac's second film, *Géo le mystérieux*, starred Grétillat, as well as Jane Marken, also active in Antoine's theater. In addition, Dulac used location shooting (*Géo le mystérieux*, *Âmes de fous*), as well as simple, authentic, yet symbolic settings and decors, drawn by hand, in order to indicate social status and relations.[95] For example, set during the French Revolution, much of her serial *Âmes de fous* was shot outdoors. For scenes requiring historical decors, Dulac used real settings, such as the Château de Versailles and Paris's Musée de Cluny (officially known as the Musée national du Moyen Âge).

Other realist tendencies were evident in Dulac's early films. For example, in one of her earliest articles, "Où sont les interprètes?" (Where are the actors?), published in *Le Film* (1918), she promoted the use of nonprofessional actors in secondary roles to enhance the realistic portrayals of her characters.[96] She also loved, owned (fish, dogs), and featured live animals (birds, fish, dogs, and a monkey) in her films. For example, in *Les Sœurs ennemies*, a child capers about with a greyhound. As the critic Louis Delluc noted, Dulac employed numerous "Asian cats and dogs" in *Âmes de fous*.[97] This convention, which anticipates Bazin's theories on the use of live animals as a realist device, is one of many proto-aesthetic realist techniques that characterizes her fiction films (e.g., *Gossette*, *Âme d'artiste*, *Diable dans la ville*, *Folie des vaillants*).[98]

Additionally, Dulac employed numerous techniques rooted in theatrical naturalism, with its penchant for authenticity and a diegetically motivated mise-en-scène, in order to communicate character psychology. For example, in the first scene of *Les Sœurs ennemies*, Dulac has a character (played by Suzanne Desprès) carry a work lamp. She uses the light and shadow cast by the lamp to express visually the woman's worry as she awaits the arrival of her younger sister for dinner.[99] Later in the film, she uses narrative elements such as the light of a gas stove, as well as a pendulum, a mirror, and steaming soup (techniques present in the work of Zola, Antoine, and Lugné-Poë) to portray the protagonist's evolving psychological state. This use of expressive diegetic lighting was contemporaneous with that of Cecil B. DeMille's film *The Cheat*, which Louis Delluc upheld as a landmark work upon its 1916 French release. In *Les Sœurs ennemies*, Dulac also links figures and objects through juxtapositions, fades, and dissolves as a means of illustrating characters' thoughts. The surviving script shows that Dulac was meticulous in her particularization of character placement and movement in relation to the elements of decor, lighting, and shot distance, as she would be in her later projects, which carefully specify effects, camera movement, and shot duration or rhythm.[100]

Dulac's use of naturalist techniques, as a means of representing character psychology, gradually gave way to more specifically symbolist tendencies, as she employed cultural references to painting and music, for instance, as well as actors whose performance styles bolstered this approach. For example, again in *Les Sœurs ennemies*, Dulac's choice to star her early muse Suzanne Desprès of Lugné-Poë's Théâtre de l'Œuvre reverberated in the film's symbolist style. In the magazine *La Rampe* (The footlights), François Crucy, called Desprès "the incomparable revealer of Ibsen's genius . . . she who in this country was the first great interpreter of this Theater of Ideas."[101] Unlike the dramatic acting of classical theater, Desprès, known for her modern and realist style and her tendency toward subtlety and simplicity functioned as a single element within a larger symbolist framework.

This context sheds light on the aspects of theater that most influenced Dulac. As the *La Rampe* critic Claude Briault wrote of this approach to mise-en-scène: "When the action developed by an author has been carried out with the very clear intention of creating an abstract ensemble whose scenic development is really an illustration and live commentary, it appears clear that, above the dramatic art and the interpretation of life, there is something dominant revealed by this very art that is of the domain of philosophy and pure thought—in short, a concept."[102] While Dulac employed some classical elements in her first film, her use of Desprès attests to her highly modern conception of the actor as one of many components in a much larger and more complex system, one interweaving into the film's open constellation of meanings.

Many of the symbolist features that would characterize Dulac's 1910s and 1920s work, and that drew inspiration from literature, painting, music, and opera (e.g., Baudelaire, pre-Raphaelite painting, and Debussy), also had links to the theater. In 1915, Dulac attended a representation of Debussy's revolutionary symbolist opera, *Pelléas et Mélisande*, based on Maeterlinck's play.[103] Inspired in part by the "oriental theater" of the poet and writer Pierre Louÿs, Debussy's original and audacious conception of harmony and rhythm, and his dramatic use of sound, silence, and interweaving themes and motifs created an impression of improvisation or instability within continuity, and a new auditory sensuality, whose visual equivalent can be found in Dulac's narrative and abstract films (e.g., *Invitation au voyage*, 1927; *Thèmes et variations*, 1929; *Arabesque*, 1929). Dulac also attended Diaghilev's Ballets russes, which had transformed the domain of ballet by making it a veritable synthesis of the arts (painting, music, dance). She was particularly inspired by the sumptuous decor and exotic fantasy atmosphere created by Diaghilev's scenic designer Léon Bakst for *Les Femmes de bonne humeur* (The good-humored ladies) at its Paris premiere (Théâtre du Chatelet, May 11, 1917).[104] Bakst's elaborate designs and vibrant colors find echoes in the intricate patterns of the costumes and decor of Dulac's exotic and erotic third film, *Vénus Victrix* (1917), which stars Stasia Napierkowska, and her fourth film, *Âmes de fous* (1918), with Ève Francis. As a letter to Albert attests, Dulac was also influenced in her use of gesture and movement by the Russian dancer, actress, and pantomime artist Ida Rubinstein, another major figure of the Ballets russes (and heir of modern dancer Isadora Duncan).[105]

Celebrated for the audacity of her spellbinding Mikhail Fokine-directed private debut performance of Oscar Wilde's *Salomé* (1908, censored for erotic indecency; an additional performance in 1912) and *Shéhérezade* (1911), Rubinstein's keen sense of expressive movement allowed her to convey an intense sensuality and deep mysticism on the stage. Correspondence with Albert, as well as film stills reveal that Dulac used Rubinstein as a model for Napierkowska's gestures and poses in the theater play in *Vénus Victrix*.[106]

Other creative tendencies in 1910s theater and literature influenced the artistic sensibility of Dulac's films. For instance, an orientalist tendency that gained popularity in the 1910s due in part to the success of Diaghilev's ballet, helped shape the Eastern mysticism prominent in many of her films, and central to *Vénus Victrix*.

In this film, a wealthy theater proprietor plans to leave his wife for the entrancing Hindu dancer, Djali (Napierkowska). At first glance, the orientalism incarnated by Djali and her potions and dances might be seen as a simple exoticization of the mysterious and unfamiliar world of the East. Indeed, Napierkowska's character states, "I come from the Indies [Indonesia], where I danced dances yet unknown."[107] Yet, as Gaylyn Studlar has argued with regard to early Hollywood cinema, such an interpretation can be reductive and limiting. On the one hand, as Studlar has noted, the use of "oriental," particularly East, Southeast, and Central Asian, themes and settings associated with the Ballets russes was used to add artistic value and status to the motion picture medium, still considered by many to be little more than a frivolous attraction.[108] On the other, and within the context of Dulac's work, this orientalism also had feminist implications. It was often associated with themes of travel and imagination, and could be seen to represent women's physical and spiritual emancipation from a fixed social category bounded by the stasis of tradition (*Âme d'artiste*, *La Folie des vaillants*, *Antoinette Sabrier*, *Princesse Mandane*). For Dulac, the allure of Hinduism, which inspired the early name for her company, Krishna Films, is also tied to her interest in the doctrines of reincarnation and multiple identities. As Albert affirms in a March 1917 letter: "The idea of diverse incarnations of Djali and the Flame are perfect."[109] A connection is apparent between Dulac's interest in both Eastern mysticism and feminism, with many of her films addressing the rebirth and transformation of women. Additionally, experimentation with East Asian and Central Asian themes permitted Dulac to push back social boundaries through her work. For example, her films *Âmes de fous* (1918) and *Malencontre* (1920), featuring the French Javanese dancer Djemil Anik, are among the earliest uses of an actor of color in a prominent role in France. She would later employ Anik as a figure of maritime fantasy in her 1927 *L'Invitation au voyage* (Invitation to a voyage).[110]

Though Dulac sought early on to delineate the cinema as a modern art free from the established conventions of classical literature and theater, she would continue to be inspired by the more innovative and liberating tendencies within modern and particularly symbolist literature and theater, inasmuch as they could help her to create a universe with new representational possibilities that would respect her conception of cinematic specificity.[111] In the early twentieth century, cinema and other arts were integrally linked through their common relation to modernity and shared vision of a "new man," as Jacques Rancière has pointed out, and Dulac's films no less dramatically depict a "new woman." In the fall of 1917, just one year after directing *Les Sœurs ennemies*, and just as she had started working on the serial *Amês de fous*, Dulac began to concretize this new vision of a cinema that she would develop during the 1920s and 1930s: that is, of a new medium capable of representing modern life and of providing a vision of a new world.

On November 12, 1917, Dulac published her first article on cinema, "Mise-en-scène," in the weekly journal *Le Film*, published by Henri Diamant-Berger and edited by pioneering literary and film critic Louis Delluc, Ève Francis's soon-to-be husband (January 1918). This early article attests to her already expansive approach to the cinema and announces the major concerns that would come to define her career, namely, cinema's potential as an art, its relation to industry and to the public, as well as, in this wartime context, its role in the propagation of French culture.[112]

In the introduction to her article, Delluc praised the innovation of this new artist who, based on her directorial debut, he asserted, "already ranks among the best." Significantly, Dulac's first film article adopted a militant tone as she defended, with strong symbolist echoes, cinema as "a new means of expression [. . .]. A new form. Perhaps a new form of art." Dulac announced her interest in creating a subtle, yet sophisticated technique that would allow her to ally realism and symbolism with the concrete and the spiritual, asking: "Isn't there a lot to be said when one can exploit the most subtle nuances of light, make gestures speak, animate forms, evoke all that which, through our eyes, address our spirit, from reality to dream?"[113] By exploiting the expressivity of light, gesture and movement, Dulac's approach would allow her to consider, often subtly and obliquely, the increasing disparity between the "new woman's" aspirations for liberty and her social reality after the war.

Yet, the article addressed a major obstacle to the cinema's development as an art and social tool: the incomprehension of the public. In the coming years, this would become the primary impetus for her development of a broad pedagogical approach to the cinema via filmmaking and activism. Dulac described this problem as twofold. She noted the passivity of popular audiences: "the unthinking mass who, like children in front of the magic lantern not so long ago, seek a simple pleasure of imagination." She also pointed to the disinterest of the elite: "people of taste, intellectuals and artists [who] flee in response to a spectacle that they are not always wrong to disdain as vulgar." Dulac took on the complex challenge of establishing the legitimacy of cinema as an art and its popularization, while in turn nurturing a struggling industry. She not only endeavored to contribute to the aesthetic evolution of cinema through her films, writings, and conferences. She also argued for the necessity of defending French cinema, and thus the French film industry, internationally as a means of protecting it from the infiltration of U.S. films; and as a means of promoting the French spirit, its social habits, and tastes.[114] Finally, she supported and defended the cinema through her ciné-club activism and her involvement in numerous national and international, social and educational organizations.

At the time of the famous *grève des midinettes* (seamstresses' strike, 1917–18), which in 1920 won Frenchwomen the legal right to belong to a labor union without their husbands' permission, Dulac took an active role in union issues.[115] She became a member (1917) and treasurer (1919) of the Société des auteurs de films (SAF, Society of Film Authors), holding the latter position until her death in 1942. During this period Dulac became one of the major defenders of the status and rights of the filmmaker in relation to screenwriters, producers, distributors, and censors. Finally, in 1921, Dulac served as vice president, alongside Abel Gance, of what is considered to be the first official ciné-club, le Club des amis du septième art (CASA, Club of Friends of the Seventh Art), founded by longtime film critic and activist Ricciotto Canudo. In Dulac's mission to elevate public appreciation for cinema and to legitimize film as an art, she helped found numerous other ciné-clubs, before becoming the founding president of the Fédération française des ciné-clubs (FFCC) in 1929. Following these efforts, Dulac would play a key role in the League of Nations' International Educational Cinematographic Institute (IECI), as well as in the founding of the Cinémathèque française (1936) and the Fédération internationale des archives du film (1938, International Federation of Film Archives).[116]

By the end of World War I, the defining elements of Dulac's career were in place. However, with the end of the war, women were called upon to return home and relinquish jobs to the demobilized male workforce, and a pronatalist movement sprang up.[117] During the postwar era, the feminist movement, already subverted by the popular sentiments of national unity and economic crisis, became less visible than it had been prior to the war. Françoise Thébaud has aptly called the interwar years a period "entre-deux-feminismes" (between-two-feminisms).[118] This shift would have a direct impact on women in the film industry, including Dulac.

While a small number of influential women, including actresses Musidora and Napierkowska, had managed to create their own production companies during the war, few continued afterwards, as women's presence in non-essential spheres of activity began to lose support. Although Dulac was one of the few women filmmakers to survive this crisis, and to continue an active career well into the 1920s and 1930s, she was not unaffected. In February 1918, just before the war's end, Louis Delluc evoked the discrimination that Dulac faced as a woman filmmaker, writing the following:

> Unmaliciously, solely by reason of her existence, she has provoked sharp debates; for Mme Dulac has energetically made herself known with three films, the first of which was much better than her confrères' second [films]. Who would dare to deny it? But the cinema is full of people, no doubt very decent people [de très braves gens]—who may not all be very brave people [des gens très braves]—who won't forgive her for being a cultivated woman. The few men of the world among us [on the home front] are perhaps humiliated simply because she is a woman, but that is jealousy more than rivalry.[119]

Within the contexts of a temporarily diminished feminist movement, a resurgent postwar conservatism, and the steep challenge of promoting cinema as a new, entirely legitimate form of art, Dulac's success was remarkable. Embracing both realism and a symbolist impressionism, she would promote the evolution of commercial and avant-garde cinema via several innovative tendencies: first in the realm of fiction, from figuration to abstraction, and later in the documentary and newsreel domain, and this not only in France, but also internationally.

PART II

Chapter 3

Negotiating Art and Industry in the Postwar Context

In the wake of World War I, the "war to end all wars," and amid large-scale economic and humanitarian recovery efforts, peace did not usher in a blithe and tranquil return to France's Belle Époque. In a postwar climate of shifting social and aesthetic hierarchies, Dulac played a founding role in the creation of a new, aesthetically groundbreaking, and socially engaged cinema. The 1920s—known mythically as *les années folles* (the crazy years)—were marked by major social fissures. There was a tremendous gap between women's desires to maintain their wartime experience of liberty and the official postwar moral discourse of pronatalism, which dictated conservative social conceptions of class, gender, and sexuality. A socialist and moderate feminist with a predilection for modern artistic tendencies, Dulac pioneered new cinematic strategies and techniques ranging from reflexive narrative structures and performance styles to symbolic technical effects and abstract visual associations. These allowed her to communicate her progressive social ideals through an elaborate signifying network based on "suggestion."[1]

We can best understand Dulac's approach to the new medium in light of France's complex postwar social context and an amplified tension between art and industry. She explored with passion the cinema's infinite formal possibilities to promote a progressive politics within a conservative social context, one that authorizes, reflects, and empowers her own evolving conjugal situation and life choices (namely, her budding love affair with Marie-Anne Colson-Malleville, whom she met in 1921, and her legal separation from Albert in 1922).[2] It is from this same perspective that she sought to fashion a more critical spectator and a more stable and flexible industry. To this end, Dulac played a founding role in the creation and elaboration of a film culture through the ciné-club movement, to which she further contributed through her prolific writings and lectures to both popular and elite publics. She also undertook numerous corporative initiatives to strengthen the French cinema in the face of Hollywood domination, as well as to defend the film director's status as auteur, or what she termed the *artiste créateur* (artist creator) within the industry.[3]

All of these elements were integral to her filmmaking strategy. It was in this constantly shifting context that Dulac developed her cinematic ideal in her commercial and avant-garde films using a wide variety of approaches, from impressionism (1919–28) and surrealism (1927) to abstract cinema (1929), before turning to nonfiction filmmaking (1930–42). She also developed a number of experimental film strategies to reconfigure and subvert formal, narrative, and generic codes (caricature, parody, *mise-en-abyme*, technical effects, multiple endings), for the purpose of social critique and the expression of her discourse on gender and sexuality, as well as a means of exploding or analyzing the film from within.

The two chapters in part 2 of this book examine Dulac's various strategies and trace the evolution of her conception of cinema as it evolved from figurative to abstract. What follows here is an account of the production and social context in which Dulac worked, so we may understand how she negotiated art and industry, developing in the process her notion of aesthetics as a means of social criticism.

Film historians, particularly in France, have tended to separate Dulac's cinema into commercial and avant-garde works, with distinct and contradictory goals (narrative immersion and escapism versus abstract contemplation and edification or enlightenment). This is perhaps owing to a view of Hollywood, in its most monolithic sense, as a reference point for a commercial entertainment-based cinema; or, on the contrary, owing to a view of the avant-garde as a formalist, apolitical cinema, whose primary interest is its aesthetics. Dulac's conception of a single integrated cinema was crucial to determining her relationship to the French industry and the breadth of her ciné-club and corporative activism, as well as the inventiveness of her filmmaking. While it is important to recognize those aspects that resisted assimilation, a global view of her films allows a better comprehension of the interconnectedness of her filmmaking and activism, and it permits a historicization of the integral relationship between her film aesthetic and her social conceptions, which has largely been ignored until now.

In the face of the immediate postwar economic crisis, and the threat from the newly dominant American cinema, Dulac, like many of her contemporaries (Abel Gance, Louis Delluc, Marcel L'Herbier), believed it necessary to defend cinema both as art—with its intellectual ideals and intentions—and as an industry, consisting of the network of institutions that helped to produce and disseminate it. From her start in the industry in 1917, Dulac actively defended these dual aspects of the cinema, a battle she would continue throughout her career. In a 1929 interview after being awarded the Legion of Honor, France's highest and most prestigious decoration, Dulac affirmed, "I've always tried hard, in the course of my production, to serve the cinegraphic industry by making commercial films, and the cinegraphic art, by making avant-garde films."[4] In her "Le Cinéma d'avant-garde" (1929), written from a historical perspective, Dulac went further, proclaiming that "the avant-garde and commercial cinema, or the art and industry of film, form an inseparable whole."[5]

This integrated approach to the cinema underscored Dulac's search for new techniques that, in light of an official discourse of governmental and social conservatism, and the modernity of the new medium, were capable of expressing her progressive, antibourgeois, nonconformist and feminist social vision, in a less threatening and more effective manner. This integrated approach also motivated her corporate and ciné-club activism, and her desire to gain legitimacy for this art among a broad public.

Dulac's political efforts also coincided with a major shift in her private life, one that could be seen to underpin many of the issues addressed through her films and pedagogical efforts: from her representation of gender, and sexuality in relation to bourgeois marriage to her promotion of a subtle and suggestive aesthetic and an active spectatorship that looks beyond surface and the official face of things. Dulac's legal separation or divorce from her husband Albert Dulac on February 9, 1922, created a space for an enduring intimate and professional partnership with Marie-Anne Colson-Malleville (née Mareau, 1892–1971).[6]

Colson-Malleville, who worked as a teacher, and later as a film programmer (*Le Marivaux*, *La Madeleine*, *Le Colisée*) alongside exhibition and film education pioneer Edmond Benolt-Lévy (uncle of cineaste Jean Benoît-Lévy) in the midteens, would become Dulac's directorial assistant in the 1920s, before working as a music director and realist songwriter (for Fréhèl and others) in the 30s.[7] In the early to mid-1940s, just after Dulac's death, she would host the meetings of the Commission de recherche historique of the Cinémathèque française in their home (46, rue Général Foy), near Parc Monceau and directly north of the avenue des Champs-Elysées, before going on to direct at least twenty-two documentary films of her own from 1948 to 1961 (alongside Georges Franju and Georges Rouquier).[8] Colson-Malleville's surname tells a story itself. Before marrying Dulac's Gaumont newsreel associate George Colson in the early 1930s (likely for legal status, but possibly as a veil for her sexuality, and domestic partnership), Colson-Malleville had been married to Paul Malleville (director of the Cinéma-Théâtre du Colisée, an early art cinema, 38, avenue des Champs-Elysées), all while living continuously with Dulac. It is not clear whether Dulac befriended Paul or Marie-Anne first or both at the same time. However, a photograph shows the three traveling together to Normandy in 1921, and Paul Malleville would remain an important collaborator throughout the 1920s, serving as a host for some of her key ciné-club initiatives.

Ciné-Club and Corporative Activism

Driven by a desire to elevate the French public's awareness of cinema's expressive capacities, Dulac played a pioneering role in the creation and development of the ciné-club movement, a major support system for the 1920s cinematic avant-garde, to which she also contributed via countless lectures and publications that developed and promoted her filmic ontology and aesthetics from her fiction films to her avant-garde reformulation of the newsreel. She also fought tirelessly to bolster the struggling French film industry, and the film director's creative potential within the industry, through championing the modernization of production conditions and advocating for the establishment of protectionist policies. In keeping with the spirit of her first film article, "Mise-en-scène" (1917), which promoted the filmmaker as auteur or "artist creator," Dulac served as member (1917), and then as treasurer (1919) of the Société des auteurs de films (Society of film authors), where she helped establish and defend the status and rights of the film director in relation to screenwriters, producers, distributors, and censors, a highly influential position she would hold through World War II.[9] Some of the meetings in the early 1920s for the Société des auteurs (not unlike those of the wartime Commission de recherche historique hosted by Colson-Malleville) were held in Dulac's first home on 24 rue Chaptal (9th arrondissement), just a few blocks from the organization's headquarters.[10]

Not only was Dulac a founding figure, but she was also one of the pillars of the ciné-club movement, as one of the most consistent long-term contributors to its development and proliferation. As noted, she was vice president of CASA, France's first known ciné-club, which according to Abel Gance was established during the war, and which aimed to improve the overall public perception of the cinema.[11] A May 1921 article by critic and ciné-club president Ricciotto Canudo designed to officialize CASA doubled as a manifesto announcing its ambitious goals: "to affirm the cinema's artistic character through all available means," "to raise the intellectual level of French cinematic production," "to attract creative talents," and "to lobby the state for equitable laws and support."[12] The group also planned to draw public attention to the "origins and evolution of cinema in France," through the organization of a *festival cinématique français*.[13] These broad pedagogical and corporate objectives conformed to Dulac's long-held moderate and pragmatic stance on reform and her belief in the effectiveness of innovating within the system, and they reflected her commitment to a dual conception of the cinema as both art and industry. CASA was met with some trepidation by distributors and exhibitors, who apparently viewed the group as "revolutionaries" seeking to disrupt the system, but in a subsequent issue of *Cinéa*, the ciné-club's "international delegate," the filmmaker René Le Somptier, reassured the commercial sector, itself a "war mutilee," by proclaiming the organization's pragmatic intentions, "*We want to build, not destroy*" (original emphasis).[14]

Dulac also contributed to the creation of France's first and largest semiprofessional ciné-club oriented toward the improvement of production conditions. In 1922, she participated in the sole, but crucial, meeting of a group called les Treize (Thirteen), along with Canudo, the journalist Michel Coissac, and the budding directors Henri Fescourt, Jacques Feyder, and Louis Delluc.[15] As the film historian Christophe Gauthier has shown, this one-off gathering "for the love and defense of a great cinema" was closely linked to the spring 1922 creation of the professionally oriented Club français du cinéma (CFC). Dulac also served as general secretary of the club.[16] Unlike CASA, whose primary aim was to publicize cinema, the CFC was an attempt by this "first cinematic avant-garde" to create a professional support system, and an alternative distribution network for their films.[17] Their agenda included the recognition of directors as film authors, their independence with regard to distributors, and their proper recognition by film critics, a program that also was closely linked to the campaign led by the Société des auteurs de films. Following the organization's official registration in December 1923, the CFC held its regular meetings at one of Paris's first art cinemas, the Cinéma du Colisée, run by Colson-Malleville's first husband, Paul Malleville.

Dulac was later a cofounder with filmmaker Robert Boudrioz, actress Yvette Andreyor (*La Mort du soleil* [1921]), and her husband Jean Toulout (*La Fête espagnole* [1920], *La Belle Dame sans merci* [1921])—as well as treasurer of the Ciné-Club de France (CCF), the product of the union of CASA and the CFC in 1924. CCF members included Léon Poirier (president), critic Léon Moussinac and filmmaker Henry Roussel (vice presidents), critic René Jeanne and filmmaker Marcel Silver (general secretaries), and Colisée director Paul Malleville.[18]

Building on the work of its predecessors, the CCF nonetheless greatly broadened its purview. It combined the CFC's goals of studying and developing the conditions necessary for the expansion of the cinematic art with the original pedagogical goals of CASA. However, its objectives were markedly international, lending support to Jacques Rancière's thesis that cinematographic avant-gardes have always been essentially international and should be considered, in their common relationship to modernity, within a transversal interdisciplinary framework.[19] A 1924 CCF brochure highlighted its broad aspirations: the "*study, development,* and defense of the *cinegraphic* art," the coordination of "all *intellectual, artistic, technical,* and *economic* forces likely to enrich the international domain of Cinégraphie," and a commitment "to seek across *all trends* to reinforce the sincere efforts of artists *of all countries* and to second them in every way possible" (emphasis added).[20] In keeping with her earlier cultural and political activism, Dulac's commitment to promoting the development and expansion of cinema in all of its dimensions is already clear at this early stage.

At the end of the 1920s, when the arrival of the sound picture threatened the future of the "silent" art, Dulac took the lead in nationalizing and eventually internationalizing the ciné-club network. In 1929, she cofounded the Fédération des ciné-clubs de langue française (Federation of French-Language Ciné-Clubs) with Robert Jarville, which became the Fédération française des ciné-clubs (FFCC, French Federation of Ciné-Clubs) under her presidency in 1930.[21] Its first congress, at the Maison des Sociétés savantes de Paris on November 13 and 14, 1929, brought together the leaders of France's eighteen existing ciné-clubs. Among those present were Charles Léger, founder of the Tribune libre du cinéma (Free Cinema Tribune) film club; Henri Clouzot, Musée Galliera director, president of the Ciné-Club de France, and uncle of the future cinéaste Henri-Georges Clouzot; and budding filmmaker Jean Vigo, director of

Les amis du cinéma (Friends of the cinema, Nice), as yet little known, who is credited with launching poetic realism in film.[22] The federation, which extended the broad goals of the CCF, served as a central organization of support and representation for the ciné-clubs, as well as for the emerging *salles spécialisées* (specialized theaters), or art cinemas.[23] In her opening speech to the congress, which coincided with the production of her own experimental shorts (1929) exhibited in these locations, Dulac cited the federation's chief aim: to educate the public to accept and support what she referred to as "evolutionary" or "research" films. She also called on the group to develop an independent circuit extending the activities of Paris's new art cinemas to the provinces, before engaging in efforts to create a "national" cinémathèque.[24]

The ciné-club movement in its promotion and conservation of both avant-garde and classic silent films and its key role in the preservation of cultural memory would be a key contributor to the creation of cinémathèques internationally. "All Western cinémathèques were born out of ciné-clubs," Henri Langlois later noted in a *Cahiers du Cinéma* interview.[25] Dulac would play an early role in the creation of the privately run Cinémathèque française (CF, 1936). Involved in the embryonic 1935 Cercle du cinéma (created by Langlois and Georges Franju at the suggestion of Jean Mitry), a ciné-club with a "quasi-religious" atmosphere, with devotees who came to view rare and silent classics that had disappeared from the screens, Dulac was a founding member of the CF, donating her films, signing its original statutes, and negotiating its private status vis à vis the state. Dulac served on its first board of directors in 1936, again from 1939 through the Occupation, a period during which, paradoxically, its liberty threatened, the CF solidified its structure and retained its collections in large part due to her efforts.[26] According to sources close to Colson-Malleville, Dulac also had exerted her influence in opening the military vaults of Paris's periphery for the preservation of films, while helping to found the larger Fédération internationale des archives du film, which plays a fundamental role in the preservation of films and film history today.[27]

Dulac's lifelong efforts to promote cinema as an art to a broad public, and to sensitize the public and the industry to the goals of the cinematographic avant-garde, fit hand in glove with her own filmmaking goals of creating an artistic cinema with an emphatic and progressive social message, not unlike independent silent era directors and social activists such as Nell Shipman in Canada and Lois Weber in the United States.[28] In order to do this, Dulac took direct measures to carve out a space for her own artistic productions and to ensure their distribution within the industry.

Early Postwar Production

The post–World War I French economic crisis called for drastic changes in film production, namely, the development of a more rational production model and a more competitive product. In an attempt to reconcile her desire to support the French film industry with her desire to develop the capacities of the cinema as a modern means of artistic and social expression, Dulac sought new and more efficient methods of production and distribution.

In the immediate postwar period, the U.S. film industry, which had come to dominate the French market, served as a model of efficiency because of its Taylorist or assembly-line mode of production; and its heavy reliance on genre made it an index of thematic and artistic differentiation. The challenge was to create a competitive, specifically French, cinema. Whereas the film mogul Charles Pathé called on French filmmakers to copy the U.S. model, Dulac advocated efficiency, but only within the framework of creating a unique national product and style, true to its cultural origins.

Dulac called for a cinema that modeled itself on reality, rather than on the films of other countries or on other art forms. In her 1919 article "Ayons la Foi" (Have faith), she wrote: "Rather than looking at ourselves, having lost confidence, we look at the efforts of others, there, in the United States, and try to model ourselves on them. The time has come, I believe, to listen silently to our song, to seek to express our own personal vision, to define our sensibility, to trace our own path. Let's learn to watch, to see, to feel. Have something to say, and eyes, eyes wide open, not on reflections, but on life itself. Let's look for ourselves, find ourselves. . . . No longer copy, but *create*."[29]

The search for a cinema based on truth and life itself was a constant in Dulac's approach to filmmaking, and it was tied to her belief in the importance of cinema as a social tool. For Dulac, a sincere cinema, based on local life, both regional and national, and put on screen according to a filmmaker's personal vision, would reveal human and social truths. She saw this as a prerequisite for the success of French films in international markets. Later in her career, this view would become the basis for her unique approach to the production and exchange of international newsreels.

New Production and Distribution Tactics

Having grasped early on that it was necessary to create an international market for French cinema, Dulac took a number of specific measures in order to improve production conditions and to give herself greater autonomy as a filmmaker, starting with the creation of an office for the international distribution of her films. In 1919, she set up a distribution office in New York.[30] Despite Léon Gaumont's wartime declaration warning of the difficulty of French film distribution abroad, and the impossibility of investing in the United States, Dulac broke into the U.S. market with *Le Bonheur des autres* (The happiness of others, 1919), a sentimental comedy starring Ève Francis, thus becoming one of the first postwar French filmmakers to distribute her films in the United States.[31]

"A first victory has just been achieved in America by the French film, thanks to the assiduous work of Mr. A. Dulac in collaboration with Mr. Silz, the publicity representative of the *New-York Herald*," the French movie magazine *Ciné pour Tous* (later *Cinéa-Ciné pour Tous*) reported in November 1919.[32] While this film, apparently never released in France, is currently considered lost, it may exist in a U.S. vault somewhere. Not surprisingly, Dulac distributed additional films in the United States, including *Malencontre* (1920) and *La Belle Dame sans merci* (1921).[33] Furthermore, it seems that Dulac's film distribution was not just confined to the United States. According to a letter from her husband, Albert, as well as an industry report by early French filmmaker Alice Guy (1873–1968), Dulac distributed several of her films through London studios in the early 1920s, at least two of which are preserved at the British Film Institute.[34] She also made films in Germany and England: her self-produced *Werther* (1922), an early screen adaptation of Johan Wolfgang von Goethe's *Die Leiden des jungen Werthers* (1774, *The Sorrows of Young Werther*), starring Denise Lorys, shot in Berlin, yet never completed,[35] and her backstage comedy, *Âme d'artiste* (An artist's soul, released in the UK as *The Heart of an Actress*, 1925), shot and distributed in London and featuring popular British actress Mabel Poulton.[36] Both of these use flashbacks and the latter also uses innovative techniques, such as *mise-en-abyme* and newsreels from distant lands, to visualize the heroine's reveries.

Given the increasing consolidation of the French film industry in the postwar period, Dulac's production of two feature films on her own—*La Belle Dame sans merci* (1921) and the incomplete *Werther* (1922)—was a considerable achievement. Yet, for the most part, she chose to work with the most independent producers of the period, including Louis Nalpas at Ciné-Studios, Henri Fescourt at the Société des cinéromans, as well as Charles Delac and Marcel Vandal, who created the unique, vertically integrated independent company Delac, Vandal et Cie, in January 1919. (The Delac-Vandal establishment brought together three major companies, Film d'art [production], Agence générale cinématographique [distribution], and the prestigious Salle Marivaux [exhibition], in an attempt to confront the industry crisis.)[37]

In 1919, Dulac's efforts to increase her autonomy as a filmmaker continued in her work with the prestigious and long-standing independent company Film d'art, for which she would make *La Cigarette* (1919) and later *La Souriante Madame Beudet* (1923). She also collaborated with one of the most modern and independent-minded producers of the era, Louis Nalpas (the former artistic director of Film d'art), who had just signed a contract to run Serge Sandberg's newly built Ciné-Studios site, the Studios de la Victorine, located in Nice, on the Côte d'Azur.

Modeled after the Los Angeles studios, and even referred to in publicity and press materials as the "European Hollywood" or "Los Angeles à Nice," the Studios de la Victorine were designed to provide film directors with a well-equipped, adaptable, and efficient production facility.[38] Louis Nalpas was one of the few artistic directors devoted to creating a wholly competitive product that was both artistic and uniquely French, at a time when American investors like David O. Selznick and Fox were setting up studios in France.[39] While Nalpas attracted a number of innovative directors to the Victorine, including René Le Somptier, Léon Poirier, Léonce Perret, Rex Ingram, Robert Boudrioz, Abel Gance, and Louis Delluc, Dulac was one of the first directors whose films he produced.[40]

Nalpas would back several of Dulac's films over the decade, including *La Fête espagnole* (1920), and *Malencontre* (1920) for Ciné-Studio, and *Antoinette Sabrier* (1927) for Nalpas at the Société des cinéromans. She would also make her self-produced *La Belle Dame sans merci* at the Victorine in 1921, before going on to direct several films for producer Henri Fescourt at Ciné-Romans, including the commercial serial, *Gossette* (1923), and the inventive period picture, *Le Diable dans la ville* (1924).

While for the most part Dulac worked with the same group of independent producers, who were relatively sympathetic to her innovative production efforts, during this period, she constantly sought opportunities for more creative freedom. In the fall of 1921, she worked with Fescourt and the filmmaker René Le Somptier, a colleague from the Société des auteurs de films to create the filmmaking cooperative L'Union cinématographique française, which the press heralded as an innovative and promising approach during difficult times.[41] (One of the first of its kind, this cooperative announced a developing trend of independent and collaborative organizational structures that would be adopted by Dulac among other French filmmakers during some of the country's most economically fragile and politically volatile periods, such as under the Popular Front government in the mid-1930s and in the aftermath of the general strike and student demonstrations of May 1968.)[42]

Dulac supplemented these efforts to create an economical production structure by seeking out the most effective technical means. In an effort to learn about the latest technologies and methods being used by U.S. studios, she made at least one trip to the United States in October 1920 with the producers Charles Delac and Marcel Vandal, and their new artistic director, Jacques de Baroncelli. The team brought back the latest "sunlights" that would supplement, and eventually supersede, the standard arc lamps of French studios.[43] Dulac also met with D. W. Griffith at his studios in New York. As *Cinéa* described it, her aim was "to study on site the working method of the great American aces."[44]

Figure 6. David Wark Griffith (second from left) and Germaine Dulac (second from right) during a film studio visit in New York (1920). Rights reserved. Collection Cinémathèque française.

Dulac expressed a general dislike for U.S. films, which, she asserted, "under a luxurious mise-en-scène, hide a profound poverty of thought." However, she appreciated the cinema of Griffith, which came from "a single will" or vision that echoed her ideal of the film auteur. In particular, she praised his use of realism and symbolism, and his use of "music that guided the measure of images on the screen." Dulac explored this aspect in her films of this period (*La Mort du Soleil*, *La Souriante Madame Beude*), both uniquely personal, yet entirely different types of production.[45]

There can be little doubt about the distinct intellectual sensibilities of Dulac and Griffith, if only in their subject matter and their portrayal of women, and the disparate scale of financial and technical resources they employed is striking. Indeed, after a conversation with Dulac's London distributors—M. and Mme Ratisbonne de Ravenelle—following a showing of *La Belle Dame sans merci* (March 1921), Albert wrote to his wife, "Mme Ratisbonne says that if you had Griffith's means, you'd surpass him. I congratulated her heartily for being of my own opinion."[46]

A New Artistic and Social Context

While Dulac was resourceful and pioneering in her efforts to carve out a place for herself where she could make personal films in a struggling industry, the constraints she faced in expressing her feminist social views in the post- or interwar period presented other challenges. Many of these would require an equally innovative response. The post–World War I period in France was fraught with contradictions concerning gender roles. During the Great War, many women experienced unprecedented personal and professional liberty. However, as a result of its devastating human cost—in France, some 1,697,800 individuals, 4.29 percent of the population, died as a result of the war—the end of hostilities saw the emergence of a widespread conservative bourgeois pronatalist discourse. It was in this context that France witnessed one of the strongest gender gaps that it had ever seen.

Having enjoyed their independence, many women of the *arrière* (rear) or "home front" were not ready to return to the home to repopulate the nation. The postwar period saw the emergence of the "new woman": more active and self-indulgent, with a new androgynous clothing style and a bobbed haircut *à la garçonne* (like a flapper).[47] As Anne-Marie Sohn notes, the new woman's most manifest and universal gain was the "freedom or allure of movement. . . . Rid of the hindrances of the corset, long and tight-fitting clothes, cumbersome hats and sometimes chignons . . ., the female body can move." It meant "a different relationship to one's body and one's self: playing sports, dancing to the rhythms of America, going out alone, exploring one's sexuality and sometimes choosing what to do with one's own life."[48]

Although the idea that the war overturned conventional gender roles and liberated women, or the thesis of the "emancipatory war," has become relatively commonplace, recent women's histories, such as those of Françoise Thébaud and Christine Bard, demand that we take into account the largely provisional and superficial nature of these changes.[49] Central to the question of post–World War I female liberation is the distinction between how the war redefined women's roles on the level of both symbolic perception and lived reality. Indeed, based on these recent studies, it has become clear that for a majority of Frenchwomen of the 1920s, the emblematic image of the *garçonne* (the French counterpart of the Anglo-American flapper, although far from equal in civil terms given the success of the U.S. suffragette movement) was predominantly a figure of fashion and fantasy.[50]

As Sohn has noted, while women gained an appearance of liberty, in most cases their daily lives changed very little: "If the twenties presented the signs of a female emancipation, short hair, *garçonnes* . . ., the daily life of women evolved little; the ideal of the woman as homemaker seems to have been uncontested, more than ever, as was the division of roles it implies."[51] The feminist historian Françoise Thébaud notes similarly that, in the twilight of a debilitating war, the "emancipated woman" was subject to widespread criticism and was thought to have negative consequences for society as a whole: "the demobilization of women [was] accompanied by a virulent critique of the emancipated woman and feminism, referred to as 'the dream of the enemy' for some."[52] For homosexual women who had experienced the Sapphist liberty of the Belle Époque, things were worse. As we have seen, Dulac and Colson-Malleville were not exempt; for reasons unknown, the latter married a second time while living with Dulac. The gap that emerged between women's desire for liberty and the official moral discourse that imposed a morally oppressive daily reality was one of the central preoccupations of Dulac's work. Part and parcel of this reality was the figure of bourgeois marriage and of the displaced male, traumatized by the war and threatened by these desires.

In Dulac's films, desire and fear evolve together, as women's liberty often develops in tandem with and is ultimately compromised by the dejected or abject male's propensity to commit suicide. The frequency of male suicide attempts in Dulac's oeuvre is telling.

Gender issues are central in Dulac's films, and the same increasingly conservative and bourgeois moral discourse that dictated women's daily existence also impacted Dulac professionally. In the commercially dependent medium of cinema, and particularly during this early period of the industry crisis (1919–23), it would likely have been professional suicide for her to express her feminist ideals directly.[53] As such, she had to make films that did not offend, but appeared to conform to mainstream and conservative sensibilities (moderated by censors and distributors), while surreptitiously injecting an underlying message that was counterhegemonic.

In this context, Dulac chose to turn to the resources of naturalism and symbolism, allowing her on the one hand, to exploit the medium's capacity to observe and record the less visible aspects of everyday reality.[54] On the other hand, drawing on her experience as a critic at *La Française* and as a wartime filmmaker, Dulac's use of a less direct, cumulative system of symbolist association supported a more subversive and liberating discourse. In her growing conviction that the essence of the cinema was to be found in life, movement, and rhythm, Dulac also used expressive techniques inspired by modern tendencies in painting, dance, and music to communicate through suggestion. To address the divide between individual aspirations and social perceptions inherent to the dramatic representation of the new woman, Dulac employed a number of experimental and highly reflexive strategies, such as self-conscious and contrasting acting styles, *mise-en-abyme* and multiple endings, hitherto unexplored in her work, before eventually turning to abstraction.

The Films: An Integrated Approach

Dulac's desire to express progressive social ideals in a conservative, pronatalist postwar context fueled her effort to innovate subversive narrative and aesthetic strategies. The aesthetic and social aspects of her work can only be understood in tandem. Her films of the postwar period demonstrate her strategy of promoting progressive gender roles, in particular, through the development of an increasingly subtle, yet complex system of signification, which she referred to as *impressionist* at least as early as 1921.[55]

The term *impressionist* requires a certain degree of redefinition in the context of Dulac's work. George Sadoul was the first French film historian to have retroactively identified and characterized what he perceived to be a coherent narrative film movement, whose principal contributors included Abel Gance, Louis Delluc, Jean Epstein, Marcel L'Herbier, and Germaine Dulac. Drawing on Sadoul's findings, the U.S. film historian and theorist David Bordwell had in his early work (1974) further characterized the movement of cinematic impressionism, or impressionist technique, as one that employs an assemblage of technical devices, including the dissolve, the superimposition, distorting lenses, and so on, as a means of expressing the psychology and subjectivity of characters.[56] Yet, this characterization, while relevant, does not fully account for the broader conception of the term by its innovators, and in its context, and the certain particularities raised by Dulac's films, such as movement and gesture, contrasting acting styles, intertextuality, and *mise-en-abyme* structures.

For Dulac, who used the designation in 1921 to describe her own films in relation to the late-nineteenth-century movement in painting (and in 1908 in reference to symbolist theater), the term corresponded to a whole system of meaning, a universe of intersecting symbols. Cinematic impressionism utilized technical effects, but it was above all a culturally specific intermedial and intertextual system of visualization and organization of both performance and mise-en-scène, sometimes augmented by pro-filmic or in-camera effects. Inspired by theatrical naturalism (and its preference for realist decors and underplayed acting), as well as theatrical and literary symbolism (and its use of a symbolic network), Dulac's repertoire included references to the modern tendencies in painting, music, poetry, sport, and dance. Yet when applied to the modern art of cinema, her approach implied a reconceptualization of performance styles and of spatial and temporal relations, as well as of narrative and looking structures; indeed, it demanded a new kind of critical viewing, as can be seen in her earliest extant film, *La Cigarette*.

La Cigarette *(1919)*

In the fall of 1919, not long before her research trip to the studios of New York, Dulac premiered *La Cigarette*, a four-part comedy based on an original script by the naturalistic filmmaker Jacques de Baroncelli, marquis de Javon, her colleague and traveling companion.[57] This film marked an important phase in Dulac's career, in that it allowed her to express her social ideals freely at a crucial moment in the history of Paris, and it planted the seeds for her development as an avant-garde artist. Baroncelli, credited in the film as Jacques de Javon, had just replaced Louis Nalpas as the new artistic director at Film d'art. A disciple of André Antoine, Baroncelli, or "the Baron," as Dulac sometimes referred to him, viewed film as the new realist art form, and his progressive attitude to gender roles made him an ideal collaborator for her.

Considered in context, *La Cigarette*, Dulac's first film of the immediate postwar period (written and shot in the spring of 1919), features one of the most patently liberated women, if also one of the most distressed and suicide-driven male heroes, of her oeuvre. Only the heroine of *La Belle Dame sans merci* (1921), an ironic and highly subversive filmic portrayal of the femme fatale, and the heroines of *Âme d'artiste* and *La Folie des vaillants*, both directed in 1925, are comparable. However, these latter films are both set abroad, in London and on the Black Sea, allowing them to reflect differently envisioned social realities—which were not possible in France.

Dulac's use of naturalist and symbolist techniques in *La Cigarette* to express the liberty of the female figure not only exemplifies her feminist perspective in very clear terms, but also lays bare the core aspects of the formal approach that she would later develop through more specifically cinematic techniques via camera work, montage, and technical effects. That this film is somewhat more didactic than Dulac's later films, however, is a result of her early liberty in the representation of progressive women's roles, a liberty that would gradually erode in the face of a more conservative moral discourse after the war.

La Cigarette tells the story of a young Parisienne, Denise Guérande, whose carefree jaunts outside of the home (and her association with the young and modern Maurice, who plays golf and dances the tango) awakens a jealous anxiety in her husband, Pierre (Gabriel Signoret), an archaeologist and curator of Egyptian antiques at the Musée d'art oriental. This jealousy leads Pierre to attempt suicide by injecting one of his cigarettes with poison. The couple's age difference highlights the gap between a tradition-bound husband and his independent-minded, "new woman" wife. Their age difference is emphasized by the husband's association with one of the museum's most recently acquired antiques, a mummified Egyptian prince who, distraught over the coquettish frivolity of his young princess, committed suicide by ingesting poisonous cakes. Denise's independence and her interest in modern dance and coed sports also contribute to her husband's insecurity. In fact, an early title card reads, ironically, "The love of antique art did not keep Pierre Guérande from marrying, despite his mature age, a young, beautiful and very modern woman."[58] Pierre's fear—later revealed to be unfounded—is emblematic of masculinity in crisis. The independence displayed by his wife and embodied in her sportswomanship contrasts with Pierre's contemplative and didactic profession, challenging traditional social perceptions of the man of action and the passive wife.

In *La Cigarette*, Denise's liberty and modernity, which are shown to exist within a conventional marriage structure, remain entirely unreformed and unpunished. This would not be the case in Dulac's later films, in which the independent woman figure would be forced to resign herself to celibacy (*Âme d'artiste*, *Princesse Mandane*), to the constraints of conventional marriage (*La Souriante Madame Beudet*, *Antoinette Sabrier*), or even to death (*La Folie des vaillants*).

La Cigarette exemplifies the strong realist and symbolist sensibility that would infuse and shape Dulac's work on almost every level of the mise-en-scène, beginning with her use of settings and acting styles.[59] In her October 1918 "Où sont les interprètes?" (Where are the artists?), published not long before she directed *La Cigarette*, Dulac compared the film director or artist creator, and his or her relationship to the reality he or she represents, to that of the realist painter, "inspired directly from nature."[60] In keeping with Jacques de Baroncelli's naturalist sensibility and using wartime cinematographer Louis Chaix, the film was shot almost entirely on location.[61] Moreover, Dulac carefully chose these locations to correspond to the specific states of mind expressed. Locations included the extant gardens of the Musée Guimet's galeries du Panthéon bouddhique (place d'Iéna), where Pierre works; an open-air space that parallels an enclosed site caught between orientalist modernity and historical antiquity, which mirrors the couple's age difference and social tension; and the Champs Elysées and other distinctively modern Parisian streets, where the male protagonist feels out of place. Dulac also situated one of the film's pivotal scenes in the modern and naturalistic setting of an urban golf course, prefiguring the important symbolic and formal role that sport and dance would play elsewhere in her films.

Along with location shooting (and in anticipation of her later films, such as *La Folie des vaillants*), Dulac also employed realist acting, which she combined with symbolist association. In her 1918 article, she called for a style of acting that distinguished itself from traditional theater by relying more on subtlety and detail, thus becoming more lifelike: "The performer who acts for the camera must forget all his notions of theater. On the stage, a gesture is better communicated to the audience when it is broadened. On the screen, it must be highly detailed. Any artifice, trick, or forced effect clashes like a wrong note. And quite the reverse, anything that is without affectation, simple, unexpected, *real and direct like life* takes on a delightful meaning, [and] creates and carries the emotion. . . . On the screen, we don't need actors. We need artists. We don't need processes. *We need truth*" (emphasis added).[62]

This more direct or realist acting style, designed to remain as close to life as possible, was central to Dulac's conception of cinema. And accordingly, the acting in *La Cigarette* is distinctly naturalistic. With the exception of the deliberately expressive display of elation by the young girls in the film's housewarming party sequence, gestures are minimal and unobtrusive. The actors's facial expressions are relatively subtle and understated. Meaning is created uniquely through the associations between actors and their environment.

Dulac frequently referenced painting and music, as did many of her contemporaries, most famously, Abel Gance in his film *La Dixième Symphonie* (*The Tenth Symphony*, 1918). However, for Dulac, these references never dominated, and like cinema's relationship to the other arts, remained primarily analogical. For instance, Dulac insisted that the director should prepare the realist actor in a pictorial manner, as a basis for the larger dramatic movement, saying: "It's in real life that these attitudes are observed before being reproduced. The preparation of the actor is essentially pictorial. Using these elements, the director should compose the dramatic movement . . . to achieve this truth in acting, just as the realist painter who finds his inspiration directly in nature."[63]

While Dulac drew on a variety of acting styles in her work, in all cases these styles were subject to a larger system of signification orchestrated by the director. In keeping with the symbolist penchant for citation, Dulac sometimes employed gesture, as a condensed visual description (within the image), as a means of associating her female protagonist with an existing archetype, which she either developed (*La Cigarette*, *La Souriante Madame Beudet*) or undercut (*La Belle Dame sans merci*).

Denise Guérande, the young heroine of *La Cigarette*, is associated with various elements of symbolist art. Denise's appearance specifically resembles the female archetype of mid-nineteenth-century Pre-Raphaelite painting. (Dulac made specific references to this school of painting in a subsequent script for *La Souriante Madame Beudet*, whose heroine is modeled, in the opening sequence, after a painting of "Ste. Cécile École des préraphaélites" [Saint Cecilia of the Pre-Raphaelite school].)[64] In addition to the long, wavy and flowing blond hair that dominates her physical appearance, Denise is presented to the spectator in the reduced Arcadian landscape of her garden, before an outdoor pond and fountain, a frequent image in symbolist art. (The presence of three swans in the fountain may be a reference to Wagner's opera *Parsifal*, where a slain swan connotes a young knight's virtue and self-castration in relation to a bewitching heroine. In light of this reference, the presence of three swans in the fountain might be read as a critique of the traditional heterosexual couple.) The heroine of *La Cigarette* is also associated with music and additional nonnarrative images of nature. Drawing on the musical analogy central to her later work, Dulac employs the figurative technique of animation—for example, she follows the image of a gramophone record with images of nature and the sky, on which she superimposes a shot of painted musical notes appearing one by one on the screen. The resulting correlation, which is rooted in the romantic associations among music and sexual desire and creativity, expresses the carefree attitude, spontaneity, and dynamism of her young heroine. Dulac contrasts this image with more modern symbolic gestures later in the film.

Dulac also creates meaning through a number of symbolist associations, which unfold almost as a string of impressions. While Denise is out learning to play golf, Pierre's anxieties about his wife's absence are expressed through a series of encounters on the streets of Paris, which serves as a direct illustration of his evolving mental state. For example, while waiting for a cab on the Champs Elysées, Pierre watches two newlyweds emerge from a church, while a young man also observing them scoffs that the dramatic age difference between the two is a sure way to be deceived. (An intertitle reads, "No hair on the cranium, must want to be cheated on.") A subsequent shot in which Pierre remarks on the young age of the couples that line the park benches of the lower Champs Elysées further emphasizes the character's feelings of forlornness and displacement. Shortly afterward, he contemplates an old photograph of himself at age twenty, and then an album with clippings from his marriage (at age forty-eight) to his young wife, again reinforcing his insecurity.

Dulac also juxtaposes these sequences with shots of Denise, which in addition to their own internal associations, further highlight Pierre's state of mind. Dulac intercuts these scenes of Pierre with his antiques, or Pierre reflecting about his age, with those of his independent young wife partaking in, as the intertitle indicates, "The pleasures of modern life" (a manicure, a golf lesson, a "tea-tango," and housewarming party at Irène's sister's *atelier de garçonne*, or

Figures 7a and 7b. Andrée Brabant as Denise Guérande and Gabriel Signoret as Pierre Guérande. *La Cigarette*, 1919. Rights reserved. Collection Cinémathèque française.

bachelorette studio). The opening title of the sequence reads "It's delightful to be a bachelor[ette] without a domestic." These scenes, which Pierre perceives from afar, lead him to suspect his wife's infidelity and her preference for the young Maurice. The oriental tissues, flowers, and perfumes decorating the atelier further represent Denise's sensual independence. This iconography of orientalism—apparent in the nineteenth-century travel literature of romanticist writer, sensuous dance critic and choreographer Théophile Gautier and his daughter, poet, musicologist, and feminist Judith Gautier, which Dulac read, as well as in the colorful performances of the Ballet russes, which she attended—also is associated with the feminine desire for liberty.[65] An earlier shot of Denise and Irène in the museum with a nude Hindu statue of a woman with three heads and six arms has additional connotations of female sexual desire and fantasy, recalling the Hindu mythologies that intrigued Dulac and her former lover, Irène Hillel-Erlanger.

Dulac's pictorial universe was largely composed of nineteenth-century symbolist references, like Pre-Raphaelite painting, as well as decorative orientalism and abstraction, the latter of which were also linked to symbolist theater through the "synthetic symbolism" and Nabism of painters like Gauguin and Vuillard, respectively. Yet, Dulac also frequently employed more contemporary pictorial and figurative references, namely, sports and modern dance.

Women's Sports in Dulac's Films

The golf scene in *La Cigarette* and the more general recurrence of women's sports in Dulac's films merit consideration within the postwar context. The early-twentieth-century development and popularization of "harmonic gymnastics" by Georges Demenÿ and "rhythmic gymnastics" by Jacques Dalcroze, along with the emergence of women's sports organizations during the Great War, heightened the widespread discourse surrounding the fears of woman's "virilization," in terms of both the female body and mind.[66] While Dulac's incorporation of these motifs was part of this broader cultural discourse, it also reflected her particular point of view as a moderate feminist.

Faced with the reality of the new woman (founded in particular on her new relationship to her body), this debate gave rise to discourses that were largely contradictory. In an article published in the illustrated sports journal *La Vie au Grand Air* in September 1918, the same year as the officialization of the Fédération des sociétés féminines sportives de France (French Federation of Women's Sports Associations), Rose-Nicole (nom de plume), author of *Les Secrets de beauté de la Parisienne*, gave a long warning that summarized fears related to women's sports: "Certainly, young women who exercise their body's strength and flexibility must be praised, but they must be safeguarded from unappealing and unnecessary excess. . . . There would be cause for alarm, if the female athlete were only an athlete and, in the fervor of her competitions, forgot her real human task: motherhood." The author's advice ultimately was ambiguous: "Accustom women to sports, fine, but reject any inclination to an exaggerated athletic movement leading to feminist sportsmanship."[67]

In contrast, other women, among them Suzanne Grinberg (vice president of Union française pour le suffrage des femmes, cofounded by Jane Misme of *La Française*, 1908), defended women's sports, arguing against the idea that women would become masculine. She argued that virilizing or masculinizing female intelligence would not make participants less womanly. On the contrary, such an effort would strengthen their willpower, which was essential for self-control.[68] Nevertheless, the general atmosphere of conservatism presented constraints for those who tried to create compliant or acceptable images. An emblematic case was that of the French tennis champion Suzanne Lenglen, who was obliged to soften, or attenuate, her appearance and display a reassuring femininity—often by adopting dance-like poses—in order to gain popular acceptance for her sports activity, which called on traditionally masculine qualities, such as physical strength and speed.[69] Just as Lenglen tempered her image, Dulac opted to present images of women practicing or contemplating more modest and accepted sports, such as golf (*La Cigarette*). Tennis, a sport Dulac practiced intermittently with Albert and Irène in Giverny during the war, nonetheless figures most frequently in her later work (*La Belle Dame sans merci*, *La Souriante Madame Beudet*, *La Coquille et le clergyman*; also an unproduced documentary project on tennis champion Henri Cochet in 1930).

Many, such as Rose-Nicole in 1918, considered tennis the "women's sport par excellence," or the most appropriate sports activity for women, because "one can determine the dose of physical exertion." A sports article published over a decade later in 1930 warned readers against "unfeminine" activities. The article's humor does not conceal its seriousness: "Sports will only be beneficial to women at the cost of a discipline which is hardly of their character. Only exercises requiring flexibility over strength are suited to them: tennis, swimming, but running, jumping or ballgames, why not fighting or boxing?"[70] In this regard, Dulac's films show her determination to use the image of the sportswoman to alter how women were perceived.

A number of Dulac's films include scenes of women playing sports, driving, or hunting. One such "new woman" is the young heroine of *La Cigarette*, Denise, who expresses her independence through athletic endeavor and has been learning to play golf from her girlfriend Irène's friend Maurice (representing the "new man"). *La Cigarette* simultaneously evokes Denise's freedom and autonomy and the anxiety that the emergence of the strong, independent new woman causes her husband, Pierre, but its nonviolent, serene mise-en-scène reassures viewers that all is well. At the end of the film, the status quo is partially upheld. When Denise returns home, she relates her manifestly innocent version of events. Her subjective narration takes the form of a flashback explicating Irène's absence from the golf lesson—she was attending her sister's housewarming party. Denise also explains how, on one occasion, having surmised her husband's plan to commit suicide, she diverted him in order to dispose of the poisonous cigarette. The husband's fears thus are allayed, at least temporarily. Despite this apparent return to the status quo, the final shot creates ambiguity and adds significance to the film's title. Throughout the film, Pierre forbids Denise to smoke, but in the very last shot, which takes place in the garden where the film began, she playfully steals a puff from her husband's cigarette, implying that things have indeed changed, however slightly, in their relationship.

Dulac's use of naturalistic or realist settings and acting, as well as her use of symbolist association through atmosphere and gesture, anticipates the approach used in her subsequent films, deemed impressionist, and the cinematic movement of the same name that her next film, *La Fête espagnole*, is credited with having launched.

Delluc and Dulac, and the Foundation of a Movement

Dulac's collaboration with Louis Delluc, whom she had met during the war through his fiancée, the actress Ève Francis, marked another important step in her development as a filmmaker. This collaboration was in many ways prototypical of future film movements, in that it grew out of a union of (in this case, two) front-line artist-critics who purposefully united their efforts to theorize, create and promote a new type of cinema, one they believed would equal and even surpass the other arts in its modernity. In August 1919, following her completion of *La Cigarette*, Dulac directed *La Fête espagnole* (The Spanish fiesta), based on a *livret* (libretto) by then-film critic Louis Delluc. In 1927, George Sadoul credited *La Fête espagnole* as the first impressionist film. However, before making this film, Delluc and Dulac had collaborated on an entirely different, yet unrealized, production for Film d'art.[71] In early 1919, Delluc had asked Dulac to direct a film based on his script and soon-to-be-released novel, *Le Train sans yeux* (The train without eyes). The action of the project, starring Ève Francis and Jean Toulout, was to take place on an express train from Paris to the Côte d'Azur.

The project had several false starts. Following a last-minute dispute over casting with Film d'art's management, Delluc abandoned the project. In April 1919, in the hope of securing more autonomous production conditions, and once again with Dulac as director, Delluc proposed the project to Louis Nalpas, who had recently left Film d'art for the Studios de la Victorine.[72] Indefinitely delayed and eventually abandoned for financial reasons, the project (which would not see the light until Alberto Cavalcanti's 1926 production), in many ways can be seen to have heralded the arrival of France's first cinematographic avant-garde, later known as the impressionist film movement.

Dulac's preparations for the project were remarkable. According to a letter from Delluc to Nalpas dated May 6, 1919, she negotiated with the Compagnie des chemins de fer Paris-Lyon-Méditerranée (known as PLM), once run by her great-grandfather Antoine Schneider, to gain access to wagons, trains, and stations, as well as model trains that could be burned. The model trains had been constructed for the re-creation of a railway accident, a theme that mesmerized the public after the great accident at the Gare Saint-Lazare in 1905.[73] Dulac's endeavor to use on-location shooting, like her penchant for realist acting (and the use of nonprofessional actors in secondary roles), to a certain extent anticipated Jean Renoir's quintessentially realist film, *La Bête humaine* (1938), in which Jean Gabin prepared his role with actual rail workers.

Delluc and Dulac's decision to direct a film centered on the quintessentially modernist symbol of the train was significant. The train as a subject embodied the movement, rhythm, and speed that fascinated avant-garde artists. Moreover, the project anticipated Abel Gance's emblematic film, *La Roue* (1922), initiated in 1920 based on a script by Elie Faure, and considered one of the foundational films of cinematic impressionism. In 1924, Dulac would venerate Gance's *La Roue* for those musical qualities that she was to develop into her own theory of the "visual symphony."[74] In this, she was not unlike Jean Epstein, who later claimed that had it not been for *La Roue*, he might never have made films. One can only speculate on what form Delluc and Dulac's homage to the train might have taken, but their project constituted an important link to the modernist projects of other avant-garde filmmakers. The railroad theme was later also valorized by Cavalcanti (1926), as well as Renoir (1938).

La Fête espagnole *(1920)*

In August 1919, following her completion of *La Cigarette* for Film d'art, and faced with continuing uncertainty about the financial feasibility of "Le Train sans yeux," Dulac directed *La Fête espagnole*, whose critical reputation largely depended on its sophisticated use of movement, both within and between the shots, as Dulac would later explain.

La Fête espagnole—based on a stream-of-consciousness script, legendarily drafted by Delluc on the paper tablecloth of a café in late 1918—returns to the theme of the postwar crisis of masculinity. The film highlights the perceived gap between men's and women's experiences, between the battlefront and the home front, or the separate dominions of the "miserable" and the "happy," as Henri Barbusse put it in his wartime novel, *Le Feu* (1916).[75] In *La Fête espagnole*, two male protagonists (Jean Toulout and Gaston Modot) fight to the death over a confident, sensuous woman (played by Ève Francis, Delluc's new wife), who appears entirely unaffected by the men and their struggle. She exits with a third male, thus capping a piercing commentary on women's liberty and pursuit of personal pleasure in the wake of masculine violence.

This reflection on the gender division created by the war would draw amply upon the medium's new formal possibilities, such as its relative synchronism.[76] Yet the challenge in examining a joint project such as *La Fête espagnole* lies in locating the individual voices of the film's creators, and particularly that of Dulac as director. Most of the film is considered lost, but an incomplete print consisting of two or three short excerpts, as well as a script, and several archival documents (correspondence and reviews) help us situate this film within Dulac's career. The fragmentary print, recovered by Langlois during an exchange with Éclair in 1938, includes several establishing shots of a Spanish village and two indoor sequences in a café and cabaret, featuring Francis, as well as a final extremely long shot of a house, which closes the film with the extinguishing of an upstairs light.[77] As Richard Abel has pointed out, one of the most salient points that can be gathered from these surviving extracts is Delluc and Dulac's joint commitment to filming on location, a foundational element of their aesthetic.[78] Places "seem less presented than incorporated into the flow of picturesque events," Delluc remarked.[79]

Along with its use of outdoor settings, *La Fête espagnole* is also marked by Dulac's use of subtle naturalistic acting. One sequence uses dance to express the state of mind of the female character, a device characteristic of a large proportion of Dulac's films. Movement and rhythm are the second and third

Figure 8. This film poster designed by Albert Puylat recalls Barbusse's references to France's wartime gender divisions. *La Fête espagnole,* 1920. Rights reserved. Collection Cinémathèque française.

important terms—after life itself —in her conception of cinema. While more than one-third of her feature films contain sport scenes, more than half contain dance scenes, all of which contribute to the films' psychological expressivity or symbolism. She also characteristically employs athletes and dancers in key roles.[80]

In the first part of the surviving extract, and very much in keeping with Dulac's prior film *La Cigarette*, Ève Francis's acting in the café scene is relatively understated. The second part, which takes place in a busy cabaret, is the most original and revealing. Intercutting Francis's sensual and increasingly erratic dance with the mounting passions of the two men, the sequence expresses the inner life of its characters both through movement "within" and "between" the shots, via a slow, but rhythmic, alternating montage, to which both Delluc and Dulac allude in their writings.

The Reception and Legacy of La Fête espagnole

As the object of collaboration of two leading cinematic impressionists, *La Fête espagnole* occupies an important terrain of contestation in film history, one that Dulac would face again in her 1927 production of a script by surrealist Antonin Artaud.[81] A consideration of *La Fête espagnole*'s reception also highlights the prejudice that Dulac faced as a woman director, echoing that against which Delluc himself had defended her. Several early reviewers, such as Surrealist poet and literary critic Phillipe Soupault, attributed the genius of the film solely to writer Louis Delluc.[82] Others went further in attributing its success to Delluc and its shortcomings to Dulac, arguing that the abstract literary style of the script and its evocation of a dynamic suite of images, surpassed the film itself.

In his 1921 review for the satirical journal *Le Crapouillot*, René Bizet omitted all mention of Dulac, while indirectly faulting her for the film's limitations.[83] "I believe that it is to Louis Delluc that we owe the best French film of last year," he wrote. "With its sober script and composition, *La Fête espagnole* could have been a masterpiece if the atmosphere had been better treated." While Delluc had not yet directed a film himself, Bizet foregrounded the young writer's skills: "As it was presented, the film was as dignified as the good American productions that Louis Delluc, who is a particularly intelligent critic, has defended so often in his columns."[84] Indeed, following the critics (perhaps also incited by the synopsis prepared for distributors), all of the major French film historians of the period, including Léon Moussinac, George

Figure 9. On the set at the Villa Liserbe of the Studios de la Victorine (August–November 1919). In the background, Ève Francis stands atop a table for the filming of the sensual dance sequence. *La Fête espagnole*, 1920. Rights reserved. Collection Cinémathèque française.

Sadoul, and Jean Mitry, similarly attributed the film's critical success to its script.[85] Delluc, and not Dulac, was thus credited when Sadoul touted *La Fête espagnole* as the first impressionist film.[86]

This critical erasure of Dulac and her key role (as director) in *La Fête espagnole*'s success, and correspondingly of her early impact on the impressionist movement, merits reconsideration. Dulac's place as a woman in a predominantly male postwar industry was precarious. Furthermore, Delluc had something of a cult following, and his premature death from tuberculosis in 1924 further elevated his mythical status. In 1916, Delluc had cofounded *Le Film*, the first and most important dedicated film journal of the era, with Henri Diamant-Berger, and he was a luminary for many young cinephiles.[87]

When examining the film's production and distribution files, this attribution of the film's success to Delluc and the erasure of Dulac's role as director, while characteristic of women's status and representation at the time, as well as of the pressures of the film distribution system, proves arbitrary. Contrary to historical accounts, Delluc, while conceding some of the project's inherent limitations, praised Dulac's direction. In an article for *Paris-Midi*, published on May 4, 1920, Delluc lauded the film as an example of perfect teamwork. "Even if it provokes fiery, but useful criticism, I strongly advise you to go see this film, for it is one of the rare examples of complete collaboration in the French cinema," he wrote. "The writer, director, and actors all worked together willingly and contributed their special talents to realize the chosen theme."[88]

Moreover, the film's critics had overlooked a number of factors, including material constraints, unaccounted for in its minimalist script. Although *La Fête espagnole* featured star actress Ève Francis, wearing a panoply of dresses, including one advertised as one of the first costumes made especially for the cinema, budget limitations prohibited the film from being shot on location, as Delluc and Dulac had desired.[89] The film's atmosphere, criticized by Bizet, was thus one clear consequence of these restrictions. "Something torrid, exhilarating and turbulent was missing," Fescourt writes. "The languor of the Riviera substituted for Iberian austerity."[90] If we listen to Delluc himself, Dulac could hardly be faulted. In his *Paris-Midi* article, Delluc praised Dulac's bravado in having overcome the lack of resources and the limitations of the film set, hailing her direction as "entirely different from the pretty needlework with which most directors ordinarily replace the script." He affirms, "In France, faith suffices where means are lacking, and Germaine Dulac captured the essence of what was needed."[91]

Similarly, while *La Fête espagnole*'s narrative line may have been more pronounced than initially conceived, if we look at Dulac's subsequent productions at the Victorines, it appears that this may have been producer-imposed. Indeed, a letter shows that Nalpas asked her to foreground narrative action in her subsequent film *Malencontre*, and that it is only in her final self-produced film at the Victorines, *La Belle Dame sans merci*, that she escaped such interference.[92] (Dulac would highlight the importance of directorial autonomy, notwithstanding other distributor-imposed restrictions, when presenting this later at CASA.)

In his article for *La Fête espagnole*'s premiere, Delluc went further in championing some of Dulac's unique and innovative contributions in the use of lighting, visual motifs, and decor, and called for her to be given the recognition she had long deserved: "We owe to her the muted, ironic passion of the lighting, the warm accentuation of scenes, the ornamental heights of which French cinema seems to be categorically unaware. Let this be grounds for us to give the director of *Âmes de fous* and *La Cigarette* her rightful place. Let this be a formal reason for her no longer to have to accept mediocre offers to make films without audacity and greatness."[93]

In fact, Delluc's only criticism regarding the film concerned its distributor-imposed intertitles. "The public should know that a film's shortcomings are not necessarily caused by the author, the director and the actors," he further cautioned.[94] So, even in Delluc's eyes, and in spite of production constraints, Dulac deserved substantial credit for the success of *La Fête espagnole*.

Since Delluc's status as primary author was based on his strengths as a writer and film critic, one may ask if the films he directed exhibited the same limitations as the one directed by Dulac. Indeed, his later films, and their reviews, provide further evidence of Dulac's unjust erasure as author. While films like Delluc's *La Fièvre* (1921) attest to his inspired use of realist decors and character types, certain aspects fall short of expectations. For example, the acting (including that of Francis, who worked with Dulac again in *Antoinette Sabrier*) appears more exaggerated in its use of facial expression and gesture, than that in the surviving extracts of Dulac's *La Fête espagnole*, and her extant films of the same period (*La Belle Dame sans merci* and *La Mort du soleil*). Perhaps due to her influences from symbolist theater, early 1920s films not only are more subtle in their use of gesture but also more frequently employ close-ups to capture detail in realist acting, a wholly modern technique in France at the time. (The notoriously satirical and histrionic acting of Alexandre Arquillère in Dulac's *La Souriante Madame Beudet* is a deliberate exception that sets her broader technique in relief.)

A final and crucial consideration is the use of movement (as a corollary to the characters' psychological states), for which the impressionist school is noted. Alongside Dulac, who became a leading promoter of cinema's modernity as a derivation of its essence in movement, was impressionist filmmaker Jean Epstein, who also foregrounded this notion, while raising crucial questions concerning the authorship of *La Fête espagnole* and the locus of its originality.[95] In a postwar critique of the first cinematic avant-garde, Epstein, while gesturing to Delluc in describing his own distinct concept of photogénie (see below), not only referred to *La Fête espagnole* as the most original of Delluc's films, but, crucially, evoked the collaboration with Dulac as a factor in this originality:

> Louis Delluc decided to call this secret quality of the phenomenon the cinema favorably transfigured *photogénie*. And it was accepted that a cinema worthy of this name should in some way be the precise location of all that was

> *photogénique*. In truth, *photogénie* and *photogénique* were still only words which vaguely designated a very poorly defined function. . . . Nevertheless, little by little, it became evident to directors and cameramen that *photogénie* depended, perhaps not exclusively, but in general and without a doubt, on movement: movement either of the filmed object or of the play of light and shadow. . . . *Photogénie* appeared above all as a function of mobility. As such, movement—this appearance that neither the drawing, nor painting, nor photography, nor any other means reveals and that only the *cinematograph* knows how to render—proved itself to be precisely the primary aesthetic quality of images of the screen. A logical conjuncture, that etymology should have allowed us to foresee, but whose importance Delluc himself doesn't seem to have given the recognition that it deserved, except in the film *La Fête espagnole*, which he made in collaboration with Germaine Dulac, and which no longer physically exists.[96]

Epstein's statement points to a wholly different conception of the historical collaboration between Delluc and Dulac than prior critics by locating *La Fête espagnole* as a privileged moment in the career of the young critic-turned-filmmaker. Epstein's account suggests that it was only in collaboration with Dulac that Delluc foregrounded movement as the essence of cinematic expression, or what Delluc and Epstein (but not Dulac) referred to as *photogénie*.[97] According to Epstein, Delluc seemed to write about movement, more than he explored it in his films (e.g., *La Fièvre* and *La Femme de nulle part*). While perhaps only a recovery of *La Fête espagnole* would help resolve the contention surrounding the film's authorship in the face of production constraints, and its role in the emergence of cinematic impressionism, its controversial position does illuminate the conditions of Dulac's directorial legacy. This celebratory attitude toward this flagship film, which Henri Langlois later calls "the key film of French film history: as important as Eisenstein's *Strike*," stands in stark contrast to Dulac's critical erasure from French cinema history, and lays bare the cultural, aesthetic, and economic factors that render a reevaluation of her films so crucial.[98]

Malencontre *(1920)*

Following *La Fête espagnole*, Dulac made two additional films at the Victorine Studios in the early 1920s. Both elucidate the types of producer and distributor-imposed constraints she faced (while working in a relatively independent context), as well as the resourcefulness and creativity with which she addressed shifting gender roles. In the winter of 1919–20, before producing a satire of the femme fatale image of *la belle dame sans merci* (the beautiful woman without mercy, much celebrated in literature), with her 1921 film of the same title, she directed the racially charged *Malencontre* (Misfortune) for Louis Nalpas Films, based on an austere and bleak novel by Guy Chantepleure (pseudonym for Mme Edgar Dussap, née Jeanne-Caroline Violet).[99]

Archival materials concerning *Malencontre* help us to reconstruct the details of this lost film. As in her earliest films, Dulac sought to express psychological states through a maximum of atmosphere and a minimum of action or plot-driven agitation, not to be confused with Epstein's notion of movement. As the critic Jean Morizot wrote in his October 1920 review, "Mme Germaine A. Dulac probably chose the novel because it is indeed a pretext *and no more than a pretext for a few paintings of souls*. Also the film is directly linked to *Âmes de Fous*, an excellent and even authoritative French work" (original emphasis).[100] According to critics, in this film, as in *La Cigarette*, Dulac combined expressive interior decors (a large room, charming pillows, a piano) with outdoor settings (animal herds on moors, flowering fruit orchards, mountain streams) from the Midi region (southeastern France). Numerous publicity and film stills of the French Indonesian actress and dancer Djemil Anik (1888–1980, born in Martinique of a Javanese mother and French father) suggest that Dulac also used expressive lighting and several symbolist gestures from dance to express various psychological states.[101] (However, unlike *La Fête espagnole*, which associates passion and death with summer heat, *Malencontre* cloaks these themes in an atmosphere of coldness.)[102]

Malencontre was subject to numerous production constraints. In a letter to Serge Sandberg requesting the immediate purchase of the rights for the novel, and at a time when Ciné-Studio was just getting on its feet, Nalpas emphasized the film's commercial potential. In a letter dated November 1919, Dulac agreed to Nalpas's request to make the film more commercial and narrative by reinforcing its atmosphere and the characters' sentiments with "more precise facts" and "more intense action," as well as by defining the film's conflict as earlier than initially planned, a shift that also had a considerable impact on the social content of the film.[103]

Malencontre addresses the theme of interracial relations through the story of a young widower, Patrice de Malencontre (Jacques Roussel), who is in love with a light-skinned half-Ceylonese woman, Gladys Savage (Seigneur), of whom his unsympathetic mother (Brindeau) disapproves. Another major character is Gladys's half-sister, the olive-skinned Hindu dancer Brinda (Djemil Anik, Ève Francis's costar in *Âmes de fous*). *Malencontre* reaches its climax when Brinda murders her light-skinned sister, Gladys, the night before Gladys's marriage, much to the satisfaction of Patrice's mother.

According to different versions of the script, Dulac responded to Nalpas's request by expanding the film's epilogue, through Patrice's eventual marriage to a Frenchwoman, Flavie Clairande (France Dhélia). This development essentially undercut the treatment of Gladys and Brinda, as well as the critique of racial discrimination in the film. However, through Dulac's mise-en-scène, arguably, the film's radical aspect was preserved, since the most prominent and captivating figure in the film is Gladys's "passionate" and "indifferent" half-sister, Brinda.

One of France's first actresses of color to appear in a major role, Djemil Anik commands the spectator's attention. In addition to the atmospheric decor, such as the incense burners and oriental pillows with which she is associated, Anik's apparently entrancing use of gesture as an expression of her psychological state no doubt heighten the spectator's affinity for her character. As Jean Morizot wrote after the film's premiere, "Mme Djemil Anik still resembles the sculpted goddess herself, but she is now a moving goddess. Her olive Hindu skin stands out extraordinarily beneath the flash of the spotlights. In her dances, her demeanor, her walk, her most frivolous gestures, she demonstrates a science of postures and eurhythmy pushed to perfection." Yet Anik's performance also

Figure 10. Isadora Duncan prodigy and dancer Djemil Anik as Brinda Savage. *Malencontre*, 1920. Rights reserved. Collection Cinémathèque française.

creates a potent atmosphere of coldness, adding to the film's fatalistic tone, and confirming the difficulties of miscegenation. As Morizot affirmed, "Djemil Anik makes us dream of death, cold and rigid as she is. In *Malencontre*, it is exactly what is needed."[104]

The centrality of the dancer figure in Dulac's films cannot be overemphasized. In her 1917 film *Vénus Victrix*, starring the dancer-actress Stasia Napierkowska, Dulac took her inspiration from the sultry gestures of Ida Rubinstein. For *Malencontre*, she was influenced by Russian dancer and actress Alla Nazimova, whom she had seen in Albert Capellani's 1919 *La Lanterne rouge* (*The Red Lantern*), in a role strikingly similar to that of Anik's Brinda. In November 1919, while adapting Chantepleure's novel, Dulac wrote to producer Louis Nalpas, "I saw Nazimova again, yesterday in *La Lanterne rouge*. And I am enthused. Her slightest gesture is the synthesis of an entire state of mind. She is beautiful, powerful and true, and she knows how to express her spirit without false means. She is great among the greats."[105] The gesture of dance as a means of expressing the immaterial or spiritual, and ultimately the social, would be a constant in Dulac's work both in its figurative form, and in its more abstract linear and arabesque renderings.

In her next film, *La Belle Dame sans merci*, Dulac further developed the use of atmosphere and gesture, as well as her conception of movement as primary means of expression. In Dulac's films of this period, movement was already central to the expression of character's psychological states, although she did not articulate this conception in her lectures and writings until later. Moreover, Dulac's use of movement was bound to her symbolist conception of cinema.

La Belle Dame sans merci *(1921)*

Written, directed, and produced by Dulac, and based on an idea by Irène Hillel-Erlanger, *La Belle Dame sans merci* is one of the director's most personal and most modern. In addition to intensifying her use of gesture and movement, of sport and dance, to express her feminist ideals, it expanded Dulac's experimental repertoire through a more salient use of reflexive narrative techniques such as caricature and parody. It was one of the first films that Dulac presented at the opening of CASA in her continuing efforts to educate the public about the art of cinema.[106] A transcript from this presentation, along with the film and film script, provides us with key insights into the singularity of her approach.

In this film, the female protagonist is distinctly different from the apparently innocent and unaware heroine of *La Cigarette*. The Belle Dame (Tania

Figure 11. Tania Daleyme as Lola de Sandoval reading love letters from admirers. *La Belle Dame sans merci*, 1921. Rights reserved. Collection Cinémathèque française.

Daleyme) is a beautiful and talented actress, who goes by the name of Lola de Sandoval. Mistreated by her former lover, the Count d'Amaury (the name of a villainous twelfth-century count, played here by Jean Toulout), this modern city woman now uses and disposes of men as she sees fit. She is presented in contrast to the traditional women of the provinces, whom she will later confront, with respect to her stigmatization as femme fatale. The film is titled after John Keats's homonymic ballad, which explores issues of representation, language, and illusion.[107] Keats's "La Belle Dame Sans Merci" (1819) tells the story of a knight who meets a woman with "wild wild eyes" in a meadow, who declares her love, only to leave him to awaken alone, abandoned "on the cold hill's side."[108] (The figure of the Belle Dame also is a favorite of nineteenth-century English Pre-Raphaelite painters, such as John William Waterhouse and Frank Dicksee, who illustrated Keats's poem.)[109]

According to pre-project notes written by Hillel-Erlanger, Lola de Sandoval's character was also inspired by the Queen of Sheba figure in Flaubert's *La Tentation de Saint-Antoine* (*The Temptation of St. Anthony*).[110] The Belle Dame of the Napoleonic era, who embodies the romantic theme of failed relationships often ending in male suicide, took on a new and correspondingly poignant significance after World War I.

Dulac's film presents the myth of the Belle Dame in a modern context (postwar Europe), which she transmits to the spectator in the condensed form of a telephone exchange during the film's prologue.[111] In this opening sequence, which uses parallel montage, a lovesick man declares his love for Lola and begs her to let him see her again, to which Lola responds, mercilessly, that she will have forgotten him "in the time it takes . . . to smoke a cigarette."[112] The young suitor's repetitive beckoning to Lola, even after she has hung up the phone, highlights his suffering and her indifference. In this sequence, Dulac brilliantly intercuts shots of the city men, bitterly criticizing her in a "night cabaret," with shots of Lola in her studio, calmly and elegantly smoking her cigarette, in a position of total repose.[113]

Through the mise-en-scène and editing of this sequence, Dulac sets up a powerful caricature of Lola that she proceeds to deconstruct. To begin this process, she revisits the stereotypes of nineteenth century art. For example, Dulac positions Lola in a manner that reflects symbolist and modernist painting. Lola's posture is a direct reference to Édouard Manet's *Olympia* (1863), a striking portrait of a high-class prostitute in repose. Manet's portrait is a remarkably realist interpretation of the classic theme of the reclining nude, made famous by the Renaissance painters Giorgione and Titian, as well as Ingres's *La Grande Odalisque* (1812). Owing to its stark contrast between model, foreground, and background, along with the confrontational gaze and resolute gestures of its female subject, Manet's *Olympia*, which was regarded as an intended parody, provoked a scandal at the Paris Salon of 1865, and also provided a stimulus for the young painters of the future impressionist movement. In Dulac's reference to Manet's modernist and realist painting, which blurred objectivity and subjectivity, she draws attention to the distinction between reality and representation, as a means of destabilizing the stereotype of the Belle Dame, or femme fatale. (A reflexive, if somewhat ambiguous, intertitle calls attention to the issues of representation and interpretation: "One must be able to differentiate between art and beauty.")

Dulac also plays on the purposefully ambiguous motives of the romantic female archetype of Keats's era, in order to comment on and challenge it. In Dulac's film, the Belle Dame's motivation remains uncertain. However, Dulac goes further in nuancing and ultimately overturning the archetype. Even unsuspecting critics are sensitive to this subversion. As J. L. Croze writes,

"This Lola, a victim of love who swears to take vengeance on men for the suffering caused by one alone, is so coldly coquettish and scheming in her attempt to hurt others that she risks being hateful; yet, one only feels sorry for her . . . we are tempted to excuse the ruthless woman for having done so much harm, with so much beauty!"[114] Dulac's deconstruction of the Belle Dame archetype relies as much on experimental narrative, as well as more directly visual means.

La Belle Dame *in the Provinces*

Dulac uses the opposition between country and city as a backdrop for her larger discourse between traditional and modern values, and between the traditional and modern woman. Once again, her naturalist and symbolist influences are apparent, and her masterful treatment of indoor and outdoor settings incites critical praise. One reviewer compares her realist treatment of the provincial setting in *La Belle Dame* and her subsequent films to the use of landscapes by the Swedish filmmakers, likely a reference to Victor Sjöström and Mauritz Stiller, whom Dulac admired.[115]

Dulac uses caricature and parody to contrast traditional and modern values, within this larger framework of realism and symbolism, and against this backdrop of the city and country. In *La Belle Dame*, she employs these techniques to specifically feminist ends. For example, following the cabaret sequence in the prologue is the parodic representation of Lola, as seen through the eyes of the countrywomen. When Lola organizes a charity event in the country, in an effort to uplift her faltering image, she is met with suspicion and fear. Here Dulac humorously employs the trope of gossip (a structural motif that she would later use in *Madame Beudet*, and that would become the central figure of *Le Diable dans la ville*). An intertitle reads, "As for the women, they are conspiring." In a provocative and rapid montage sequence, which is set off from the rest of the film by its gothic intertitles and the static, frontal, austere, and wholly artificial character of its compositions, Dulac intercuts evocative and detailed images of Lola with shots of the gossiping women imaginatively describing her. This sequence, which includes an image of the courtyard of Lola's hotel, stocked with lion cubs, and a shot of four black slaves rigidly and symmetrically arranged within the frame, has the effect of undermining the countrywomen and rendering their musings absurd.

Dulac renders the country sequence more discursive by inserting a shot of three elderly women sitting in rocking chairs, engaging in idle talk while

Figure 12. Tania Daleyme as Lola de Sandoval and Jean Toulout as the Count Guy d'Amaury, driving to the provinces. *La Belle Dame sans merci*, 1921. Rights reserved. Collection Cinémathèque française.

crocheting, followed by a graphic match of three parakeets in a cage (distinct from the triangle of swans in *La Cigarette*). This device is similar to, although arguably more self-reflexive and critical than, a famous sequence in Erich von Stroheim's later film, *Foolish Wives* (1922). In that film, Stroheim illustrates the misogynistic point of view of the lead protagonist (which he played) with a shot of a group of women around a washbasin, followed by a graphic match of chickens encircling a puddle.[116] Dulac's exaggeration of the traits and views of her country women, through mise-en-scène and editing, conveys the rigidity, fixity, and ultimately the absurdity of conventional conceptions of female domesticity, before going on to introduce, naturalize, and celebrate women's liberty, mobility, and creativity. This stereotypical representation contrasts with Dulac's more nuanced representation of Lola and the Countess, whom Lola influences, in the film's broader framing narration.

Dulac's Aesthetic

Dulac goes further as she steadily deconstructs and redefines the Belle Dame archetype through purely visual means, such as decor, character gesture and staging, cinematography and editing. From the outset, Lola undeniably is a temptress. Shortly after her arrival in the provinces, the Belle Dame sets up the Count d'Amaury so that his wife, the Countess (Denise Lorys), suspects them of having an affair. During a visit from the count to sign a contract stating that he is her protector but not her lover, Lola receives the countess in her studio, along with one of the orphans (who figure frequently in the postwar period) for whom the charity event has been organized. When the countess arrives, the count hides, but Lola plants his cane so that his wife will see it. This sequence, in which Lola gets back at the count for her unrequited love following a past affair, becomes a narrative pretext for the countess's subsequent transformation and quest for liberation and self-determination.

In a showing of the film at CASA in 1921, Dulac explained her use of atmosphere and gesture to convey the influence that Lola had on the countess: "Will the Countess also allow herself to be charmed by Lola[?] . . . The ambiance, the incense burner, and the flowers are what matter. . . . Will she give up fighting with her rival? This question is left unanswered. As such, these things show her evolution, her decision to accept defeat. The bent body position indicates her state of mind."[117] Dulac had conceived of body posture as a more naturalist aspect of performance, centered on inner movement. However, at other moments, she also employed it as a symbolist, outer expression of visual style and form.

For example, in one sequence, Dulac uses graphic relations and what she refers to as the "play of volumes" or the spatial relations of set elements, to express the countess's isolation amid the lavish decor of her large apartment. In the sequence, an image of the petite countess is followed by wide shots of the large table, where the husband's place setting has been lifted and the son's vacant setting remains, emphasizing the isolation and loneliness of her domestic life. Dulac explains:

> I wanted to demonstrate the solitude of the Countess of Amaury's life—I was able to create this impression by creating a contrast between the architectural dimensions of a vast dining room and the small size of the woman, shown alone in the frame and through extreme long shot. There, *proportion* replaced *acting* and the luxury of details underlined the melancholy of solitude amid wealth. The role of the two empty place settings is as important as the attitude of the countess. Without anyone constituting the drama, the place settings of the son and the father, and the association of these inanimate things, with a motionless thinking being, comprises all the action of the scene. (emphasis added)[118]

Dulac conceived of these techniques, which created meaning through spatial relations (in the first example, through atmosphere, decor, and gesture; in the second, through shot length and the play of volumes) as part of a larger network or system of associations. Here, this system, which in many ways anticipates aspects of 1920s Soviet montage, is used to express the theme of women's emancipation in the face of conjugal oppression.

In a third sequence of *La Belle Dame*, envisaged as a synthesis of the prior two, Dulac shows the final evolution of the countess, who relaxes in the garden, the place of her many meetings with her true love, the marquis of St. Erasmus. Dulac states, "in contrast, after a solitary lunch, this neglected woman stretches in the heat of the sun. . . . Thus she understands the voluptuous meaning of things. After the importance given to the two isolated place settings, this stretching movement shows the evolution that is beginning."[119] In this sequence, the character's progression is expressed through gesture, and more specifically through the arabesque of the female protagonist arching back (a visual echo of the cabaret dancer in the prologue of *La Belle Dame*, and of the woman golfer in *La Cigarette*). Like the nineteenth century decorative style, the ballet dancer, and the musical structure of symbolist composer Debussy, the arabesque would become a recurring motif in Dulac's narrative films, and anticipate their evolution toward abstraction.[120] In her further insistence on the synthesis of these sequences, Dulac refers to the "shock" of images, an entirely modern conception that prefigures Eisenstein's idea of montage: "Two place settings, the stretching movement, how does one read this. . . . It is the convergence of images and the shock of gestures that create meaning. It is very short and it is crucial to the plot of the film."[121] Dulac would develop this technique further as a basis for creating a broader system of meaning in her films, notably in *La Souriante Madame Beudet* and *La Folie des vaillants*.

By all appearances, it is in *La Belle Dame* that Dulac first refers to the signifying system she employs as "impressionist," doing so before her colleagues and contemporary historians, and much sooner than contemporary historical accounts suggest.[122] In her 1921 presentation of *La Belle Dame*, Dulac compares her approach to that used in impressionist painting: "My film is not a film of action. Following an impressionist method, I employed notations. And for an impressionist painting to come together, one shouldn't show a small parcel of colors, but all colors, and each one separately is such a small touch that we only see its significance in the blending of the ensemble." She describes her method of depicting the countess's state of mind, and her broader cinematic approach in a similar manner, writing, "Impressionist in the things that it unites in order to create an inner whole, such is my vision of the cinema."[123]

In contrast to her prior films, *La Fête espagnole* and *Malencontre*, which were subject to various material and producer-imposed constraints, *La Belle Dame* also is Dulac's first freely developed example of her cinematic conception, based on the protracted expression of inner states through the delay of exteriorized action and resolution. Dulac explains the film's denoucment, which begins with the attempted suicide of the Countess's son Hubert, following his rejection by the Belle Dame:

> When the drama explodes, when, as we say in theater, there is action, (I'm referring to the Countess of Amaury's plans to flee and to young Hubert's suicide), the film is almost over. As I see it, the drama is nothing, the psychological facts that are brewing are everything; and when the drama actually unwinds I tried to express this with the utmost simplicity, without the facial expressions of the actors, without haste or agitation, always beginning with the principle that in life we exteriorize our thoughts very little, and that cinema should be true above all.[124]

Dulac's method of privileging character psychology and its development and resolution over time constituted a wholly modern approach to plot construction, one that went against the moralistic, action-oriented, and suspense-based dramas of dominant filmmaking modes of the time (e.g., D. W. Griffith, Thomas Ince, and Louis Feuillade). In Dulac's film, narrative resolution became secondary to the protagonist's self-realization. Through associative references and a specifically cinematic construction of spatial relations, which favored the expression of interior thoughts while preserving and respecting exterior realism, Dulac managed to achieve the psychological and social realism exhibited by the masters she lauded in her prewar theater reviews. She used this realism to promote a modern and even subversive conception of gender relations.

Dulac's conception of cinema as an associative whole, in which character psychology is expressed through atmosphere, gesture, and the relationship between the shots and sequences, is more developed and better illustrated by *La Belle Dame* than by her earlier films. As with impressionist painting, this approach also places a greater burden of constructing meaning on the spectators' capacity for observation. What one observes through Dulac's films is a relationship among images that invites a reading of homosexual subtexts. For example, in the final garden party scene of *La Belle Dame*, in which the countess is mentally preparing herself for her departure with her true love, the baron, she adopts an air of confidence and flirtation, dances with other men, and smokes a cigarette (in that era, a sign of her liberation). In a subsequent shot, she thanks Lola for having taught her something essential about life.

During the conversation, the two stand at an entryway or threshold. Their shared confidence and close visual relationship connotes their final bonding as women. Yet, Lola is on the outside of the threshold, adjacent to the garden, and the countess is on the inside, confined to the domestic space, an arrangement that prefigures their final destinies. The patently symbolist system of association in this film foretells Dulac's construction of more manifestly homosexual subtexts in her later films (especially *La Coquille et le clergyman*, *L'Invitation au voyage*, and *La Princesse Mandane*).

It also is with respect to *La Belle Dame* that Dulac first details her conception of movement. Dulac frequently differentiates between what she called inner and exterior life, or thought versus action. While life (which was closely tied to her penchant for realism) is the first term of her cinematic approach, movement is the second essential term. Citing an apparently influential encounter with the Italian actress Eleonora Duse (1858–1924), Dulac explains her conception of cinema as the locus of alternation between silence and what she refers to as "kaleidoscopic movement": "'Cinema is the moment of silence,' La Duse once said in my presence. After having spoken and acted a lot, that moment when the soul turns in on itself, when the flux and reflux of intimate sentiments agitate it, beyond facts . . . that is for the cinema to express. The silence of the soul amid the kaleidoscopic movement of things; the multiplicity of movements of a heart amidst the calm of a life.—Movement and silence, that is my personal vision of cinema."[125]

Drawing on her modernist musical influences, Dulac also viewed her conception of movement within a larger system of interconnecting significations in which rhythm plays a part. Her notion relied on the creation of a network of visual associations around and between characters, as opposed to direct expression, action and interaction. Of *La Belle Dame* she asserts: "I tried then to make my characters and the conflicts that divide them known in the silence of each one's soul. . . . They interact by parallelism then, and not directly. It's each individual stroke, rather than the general development, that composes the dramatic rhythm."[126] Dulac's conception of cinema as an intricate visual network—based on life, movement, and rhythm, and inspired by the impressionist music of Chopin and Debussy—is already evident in *La Belle Dame*, although it would only achieve its fullest development in her later writings and films.[127]

Despite Dulac's convictions, in *La Belle Dame* narrative action did ensue, even if Dulac viewed it as a concession. The film's ending, which constitutes a complete reversal of the psychological development of the female characters up until that point, reflects the demands of commercial cinema at the time. In effect, after having avenged herself on the count and liberated the countess, who decides to leave with her true love the marquis, Lola intentionally lures the couple's only son, Hubert d'Amaury, into attempting suicide. The fact that the young boy is captivated by Lola's beauty and dynamism is again expressed through sport. (In earlier sequences, Lola had intimidated the boy with her skills in deer hunting, as well as with her speeding automobile, which almost runs him over.) In the film's denouement, Lola, knowing that Hubert is eavesdropping on her conversation with the count, states that the only way for a man to prove his love to her would be "to kill himself or another." (This scene echoes the hunting sequence in which she boasts of having shot a deer "right in the heart.") As Dulac states in her ciné-club talk, Hubert's subsequent suicide attempt in front of Lola is the moment of action that triggers the film's resolution.

The young boy's suicide attempt ushers in a dramatic turn of events. The film's final act, which is a double ending of sorts, displays the polysemic nature of Dulac's films. In the last moments, the countess, who has yet to hear of Hubert's suicide attempt, is already torn between her responsibilities as a mother and wife (expressed by a painting of a mother and child), and her desire to run off with her true love (signified by an eye-line match to a shot of a clock, emphasizing the urgency with which she must take action). Just as the countess finally decides to flee, she learns of Hubert's desperate act, which seals her fate, or the destiny that society has imposed on her. At the film's end, order is restored: the countess returns to her husband, and the son reunites with his fiancée, while the film's last shot, a close-up of Lola, implies that the destiny of the Belle Dame herself remains ambiguous.

Yet, as the archival transcript from Dulac's presentation of the film attests, the final scene, which constitutes an epilogue or double ending, is a result of distributor-imposed constraints. Significantly, despite the liberty that Dulac had in writing, directing, and producing this film, and in elaborating her complex approach, she acknowledged her need to submit to certain commercial restrictions, such as a conservative, happy ending for the film: "This doesn't preclude certain concessions to tastes or even prejudices. At the end of *La Belle Dame sans merci*, there are a hundred or so meters [of film] that are there so that the story has a happy ending. We should take great care to take into account, the small obligations imposed from a commercial standpoint. They don't matter." Significantly, in her presentation, Dulac also encouraged a sort of textual poaching, in response to this compromise. Reaffirming her belief in the cinema's need to show the truth, she cautioned film spectators to be attentive to such concessions. She warned: "We shouldn't scorn them, any more than we should follow them blindly. However, there is a law that we should never abandon, an essential principle that we should never forget: BE TRUE."[128]

Dulac's statement clearly reflected her aspiration to open up spectators to the polysemy and complexity of her work through education, and to encourage them to see beyond the most obvious and superficial aspects, such as the ending of commercially released film most often dictated by the moral norms of the time. In future films, she would undermine such concessions in more direct ways (within the texts themselves), through the doubling and parodying of the official ending (e.g., *La Souriante Madame Beudet*), or through *mise-en-abyme* (e.g., *Le Diable dans la ville* and *La Princesse Mandane*). In her independent film *La Folie des vaillants* (1925), she would develop a new solution to the constraint of the happy ending, through the creation of multiple endings available on demand.

La Mort du soleil *(1921)*

In her next film, *La Mort du soleil* (The death of the sun), shot in the fall of 1921, Dulac continued her search for a judicious cinema-specific language that she could use to advance her progressive social ideals. In particular, she explored the use of technical effects as a means of creatively and effectively addressing the controversial issue of women's labor in a postwar context. It was also during this period that she produced her unfinished, ostensibly lost adaptation of Goethe's *Werther* (1922), which marked the end of her production company Les Films DH. Both works star the subtle actress Denise Lorys, who played the countess in *La Belle Dame*.

In *La Mort du soleil*, written and produced by André Legrand, Lorys plays out a new conflict as Marthe Voisin. In this film, she is caught between her duties as a mother and wife and her career as a scientist; she assists the famous Dr. Faivre (André Nox) at an orphanage for children with tuberculosis, a theme that recalls Dulac's 1907 portrait of Madame Poilpot for *La Française*. It is notable that the film, which was shot one year after the death of Dulac's sometime companion, Irène Hillel-Erlanger, from tuberculosis, a major health concern of the period, was funded in part by the American Committee against Tuberculosis, as noted in the film credits.

Figure 13. Denise Lorys as mother and scientist Marthe Voisin. *La Mort du soleil,* 1921. Rights reserved. Collection Cinémathèque française.

In this work, Dulac cleverly addresses the question of women's liberty by aligning it with efforts to combat this widespread and anxiety-provoking disease, which she sets in opposition to the heroine's conjugal and domestic duties. Yet, this tale of a jealous and unsympathetic husband who forces his wife to choose between family and career and, when she opts for the latter, deprives her of her daughter, struck at the heart of women's social reality during this period. At the end of the film, Marthe, who has helped the dying Dr. Faivre complete his work, returns to her family. Yet despite the ending that capitulates to commercial demands, all of the spectator's sympathy and praise is for Marthe's courageous work as a scientist, and one can't help but feel regret when she relinquishes this path.

In addressing the question of women's liberty and duty in the postwar period, Dulac's film marks a shift both inward (personally) and indoors, as she explores the use of technical effects, such as dissolves, superimpositions, masks, and out-of-focus shots, as a means of portraying the psychological states of her protagonists, who are more frequently confined to interior spaces. With respect to her next film, *La Souriante Madame Beudet*, these effects, to which she attributes "a suggestive value equivalent to musical signs," and which prefigure her ideal of a "visual symphony," are clearly rooted in her musical background.[129] Yet they are only one aspect of her impressionist technique, whose principal aim is to express inner states through a global system of associative elements. In a February 1922 interview for *Cinéa* provocatively titled "*La Mort du soleil* et la naissance du film" (*La Mort du soleil* and the birth of film), Dulac reaffirmed her conception of cinema as a site of interplay between interior and exterior life and movement: "My effort in *La Mort du soleil* was to describe the interior movements of the soul, in accordance with the theme of the action . . . yet, above all, beyond acts. My vision of the scale of cinematographic values is as follows: exterior fact . . . soul . . . physiognomy, the impression reacting against the soul before appearing on the face. But again . . . being simple, true and *mobile amid the immobility* of things and the apparent calm of beings" (emphasis added).[130]

Despite criticism regarding the script of *La Mort du soleil*, Dulac was widely and consistently praised for her new and original visual treatment, and indeed for her innovation in the domain of cinematographic language.[131] A 1922 film review by Lionel Landry, who later collaborated with her at the CFC, reaffirmed the pertinence of Dulac's creativity and resourcefulness in this regard: "In this work, and beyond its social value, there is something else: the subtle and audacious interpretation of Mme Germaine Dulac has produced one of the most ingenious and interesting attempts of creating a cinematic language whose future development alone will give the seventh art an autonomous life."[132] While the review acknowledged the social portent of Dulac's work, it made no mention of its feminist character, clearly perceived as a threat. Dulac herself never discussed her feminism with respect to her filmmaking. Yet, if one had any doubts about the grassroots feminist convictions that lay behind her outward discourse on film form, Dulac's next film, a little-known docu-fiction project on women's labor, further substantiates her social engagement.

Jenny l'ouvrière *(1922)*

Following up on the theme of women's work in *La Mort du soleil*, Dulac directed a series of fictionalized newsreels, collectively titled *La Femme au travail* (Women at work), for a small commercial company, Triomphe films. This series of five short films (approximately 120 meters or 400 feet or five minutes each), which was associated with a national competition recognizing "la jeune fille la plus méritante de France" (France's most deserving young woman), screened at the Palais de la mutualité on June 7, 1922.[133] Also known as *Jenny l'ouvrière* (Jenny the worker), a title that plays on the serial craze of the era, this series was described as showing "in an appealing form, the multiple jobs that a young girl with a limited income might be able to fill."[134]

In these five films, currently considered lost, Dulac showed women working in a variety of different occupations, among them a fashion model, a taxi driver, a saleswoman, a nurse, and an agricultural engineer. The films also featured an array of popular French actresses, including film stars Musidora, and Suzanne Bianchetti, as well as several of her regular actresses Denise Lorys, Marthe Régnier, and France Dhélia, soon-to-be-star of the provocative banned film *La Garçonne* (Du Plessy, 1923).[135] Yvette Andreyor, who later costarred in Dulac's 1925 film *Âme d'artiste*, played the provocative role of a conductress on the *métro* (although Dulac was apparently unable to finish that segment because of difficulty obtaining permits).[136] Dulac's attention to women's work, even in this essentially commercial production, exemplified her effort to promote a feminist ideology on a practical level, even if certain of these occupations (with the exception of those of taxi driver and, perhaps, agricultural engineer) are considered conventionally feminine.

A 1922 interview for *Cinéa* gives further evidence of Dulac's comprehensive negotiation of art and industry, showing how she strove to tackle economic and social concerns, even if it meant temporarily placing her avant-garde aspirations on hold. Just before the public premiere of *La Mort du Soleil*, and as she embarked on this commercial project, Dulac spoke out about the necessity of pursuing one's goals on all fronts, even financial: "The subject of my current preoccupations is the good, very commercial drama *Jenny l'ouvrière*. . . . The fight for an avant-garde ideal is over. Money, the god of today, invites us to pursue other pleasures. . . . Money creates power and force; and power and force = self-realization later on; that is, for the philosopher who knows how to wait . . . and to grow while waiting."[137]

While Dulac emphasized the commercial aspects of *Jenny l'ouvrière*, the project clearly fulfilled an important feminist role (although unstated by Dulac), one that contributed to her ideal of a socially relevant cinema for the masses. During the fall of this same year (1922), after trying to set up L'Union cinématographique française, with Henri Fescourt and René Le Somptier, and after her research trip to the United States, Dulac continued her efforts to gain autonomy through the creation of her own production studio. Following this commercial endeavor, Dulac created opportunities to develop a more aesthetically complex, and socially relevant cinema, beginning with her celebrated *La Souriante Madame Beudet*, produced by Charles Delac and Marcel Vandal's long-standing, esteemed and independent company, Film d'art.

Chapter 4

Dulac's Aesthetic Matures

In mid-1920s France, a consolidated production environment and a persistent pronatalist conservatism called for yet greater entrepreneurship and more inventive rhetorical strategies on Dulac's part. In the wake of her separation from Albert, her new romantic and professional partnership with Marie-Anne Colson-Malleville brought with it new liberties, while bolstering her productivity, and the creative complexity of her collaborations during this period. Her films of the mid- to late-1920s, while containing echoes of her own life experiences, offer a new approach to the politics of film form through a highly critical vision of traditional gender roles and hetero-normativity, associated with bourgeois marriage, as well as a critique of the conventions of linear and invisible narration that support it.

Dulac's fiction films from 1923 to 1929 show an increasingly sophisticated integration of contemporary sociopolitical concerns with complex narrative forms. Her maturing aesthetic—the loosening of filmic narration from the constraints of linear plot and heavy subtitling, in favor of wordlessness and visual association—contributed to her efforts to develop a stronger, more effective barrier to political censorship through a more modern, symbolist-inspired visual style, one that grows and develops from narrative figuration toward contemplative abstraction.

La Souriante Madame Beudet (1923)

Dulac's independent production *La Souriante Madame Beudet* (1923) marks a turning point in her work. Although not her first feminist film, it is one of the most sophisticated in its portrayal of female subjectivity through specifically cinematic means, ranging from intimate and mobile compositions to associative editing and technical effects. In the fall of 1922, at the suggestion of the playwright André Obey, Charles Delac and Marcel Vandal had offered Dulac the project of directing a film based on the successful avant-garde play by André Obey and Denys Amiel *La Souriante Madame Beudet*, which had premiered at the Nouveau théâtre a year earlier (April 16, 1921).[1] In a letter to Vandal, dated November 8, 1922, Obey wrote "the cinema is what interests me most and, while I am a writer, I would give all of French theater for a small projection room. [. . .] Would you allow me to collaborate on [the] production, under the supervision of your director, [. . .] I would be happy if it were Madame Germaine Dulac!" Obey, a sportswriter as well as a lover of music and cinema, worked with Dulac to adapt the script for the screen.[2]

The film tells the story of Madeleine Beudet (Germaine Dermoz), an intellectually curious young woman with modern aspirations, who seeks to escape from her oppressive marriage to a stodgy accountant, with classic bourgeois tastes (played by the *grand boulevard* actor Alexandre Arquillère).[3] The film's highly original juxtaposition of diverse classic and modern elements can be traced back to the influence of the realist and symbolist movements upon Dulac, who draws upon a variety of techniques in *La Souriante Madame Beudet* including associative montage to express her feminist vision, while developing her idea of gesture in movement and rhythm within the image. Shooting on location, natural lighting, and Germaine Dermoz's understated acting convey the heroine's bleak, unpromising petit bourgeois marriage. Montage, technical effects, and allusions to symbolist music, painting, and poetry translate her interiority and her modern dreams and desires. The contrasting acting styles and the self-reflexive strategy of *mise-en-abyme* highlight cinema's superiority as a medium better able than theater to express Dulac's ideals.

Realism in *Madame Beudet*: The Provincial Setting

As a young woman, Dulac had developed an aversion to the countryside, and it is thus not surprising that in *Madame Beudet*, she adopts a realist approach to convey her heroine's dismal provincial existence as directly as possible. While the film takes place almost entirely indoors, emphasizing its female protagonist's sense of imprisonment, it opens and closes with an impressionistic montage of the then conservative and religious town of Chartres, where it is set. As specified in Dulac's shooting script, the prologue contains a series of austere shots of a "hazy church tower," a "deserted path," an "isolated canal," a "courthouse," and a "prison entrance"—all shots of equal lengths taken from low or level camera angles, before moving onto the oppressive interiors of the Beudet home. In order to further emphasize the dreariness and desolation of the milieu, Dulac suppresses several of the characteristically attractive or superficially appealing elements, such as the "Parisian-style shops" from Obey's original opening.[4]

Indeed, the allure of urban modernity, embodied by the character of Lola in *La Belle Dame sans merci*, is entirely absent from the domestic setting of *Madame Beudet*, which as musicologist and film critic Émile Vuillermoz notes, avoids "the facile coquettishness of the trade that would have distorted its character." It undoubtedly avoids the rich lighting and glamour shots and eye-catching settings that were a part of contemporary practice. According to Vuillermoz, distributors criticized the film for its "grayness" and pessimism, but these very elements supply its force.[5] Most critics praised Dulac for this realism, integral to the film's feminist premise. Claude-Fayard (nom de plume) compares her cinematic realism to that of her Nordic contemporaries (e.g., Victor Sjöström, Mauritz Stiller): "What Swedish filmmakers did in the rural domain, Mme Germaine Dulac has done in the provincial domain. She did it with a quiet realism, all in rapid, discrete, gray touches. Gray like the small town through which the Belle Dame passed and in which Mme Beudet grew old."[6] The association between the film's grim exteriors and the interior of the prison-like home is strikingly captured through shots of Madame Beudet staring blankly out the window, visually expressing her oppression and her lack of real alternatives.[7]

The originality and accuracy of Dulac's realism are also evident. "I suspect Germaine Dulac to have experienced life in the provinces, to have suffered from the stagnation of habit and hours without enthusiasm and excitement," Claude-Fayard wrote. "For no one has translated it to the screen with exactness and sensibility better than her. And it is this creation of atmosphere that strikes one, above all, in the work of this director."[8] Dulac had indeed despaired in 1905 at having to spend six months in the agricultural provinces, where Albert had been working. This association between provincial life and marital repression would have had added relevance for Dulac in 1922, the year of her legal separation.

Symbolist Associations

Dulac uses realist settings to heighten *Madame Beudet*'s broader social dimension and employs symbolist thematic references and visual motifs to structure the inner life of her heroine. The modernity of Dermoz's acting stands in stark contrast to Arquillère's broad theatrical gesticulation in the role of M. Beudet. It permeates every aspect of the film. Dulac has Dermoz perform the role of Madame Beudet with restraint. According to Dulac's unpublished book manuscript, this new privileging of inner action over outer action marked a major shift in her work. "Only think, feel without letting any muscle in your face move; you will see that your performance united with the rhythm of your images and your thoughts will fine-tune precisely the emotions you need to convey," Dulac says of her direction of Dermoz. "In 'The Smiling Madame Beudet' [there is] no or little action: [it depicts] the life of a soul. The film marked a great turning point for me."[9]

The first time we see Madeleine Beudet, she is playing the (symbolist-inspired) impressionist composition, "Jardins sous la pluie" (Gardens in the rain) by Claude Debussy. The director again uses symbolist pictorial references to represent her female protagonist visually. She follows a frontal close-up of Madame Beudet, as she plays the piano, with a back-lit shot of the heroine in profile, which results in a halo effect. This second shot of the heroine, inspired by a Pre-Raphaelite painting to which Dulac makes reference, is likely J. W. Waterhouse's 1895 *Saint Cecilia*, a painting that portrays the heroine reading in a seaside garden, and listening to the sounds of two violinists.[10]

The film's script reads: "Mme Beudet is shot in profile (Ste. Cecile School of the Pre-Raphaelites). She writes on the piano score and then plays 'Jardins sous la pluie.'"[11] Dulac evokes Madeleine's melancholy by following these shots with images of nature, light, and water, which are the visual equivalent of the music she is playing on the piano. While Dulac already had forged a link between music and nature in *La Cigarette*, here these images, associated with Debussy's composition, can be seen to correspond to Madeleine's inner world, as well as to the space of her imagined liberty. This sequence also anticipates Dulac's conception of a pure or integral cinema based exclusively on life, movement, and rhythm, and her film, *Arabesque* (1929) in particular, inspired by Debussy's two arabesques.

In a later sequence, Dulac also references Baudelaire's poem "La Mort des amants" (The death of lovers). In this sequence, she intercuts a shot of Mme Beudet reading the poem with the text of its first passage. Dulac illustrates Baudelaire's textual references to "strange flowers" and "divans as deep as tombs," with artificial flowers and the Beudets' conjugal bed. Through these associations with symbolist painting, music, and poetry, Dulac is drawing parallels between the expressive capacities of cinema compared to the other arts. Although these techniques provide a productive analogy for the filmmaker, they do not afford her the immediacy for which she was searching. They are, however, crucial in informing and shaping her specific cinematic choices.

Dulac already had begun developing a specifically cinematic approach through the use of parallel editing, graphic matches, and in-camera technical effects (e.g., dissolves, superimpositions) in her earlier films, such as *La Cigarette*, *La Belle Dame*, and *La Mort du soleil*. However, in *La Souriante Madame Beudet*, her recourse to cinema-specific qualities and techniques is more pronounced. In her 1924 ciné-club lecture, "Les Procédés expressifs du cinématographe" (cinema's expressive techniques), Dulac described her use of symbolist associations in *Madame Beudet* leading up to this Baudelairean reference: "Until now, everything has been distant. People have only acted in relation to things. . . . We see them evolve, and position themselves. . . . Movement. We sense that poetry and reality are going to collide."[12] Here Dulac is referring to her transition from the symbolist allusions in *Madame Beudet*'s mise-en-scène inherited from theater and the other arts to the specifically "cinematic" expressive techniques that make film an art in itself.

Dulac called attention to two signifying strategies in particular, which could be seen as an extension of her use of symbolist references, and which anticipate the more direct confrontation of disparate realities (e.g., the interior and exterior realities of an individual, or those of different individuals) through cinematic processes in her later films. These strategies included associative montage, as well as cinema-specific "technical effects." For Dulac, in the first case, the distinct realities of her two protagonists collided to achieve a new level of signification through montage, a technique for which D. W. Griffith earlier and the Soviet theorist and filmmaker Sergei Eisenstein later would gain renown. Similarly, in the second case, the objective reality recorded by the cinematic lens or *objectif*, which Dulac later referred to as the *œil puissant* (powerful eye) of the camera, and the subjective reality, which, as Dulac writes, is seen through the "eyes of [Madame Beudet's] imagination," were united through technical effects.[13] Indeed, the technical effects, with which impressionist filmmakers such as Gance, Delluc, Epstein, and Marcel L'Herbier have been most closely associated, can be seen not only as an extension of associative montage, but also as a manifestation of the larger system of symbolist references, integral to artistic filmmaking today.

A Cinematic Aesthetic

In *La Souriante Madame Beudet*, Dulac employed a specifically cinematic system of signification based on the isolation and the opposition or synthesis of expressive gestures, which she used as social critique. She had already made frequent use of the close-up in her earlier films, from *La Cigarette* to *La Mort du soleil*, but here she turned to the extreme close-up, which she utilizes in a discretionary, yet more intensive manner, in order to isolate individual gestures marking an evolution of character. Dulac viewed each shot as a "notation," having a value similar to a musical note, yet representing a specific concept or ideal, which she subsequently juxtaposed.[14]

As Dulac explains in "Les Procédés expressifs du cinématographe," "The characters are posed by isolated shots of different gestures captured as such in relief and placed in opposition." In the film's prologue, she juxtaposes an extreme close-up of Madeleine's hands playing the piano with a shot of M. Beudet's hands counting money. Similarly, in a subsequent sequence, she cuts from Madeleine's hands holding a book to those of M. Beudet examining fabric samples. Dulac explains that these shots confront two different ideals, "intellectualism" and "materialism."[15] Dulac further defines the characters by juxtaposing shots of the couple eating, which contrast Madame Beudet's good manners with the vulgar ones of her husband. Dulac's critique of the bourgeoisie is close to that of feminist and radical socialist Jules Guesde (1845–1922), a founder of the Parti ouvrier français (French Workers' party) and the Section française de l'internationale ouvrière (SFIO, French Section of the Workers' International), who spoke out against the oppressive effects of bourgeois marriage on women in 1921–22, much in the ways that Dulac had in her days as a journalist and critic at *La Française*.[16]

Dulac's efforts are echoed in Eisenstein's much later principle of "intellectual montage," and his 1925 film *Battleship Potemkin*, which employs similar oppositions.[17] Dulac refers, with respect to *La Belle Dame*, not only to the shock or collision of images, but also to their conflict and synthesis, all of which would be central to Eisenstein's conception.[18] In *La Souriante Madame Beudet*, however, this synthesis often is achieved through a long shot, or *plan d'ensemble*.[19] For example, in the prologue of *Madame Beudet*, Dulac follows the above-mentioned opposing shots with an ensemble shot that unites the characters in order to emphasize or intensify the conflict. "All of a sudden, a long shot reunites the two beings. Brusquely, all the disparity of a marriage appears," Dulac writes. "It's a coup de théâtre [a stroke of theater]." Gesture, or figuration, again plays a central role in Dulac's impressionist system of signification and its use of symbolist references, associative montage, and technical effects.

The Musicality of Gesture

Once again Dulac turns to what she sees as the essential, as well as "suggestive," qualities of cinema. The liberation of gesture (life in movement) and its development in duration, or through rhythm within the image, is one of the primary means through which she externalizes Madame Beudet's inner desires and her fantasy of emancipation. In her earlier films, the gesture, in its very lines and forms, is not only visually expressive, but also takes on significations that are psychological and social. Yet, for Dulac, it is specifically "rhythm" (with all of its musical and abstract connotations), the third essential term of her conception of cinema, that reveals what she calls the "source" of movement, in other words, its cause, or the social reality that provokes it. While these two terms are effectively key concepts for many 1920s avant-garde filmmakers, Dulac's originality stems from her belief that these can reveal the "inner life" of its characters, and consequently, their social conditions.[20] In the first (and, alas, only) issue of her journal, *Schémas* (1927), Dulac writes: "When a hand poses itself on another hand. Movement. Dramatic line, analogous to the geometric line that links one point to another. *Action*. Whether this hand realizes its gesture, slowly or rapidly, *rhythm gives the movement its inner meaning*" (original emphasis).[21] This link between gesture, movement, and rhythm will be central in her move toward abstraction as a means of social expression.

It is not surprising that, in *Madame Beudet*, the heroine's will to escape from her Chartres apartment and bourgeois husband is expressed at decisive moments through sport (as an expression of movement) and music (and its relation to rhythm).[22] In effect, Madame Beudet's sole means of escape are the piano, on which she plays the modern music of Debussy, and her illustrated journals, whose images of sports and automobiles evoke a modern world in which existence appears to be freer and more active.[23] After she refuses to accompany him to see an outdated and caricatured production of *Faust* at the theater, her husband locks the heroine's piano, depriving her of music, which in romantic traditions is associated with desire and creativity.

Figure 14. Olympic athlete Raoul Paoli as tennis player Charlie Adden. *La Souriante Madame Beudet*, 1923. Rights reserved. Collection Cinémathèque française.

The next day, it is through the symbolic figuration of a tennis player's gesture that she imagines her liberation. In this fantasmatic vision, we see the tennis player Charlie Adden (played by the athlete Raoul Paoli) spring from a newspaper page to liberate Mme Beudet by ridding her of her husband.[24] Set against a black background that matches the page, Adden enters the Beudets' living room, his arm extended above his head holding his racquet, which he brings down in a fluid gesture, filmed in a single slow-motion shot.[25] Madeleine laughs, her head falling back in an expression of ecstasy, while Adden, whose athletic appearance is not without connotations of sexual potency, lifts and carries her husband from the room.

The character of Charlie Adden, who embodies virility and dynamism, represents another possible life for Madeleine, unlike that with her oafish, immobile husband. His move with the racquet, resembling an arabesque, and recalling the chrono-photographic studies of Étienne-Jules Marey and Georges Demenÿ, is associated visually and symbolically with the liberty that Madeleine seeks.[26] The representation of gesture also has a quasi-musical quality (an idea that Dulac develops in her later films and writings). In her 1927 article "Du Sentiment à la ligne" (From sentiment to line), a manifesto of sorts for her "pure cinema," Dulac declares, "movement is not only displacement, but also and above all, evolution, transformation."[27] In a text that comments on the article, she similarly affirms that the "mathematic combinations of movement, thus broken down into rhythms" are linked by "a 'sentimental and suggestive' inspiration, analogous to musical thought which guides the coordination of sounds."[28] We find this association of the sports gesture and music in André Obey's essay "Danses dans l'herbe" (Dances in the grass) for his

Figure 15. Germaine Dermoz and Alexandre Arquillère as Madame and Monsieur Beudet. *La Souriante Madame Beudet*, 1923. Rights reserved. Collection Cinémathèque française.

book *L'Orgue du stade* (The organ of the stadium), published during the 1924 Olympic Games in Paris.[29] Dulac's predilection for "visual rhythms," expressed through the lines and forms of sports gesture, makes dance an ideal figure in her work, as well as a footbridge for her move toward abstraction.

The sequence of Mme Beudet's imagined liberation by the sports figure is followed by her husband's recurrent feigned suicide prank. However, it is only with M. Beudet's final mock attempt, after she has secretly loaded her husband's empty gun, that the film's story finally unravels. When in a brusque gesture he instead fires the loaded gun at Mme Beudet (missing her and instead breaking a vase, whose placement has been a point of contention between the two earlier), the uncomplicated M. Beudet infers that his wife wanted to kill herself. This turns out to be a convenient explanation for both Mme and M. Beudet, whose attempt to console her is met with great relief. As narrative conventions of the period would have it, the couple appears set to live happily ever after. Nonetheless, the portrayal of the heroine's repression is so strong it seems that only the most credulous of spectators, like M. Beudet himself, could believe in a "happy" resolution. As a synopsis from the distribution company Louis Aubert recounts, "Life continues, based on this lie, sweetened for now—but for how long?"[30] Indeed, Dulac further undercuts the film's abrupt and incongruously false "happy ending" with a highly reflexive use of *mise-en-abyme*.

Mise-en-Abyme

Dulac employs a second theatrical sequence to create a form of *mise-en-abyme*, recalling the static, caricatured shots of the players in the theatrical performance of *Faust* attended by M. Beudet. This sequence directly follows the film's climax and its psychological reversal, which come when the gun goes off and the tyrannical M. Beudet reveals himself to be in love with his wife. The image of a boat, recurrent in Dulac's films, evoking the idea of travel and liberty, dissolves into a marionette theater. Two *guignols* (puppets) appear in a picture frame above the heads of the two characters, whose action they double. The script reads, "In the masked area of the screen: the marionette theater, where two puppets cuddled to the same rhythm as the Beudets."[31] The stage curtain drops before the two reconciled puppets on the upper half of the screen. Then, the word "Theater" briefly appears, only to dissolve into the intertitle "Province," echoing the film's introductory title and framing the entire film as representation.[32] The title announces the film's final sequence, shot outdoors, in which a priest waves to the couple, whom we see from behind, and continues on his way. This sequence, which originally was also to include two "town notables," attests to their social propriety.

Through the puppet theater sequence and the final exterior sequence or epilogue, the story of the couple becomes a self-reflexive *mise-en-spectacle*, or parodic exhibition. Its protagonists become players or actors in a system, that of early-twentieth-century society, which, not unlike today, imposed a social appearance, particularly concerning the issues of bourgeois marriage (as Dulac and her partner Marie-Anne Colson-Malleville would experience). The final exterior scene of reconciliation is a scene that is played out as an obligatory part of this representation of social appearances. Yet aside from her pensive eyes, Madame Beudet remains solemn and expressionless through to the film's end, resisting this conventional ending of reconciliation and reinforcing the irony of the film's title.[33]

The film's epilogue is illustrative of Dulac's highly original juxtaposition of her two conceptions of cinema: one realist, conveying the dismal life of the female character in her petit bourgeois marriage; the other symbolist, revealing her dreams, and desires, in which the figure of the modern athlete delivers her from her boorish husband. In the last image of the film, the street that the couple treads appears to have no end, and the young woman, attached to her husband's arm, appears no less trapped within the walls of habit. The priest with whom they cross paths further accentuates the weight of the traditionalism and conservatism of the bourgeois society of which the young woman is a victim.

Notably, while it is absent from the French and Swiss prints of the film (Cinémathèque française and EYE Film Instituut Nederland), in both the original and final scripts, the puppet theater sequence was followed by a shot of young spectators laughing and clapping after the final reconciliation. This shot, which derided the public and its demand for facile, escapist resolutions, appears to have been removed by distributors. Yet it is a trope that would reemerge soon in the prologue of *Âme d'artiste* (1925). Dulac's critique of the public, which she saw as responsible for retarding the artistic development of cinema, was amplified in both her writings and films of the mid-1920s, and with due cause. Following the making of *La Souriante Madame Beudet*, Dulac was obligated, for financial reasons, to turn almost exclusively to commercial filmmaking from late 1923 to 1926, and again in 1928.[34]

Throughout her commercial films, Dulac employs a variety of experimental, self-reflexive narrative strategies to invoke a more active spectator, including unreliable narration in *Le Diable dans la ville* (1924) and *mise-en-abyme*, through both the theater-within-a-film and film-within-a-film structures, in *Âme d'artiste* (1925) and later in *La Princesse Mandane* (1928). Dulac's commercial efforts from the mid-1920s show that she never gave up on her desire to make films of artistic merit.

Commercial Films (1923–1925)

In 1923, having been unable to complete her self-produced *Werther* (Germany, 1922), Dulac directed a series of more "commercial" productions, all of which were adaptations, a convention that ensured the producers that a film would draw a substantial public. Dulac's closeness to the filmmakers René Le Somptier and Henri Fescourt, her collaborators at the L'Union cinématographique française, facilitated her first two projects. After writing the screenplay for an adaptation of René Le Somptier's *La Porteuse du pain* (The bread peddler; Germany, 1924),[35] she was hired to work, thanks to Fescourt's intervention, at the Société des cinéromans, which had also just hired Louis Nalpas as artistic director.[36] While in her commercial productions Dulac was unable to fully explore her conception of cinema as "visual symphony," she nonetheless investigated many of the ideas that were dear to her. Indeed, despite producer-imposed constraints, these films were all innovative within their respective genres.

Dulac's first film for the Société des cinéromans was *Gossette* (1923), a six-episode serial, based on a novel by Charles Vayre. Serials aimed at attracting a faithful public interested in simple emotional or escapist fare contributed largely to the stability of the film industry of the 1920s.[37] In *Gossette*, Dulac experimented with and designed a number of special lenses and prisms to produce a variety of effects and multiply the expressive means that translate the characters' visions and mental states. She also reversed class and gender roles when the female orphan character Gossette (Régine Bouet) comes to the aid of the antihero, falsely accused of murder, Phillipe de Savières (Georges Charlia).

Although the success of this film allowed her to introduce a broader public to the art of cinema, Dulac considered it to be far from her cinematographic ideal.[38] For Dulac, who hoped to contribute to the evolution of public taste,

Figure 16. Poster for six-episode ciné-roman. *Gossette*, 1923. Rights reserved. Collection Cinémathèque française.

such films—inspired by stories or novellas that were published simultaneously—served to help familiarize the public with avant-garde technical effects.[39]

Dulac's next two films were the social satire *Le Diable dans la ville* (The devil in the city, 1924) based on a script by Jean-Louis Bouquet, also made for the Société des cinéromans, and *Âme d'artiste* (1925), made for Ciné-France-Film. Both of these films are innovative in their self-reflexive use of narration and *mise-en-abyme*, and both employ Dulac's preferred framing device or structuring paradigm of reality versus illusion. In *Le Diable dans la ville*, Dulac employs unreliable narration in a highly original way, expanding significantly on the manner in which this device had been employed in Robert Wiene's landmark German expressionist film (*Das Cabinet des Dr. Caligari*, 1920).

Le Diable dans la ville is the story of a philosopher with modern ideas who after his arrival in a medieval village is treated as an outcast when he is seen to bring misfortune and even madness or folly to certain of its inhabitants. In keeping with her belief in the cinema's ontological function of recording reality or "life itself," Dulac employs outdoor settings but is also meticulous in her use of historical decor. Moreover, through the trope of superstition, as well as gossip, previously employed in *La Belle Dame*, she sets up opposing narrations. One narration is presented through realistic portrayals of setting and character; and another through deformations and superimpositions, which express the subjective visions of the affected villagers or madmen. In the end, our knowledge and vision as spectators are undercut when we discover, not only that the madmen were never mad, but also that, much as in Alfred Hitchcock's *Stage Fright* (1950), the "visions" that we have witnessed with our own eyes never existed. In this film, Dulac does not simply show character subjectivity, but more importantly, questions and undercuts the dominant ideology, as well as destabilizes and breaks open the narrative conventions that govern film language.

Dulac's film *Âme d'artiste* (1925), whose working title was "Rêve et réalité" (Dream and reality), based on the play *Opad!* by the Danish poet and playwright Christian K. F. Molbech (1821–1888), is also highly reflexive. Starting with its opening sequence, this backstage drama uses *mise-en-abyme*, to highlight the specificity of cinema in relation to theater in a way reminiscent of the *guignols* of *La Souriante Madame Beudet*'s epilogue, as well as her lost film *Vénus Victrix*. After a few impressionistic shots of London and a theater marquee, *Âme d'artiste* begins with a scene of domestic violence, which retrospectively is found to be a theatrical representation when the camera pulls back to reveal the stage. Per the film and emphasized in Dulac's script, the

Figure 17. Commedia dell'arte style costume ball featuring cross-dressed extras from the Paris Opera. *Âme d'artiste*, 1925. Rights reserved. Collection Cinémathèque française.

audience is shown applauding vigorously, and in an exaggerated fashion, in a reverse shot that sets the illuminated hands of the audience against a black background.[40] This is followed by a shot of the young, emotionally fragile poet, who is smitten with the beautiful, independent actress of the play. The shots simultaneously present the film's lead protagonists and subject, echoed in its commedia dell'arte subplots parodying the performance of everyday life, as well as announce its inversions and role reversals (audience and players; representation versus reality; even masculine and feminine—in the "womanly" aspects of the male poet's character). The opening shots, which pull back to reveal the facade of the theatrical representation of violence, also mark Dulac's shift to a specifically cinematic technique.[41]

La Folie des vaillants (1925)

Not surprisingly, in mid- to late-1925, after directing this series of commercial pictures, Dulac was uncompromising in her attempt to realize her concept of an art cinema unhindered by commercial conventions. According to Colson-Malleville's recollections, Dulac boarded a bus with an enthusiastic group of Russian immigrants happy to work as extras for twenty francs and a sandwich, and traveled to the Midi region (south central France) to make *La Folie des vaillants* (The folly of the brave).[42] This low-, almost no-budget, independently produced movie, which Dulac regarded as her *film roi* (king film), according to Colson-Malleville, is distinguished by its unusually bold treatment of the theme of women's independence and its innovative production and distribution strategies.[43] It was also the first occasion, since *La Souriante Madame Beudet*, in which Dulac was able to explore more openly and fully her notion of a cinema free from the other arts, based on life, movement, and rhythm. *La Folie des vaillants* marked the crux of the aesthetic and epistemological shift in her fiction films—to the use of "rhythm within and between the images," and from narrativity to nonnarrativity, as announced in *La Souriante Madame Beudet*. As such, it went the furthest among Dulac's "narrative" fiction films in the fulfillment of her cinematic (and decisively symbolist) ideal of what she termed a "visual symphony," concretizing key concepts in her more explicitly "theoretical" writings of the mid-1920s.

La Folie des vaillants is based on the symbolist story "Makar Tchoudra/ Makar Chudra" (1892), published in French as "Radda" (1902), written by Russian author and founder of the socialist realist literary method Maxim Gorky (1868–1936).[44] The film tells the story of a passionate love between

Figure 18. Raphaël Lievin as Loïko. *La Folie des vaillants*, 1925. Rights reserved. Collection Cinémathèque française.

Figure 19. Lia Loo as Radda, and Raphaël Lievin as Loïko. *La Folie des vaillants*, 1925. Rights reserved. Collection Cinémathèque française.

two gypsies named Loïko and Radda. For Gorky, the gypsy represented the ideal socialist: that is, rebellious and hence naturally radical, outside of the borders of capitalism, and thus free from all moral and material attachments. Gorky's tale provided Dulac—for whom social issues had always been fundamental, and who officially joined the SFIO in 1925—with an ideal framework in which to consider an alternative social construction of gender roles.[45] Of course, Dulac would radicalize Gorky's story to further her own agenda.

La Folie des vaillants takes place on the shores of the Black Sea, where Loïko is a roving, Orpheus-like vagabond who rides around on his high-spirited horse mesmerizing men and seducing women with the sensuous sounds of his violin. When he sees the lovely Radda, Loïko falls in love. However, unlike the willful gypsy woman of Gorky's original tale, Dulac's Radda repeatedly rejects Loïko, only further enflaming his passion. When Loïko asks Radda's father for her hand in marriage, the self-reliant Radda again refuses. Later, realizing that she loves the untamed Loïko, Radda consents, on the condition that he humble and indeed humiliate himself before her tribe by relinquishing his beloved horse (which embodies his freedom and power) and by breaking his violin (which evokes his promiscuity and seductiveness). Loïko does both these things and then kneels before Radda in submission, kissing her feet.

But as he rises he stabs her in the heart and then kisses her on the lips as she expires. Radda had demanded that Loïko give up the kinds of things that women were typically expected to relinquish when marrying men. Radda's transgression was to reverse this configuration, and to use desire to demand a similar self-sacrifice from a man. Her punishment is death. Indeed, only by killing Radda can Loïko possess her; alternately, one might argue that, with her death, he in fact never possesses her. In the final moments of the film, in another departure from Gorky's tale, Loïko falls onto the knife, ending his own life, a gesture that punctuates his refusal to concede to Radda's egalitarian demands, along with being a rejection of marriage.

The film's violent ending would have had special resonance for those with feminist ideals in France of the mid-1920s. Radda's absurd demands on Loïko—that he give up all that was important to him and humiliate himself in subjugation to her—reversed the terms of contemporary marital power relationships in France and, in so doing, highlighted existing inequalities based on gender. In 1925, the very year of the film's production, and of the leftist Socialist (SFIO) and Communist party split, feminists had launched a proposal to revise the Napoleonic code, which severely curbed women's access to their own finances, institutionalized spousal inequality and paternal authority, and generally restricted women's personal liberty. Dulac's reversal, of course, cast into sharp relief the injustice of those provisions of the Napoleonic code that so constrained women's freedoms. Moreover, from a narrative point of view, we also see in the film's provocative ending a refusal of the neat, narrative closure that leaves the audience smugly satisfied and the dominant and reassuring ideological formations intact.

Dulac was forced to negotiate her feminist and aesthetic goals in a relatively constrained financial environment. Significantly, *La Folie des vaillants* was an independent film, financed by a patron of the arts, Baron de Stryk, who resided in Nice.[46] While the film was made on a shoestring budget of 78,000 francs—less than one-tenth of the average French film of this period—the production contract granted Dulac "complete artistic freedom."[47] This gave her liberty with respect to narrative and aesthetic choices, if the film was to run in commercial distribution circuits, although she was still forced to negotiate the issue of "public taste."

With regard to the film's feminist narrative, this negotiation took the form of preparing multiple endings. Dulac shot at least two endings for *La Folie des vaillants*, one the radical and feminist ending just described, and then a more commercial ending, which theater owners could order on demand, in which Loïko and Radda happily marry. Despite market imperatives, publicity brochures and articles from the period show that Dulac boldly chose to take the risk of releasing the film without the commercial ending. One critic commended Dulac precisely for this combination of artistic audacity and commercial prowess in creating multiple endings: "One can only praise the director who, working according to her inspiration and personal ideas, does not neglect the mentality of the public, which, shaped by the abundance of films presented to date, cannot be expected to change so quickly."[48]

While the alternate happy ending of *La Folie des vaillants* might be seen to represent Dulac's capitulation to the commercial market, the more radical and direct ending was made, and, in fact, widely distributed. Dulac reserved for herself the option and freedom of creating this alternative ending, even if it meant supplementing it with a more popular version later on. Dulac continued to navigate between the requirements of art and those of the film industry.

The "Visual Symphony"

La Folie des vaillants was also a product of Dulac's approach to film ontology and film form. While narrative considerations and the demands of the market necessitated a degree of acquiescence from Dulac—after all, she had to have a story and had to develop characters—she reserved for herself a considerable range of freedom in realizing the film's aesthetic dimensions. The independent financing and the directorial autonomy that this film provided offered her an unprecedented opportunity to realize her concept of cinema as a "visual symphony."

Although film critics such as Ricciotto Canudo and Émile Vuillermoz remarked on the close relationship between music and cinema as early as 1911, Dulac was the first to speak of music as a model for organizing a film in its entirety.[49] In her 1925 article "L'Essence du cinéma. L'idée visuelle," she wrote: "The integral film that we are all dreaming of composing is a visual symphony made of rhythmic images, which only the sensation of an artist can coordinate and cast onto the screen. . . . There is the symphony, pure music. Why wouldn't the cinema also have its own symphony?"[50]

According to Canudo, he and Dulac had even discussed the musical qualities of cinema during the war, at a time when she was preparing a project on Chopin, which would finally see the light in 1929, with her nonnarrative "abstract" film *Disque 957*.[51] However, unlike Canudo, who saw cinema as the confluence or synthesis of the arts, Dulac believed in the purity of film's specificity, or a cinema that owed nothing to the other arts.

In her writings, Dulac highlights the specifically cinematic character of the visual symphony, insisting that the relationship between it and the musical symphony is purely analogical. In 1927, paraphrasing her "L'Essence du cinéma," she noted, "Why shouldn't the cinema have its own symphonic school? the term 'symphony' being employed here only as analogy [*par analogie*]."[52] The "visual symphony" responded to her ideal of a "pure" cinema. Again, for Dulac, life, movement, and rhythm embody the purity or essence of cinema.[53]

While the other arts imitated reality and nature, film's relationship to reality was qualitatively different; in her words, film gives us "la Matière-vie elle-même" (the material of life itself).[54] Similarly, in her 1924 lecture and article, "Le Mouvement créateur d'action" (Movement, creator of action), she claimed that film does not offer an illusion of movement, but *is* movement.[55] Here she noted that in film, there is movement both *in* the image and *between* the images.[56] Her description of movement here parallels Eisenstein's theories of montage. With music and movement there is rhythm—the third definitive feature of film, according to Dulac—and film's formal qualities must acknowledge this important aspect of the rhythmic movements within shots (moving figures) and the rhythms created by editing. So central to Dulac's definition of cinema were the concepts of rhythm and movement that she argued that movement should not serve the story; the story should serve movement. "Movement, the creator of action, is never vain, never superfluous, an intention guides and arranges its development, to express a fact, depict its character, reveal a problem, and, above all, release emotion," Dulac affirms in "Le Mouvement créateur d'action."[57]

As noted previously, one of the films that had most inspired Dulac during this period was Abel Gance's 1922 *La Roue*, made in association with avant-garde poet Blaise Cendrars; the film has a relatively minimalist scenario similar to that of *La Folie des vaillants*.[58] Dulac described the film's famous train sequence, which expressed a man's passionate jealousy through movement and rhythm, as a "visual orchestration" of "eyes, wheels, landscapes, quarter notes . . . half notes and sixteenth notes," and likened the film itself to a "grand symphony."[59]

With her theory of a "visual symphony," Dulac approached her ideal of a "pure" cinema, grounded in her filmic ontology of life, movement, and rhythm, by maximizing the association between the images and by minimizing the importance of acting, plot, photography, and decor. "It is not the character that is most important in a scene; it is the relativity of images amongst themselves," Dulac asserts in "L'Essence du cinéma."[60] In the same vein, Dulac said of *La Folie des vaillants* in a 1926 article titled "Tout Film ressort d'une esthétique" (Every film springs from an aesthetic): "Searching for a new directive, I avoided all that was yesterday's avant-garde. In reaction, I simplified the theme as well as the acting, photography, and even the decor to their extreme."[61]

The concept of rhythm in *La Folie des vaillants* represented, for Dulac, a new aesthetic against which everything else became secondary. She claimed that the film was "one step toward habituating the public to the visual symphony where so-called 'theatrical' action will be nothing, and sensibility . . . everything."[62] Dulac used on-site outdoor locations for the story, little-known Russian actors in the lead roles, and nonprofessional actors from a colony of Russian immigrants, who not only worked for little money, but also contributed to the film's realism.[63] Shooting on location also added to this realism, a realism that at first glance might seem to contradict the notion of film aspiring to symbolist abstraction. But for Dulac, the actual locations and convincing vernacular characters in *La Folie des vaillants* freed the film from the theatrical tradition, with its reliance on stage settings and well-known actors, thus ultimately serving the purity of the medium.

Furthermore, Dulac chose to keep the film's plot minimal. For her, cinema, unlike literature, should not be recountable, but should "draw upon its active or emotive principals in images of visual vibrations alone." Of the rhythm of the images, Dulac states: "Their emotional value became so great, and the link between them so logical that their expression alone had value without the assistance of a text."[64] An elaborate plot structure would have obscured the genuine sensations and emotions of her characters that the rhythm of the images and their sonority expressed. Indeed, she referred to the characters themselves as "souls." Dulac's ambition was to eventually create an "integral" or "pure" cinema in which there would be no characters, no plot, and only natural settings. On the one hand, the musical analogy explored in *La Folie des vaillants* would not only provide Dulac with a footbridge to a nonnarrative and nonfigurative cinema, but would also permit her to qualify the movement and rhythm essential to cinema, with its spiritual dimension, or what she referred to as the *insaisissable* (imperceptible, intangible, or elusive). In her 1928 article "La Musique du silence" (The music of silence),

Figure 20. Ève Francis as Antoinette Sabrier and Paul Guidé as Roger Dangenne. *Antoinette Sabrier* (1927). Rights reserved. Collection Cinémathèque française.

Dulac wrote: "The cinema can certainly tell stories, but one must not forget that the story is nothing. The story is a surface. The seventh art, the art of the screen, is the depth that extends beneath this surface made perceptible: the elusive musical [*l'insaisissable musical*]."[65]

In the years that followed, Dulac devoted herself more wholeheartedly to films that approached her ideals. After *La Folie des vaillants*, she would make two commercial films for the Société des cinéromans: a theatrical adaptation, *Antoinette Sabrier* (1927), and an adventure film *La Princesse Mandane* (1928).[66] The rise of art house theaters (*salles spécialisées*) in the late 1920s, and the growing interest in experimental cinema by art patrons and the public alike, each propelled by the ciné-club movement, provided Dulac with a more favorable environment for the creation of a series of experimental films. In this context, she would also direct *L'Invitation au voyage* (1927), a low-budget independent short whose title evokes the symbolist poem of the same title by Baudelaire, and *La Coquille et le clergyman* (1927), based on a script by Antonin Artaud, before making three musically inspired "abstract" or "pure" films in 1929.

La Coquille et le clergyman (1927)

La Coquille et le clergyman (*The Seashell and the Clergyman*) has been extensively written about in terms not only of its psychoanalytic and feminist significance but also of its controversial authorship and production and reception histories.[67] It can also be reread, in the context of Dulac's larger body of work and her conception of cinema, as a study in figuration, performance style, and social representation, and as an essay on rhythm.[68]

In Dulac's visualization of Artaud's script, the film's title takes on its full meaning. The seashell or celestially formed nautilus is the arabesque, Dulac's line (of sensation) in movement and rhythm, which can be taken as a signifier of the clergyman's uncertain destiny and of his path to liberation.

If the film's surrealist script is not necessarily typical of the type of films Dulac made up to that point and even afterward, her interpretation and visualization of the script are entirely characteristic. The film's initial and sole subtitle, "This is not a dream, but the world of images itself" (inspired by Artaud) is entirely in keeping with Dulac's conception of cinema as a series of images that should be interpreted collectively: not exclusively as one character's psychology, but as the representation and realization of a spiritual and social struggle.

The film encapsulates a paradigm that is central to all of Dulac's work. That is the search for the self (or for identity), as realized by the lead protagonist (or in a film like *La Belle Dame*, the heroine and her double). Artaud and Dulac both claimed that *Coquille* should not necessarily be understood in psychoanalytic terms. That is, for example, the negotiation of the id, ego, and superego articulated through the forbidden desire of the clergyman (Alex Allin) to conquer the woman (Génica Athanasiou, Artaud's fiancée), to destroy his sword-carrying rival (Lucien Bataille), and ultimately to defeat the social structure that contains him.

In its original version, beautifully restored by the EYE Film Instituut Nederland, *La Coquille et le clergyman* opens with the clergyman (Allin) using a seashell to pour liquid into various transparent and shattering glass vessels.[69] The film traces the clergyman's course and his pursuit of the woman (with his eventual eradication of the officer) across various painterly and architectural landscapes, rural (recalling Monet's garden paths and canal poplars) and newly urban (evocative of the city symphony film, with its winding streets, horse-drawn carriages, and angular buildings). The film takes us through a

Figure 21. Rhythmic movements of maids cleaning. *La Coquille et le clergyman*, 1927. Courtesy of LightCone Film.

series of interior doorways, halls, and passages, and finally into a ballroom of orthodoxly and rigidly posed and then choreographed dancing female servants, in which figures a large transparent glass globe showing the visage of the clergyman, which is subsequently shattered. The film ends with an image of the clergyman drinking from the seashell. He is drinking an image of himself. The seashell encapsulates the path of the clergyman, and eventually his and arguably the spectator's liberation through the self.

Dulac differs from Artaud in her radical gendering of the film's subject matter, through her particular casting choices (notably of the antiheroic Allin), contrasting performance styles, and in her pure cinema approach to the film's visualization (e.g., her work on the plasticity of the image, its movement, and rhythm). Artaud was set to play the clergyman until the last moment when his protracted commitment to playing the monk Massieu in Carl Theodor Dreyer's *La passion de Jeanne d'Arc* (*The Passion of Joan of Arc*) prevented him from participating in Dulac's scheduled film shoot in July 1927. The choice of the meek, human, and antiheroic Alex Allin to replace Artaud in the role completely undermines surrealist notions of virile masculinity. There is also a stark contrast in *Coquille* between the realist performance of Génica Athanasiou—who played in Jean Grémillon's 1928 proto-poetic realist drama *Maldone*—and those of the burlesque-trained actors Allin and Bataille (an early French Ernest Borgnine type), much like the contrasting acting styles in *Madame Beudet*. At one point, Allin's gripping, claw-like gesture recalls that of Max Schreck in Murnau's *Nosferatu* (1922), and a shot of Allin waddling away from the camera and spinning a key evokes Chaplin twirling his cane, an image famously reproduced in abstract artist Fernand Léger's "pure film" *Ballet mécanique* (1924).

Above all, however, the film can be seen as an essay on "rhythm." Indeed, Dulac said of it that

> my entire effort has been to search the action of Antonin Artaud's script for the harmonic points, and to link them through well thought out composed rhythms. . . .
>
> Two sorts of rhythm exist: the rhythm of the image and the rhythm of images. That is, a gesture should have a length that corresponds to the harmonic value of expression and that is dependent on the rhythm that precedes or follows it: rhythm in the image. Then, rhythm of images: a chord of several harmonies. I can say that not one image of *The Clergyman* was delivered by chance . . . the effects had less importance for me than the tempo, rhythm and visual orchestration, of which they were only one component.[70]

Dulac's emphasis on rhythm adds a refreshing opening and new dimension to the extensive debates over her alleged betrayal of Artaud's script, and it broadens the myopic focus on the authorship of this film, which has come to overshadow her diverse oeuvre. The experimental film specialist Rudolf Kuenzli has gone so far as to argue that *La Coquille et le clergyman* can be broken down into two distinct components: Artaud's surrealist phallocentric iconography and Dulac's "pure," rhythmic images.[71] Kuenzli's proposition is one effective means of resolving the long dispute between the two authors, detailed in a lengthy study of the film's reception by the French critic Alain Virmaux, starting with the famous and much-hyped scandal, a staged attack on the film and Dulac that took place at its February 9, 1928, opening at the Studio des Ursulines.[72] The film, which Marie-Anne Colson-Malleville deemed the least characteristic of Dulac's oeuvre, seems destined to remain a site of debate, as critics weigh its substantial fidelity to Artaud's script against its ultimately Dulacian visual arrangement.[73]

Of course, for Dulac, rhythm was more than a visual orchestration. Rhythm was crucial as a means of broaching social taboos that could not be conveyed directly. Thus, in this period in which Dulac and Colson-Malleville were spotted dancing in the cafés of Montmartre, it is not surprising that dance figured so centrally in Dulac's films. Dance was particularly important in her commercial and experimental films of the late 1920s, where it remained a key device for the expression of inner states.

The Use of Dance in Dulac's Films

As with the traditional sports practices featured prominently in many of her early films, Dulac used dance to express women's "interior life" metaphorically and lyrically. However, she seems to go further in her use of this "art of gestural harmonies" to subvert gender conventions.[74] To this end, and particularly in her films of the late 1920s, while she and Colson-Malleville frequented the lesbian hotspots of rue Lepic (Montmartre), Dulac used the rhythm of cinema and dance to tackle more socially controversial issues, such as homosexuality (or arguably what gender theorist Judith Butler today designates more broadly as "queerness" in opposition to any prescribed, normative sexual identity).[75] The independent short *L'Invitation au voyage* (1927) and the commercial feature *Princesse Mandane* (1928), both of which integrate dance, as an expression of social constraint and liberation, are perhaps the most explicit examples of a queer text in Dulac's expansive oeuvre (indeed, certain shots go beyond simple subtext).

In Dulac's 1927 *L'Invitation au voyage*, made just months prior to *La Coquille et le clergyman*, dance is linked to the emancipation of the female protagonist, who, one evening, during her husband's absence, goes to a cabaret. More broadly, the film returns to Dulac's preferred paradigm of social reality

Figure 22. Set photo. Women in center row (left to right): Marie-Anne Colson-Malleville, Germaine Dulac, unidentified extra (trinket seller), Emma Gynt. *L'Invitation au voyage*, 1927. Rights reserved. Collection Cinémathèque française.

versus illusion, which she explores here with precision, restraint, fantasy, and humor. In this film, heterosexual and homosexual longing, feminine passivity versus illicit desire, are set in opposition and rendered through metaphors of transport (taxi, ships, dance), orientalist exoticism (musicality, associative superimpositions), looking patterns (homosociality/homoeroticism, direct camera), authorial intertexuality, and rhythmic abstraction.

The female protagonist of *L'Invitation* (Emma Gynt) can almost be seen to take up where the heroine in *Madame Beudet* left off. Her home environment, sparsely decorated, and characterized by banal routine and the recurrent theme of an uninterested husband leaving on a business trip, is expressed through various shots of his footsteps, a daily calendar, a clock ticking, and her embroidering. Instead of staying home and escaping through music, poetry, and magazines like Madeleine Beudet, in *L'Invitation*, the heroine dresses incognito in a long white high-collared fur coat, ventures out in a taxi, and slips into a local cabaret, whose illicit character is conveyed by the image of young teens being shooed away by a police officer (played by a woman). Upon the heroine's arrival, the movement and rhythm of the location create a strong contrast

Figure 23. Emma Gynt as La femme (the woman) and Paul Lorbert as Le matelot (the sailor). *L'Invitation au voyage*, 1927. Rights reserved. Collection Cinémathèque française.

with the austere universe in which she lives. From the opening sequence, the "bellboy," a woman in drag, who monitors the door of the cabaret, clearly announces that the sex roles will be disturbed, or that there will be "gender trouble." Here, the notion of social transformation is accentuated by the fact that the heroine enters the cabaret through a revolving door (one of a number of recurring circular motifs in the film, which also reappear in Dulac's later abstract works, such as *Disque 957*).

The first thing that the young woman sees upon entering is a dancing sailor (Paul Lorbert), whose movements from the outset express the liberty of the location. In opposition to the relaxed, lightly dressed female clientele, the young woman's gestures are rigid, and under the gaze of several men she hesitates before sitting down, taking off her coat and eventually ordering a drink. While awaiting a cocktail order, she recalls her monolithic home environment, and gazes at a young brunette woman daydreaming at the bar. During the course of the evening, she accepts an invitation to dance with a handsome young marine (Raymond Dubreuil) who is slightly shorter than she and who has an androgynous, even faintly feminine, Rudolph Valentino–like physique. This sequence constitutes a key turning point in the film. Even as the frequent displacement and circular movement of the camera contributes to creating an atmosphere of instability throughout the duration of the film, the movement and rhythm of dance, in this crucial sequence, permit a shift or slippage of gender roles. Although the couples on the dance floor are ostensibly heterosexual, their bodies turn in a vertiginous way, destabilizing their sexual identity; Dulac uses montage to juxtapose the close-up of a woman closing her eyes with a fleeting or fugitive circular panning shot showing the legs of two or more female couples dancing, which we can read as her fantasy. Here, it is through the speed of the dancers' bodies, which merge or flow together, an effect accentuated through Dulac's use of the blur, that the heroine's most illicit desires are revealed.

Alongside the atmosphere and mise-en-scène, the film's complex looking patterns also support a reading of this key sequence as one of homosexual desire. In one of the earliest sequences in the cabaret, the heroine, after refusing the advances of a first male suitor (Robert Mirfeuil), rests her gaze on the young brunette with a bobbed haircut sitting at the bar, who is positioned as the object of her desire. A subsequent shot of the Valentino-like character inviting her to dance, followed by an "insert shot" of her looking askance and delicately waving a fan, caricature her imposed passivity. Similarly, a fantasy sequence of the couple on a ship, marked by the repeated gesture of her looking passively over her shoulder is offset with a parodic construction of female sexuality (represented by several images, among them a nude bosom and ripe fruit), then male sexuality, in a sequence whose virile climax is denoted by a rhythmic shot with seven massive ships popping up one by one on the horizon. At a strategic moment, the appearance of a female seductress (Tania Daleyme of *La Belle Dame sans merci*) who lures away the male suitor, functions, both textually and intertextually, as a disruption of the pair's sexual reveries. The heroine's disillusionment following this incursion is expressed through her despondent gaze at an abandoned trinket, a miniature boat marked with the words *Invitation au voyage*. Subsequently, the image that drifts across the room of an exoticized Hindu dancer (Djemil Anik of *Malencontre*), framed in an oval mask, is followed by a matching shot of the heroine (Emma Gynt). Like that of the dancer, the latter image echoes the heroine's blossoming erotic desire and its ultimate containment. Again at key moments, gender and sexual representation are expressed through the movement and rhythm of dance.

In *La Princesse Mandane* (1928), a commercial film adapted from a novel by Pierre Benoît, Dulac evokes the constraints of the female condition through classical ballet. The film tells the story of a young man who, having seen the great adventure film *Michel Strogoff* (Victor Tourjansky, France, 1926), imagines a voyage to the country of the Tartars, where he will attempt to rescue a princess sequestrated in her palace. Here, Dulac uses the simple linear figure of an immobile ballerina to evoke the social condition of the captive princess.

In one of the film's most visually striking scenes, the ballerina, who stands immobile aside from a few restricted and controlled poses, is isolated in the center of an immense room, surrounded by her guardians and the spectators gazing at her. This composition translates the visual representation of the young heroine, as well as her sequestration in a masculine image. The image of the princess—the mise-en-scène of her femininity—is the object of a masculinist

Figure 24. Edmonde Guy as Princesse Mandane. *La Princesse Mandane*, 1928. Rights reserved. Collection Cinémathèque française.

Figure 25. The restricted poses of a ballerina are used to evoke the princess's captivity. *La Princesse Mandane*, 1928. Rights reserved. Collection Cinémathèque française.

fantasy, just like the fragile and ephemeral body of the ballerina.[76] In Dulac's film, this representation is accentuated and subverted, at the same time, by a homosexual subtext (or arguably just plain text), which sends an unconventional and unexpected image to the male protagonist and the spectator as follows. At the time of her liberation, the princess appears to regain control of her image. First, her liberty comes through cross-dressing, a recurring motif in Dulac's work (e.g., *Âme d'artiste*, *L'Invitation au voyage*). Then, at the film's climax, the princess, after being aided in her liberation by the young adventurer, rejects him. She presents him her crown, as a token of her gratitude, and leaves off-screen with another woman. Arguably, the gaze of the adventurer directed off-screen, followed by his expression of horror, renders the homosexual subtext explicit. Afterward, the young hero, "victim of the cinema," wakes up from this unexpected adventure, happy to be reunited with his wife. This framing narration, which restores heteronormative social roles at the end of the film, no doubt allowed Dulac to satisfy a broader, more conservative public at the time.

From Figuration to Abstraction

While in her narrative films Dulac often expressed the emotional and spiritual states of her characters through the movement and symbolism of dance, in her self-financed *films d'essais* (research films) or experimental films (1929) dance and gender took on their full significance on a formal level. Dulac foregrounded dance as a form of movement that was ideal in its expressivity, and its capacity to signify. In 1927, in her search for a pure cinema, she expanded on her concept of a "visual symphony" that minimized plot and simplified decor in favor of rhythm and sensation. Dulac became convinced that the lines and forms of gesture and figuration, central to her narrative films, could move the spectator without actors or characters.[77] She directed three (of four planned) abstract films, all inspired by music and nature, and intended to be played silent, and all described as dances.[78]

The role of nature essential to Dulac—like Debussy, who was an enduring source of musical inspiration to her was also crucial to the theories of modern dance in its attachment to nature and the unity of gesture. U.S. dancer Isadora Duncan (1877–1927) had summarized the essence of her own personal conception in her prewar article "La Danse et la nature" (Dance and nature): "The sole, great principal which I permit myself to invoke is the constant, absolute, universal unity of *form* and *movement*, a *rhythmic* unity which can be found in all manifestations of *nature*" (original emphasis).[79] "Pure cinema" according to Dulac echoed this conception in its formulation of movement and rhythm as essential qualities. Moreover, cinema did not content itself with imitating nature, because it provided "La Matière-vie elle-même" (the material of life itself).[80]

Contrary to other filmmakers of the abstract movement, such as Viking Eggeling and Hans Richter, who long defend a nonfigurative and nonreferential approach derived from painting, for Dulac (who was inspired by precinema, time-lapse scientific films, as well as by the medium's experiential

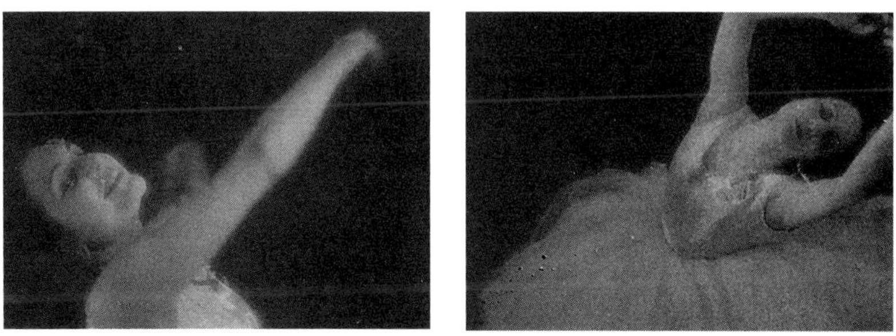

Figures 26a and 26b. Dancer Lilian Constantini, granddaughter of Communist Party founder Jules Guesde and future wife of Dulac's cousin iron baron Charles Schneider. *Thèmes et variations*, 1929.

approximations of duration), *cinégraphie* remained present in its most tangible forms: the visualization of life itself, in movement and rhythm.[81]

In her film *Thèmes et variations* (1929), Dulac makes dance a central theme and creates a series of comparisons and contrasts, or variations, between the marionette-like gestures of female dancer, Lilian Constantini [pseud.] (as line and form), and the mechanized movements of the machine.[82] According to the original synopsis, Dulac's film was also to contain various distinct material forms found in nature.[83] Beyond an isolated sequence, which presents shots of germinating plants, clouds, flowers, and trees in what Dulac refers to as a "ciné-dance," only the figure of the dancer and the machines remain.

Of the images from nature (as Paula Amad has pointed out with respect to the children's screenings of scientific films at the Albert Kahn archive and Musée Galliera), the time-lapsed tendrils of Dulac's germinating bean plant, rhyme with the ballerina's spiraling arm movements, and like the scientific films from which they are inspired, evoke a sense of touch and a mimetic pleasure that through sensorial saturation can trigger a haptic extension of the visual experience.[84] Dulac, who often illustrated her lectures with scientific films of "cristallisation" or of a "germinating grain of wheat" (from M. Colette), sought to avoid "premeditated evolutions" and "catalogued knowledge," and instead to "offer the spirit a *sensation*, which through movements is rhythmed by forms, whose undefinable structures vary incessantly following a given rhythm" (emphasis added).[85]

In *Thèmes et variations*, the silhouette of the dancer evolves through numerous oblique postures (*grands* and *petits pliés*, jumps, kicks). These developments are juxtaposed with the rhythmic movements of the machines (the play of a pivot, pistons or valves, connecting rods, perforators). Moreover, the variations of the lines and interior movement within each shot are often accentuated by slanted camera angles, which create interlacing linear and diagonal motifs. The use of slow motion, superimpositions, blurs, and dissolves render these elements even more complex. Through this elaborate schema, the image of the dancer leaves the domain of the photographic and attains abstraction, in order, according to Dulac, "to create, through the rhythm that it espouses, a suggestive aspect that goes beyond form."[86] (The film's sensual appositions apparently inspired novelist Henry Miller, who also had viewed and loved *Madame Beudet*.)[87]

Like the prior project, *Disque 957* (Record 957), subtitled "visual impressions of Germaine Dulac in listening to Frédéric Chopin's Preludes 5 and 6," and described as a "classic dance," also draws on music, nature, and the figurative in its move toward abstraction. The film originated in Dulac's 1918 narrative project on the romantic composer that never came to fruition.[88] With a prologue that recalls the blinding turn-of-the-century and wartime spectacles of Loïe Fuller, Dulac's *Disque 957* announces itself as visual music from the outset. The first image of the film is that of a hand placing a phonograph needle on a spinning record. After a series of multiple exposures and masking effects, the image of the record dissolves to a radiating pattern of abstract circles of light that fill the screen, in Dulac's words "taking the appearance of an idea."[89] The literalization of the film's musical metaphor through the play of light on the record introduces the film's dominant circular motif and sets the tone for its visual development both formally and thematically: namely, an interplay of easily discernible material forms that recall her earlier films (a clock, a pair of hands playing the piano), and more abstract forms (swirling light, raindrops on leaves, on a lake, a puddle, etc.) The visual elements follow a mathematically determined, classical rhythmic pattern, the shot lengths varying by evenly spaced increments. The circular motif, introduced by the light on the *disque*, and visually echoed in the patterns created by the rain, draws on the seminarrative pretext found in Chopin's Prelude 6, noted in Dulac's 1918 project.[90]

Dulac's faith in the materiality of the filmic image distinguished her approach early on from other members of the "abstract" movement. In "Du sentiment à la ligne," published in her 1927 journal *Schémas*, she responds directly to two of its featured articles (Miklos Bandi's "La Symphonie de Viking Eggeling" and Hans Richter's "Mouvement"), which promote a nonfigurative and nonreferential approach found in painting in which line and form, in order to remain pure, relinquish all references to the world (see, e.g., Eggeling's *La Symphonie diagonale*, 1920–24, and Richter's *Rhythmus 21*). Defending the notion that *cinégraphie* is still present in more tangible forms, she writes, "What I'm fighting is the narrow idea that one generally has of movement . . . why banish from the screen some of its purest forms, forms that, more than any others, *may hide within them the secret of an art nouveau*. Lines, volumes, surfaces, light envisaged in their constant metamorphosis are liable to affect us like a growing plant . . . *since the movement and rhythms remain, even in their more material and meaningful incarnations, the intimate and unique essence of cinegraphic expression*" (original emphasis).[91]

If for Dulac, photography gives the cinema direct access to nature, by providing it with its technique, or with "the scientific aspect of its material expression," music inspires its aesthetic, and releases it from its imitative function in relation to other arts, allowing it to "use its technique to express the spiritual."[92]

Because it draws from nature (and from music in the case of *Disque 957*), the cinema, argued Dulac, can create emotions with images much like music does with sound. In 1925, echoing a passage by Chopin's biographer Edouard Ganche, Dulac writes: "Exterior facts have no interest except in the interior expression of souls."[93] An early script for *Disque 957* shows that Dulac intended to demonstrate her concept of "interior expression" quite literally. At one point, she had planned to include a shot where the image of a woman (standing in for Georges Sand) was superimposed over a spinning record. Dulac's approach of *composing* abstract patterns based on visual impressions taken from Chopin and Sand reprises certain optical effects used in her Impressionist films, as well as in her Surrealist *La Coquille et le clergyman* (1927). A point of tension between the figurative and the abstract, it also echoes the film's prologue, creating an overall circular structure that the motif of the disque invites.[94] The film itself ends with the shot of a path, which seems to refer to Sand's fabled absence. The circular motif of the *disque* in this experimental film gives way to more abstract and complex motifs in the subsequent films of the trilogy.

In *Étude cinégraphique sur une arabesque* or *Arabesque* (1929), subtitled *Ballet cinégraphique* and inspired by Debussy's piano composition "Two Arabesques," the form of the arabesque, which comes from music, decor, and choreographic dance, furnishes these elements with the accord that they are seeking in nature, as in her film *Disque 957*, where the principal materials are water and light.[95] With the exception of some motifs, which recall *Disque 957*, the visual structure of the film is composed essentially of variations on the arabesque: arcs of light, water spouts, spiderwebs, burgeoning trees, flowers and foliage, a woman's face, arms stretching, a leg that rhythms a rocking chair. Like the more free-flowing tendency of the arabesque decorative style that employs varied elements of foliage (such as flowers, stems, and leaves), the lines and forms of Dulac's *Arabesque* maintain a more or less figurative appearance. Yet, in keeping with the arabesque motif that Debussy's suites inspire, the film, as a whole, tends more toward abstraction than *Disque 957*. Dulac often uses photographic techniques such as blurs, masks, dissolves, multiple exposures, and multiple lenses to render the natural elements more abstract. However, the elements from nature that she does include, such as light, mirrors, water, and wind, also serve to distort or blur the various elements or to intensify their design. We find tree branches reflected in water, blurred streaks of light on a spinning mirrored globe, the reflection of flowers

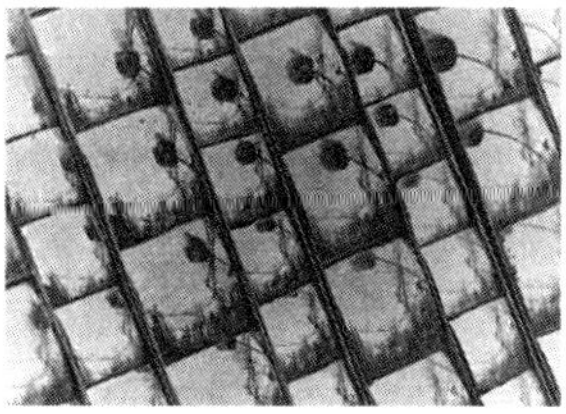

Figures 27a and 27b: A tulip dances, its reflection multiplied and reproduced in a mirrorball. *Arabesque(s)* or *Étude cinégraphique sur une arabesque*, 1929.

arched in a mirror (which Dulac refers to as a "dance of tulips"), water jets bouncing off trees, wind blowing a scarf, the reflections of light from the mirrored globe on a scarf, and so on. Recognizable figures give way to more abstract forms.

Remarkably, the literal and abstract motif of the "arabesque" is also mirrored in the film's overall editing structure. The film's first arabesque, which Dulac likened to a dance, in which lines of light and rhythm play the lead, corresponds to the second arabesque of Debussy's suite. The film's second arabesque corresponds to the composer's first.[96] Following Debussy's composition, the duration of the shots, when plotted on a graph, form two arch-like suites of rising and falling notes, shedding light on the broader formal conception and construction of Dulac's films. The technique of abstraction through light, movement, and rhythm was close to the serpentine dances of Loïe Fuller, whose body was eclipsed behind the electric lights. In February 1928, on the occasion of an homage to Loïe Fuller for the Union des artistes (Artists' union), Dulac evoked this very absence of the body: "An invisible body that dissolves into the diaphanous and transparent tissues from which a head emerges . . . a mind carried by light."[97] In "Du Sentiment à la ligne," published two years before she began making her abstract films, and without reference to any particular film, Dulac described her notion of abstraction through the motif of the female dancer, which she sees, like the *flourishing* "grain of wheat" of her early writings and of the bean plant in her film *Thèmes et variations*, as an ideal cinegraphic form.[98] She writes: "I evoke a dancer! A woman? No. A line bounding to harmonious rhythms. I evoke, on the veils, a luminous projection! Precise matter? No. Fluid rhythms. The pleasures that movement procures in the theater, why scorn them on the screen? Harmony of lines. Harmony of light. Lines and surfaces evolving at length according to the logic of their forms and stripped of all meanings that are too human to better elevate itself toward the abstraction of sentiments leaving more space for sensations and dreams: integral cinema."[99]

If this passage is famous, the source of its inspiration is unknown. A first draft of this article indicates more specifically how the filmmaker went from figuration (in her impressionist films) to abstraction (in her experimental films): "I evoke Isadora Duncan. A dancer. No. A line bounding to harmonious rhythms. I evoke Loïe Fuller. Veils. No. Fluid rhythms of light. The pleasures that movement procures that we like in certain forms in the theater, why banish them, in certain others on the screen. With Isadora a harmony of lines, with Loïe Fuller a harmony of light. Lines, surfaces stripped of all meanings that are too human to better elevate itself toward the abstraction of sentiments: integral cinema."[100]

It was with modern dance that women, and notably Duncan and Fuller, created their own choreographies for the first time, revolutionizing dance as Dulac would the cinema. (As art historian Anne Higonnet has argued, it is in this way that women "take control of their visual identity and free it from the limits within which it had been confined.")[101] It was also with modern dance that the body of the woman liberated itself from classical ballet to adopt an unfettered lyricism. In this sense, certain women perceived modern dance as possessing, through the body, a transcendental capacity. For example, in 1903, Isadora Duncan wrote of the new dance: "The dancer of the future must be a woman whose body and spirit have developed in such a harmonious manner that the movement of the body is the natural language of the soul."[102] Of this transcendental aspect, Gabriele Klein observes: "It is not surprising that the reflection of the dancer of expression on the world of affect . . . is celebrated as the veritable emancipation of women," even as she notes that the ideological conventions of expressive dance remained historically restrictive in terms of gender as well.[103]

Yet, in Dulac's ideal of a "pure cinema," the body only existed as an abstract or fleeting form. With the almost complete disappearance of the female figure, one might ask what happened to her feminist project. Loïe Fuller seems to have been Dulac's preferred model. She was preferred precisely because she was not content to desexualize the body, but to make it disappear, as Dulac stated in "Du Sentiment à la ligne," "to better elevate itself toward the abstraction of sentiments leaving more space for sensations and dreams."[104] While in her narrative films, the figure of the dancer evoked the liberty of women in the face of modernity, in her "abstract" films, the model inspired by modern dance, for one, offered new possibilities of gender and sexual identification. In other words, with her pure cinema, Dulac created a modern cinema that opened up new possibilities for the spectator to create his or her self.

Dulac's approach set her apart within the 1920s avant-garde film movement, and her work anticipated some of the most significant cinematic tendencies that followed. Her penchant for a "pure cinema" that retained its origins in the "material of life itself" would prove appropriate as the goals of the experimental film movement were transformed to meet the social concerns of the period.[105] With the move toward synchronized sound in France in 1929, and an increased consolidation of the film industry in the 1930s, Dulac with her interest in a "direct," "more objective" approach, went on to contribute to the newsreel, or *cinéma d'actualité*, which, she argued, was the sincerest and purest of cinema's many applications and forms.[106]

Figure 28. Lilian Constantini. Unidentified shot, ca. 1929–30. Rights reserved. Collection Cinémathèque française.

Dulac carried the key social and aesthetic premises of her narrative impressionist and music-inspired abstract cinema, based on life, movement, and rhythm, into the 1930s through her own social realist musical shorts or "illustrated records," as well as through her extensive work as a director of newsreels. Moreover, such innovations, often dismissed as too experimental at the helm of the 1920s avant-garde, constitute some of the fundamental modernizing principles, techniques and practices of the 1930s poetic realist movement, often referred to as the golden age of French cinema, and ushered in by Jean Vigo, to whom Dulac gave his start. At stake is an acknowledgment of the vital role of impressionist cinema as a harbinger of the symbolist poetics of French aesthetic and poetic realism, and more broadly of a contemporary, contemplative global art cinema today.

PART III

Chapter 5

Fiction, Newsreels, and Social Documentary in the Sound Era

Germaine Dulac's work of the 1930s has long been dismissed as a radical departure from her earlier days as an avant-garde filmmaker. Most studies of her work assume that the Dulac of the 1930s is not the same as the avant-garde filmmaker of the 1920s, or at least, not one deserving the same kind of attention she had received earlier.[1] Yet this is far from the case. In fact, during the 1930s, Dulac made a number of important contributions to the evolution of cinema. These innovations are not only an integral part of her film career but are also crucial to gaining a broader and more comprehensive understanding of her aesthetics and social commitment.

In consideration of the medium's specific historical, aesthetic, and social aspects, and in keeping with her humanist, internationalist, and pacifist goals, Dulac elaborated a unique theoretical and practical approach that greatly contributed to the renewal of nonfiction filmmaking. Her creative and practical innovations in the domains of the documentary and the newsreel included the choice of more intimate and personal subjects that reflected the everyday, as well as the communication of this everyday and its universe of symbols in as direct and sincere a manner as possible. These aspects corresponded to her goal of promoting greater understanding among different peoples. In addition, Dulac sought to expand the potential and influence of nonfiction films by creating more effective and efficient production and distribution methods. In her unwavering efforts to promote a visual and socially engaged cinema threatened by the hegemony of the talking picture and Hollywood, Dulac also contributed to the elaboration of a broad cultural policies that through their guiding principles and institutions formed the basis for what is known today as the "French cultural exception."

This third part of the book (chapters 5 and 6) examines Dulac's wide range of activities and the evolution of her aesthetic and social conception of cinema in light of the rapidly evolving economic and socio-political contexts (feminist, socialist, and pacifist) of this era, expanding our perception of what would be a lifelong commitment to the cinema. It begins with her first synchronized sound films in 1930 and ends with her final documentary and fiction projects, some of which were written in the months before her death (from natural causes) during World War II in July 1942.

The French Film Industry in the 1930s

Dulac had directed her last fiction films in the spring of 1930, a year that marked the French film industry's more sure-footed commitment to the conversion to sound (a conversion that would be completed in 1934). These took the form of six "illustrated records" for Columbia Music and Isis Films, which were essentially post-synchronized silent shorts, designed to accompany a variety of classical and popular music recordings, as Edison had dreamed. Several of these films (e.g., *Autrefois . . . aujourd'hui*, *Celles qui ne s'en font*, and *Ceux qui s'en font pas*) featured working-class subjects in provincial settings living their daily lives, or, in some cases, reflecting, with hope or despair, on the possibility of achieving their dreams. Some were paired with popular French melodies by realist female singers like Damia and Fréhel, whom Dulac and her partner Marie-Anne Colson-Malleville knew personally. Colson-Malleville, who has a cameo as a café patron in *Danses espagnoles*, featuring Carmenita Garcia, wrote working-class songs for singers during this period, and at least one song for Fréhel, before going on to make her own poetic and social documentary shorts in the postwar period (ca. 1946–61).[2] One of the most fascinating of these 1930 short films is Dulac's *Celles qui s'en font* (Those [women] who worry), which features the paradoxical figure and enigmatic ballerina Lilian Constantini (née Volpert) of *Thèmes et variations*.

(Constantini [1902–1982], the granddaughter of Marxist Jules Guesde, married in 1943 Dulac's capitalist cousin Charles Schneider [1898–1960], Gaumont administrator, Maître de forges [iron and steel master], and heir to Le Creusot metallurgical empire, known in the postwar period as the *marchands des canons* or canon sellers. In her Parisian home, overlooking the Luxembourg gardens, their daughter Dominique Schneidre [pseud.] has marble busts of Schneider and Guesde sitting side by side, but appropriately facing in opposite directions.)[3]

Figures 29. Lilian Constantini in *Celles qui s'en font*, 1930.

The two-part film *Celles qui s'en font* is presented as Dulac's "cinegraphic impressions" based on two French realist song recordings made famous by Fréhel in this discophilic age: "Toute seule" (All alone) and "À la dérive" (Drifting). "Toute seule," the first so-called illustrated recording, or musical short appears to have been shot on location in Aubervilliers (in the direction of the still extant Le Bourget airport, as signaled in the film), a busy working-class northeastern suburb of Paris. A slightly canted shot shows a disheveled, impoverished young woman sitting alone, drinking, at a café terrace, as families and couples pass by. Her naturalist acting style echoes the song's lyrics and beautifully captures her disposition, which fluctuates from expressions of deep sadness and regret to inebriated joy. The camera simply follows her wandering, singing, and crying until she walks alone down an urban path into the distant horizon, an image that captures the new modern plight of urban isolation.

The second "illustrated record" or music visualization, "À la Dérive," presents a different young female character (also played by Constantini), more carefully coiffed, first shown seated on a park bench in distress, beneath a verdant, shimmering tree that recalls Dulac's earlier Pre-Raphaelite-influenced imagery (*La Cigarette, Madame Beudet*). The woman visits male clientele at the bar of the Hôtel l'Aveyron and is violently rejected by one who physically intimidates her while leaving with another woman. Dejected and distraught, she leaves and wanders down to the riverbank, her journey punctuated by images of reflections in the river, echoing the title of the piece. Her final descent of a quay staircase dissolves to show her disappearance from the frame, understood as her suicide. This film in its on-location shooting, natural lighting, beautifully understated acting, and feminist and social realist themes give us a sense of what Dulac's subsequent fiction projects of the 1930s might have looked like.

Dulac's "illustrated records," which take a distinctly social-realist and semidocumentary form, are not swan songs signaling the end of her interest in fiction films. In the 1930s, she took multiple initiatives to write, direct, and produce narrative fiction features and shorts. When conditions proved unfavorable, however, she turned to the less-regulated domain of nonfiction filmmaking. She contributed to the evolution of the nonfiction film through her activism in various cultural and political organizations, as well as through her own innovative work as artistic director and director of newsreels at Gaumont-Franco-Films-Aubert. Extending her earlier avant-garde vision of a pure cinema, Dulac promoted and adopted what she referred to as a more "sincere," "intimate," and "direct approach" to nonfiction filmmaking, which emphasized the camera's capacity to surpass human vision and, thus, to bring us closer to "objectivity" or cinematic "truth."[4] Her conception intersects in some ways with that of Soviet documentary filmmaker and theorist Dziga Vertov's *kino-pravda* (film-truth, or cinéma-vérité) doctrine, outlined in the early 1920s, which foregrounded the superiority of the camera-eye. Yet, in many ways, Dulac's conception provides a more concrete stylistic precursor of "direct cinema" of the late 1950s and early '60s in its less constructed and more overtly spontaneous character.[5]

Moreover, Dulac's approach and her specific formal concerns, evident in her fiction filmmaking, help us to understand her newsreels and documentaries, as well as encourage us to ask questions about feminist filmmaking in the nonfiction realm.[6] In particular, one is invited to consider what a pure or objective approach to nonfiction filmmaking offers in the construction of social and gendered identities. The question of such identities is addressed in part 2 of this book, as well as in other work on Dulac's abstract fiction films.[7] However, here the question is extended to the domain of nonfiction. Dulac's *Le Cinéma au service de l'histoire* (Cinema in the service of history, 1935) raises similar questions about the construction of social identities (e.g., class, nation) with respect to issues of historical representation and the relationship between film and history.

This chapter examines Dulac's work as artistic director and nonfiction filmmaker at Gaumont from 1930 to 1935. Chapter 6 focuses on her cultural and political activism and her film work between 1936 and 1942, from the Popular Front era to the end of her activities under the Vichy regime, when her pacifism and belief in the unifying capacities of cinema led her to adopt a somewhat compromising political stance, which needs to be examined in context.[8]

The French Film Industry in Crisis

The early sound period brought with it new challenges for Dulac. At the end of the 1920s, paralyzed by the changes that came with the conversion to sound, the French industry suffered a marked decline in production.[9] In 1929, the year in which she directed her three experimental shorts or "abstract" films, Dulac, like many of her colleagues, faced extreme financial difficulties and unemployment. In a letter to film critic Léon Moussinac, Dulac lamented, "At present, loving the cinema and devoting one's strength to it, one is destined for fatigue. This unemployment is unbearable, annihilating. . . . When will it end? . . . Our faith is being tested."[10] In this same period, we see a diversification of Dulac's creative activities. In 1928, she had shot a film that served as the background for Sylvio Lazzari's opera *La Tour de feu* (1928). The following year, to help make ends meet, Dulac wrote and published a ciné-roman: a novelized version of Kurt Bernhardt's film *Les Bêtes humaines* (The human beasts, 1929), for the Société des cinéromans, for whom she had directed her last commercial film, *Princesse Mandane* (1928).[11] Dulac's increased activism, and her efforts to continue production during this period despite these difficult circumstances, attest both to her perseverance and to her adaptability.

Dulac undertook a range of activities in her efforts to defend the cinema as both art and social tool during this period. In December 1929, she cofounded the Fédération française des ciné-clubs with Robert Jarville. In an attempt to strengthen and expand her earlier ciné-club activities to sensitize a broader public to the role of cinema, she also lectured widely on a variety of issues vital to both the art and industry of cinema: such as the responsibility of the public to defend and support the visual evolution of cinema in the face of the "100% talking picture," the industry's need for greater protectionist measures (i.e., foreign film quotas), and a better commercial organization of the industry, to name a few.[12] In late 1929, unable to find work in the faltering industry, Dulac took steps to form her own private production company to produce her own creative projects. The company's name, L'Essor cinématographique française (the rise of French cinema), affirmed her faith in the cinema, as art and industry, and in its capacity to recover. It also attests to her intentions to continue to play an important role in the resurgence of this art form.

Early Fiction and Avant-Garde Endeavors

L'Essor cinématographique français

In the spring of 1930, Dulac established a precontract to create L'Essor cinématographique français in collaboration with the filmmaker Robert Boudrioz, and financial partners, writer Alfred Machard, and banker Albert Arnould.[13] Its broad mission included the production, purchase, sale, and distribution of films.[14] Dulac and Boudrioz, who shared responsibility as production managers, were granted exclusive directing contracts that highlighted their autonomy and freedom of expression.[15] Each was given full control over the production process, from the script, filming, and *découpage* (cutting), to the editing and creation of sound tracks for their films. Dulac and Boudrioz were to direct three feature films each, for a total of six per year. They were also to direct several short films, including documentary sketches and advertising films for public and commercial institutions, designed to augment the company's starting capital. Despite the fact that many of the alternative distribution circuits that supported experimental filmmaking in the 1920s had begun to collapse,[16] Dulac still maintained her commitment to cinematographic innovation and the creation of "personal research films," as she affirmed in a contract clause.[17] Unfortunately, however, due to the unstable economic climate in 1930 and despite her continued efforts into early 1931 to establish this independent film company, insurmountable financial obstacles prevented L'Essor from getting off the ground.[18]

Gaumont-Franco-Films-Aubert

In her subsequent work for Gaumont-Franco-Films-Aubert (GFFA), one of France's largest and longest-standing production houses, Dulac realized some her most innovative nonfiction work. In the autumn of 1930, Dulac was offered the position of assistant artistic director at Gaumont.[19] While the higher financial stakes that came with the conversion to sound compounded the usual constraints and prejudices that plague the industry, Dulac, fortified by her experience in the 1920s as an avant-garde and commercial filmmaker, once again found ways to circumvent these restrictions, creating a space that would allow her to innovate on many different levels. The initial limitations she faced at Gaumont only highlighted such innovation.

Unfortunately, even though her contract promised her a considerable degree of responsibility in a variety of areas, in reality she was given very little control over the actual productions. Traditionally, the larger commercial film industry in France left little room for avant-garde filmmakers and filmmaking. Indeed, it is not by chance that most of Dulac's commercial work of the 1920s was done for semi-independent producers, such as Louis Nalpas's Société des cinéromans and Film d'art, as opposed to larger corporations. However, as history has shown, the commercial system has tended to leave even less space for women film directors. While Dulac's reputation as one of the leaders of the 1920s French cinematographic avant-garde was undoubtedly a factor in her recruitment as an artistic advisor, it may have contributed to why Gaumont did not give her responsibilities as a full-time film director. In addition, her uncommon status as a female filmmaker seems to have exacerbated these prejudices.

Several archival documents strongly suggest that Dulac's gender was an even greater handicap for her in the 1930s film industry than it had been prior. Despite her qualifications and the stipulations of her contract, during her first years at Gaumont, Dulac was not given the opportunity to carry out the principal production activities for which she was hired.[20] A complaint that she and her lawyer filed with the company's legal department in July 1931 catalogs the limitations she faced as the artistic supervisor during the 1930–31 season: "Germaine Dulac never chose a script . . ., never made decisions about a role or the use of sound; never intervened as supervisor on a set; never created a shooting script, although in reality these were amongst her qualifications." The report further claims that Gaumont had completely disregarded Dulac's specific talents and attributes, particularly her training as an avant-garde filmmaker and activist: "Germaine Dulac (as her numerous films prove) is above all skilled in *découpage*, cinematography, directing, and editing. She is a specialist of the image and of rhythm." Yet, as the letter states, in over a year, no one at GFFA had ever called upon her "true qualities, nor the influence that she could use to serve the company externally."[21] The discrepancy between Dulac's official contract and her actual duties highlights the frequently undetectable nature of this prejudicial treatment of both avant-garde and female filmmakers. While the inner workings of these injustices are not always visible to film historians, Dulac's registered complaint provides irrefutable evidence of her resistance to this type of institutional discrimination.

Throughout her career at Gaumont, Dulac persevered in her attempts to carve out a niche for herself, so that she might contribute her own ideas to filmmaking. Unchallenged by the tasks that she was initially given as an artistic director (primarily pre-production work such as script revision and, on occasion, advising filmmakers off-set), Dulac sought to broaden her role in the company.[22] In January 1931, she wrote a letter formally proposing her services in the following areas: supervision of young filmmakers; supervision of French versions of dual-language films shot abroad; execution of the production activities specified in her contract; and replacement of directors, who for any reason, were unable to complete their films. For these services, she requested no additional salary. Moreover, in the case of financial constraints, Dulac offered to direct a shorter and lower-budget film than was stipulated in her contract, again without any salary assurances beyond the percentage guaranteed.[23]

Early Days at Gaumont: From Supervision to Realization

In response to her January 1931 request, Gaumont gave Dulac the responsibility of supervising the films of several budding directors. In 1927, she had supervised *Mon Paris* (My Paris), a picturesque drama directed by an early disciple of Dulac's avant-garde work, Albert Guyot; and in 1930, *Valse d'amour* (Love waltz), a French-language version of a Wilhelm Thiele musical produced by Eric Pommer for the German company UFA.[24] In 1931 she was credited with supervising *Bombance* (Feast), a working-class satire shot in outdoor settings and directed by Pierre Billon; and in 1932 *Le Picador*, a dramatic bull-fighting fable on the eternal theme of paternal jealousy, directed by Lucien Jacquelux.[25]

It is difficult to measure Dulac's real influence on these films because, while she is officially listed as supervisor in the credits, her actual responsibilities appear to have been extremely limited, particularly with regard to the films made at the Gaumont studios in France. Of Billon's *Bombance*, for example, the first of the Gaumont films, shot in the spring of 1931, Dulac complained that she was only brought in for the final outdoor shots (approximately 150–200 meters, or 495–660 feet), at which point the film was already two-thirds complete.[26] Aside from its working-class theme and outdoor setting, Billon's film is not of great interest.[27] The lackluster script and mediocre acting, coupled with Dulac's limited role during the various stages of the production process from script to on-location shooting to editing, no doubt frustrated Dulac, and the experience eventually led her to search for other avenues.[28]

Despite the fact that Dulac was not granted creative freedom in the domain of fiction, she still found ways to do what interested her and continued to play a key role in newly emerging movements. During this period Dulac attempted to create links between Gaumont and the avant-garde. Specifically, she identified a number of young independent filmmakers she saw as representing new hope in the still undeveloped and uninstitutionalized realm of documentary filmmaking, and tried to provide them with an opportunity to produce and distribute their work in this less-regulated domain at Gaumont. She also directed several documentary films herself before creating her own Gaumont subsidiary in the area of newsreel production in 1932.

In late 1930, in her dual role as founding director of the FFCC, and as Assistant Artistic Director at Gaumont, Dulac attended the second Congrès international du cinéma indépendant (CICI, or International Congress of Independent Cinema) in Brussels.[29] The five-day event, which opened at the Studio du Palais des Beaux Arts from November 27, proved to be a turning point in the evolution of the nonfiction film.[30] Dulac played a crucial role in the congress by offering young independent filmmakers an outlet for the production and distribution of their films. This role, in conjunction with her conceptualization and promotion through her lectures and publications of a new way of filming reality (which coincide with her authorship of some of the first historical writings on the 1920s avant-garde), make her a key contributor to an emerging documentary tendency that would have a tremendous long-term impact on film history.[31]

The congress featured twenty-five avant-garde films (many of them premieres) and included workshops on issues such as the development of ciné-clubs, the combat against censorship, and the establishment of a network for the creation of and exchange of independent international newsreels.[32] Above all, it brought together a number of young and inspired European filmmakers, who would contribute to a new current in documentary filmmaking in the context of the increasingly volatile political situation of economic instability and emerging nationalisms. Dulac's role in the development of the movement was essential. She offered several of these filmmakers a means of financing and distributing their films through Gaumont, which at the same time assured their diffusion to a broader public. Congress attendees included Hans Richter, Jean Vigo, Jean Lodz, Jean Painlevé, Boris Kaufman, Joris Ivens, Charles Dekeukeleire, Henri Storck, and Oswell Blakeston, many of whom had brought their first films for Dulac's consideration.

At this congress, Dulac, whose goal had always been to create one unified "Cinema," or to bring the avant-garde to the masses, achieved something entirely new in the domain of the documentary: the association of independent and commercial production. As Storck later attested, during the third and final CICI in 1963, "while La Sarraz had been an isolated encounter [literally cut off from the production world in the mountains of Switzerland], Brussels established the first real contact between independent cinema, that is to say, an isolated cinema, and commercial production. Germaine Dulac came to see the works and make her selection: it was for us a unique occasion."[33] As this event confirmed, the divide between commercial and avant-garde in Dulac's work, when considered as an aesthetic and philosophical continuum, is again not as sharp as scholars have suggested. Dulac opened up a space for the production and distribution of a number of important short and feature films by young filmmakers, including Pierre Billon, Jean Painlevé, and Jean Grémillon, all of whom were commissioned to make films for Gaumont; in doing so, she introduced into the mainstream new ways of filming that would change the face of cinema.[34]

Among the many fruits of this union is the work of the filmmaker Jean Vigo.[35] His daughter, Luce Vigo, credits Germaine Dulac with his entry into cinema.[36] The encounter between Dulac and Vigo is significant for a number of reasons. For Dulac, he was someone who would contribute a unique and modern vision to cinema. In her December 1930 lecture at the Salon d'automne, organized by her colleague Robert Jarville, Dulac singled out Vigo's *À propos de Nice* (About Nice, 1930) for its social and aesthetic prowess. She writes: "The documentary *À propos de Nice* leads us to make a biting social critique, without a word, through the simple opposition of images gathered and formed in their substance by life itself."[37] Dulac's affinity for the use of social irony in Vigo's work is not surprising; the use of irony and caricature, already present in her work of the 1920s, also characterizes her documentary and newsreel work of the thirties.

In 1931, on Dulac's initiative, Vigo was hired to make a short documentary on the swimming champion Jean Taris, the first in a series of shorts focusing on famous sports figures, marketed under the title *Journal vivant* (Modern journal, or living journal).[38] The subject matter itself was significant for both Dulac and Vigo. Dulac, for whom the essence of cinema was "life," "movement," and "rhythm," employed sport and dance, athletes and dancers in her films of the 1920s, and turned frequently to sports in her work in the thirties. Her own newsreel work for Gaumont continued along this trajectory, and led to a number of innovations in the filming of many of the country's most important international sporting events, including the 24 Heures du Mans (automobile race), the Davis Cup (tennis competition), and the Tour de France (multistaged men's bicycle race).[39] For Vigo, the subject matter anticipates his work in his masterpiece *L'Atalante* (1934), in particular its memorable underwater sequence.

Dulac's role in the International Congress of Independent Cinema in Brussels marked a significant juncture in the history of cinema. Her unification of "independent" talents and "commercial" means opened the door for the production of a number of films, like Vigo's *Taris*, that probably would not have existed otherwise. Moreover, her esteemed position within this avant-garde milieu, and her personal engagement in this shifting social context foregrounded Dulac's own unique and important contributions, if not to the emerging social documentary movement, through a reconceptualization of a means of filming reality.

La Fée du logis (1931)

In the spring of 1931, before publishing her first major article on nonfiction filmmaking in December of the same year, and founding her newsreel journal at Gaumont, Dulac directed a documentary short *La Fée du logis* (The fairy of the lodge). Since the term *fée du logis* can also mean "housewife," the title held obvious irony for the feminist Dulac, given her earlier films; she might have chosen it in reference to the small tasks she was given at Gaumont, as well as to make a more general point about women's unacknowledged contributions. The film, currently considered lost, was a nine-minute documentary sketch designed to open the gala event featuring F. W. Murnau and Robert Flaherty's docu-fiction *Tabu*, as well as to welcome spectators to the newly renovated and reopened luxurious sound theater, Gaumont-Palace, on June 17, 1931. Dulac never missed an opportunity to innovate, and her ode to this monument to cinema was highly inventive in its blend of social reality and fantasy, documentary and fiction, as well as its use of the star female figure, the actress Tania Fédor.[40] In this film, Dulac calls attention to the theater (and the woman) as a site of fantasy and illusion. She wrote: "She is the fairy of the lodge, the fairy of this new domain, GAUMONT-PALACE, rebuilt and restored to cradle the dreams of all through the most modern inventions."

She also uses the female figure to introduce the social documentary section on the metamorphosis of the theater, or more precisely on the workers, and the work that took place behind the scenes. Dulac wrote: "The woman evokes the construction work, everything that is happening behind the railing," she asserted. "The fairy of the lodge disappears, giving way to the evocative images and voices of the workers."[41]

On the one hand, *La Fée du logis* announced a new trend in theatrical presentation. A memo from Paul Kastor (GFFA Distribution) to Dulac expressed the company's admiration, and its desire to make similar presentational films for Gaumont theaters in cities across France, as well as to distribute the documentary component to theaters abroad.[42] On the other hand, this short, ephemeral, and forgotten film, *La Fée du logis*, not only bridges the two major tendencies of Dulac's work—fantasy and realism—but it also exemplifies her position as one of the most severely silenced heralds of the broader shift from avant-garde to social realism in French cinema during this period.

Le Tour de France, or the Silenced Innovations of an "Image-Huntress"

Dulac's film of the monthlong July 1932 Tour de France offers a prodigious example of the types of innovation that she brought to the field.[43] This was an important step in Dulac's career, for with her film *Le Tour de France* she went from being a studio-bound artistic advisor and maker of film-sketches, to taking her camera out into the field, as a producer and director, whose efforts took on national and international importance.

Dulac's was the first film ever to follow the Tour de France daily. She had a highly innovative approach to both the filming and the distribution of this event. A few years later, in an entirely different ideological context and using different economic and technical means, Leni Riefenstahl would film the Olympic Games in Berlin; she is generally regarded as the first filmmaker to bring a modern approach to filming sport. Yet, to a certain extent, Dulac preceded her. Dulac's interest in the filming of sports recalled many of the issues she explored in her avant-garde work of the 1920s concerning the representation of the body in movement as an expression of what she termed *la vie interieure* (inner life, or spirit).

Dulac had already innovated technical means for filming (lighting, lenses, prisms, in-camera effects), as well as distribution and exhibition strategies (such as made-to-order endings, illustrated lectures). Her filming of the Tour de France was dictated by the specificity of the live sporting event, and the movement it embodied, as well as by her desire to capture and deliver it rapidly to the public. Dulac's technique was also linked to her conception of a "pure" and "expanded" cinema, able to capture reality better than the naked eye, a conception that she would develop in her writings on the newsreel and documentary. In her effort to show the immediacy of a live event, she employed state-of-the-art lighting, cameras, and sound equipment. In her newsreel work in general, she sought to capture what she referred to as the *insaisissable* (imperceptible), that which we cannot see with our naked eye. In a 1932 article, "Caméréclair 300m," the author notes Dulac's acquisition of two new cameras that permitted better handling and greater mobility and allowed for "shots and sound unattained to date."[44] In her newsreels, Dulac constantly sought the means essential to creating an authentic cinema, one whose rules or techniques (mobility, immediacy) were dictated by the reality she sought to capture.[45]

Dulac was also innovative with the distribution of her film on the Tour de France. She understood that in order for sports news to be interesting to the public, it needed to be distributed quickly and to be as close to "live" as possible. Dulac's unprecedented efforts for the rapid distribution of each documented leg of the Tour de France made cinema competitive with other media forms, such as the newspaper and the radio. According to the newspaper *La Liberté*, each day a film of about 100 meters, or 330 feet, was shot and projected to show the evolution and results of that leg of the race. The film was projected the same evening, free of charge, in the town where the cyclists had arrived, and then the next day in the Gaumont circuit and the newsreel cinemas of Reginald Ford, delivering the event to the public with unprecedented speed, providing a sense of immediacy in terms of time as well as space.[46]

However, the modernity of her approach, as demonstrated by the mobility and speed that she brought to the production and distribution of her film, did not shield her from the constraints of tradition, particularly where gender was concerned. Dulac's masculine attire and habits, such as smoking and driving, and her work as a woman in the male-dominated fields of both filmmaking and sports, were noted by her contemporaries. An article titled "Following the 'Tour de France'" featured a large and unusual photo of Dulac in a convertible, wearing racer's goggles and a leather racing cap.[47] Another journalist portrayed her almost as if she were a participant in the race, a phenomenon as intriguing to the press as the competitors themselves: "A parked car is surrounded, in it is Germaine Dulac who is working. We have enough time to ask her some questions."[48] When journalists remarked on the "torpedo-like speed" of the tour, and said that filming it must be tiring for her, a comment reporters wouldn't likely make to a male filmmaker, Dulac denied having any physical fatigue, instead highlighting her concern for the effective production and timely distribution of the film. Her businesslike approach and commanding presence, and particularly her facility in giving orders (perceived as masculine behavior), made a clear impression.

Despite contemporary recognition of her considerable abilities in organizing and executing the shooting and distribution of the Tour de France, Dulac was never entirely accepted as an equal by her colleagues, and as a result she faced a number of practical difficulties. On one occasion, she was not allowed to enter the stadium where the riders were arriving, under the pretext that women were not allowed into the cyclists' headquarters. She was forced to send her cameraman in her place.[49] While she had long downplayed her gender and her feminism in the male-dominated field of filmmaking, Dulac did not hold back in speaking out against the treatment she received as a newsreel director in this often-unaccommodating nonfiction domain.[50] Her perseverance in this field and her efforts to innovate on both a theoretical and a practical level seem all the more extraordinary under such unfavorable circumstances.

Dulac's Weekly Newsreel, *France-Actualités* (1932–1935)

After *La Fée du logis*, Dulac had quickly moved into the less-regulated domain of documentary filmmaking, which not only offered her more freedom as a female filmmaker, but also allowed her to explore key ideas she had concerning what constituted the essence of cinema. In this new domain, she developed her theoretical ideas regarding cinema's relation to the "real" and sought new methods better adapted to filming this reality. Dulac's notions about the artistic qualities of the purity of film form led her to forge new techniques that privileged noninterference, spontaneity, and immediacy, as a means of approaching objectivity and universality, which she hoped would ultimately serve the pacifist cause.

In November 1931, Dulac had launched a project to create an internationally competitive documentary and newsreel company, in a period in which both of these forms were gaining unprecedented importance.[51] Dulac established France-Actualités as a "French Company of Talking Newsreels and Documentary Films." The company's capital of 4.5 million francs was donated by several large industrial organizations, including Schneider-Creusot, founded by her great-uncle a century prior. France-Actualités (69, rue de Monceau, Paris 8th) was one of only five or six major international newsreel journals at the time, which included the U.S. newsreels Paramount and Fox Movietone and their French counterparts Pathé Natan and Éclair Journal. While Dulac's France-Actualités is best known for its weekly newsreel journal of the same name, founded in September 1932, the company also made several documentaries. The project titles, listed in the archives, include several newsreel-based films documenting sports events, such as *Le Tour de France* (1932) and *Les 24 Heures du Mans* (1934), or industrial activities, such as Dulac's *Le Port de Strasbourg* (1934).[52]

Following her experience of filming the Tour de France, Dulac not only brought a number of practical innovations (such as the coverage of small news items, and of the lives of ordinary people) to her weekly cinematographic journal, but also conceptualized and theorized the social and aesthetic qualities of the newsreel in a highly original way. In September 1932, more than one year after the French film industry's shifting economic climate had brought Gaumont's first weekly newsreel journal, *Gaumont-Actualité*, to a standstill, Dulac's launching of the weekly sound newsreel journal *France-Actualités* revitalized the field. She was its sole director, overseeing three to four production teams, one led by Paul Parguel, who was one of her go-to cinematographers during the 1920s.[53] Yet despite the considerable number of staff working on these projects, her approach to the newsreel remained highly personal, much closer to that of a documentary filmmaker than of a newsreel director. Dulac sought to modernize newsreel filmmaking through the use of the latest technologies and production and distribution methods, and by creating a thoughtful and relevant journal. Dulac's newsreel was much less consensual than traditional journals, thanks to the diversity of its subject matter, its humanist and universalistic point of view and its analytical form.

The subject matter of *France-Actualités* was entirely new. For the most part, French news journals remained surprisingly homogeneous in their subject matter from their beginnings to the Second World War.[54] During the two wars, and even in the years between them, the newsreel almost always adopted the point of view of the ruling power, and its subject matter generally reflected the interests of the bourgeoisie and of private industries and government institutions that owned it. As numerous historians have shown (the early Lumière films notwithstanding), their discourse was largely complicit with the ideologies of their investors and supporters, rather than critical of them.[55] Common topics include official ceremonies, important meetings of heads of state or, alternatively, sensational events such as funerals, car and train accidents—all of which encourage a coming-together under the rubric of statehood, grief, or horror—or sports, which tend to rally the public. French newsreels, like those of most Western countries, with the exception of the Soviet Union, did not use a discourse of revolution or class critique.[56] Aside from the exception of the replacement of subtitles by voice-over commentary in the sound period, their extremely codified presentation (format, framing, style of commentary) remained constant throughout the years.

Dulac also integrated more local and specifically working-class subjects. As Siân Reynolds has noted, alongside national topics (such as the building of a dam and the execution of the gangster Gorguloff), Dulac included rural subjects; one reviewer, commenting on her third journal, took note of her coverage of public fêtes and "moto-ball," an unusual sport in which young men on motorcycles use their wheels to play football.[57] The integration of these working-class subjects was considered exceptional and unexpected. One journalist, commenting on her coverage of the popular and traditionally working-class Fireman's Ball, questioned why a journal of such talent and prestige chose to film ordinary subjects: "[T]his company is involved in a curious activity: it has intelligent and tasteful cameramen and editors who get 'the most out of minor news' items such as the Fireman's ball of Fontenay-aux-Roses—yet it resolutely confines itself to small news, neglecting major events. Why?"[58] Dulac gave an indirect response to this question in an article years later: "Filmed news reporting is the most interesting of jobs. . . . If you knew how working constantly with people, who live real lives, who truly suffer, work, and love, can change the point of view of a director used to confronting more or less fictitious beings! In the news report, all things are real, undistorted by the imagination or by reasoning acquired from books. A lesson is given to us daily through the necessities or even the turpitudes of man caught in action."[59] The purity that Dulac found in the lives of ordinary beings was central to her theoretical conception of a "pure" and "sincere" cinema and her vision of the newsreel as an ideal cinematic form.

Figure 30. Moto-ball, a new game in which motorcycles meet soccer, makes its debut at Elisabeth Stadium in Paris. © 1932 Gaumont Pathé Archives, collection Gaumont.

Dulac's Cinematic Theory: "Pure Cinema" and "Expanded Cinema"

Dulac was one of the few intellectuals and filmmakers, alongside Soviet documentary filmmaker and theorist Dziga Vertov, not only to work on the newsreel but also to write about it theoretically. The originality of Dulac's approach is clear from her reflections on "pure cinema" during her earlier avant-garde work and from the way in which she adapted these ideas to the newsreel and documentary domain. Dulac's writings, when considered in relation to her films, allow us to trace her conception of the newsreel from that of a "pure cinema" of life, movement, and rhythm in the 1920s, to that of an "expanded cinema" in the 1930s, which not only has the capacity to see more than the human eye, but which through its inclusiveness can attain a certain level of objectivity that, if used judiciously, can serve as a powerful social and pacifist tool.

In her writings in the 1930s, Dulac argued that, of the cinema's many applications, the newsreel form was the "most sincere" and "pure."[60] For Dulac, it was its liberty from the dominant fiction forms of cinema that gave the newsreel its unique and unequaled capacity to capture reality. In her December 1931 article, "Le Sens du cinéma"—which might be translated as the *direction* or *meaning* of cinema—Dulac drew on her 1920s call for a pure cinema "free from the other arts." Yet, in that article, she went further in her criticism of both "artistic" and "entertainment" films (which we can equate with avant-garde and commercial cinema, respectively) for their links to the narrative and formal traditions of theater, literature, and painting, which she said only transpose but do not give us the "real" (or that which exists in the world). Significantly, Dulac adorns her usual reference to pure cinema with a more seasoned reference to film "truth" (or what she considered to be a less contrived form of the medium) that better emphasizes its relation to the reality it seeks to represent.[61] Dulac's quest for the essence of cinema and "the truth of the cinematographic art" had given way to a more radical conception, which she found in the domain of nonfiction.

In her writings of the mid- to late-1920s, and more generally in her reflections on the specificity, purity and truth of cinema, Dulac consistently argued that the "essence" of cinema is "movement." But this is not just any form of movement, but specifically that which we find in the "material of life itself."[62] For Dulac, movement, found in life itself, movement which could be found in the concrete world, and which could be captured through photographic means, was not only the core being of cinema, but also its means of formal and artistic expression. In "Le Sens du cinéma" (1931), Dulac reaffirms this idea when she writes, "The truth of movement . . . is the scientific and artistic contribution of cinema."[63] While this idea is central to her "avant-garde" films, such as *La Folie des vaillants* (1925), where she first attempted to apply her theory of a "visual symphony," and more particularly to her "abstract" or "pure" films, in the context of her work for Gaumont in the 1930s, this notion of movement found in the real would be crucial to her conception of the nonfiction film.

Dulac also emphasized (along with Vertov) the unique capacity of cinema to show through visual means that which is not perceptible to the human eye. In the 1920s, Dulac had actively contributed to the development of a "visual cinema" capable of expressing "interior life."[64] In her 1930 lecture "La Nouvelle Évolution" (The new evolution), she described her *La Souriante Madame Beudet* as an example of cinema's ability to "extend the facts of an interior and invisible life."[65] With the coming of sound, she extolled the cinema's unique capacity to visualize the ineffable or that "inexpressible" by other means.[66] Echoing her article "L'Essence du cinéma" (1925), in which she emphasized the mobility and ubiquitous vision of the cinema (evoked by the futurists, and later the surrealists),[67] Dulac writes: "We cannot deny it: the cinema multiplies our knowledge. It continually throws us outside of our milieu, outside of our familiar thoughts, outside of our acquired knowledge, into ignored worlds. It moves, it seizes *forms*, their *rhythm* and their *spirit* by attacking the nuances that reveal instinct. It is a *powerful eye*, which adds itself to our own much too limited eye" (emphasis added).[68]

Dulac's faith in the superiority of the moving image led to her ideal of a nonfiction cinema that could go beyond the constructed nature of fiction (not to escape logic and reason, as in the case of the Dadaists and Surrealists, but to penetrate further into the real, in its most unadulterated form), an ideal that can also be found in Vertov's 1922 writings on his newsreel journal *Kino-Pravda*.[69] Dulac stated that "What we would like to combat is the artificial; what we are searching for is the real." Her conceptions of the real and of the "powerful eye" come together in what she referred to as a *cinéma élargi*, or expanded cinema.[70]

One of the most concrete manifestations of her idea of a pure cinema based in life and movement and of an expanded cinema, which captures the world in its most microscopic and conspicuous forms, is the scientific film. The scientific film bridged her 1920s and 1930s conceptions of cinema and played an important role in her conception of the newsreel. Dulac evoked the scientific film in her articles and ciné-club lectures on numerous occasions. In her 1925 article "Théorie et practique," she wrote: "In the library of M. Colette (Pathé-Consortium), you can see two films: *La Germination du blé* [The germination of wheat] and *Cristallisation*. All that appears on the screen are lines and rhythms, without decor, and the success of these two films, at public screenings, shows that spectators are not that far from a conception where the literary and dramatic idea will be replaced by a purely visual idea."[71]

Dulac referred to these two films on several occasions to demonstrate her idea of a pure cinema in 1927, and even used images from them to illustrate her historical "Le Cinéma d'avant-garde" (1932). In this article, she also evokes a variety of images that recall, in particular, the documentaries of the prominent scientific filmmakers Lucien Bull, Dr. Jean Comandon, and Jean Painlevé, which can be seen to characterize her new conception of pure cinema. She wrote of "the formation of crystals, the germination, growth, and blossoming of flowers and plants, the trajectory of a ball and bursting of a bubble (pure rhythm and how moving, these admirable syntheses of the evolution of microbes and insects, in their expression and their life)."[72]

For Dulac, the scientific film perfectly illustrated what she perceived as the cinema's objectivity, or its capacity to record reality in order to provide proof of scientific truths.[73] On the one hand, the scientific film, grounded in the real, rendered visible those things that human perception could not capture. On the other, through its ability to provide "truths," it demonstrated the cinema's capacity for objectivity. In this sense, the scientific film, with its original function of exposing or analyzing the real—much in the way that pre-cinema pioneers Eadweard Muybridge, Étienne-Jules Marey, and Georges Demenÿ had done through their stop-motion, chrono-photographic, or motion studies, respectively—was also fundamental to Dulac's argument regarding the objectivity of the newsreel.

The Objectivity of the Newsreel

Dulac's approach to the newsreel can be seen as a synthesis of her conceptions of a "pure" and "expanded" cinema, already present in embryonic form in her avant-garde films of the 1920s, and in her idea of an "objective" cinema. Dulac's belief in the objective capacity of the newsreel, which is closely linked to her practical experience as a newsreel filmmaker, can be understood in terms of three main aspects of the filmmaking process: the specificity of the cinematographic apparatus; the approach to, or process of, filming reality, and the nature of the subject or material to be filmed. Her conception of the apparatus is primary. For Dulac, the camera lens and microphone deliver the real. They invent nothing. It is significant that the French translation of "lens" is *objectif*, which also means "objective." With respect to the newsreel, Dulac asked, "What is the newsreel? It's the event of the day, captured in its movement and life, thus *in its truth* by the camera and the microphone" (emphasis added).[74] Dulac's belief in the capacity of the apparatus is an extension of the ideas of cinematographic realism that emerged with the first film experiments of the frères Lumière. The Lumière brothers were Dulac's constant reference point when she discussed the camera's capacity to record reality, and she was in close contact with Louis Lumière (1864–1948) in the early 1930s, when she assisted him in the creation of France's first major film school, L'École cinématographique et photographique de la Ville de Paris, or L'École Louis Lumière (rue de Vaugirard), and where she taught courses on "découpage" and "rhythm" as late as 1942.[75]

Beyond her validation of the capacity of the apparatus, Dulac also emphasized what she considered to be the improvised nature of the newsreel filmmaking process. In her 1934 article "La Portée éducative et sociale des actualités" (The educational and social significance of newsreels), she states, "The newsreel is created day by day, it is not premeditated. It captures the events of which it is an exact reflection."[76] For Dulac, this spontaneity or absence of premeditation reinforces the newsreel's capacity for objectivity or its ability to deliver truth. This approach to filming constitutes a major difference from Vertov. While Dulac did not exclude the search for a cinematographically expressive reality, or the careful placement of the camera and other forms of creative intervention (such as associative montage), which transform reality, she deemphasized the idea of preparation or organization of the material, and highlighted spontaneity, which she saw as reinforcing the authenticity or sincerity of the image. In a 1936 interview, she said:

"A newsreel—and that is the great power of cinema—can only be sincere, because it is the faithful reproduction of an event. *The lens cannot transform a fact, because it records in passing, as it is, without preparation.* The image is always sincere" (emphasis added).[77]

Central to Dulac's conception was the unpredictability of the subject matter itself. In her desire to create an objective cinema, Dulac emphasized the necessity for restraint in newsreel filmmaking and, in this way, clearly anticipated the proponents of the cinéma-vérité trend in filmmaking, and more specifically the direct cinema movement. However, Dulac's hands-off approach differs from Vertov's concept of *kino-pravda*, which inspired the French term *cinéma-vérité* and is considered its precursor. In fact, the founder of the cinéma-vérité movement, the late anthropologist and filmmaker Jean Rouch, who first used the term in his film *Chronique d'un été* (*Chronicle of a Summer*, 1960), was the first to acknowledge that his film is based on a highly personal and subjective conception of "truth." (Dulac's theoretical position can be situated chronologically between the work of Vertov in the 1920s and the theories of French critic André Bazin in the 1940s, both of whom write extensively on the "real.") While many of Dulac's ideas intersected with those of Vertov, her emphasis on improvisation and the minimization of authorial intervention in the activity being filmed make her a more obvious precursor of direct cinema.

Dulac's theories of the newsreel are evident in every aspect of her practice as a newsreel filmmaker. In a note to her supervisor George Colson, who owing to financial difficulties threatened to reduce the supply of celluloid for her newsreels, Dulac asserted, "One mustn't forget that the newsreel is the unexpected, that it is not prepared like a studio scene." While she was always sensitive to industry conditions, Dulac showed her resolve on this issue, by offering a maximum reduction of 1,000 meters per newsreel or her resignation.[78] In her desire to create an objective cinema, Dulac emphasized the necessity for restraint in newsreel filmmaking, through improvisation and the minimization of authorial intervention.[79] To this end, Dulac's cinematic techniques, such as her approach to shot choice, are revealing. When Dulac placed a camera on a moving vehicle in her filming of the Tour de France, her choice was dictated by the event and by her desire to capture the cyclists in action, en route across the French countryside. And when she did emphasize organization, it was as a means of *not* interfering with reality or the filmed event. According to an interview given just before she began newsreel filmmaking, Dulac explained how for one of her "illustrated records," featuring an outdoor summer dance (1930), she had hidden the camera from her subjects in order to encourage them to remain natural and therefore to obtain greater realism, much as she had in her 1923 film *Madame Beudet*. Dulac's deep-rooted realism not only influenced her ontological conception and her practical approach to the newsreel, they also impacted her position in a highly publicized and contentious landmark legal case on the freedom of the press, as well as her approach to political filmmaking (as we see in her 1935 historical documentary).

Liberty and Objectivity

Dulac's belief in the "direct" or "objective" nature of the image was taken to task in early 1934, after one of her newsreels was the subject of a libel suit. This case would lead her to ardently defend her conception of the image, as well as her belief in the importance of the liberty of film media. The newsreel concerns the mysterious death of Assistant Prosecutor Albert Prince, who was in charge of a judicial report concerning the 1934 affaire Stavisky, a colossal political and economic scandal involving government fraud (the embezzlement of 200 million francs of public funds, allegedly with the aid of Premier Camille Chautemps) and assassination, which helped discredit the entire political scene. Dulac had supervised several newsreels on the Stavisky and Prince scandals, the subsequent "February 6 riots" of right-wing extremist groups (Camelots du roi, Croix de feu, l'Action française), and the ensuing counter-manifestations and strike organized by the Left.[80] The accusation against her company regarding the affaire Prince concerned the single shot of a medical clinic of a Dr. Charles Pfeiffer, which appeared in the extended version of a newsreel projected in mid-April in the city of Dijon, where Prince's body was found.[81] While the print media had already connected him to the affair, Pfeiffer alleged that the shot of his clinic, and its association with the surrounding images, implicated him in the assassination, and placed his practice in jeopardy.[82]

Dulac had complete confidence in the cameraman who had filmed the sequence in question, her long-time collaborator and former World War One newsreel operator Paul Guichard, who had shot most of her late 1920s films (e.g., *L'Invitation au voyage*).[83] Moreover, she defended his choices on the grounds of the freedom of the press and the right to show images for informational purposes. Charles Delac, the president of the Chambre syndicale française de la cinématographie (French Cinema Employers' Union), insisted on this point when he defended her in his filmed statement for Éclair Journal newsreels: "For the first time in the existence of the filmed press, a newsreel journal, *France-Actualités*, directed by Madame Germaine Dulac, has been sued for and convicted of libel, because, in an account of the Prince affair, it shows a clinic in Dijon, and what's more, it does so without any commentary. If the appeals court confirms this judgment, it will become impossible to show freely on screen that which all other journalists publish. It will no longer be possible to give you the news to which you are entitled and which we daily strive to render more interesting."[84]

Dulac was fined by the court, which had the effect of easing the concerns of Dr. Pfeiffer, but on appeal she was acquitted of any intentional wrongdoing. The fact that she eventually won the case created a precedent in the history of film journalism. Further, the case not only strengthened Dulac's already strong anticensorship position, it also reinforced her convictions regarding the importance of the newsreel, with its unique capacity to provide extended visual evidence, as a source of information.[85]

Inclusiveness

In a context of increasing international tensions and rearmament, Dulac elaborated her conception of the objective capacity of the newsreel in more specific terms. She maintained that the newsreel, in recording life, not only provided essential and powerful visual evidence that could not and should not be denied or ignored, but that each of its elements functioned (as in her notion of the fiction film) within a broader system of information and signification, whose ability to approach the "truth" and increase human understanding depended on its very inclusiveness.

For Dulac, the capacity of the newsreel for objectivity depended not only on the recording of the authentic but also on the maximization of diverse points of view and the minimization of commentary. Dulac referred to a letter forwarded to her by Magdeleine Paz (with whom she worked on the cultural commission of Mai '36), as a means of illustrating her ideas on the "sincerity of the image and the tendency of commentaries."[86] In the letter, a suburban spectator, who is the mother of two young girls, expresses her indignation with regard to the way that military weapons, tanks, and images of a certain Führer met by enthusiastic crowds were shown without any condemning commentary or "call to good sense, and reason."[87] In response, Dulac defended the necessity of showing these images, on the basis that they were direct representations of what existed. She wrote: "We cannot object to the events presented. If newsreels depict the world and its folly of arms, it means that this disturbing folly exists—even in newsreel compilations. . . . Newsreels collect alas! and the fact is true, real." Dulac emphasized the neutrality of the newsreel filmmaker and, as in her 1920s theories of pure cinema, the active subjectivity of the spectator: "The film journalist invented nothing. He observes, that's all. It is up to us to understand the lesson of the images!"[88]

Sound and Commentary

One of the most original and significant aspects of Dulac's approach to the newsreel at the time was her view of sound and the use of commentary. Her position resulted from a belief, which she promoted and defended throughout the 1920s, in the exceptional capacities of the cinematographic language. Like many of her contemporaries, Dulac was adamantly against the "100 percent talkie," which she regarded as one of cinema's greatest threats to the visual. In a conference at the Salon d'automne in December 1930, recalling her conversation with an associate (a playwright's son) who envisaged talkies as a means of recording theatrical works, Dulac warns of the perils of the spoken word: "The danger, you understand, is there—it is the death of cinematographic art."[89] Yet, she also believed, that sound could play a positive role if used judiciously. She particularly admired the use of sound in Walter Ruttman's *Melodie der Welt* (*La Mélodie du monde/Melody of the World*, 1929), which she saw as a model for her future productions.[90]

Dulac's viewpoint was the result of her reflections and convictions regarding the fiction film. Just as she had fought in the 1920s against the overuse of intertitles, and an overdependence on story and decor (inherited from literature and theater), Dulac minimized the use of descriptive and interpretive commentary in her newsreels. One critic, reviewing the newsreels of four of the five major companies (Pathé-Natan, Paramount, Fox-Movietone, and Gaumont—the fifth was Hearst-Metrotone) pointed to the uniqueness of Dulac's approach: "Maybe distributors will understand one day that it is useless to tell us: And, in the flag-decorated town, the length of old picturesque roads, people celebrating, etc. . . . We see it, we understand, we are neither blind nor deaf. France-Actualités seems to have understood and has not fallen, thus far, into these errors."[91]

For Dulac, commentary is subjective and breaks down the balance of truth. "If the image is true, the commentaries that accompany it, as objective as they might be, and for which it has no need, already impose on this truth an element of interpretation," she wrote. "An adverb, an adjective can raise questions about that which is unquestionable in the image." While words restrict meaning, images bring truth, which can be open to interpretation or understanding. "The imprecision of words can be fatal. Cinematographic precision brings clarity and truth."[92] Dulac's effort to bring objectivity to the newsreel film stands in stark contrast to the sensationalism that dominated the newsreel at the time, which focused on government officials, parades, accidents, and crime, presented with little analysis or contextualization. She was well aware that the newsreel could be and often was didactic and propagandistic. However, her view that a newsreel filmmaker, or what she refers to as a *cinéaste journaliste* (journalist-filmmaker), should strive to be as neutral as possible is not only entirely modern, but is also central to her larger view of the role of the newsreel in a shifting international context.

Dulac's Objectivity in Context

Dulac's proto–direct cinema belief in the newsreel's potential for objectivity may appear naive since it does not seem to account for the subjectivity already inherent in shot choice and montage. However, considered within the context of her broader career, as well as in its sociohistorical context, it is revealing of her profoundly humanist conception of cinema. In particular, it corresponds to her idea that the cinematic image can play an important social, political, and historical role.

Dulac's conception of the newsreel as an educational and social tool was as a logical extension of her long-standing commitment as an activist for women's progress, pacifism, and the cinema. Her activism included her internationalist lectures at the Alliance française in the 1900s, her promotion of the cinema as art and industry, and her defense of director's rights through the Société des auteurs and the ciné-club circuit beginning in the late 1910s. Additionally, she maintained a pacifist stance as vice president of the Comité du désarmement moral par les femmes (Women's Committee for Moral Disarmament) and her participation in the educational congresses of the Cinémathèque de la Ville de Paris in the mid- to late-1920s.[93]

In the 1930s, she defended and promoted the newsreel as an educational, social, and pacifist tool (with strong gender, as well as more broadly humanist implications) in her role as president of the cinema section of both the Conseil national des femmes françaises (CNFF, National Frenchwomen's Council), beginning in 1932, and for the International Council of Women, as of 1936. In the late 1930s, as her responsibilities at Gaumont lessened, her activism intensified. In 1937, she continued to serve on the Ligue du désarmement moral under the League of Nations' International Committee of Intellectual Cooperation, alongside the German filmmaker G. W. Pabst, Charles Delac, president of the Chambre syndicale (French Film Syndicate), and Laura Dreyfus-Barney, president of the CNFF.[94] In this same year, she was also the official French representative on the League's Film Education Committee (alongside Gilbert Murray for the United Kingdom and CBS's Edward R. Murrow for the United States) and was responsible for the development of the newsreel on the Committee for the Utilization of Modern Means of Broadcasting in the Interest of Peace.[95] In the context of these sociopolitical activities, which merit a separate in-depth study, Dulac adapted her cinematic approach to the needs of a rapidly shifting social climate.

Dulac believed that newsreels had the potential to create greater social understanding. In an undated and unpublished lecture titled "La Question des actualités" (The newsreel question), she stated: "The newsreel, which through its moving images brings closer those who do not know each other, by recounting life through its lens, couldn't it bring together viewpoints that oppose each other, couldn't it replace the abstractness of words, which separate, with life, which unites? The newsreel is always social, but couldn't it be so in another more deliberate, scientific, voluntary way?"[96]

The special economic and documentary status of the newsreel was important. While gaining influence with the recent creation of specialized news and documentary theaters, newsreels were not subject to the same commercial constraints and artistic preferences as the fiction film or even the documentary. According to a note in Dulac's book manuscript, until World War II, newsreels circulated freely within international newsreel circuits and were less subject to the laws of supply and demand.[97] Moreover, the freedom from the constraints of narrative and fiction films gave them the liberty to capture with more sincerity, the true more "universally human" and visual characteristics of the cinema. In her 1931 article, "L'Action de l'avant-garde cinématographique," Dulac declared: "With the cinema, the human being surpasses himself. He regenerates his force through his contact with the entire earth, if he knows exactly how to experience the meaning of images made of truth which the cinema offers him; he becomes a conqueror, who moves forth through the universe conscious of not being the center of the world."[98] This universalism was crucial to Dulac's unique social conception of the newsreel.

Part and parcel of this universalism were Dulac's efforts in the domain of international newsreel exchanges. Dulac worked actively to create links with the newsreel companies of other nations and actively promoted their necessity. On several occasions, she expressed her future hope, "Almost every country, even if it has no film industry to speak of, will have newsreel companies. So international links have been established that make it easier to get news from distant places."[99] While she promoted the idea that each nation should have its own cinema, she spoke out against "nationalisms," and was against the domination of any single national cinema: "We shall have to wish that works of each national school can equitably share the world's screens."[100] This idea is closely linked to her long-standing defense of the French cinema, which was threatened in particular by the domination of Hollywood. Yet it is also related to her view of cinema as a universal language, comparable to music, a notion closely linked to her dislike of verbal commentary, which is language specific and fixes meaning.

Dulac invoked the musical analogy, central to her concept of pure cinema, to speak to the medium's universality, and its ability to transcend national barriers: "Each film remains . . . national. Rhythm is an expression of origin. But cinema must also be international, like music, whose potential for pathos touches human sensibility more broadly."[101] As with her pure films, this universal aspect is what allows us to go beyond official ideological and institutional discourses to gain an "intimate" understanding of beings: "The newsreel, which concerns us here, is the great modern social educator. By opening communication, between the most diverse minds, the most distant peoples, with a magnetic current, it encircles the world. Doesn't it reveal to each the intimate face of the country and beings, behind the official face of tradition and historical imagination?"[102]

Dulac saw the newsreel's immediacy and its direct relationship with reality as crucial in an international context marked by a rapidly shifting political climate. In a 1934 lecture before the League of Nations, she stated: "Like the scientific cinema, the newsreel unveils the truth of universal life, which we are unable to guess through commentaries, books, newspapers and manuals. The cinema thus considered is an individual experience, which permits each person to see and live, rather than 'to evoke.' Through the newsreel, classes and races mix directly, without intermediaries. Sentiments, gestures, joys;

humanity rises above particular characteristics, and the spectacle, bringing comprehension, makes one forget little by little the hatreds."[103]

This 1934 statement, which extols the virtues of the newsreel for its superior capacity to transmit life as a form of shared experience that can promote universal understanding, also announces the principle tenets behind the historical documentary that she undertook in 1935, during her last year as a full-time artistic director at Gaumont.

Cinema and History: *Le Cinéma au service de l'histoire* (1935)

Due in part to personal health concerns limiting her mobility, as well as to the company's financial decline, Dulac's production activities as newsreel director of Gaumont officially ended in late 1934. While continuing to serve as the company's artistic and technical advisor, a position that she would occupy only on a part-time basis after 1935, Dulac quickly turned to more independent and personal projects. In 1935, she made her first sound feature, *Le Cinéma au service de l'histoire* (Cinema in the service of history), which, while independently financed, can be seen as the culmination of her creative efforts as newsreel director, before embarking on other promising projects during the Popular Front period (1936–38).[104]

Commissioned by the producer Georges Macé, a former military commander, and Albert Thierry, a well-known journalist at *Paris-Soir*, for the opening of an "all-newsreel" theater, the Cinéma-Actual, *Le Cinéma au service de l'histoire* is a compilation film that traces the social and political events of the decades leading up to and following World War I in an effort to deter a repetition of this cataclysm.[105] This film is coherent with her broader cinematic approach and her ability to carry out highly personal projects regardless of genre, format, or production conditions. *Le Cinéma au service de l'histoire*, aptly referred to as a "monument to cinema," can be seen as a product of Dulac's theoretical reflections on the medium in the 1920s, and her practical experience as newsreel director in the 1930s, in which she worked with archival footage.[106] It is also rooted firmly in the specific historical context of 1935, that of widespread economic and political incertitude, stemming from pervasive unemployment in France, the rise of dictatorships in Europe, and the threat of another devastating war.

Dulac envisioned *Le Cinéma au service de l'histoire* specifically as a historical film that would be built from archival footage shot over the course of forty years from 1895, the year of cinema's birth, through 1935.[107] This history plays out on several levels. The film takes a chronological approach, that of events and their consequences unfolding over time, as well as a global perspective, that of France's national situation within the broader international context. Through its own formal organization, as well as through multiple visual and verbal references, the film also reflects on the role of the cinema in history.

For Dulac, cinema and history (and indeed the history of the cinema) were organically linked. From her first article in the late 1910s on cinematic mise-en-scène to her 1930s writings on the newsreel as "pure cinema," she had repeatedly praised the cinema's unique capacity (from the first Lumière films) to record and transmit "the material of life itself." In the mid-1930s, a period whose unstable political climate inspired a great deal of retrospection, she reveres the cinema as the ideal instrument for writing history, based on this same distinctive capability. In an unpublished lecture, she stated: "The newsreel is life transmitted. The newsreel is the machine that writes history."[108]

Not surprisingly, just as many of Dulac's 1920s films (*La Souriante Madame Beudet*, *La Princesse Mandane*) contain references to early film history (from Marey and Méliès to DeMille and Eisenstein), *Le Cinéma au service de l'histoire* was originally set to open, in homage to the Lumière brothers, with excerpts from *La Sortie des usines* (1895, *Workers Leaving a Factory*) and *L'Arrivée d'un train en gare de La Ciotat* (1895, *The Arrival of a Train at La Ciotat*).[109] The voice-over commentary, written by René Celier with Dulac, in homage to the cinema's origins, reiterates this link between history and the cinema: "Cinema records history every day. Wasn't the [Lumière] train a historical fact in that it showed us the people of 1895? Cinema has gone everywhere since; there have been no historical facts, great or minor, for which it has not been there."[110]

When the rights to the Lumière sequence proved too expensive, it was eliminated and replaced by an equally evocative and reflexive opening shot, reminiscent of Vertov's *The Man with a Movie Camera/L'Homme à la caméra* (1929). The film opens with an immense camera peering out across a large oval sports stadium, a cinematic site of life, movement, and rhythm. This prologue not only conforms to Dulac's ideal of the 1920s but also calls attention to the cinema's material and technical dimension, highlighting its role as a witness or chronicler of history.

Nonetheless, as suggested by the word *service* in the title of *Le Cinéma au service de l'histoire*, the cinema's role should not be limited to accounting for history. For Dulac, this art for the masses can also be an actor in history. That is, in relating history, the cinema also has the capacity to change the course of history. As such, the placement of the camera in the center of the oval stadium (with its circular racetrack) in the film's prologue also expresses the inauspicious notion that history, like life, occurs in cycles, sometimes repeating itself. The film is appropriately organized (and was also distributed) in two parts: the decade or so leading up to the Great War (which was perhaps the most significant turning point of the twentieth century) and the years that followed. The film's prologue and structure thus reflect the film's central function as a terrain of reflection on and analysis of the past, present, and future. Dulac does not content herself with simply accounting for past events through a visual chronology. She organizes and assembles the footage in a way that reveals its interpretive capacity, and makes the complex social reality it seeks to present better understood.

As in her impressionist and abstract films of the 1920s, and in her newsreels of the early 1930s, Dulac does not create a didactic political film, but instead offers the viewer a universe of symbols, an open system of signification composed of ideas, issues, and observations, which are often confrontational. The first half of the film, which covers the period from 1903 to 1918, celebrates the notion of progress, the theme of man and the machine. At the same time,

Figure 31. *Le Cinéma au service de l'histoire.* © 1935 Gaumont Pathé Archives, collection Gaumont.

it shows how a number of technological inventions (e.g., the assembly line and aviation), have also had adverse consequences, namely, modern warfare, with its effects of industrialized wars and mass destruction.

The second half of the film, which covers the period 1919–35, focuses on the many elements of the era of recovery following this great cataclysm. It traces the arrival of an unprecedented economic crisis and widespread unemployment in the United States, Italy, France, and Germany; the appearance of new political leaders in the shape of Mussolini, Stalin, and Hitler; and the ensuing uncertainty that came with the nationalism these leaders promoted.

The epilogue echoes some of the film's most powerful images in its enumeration of the West's diverse political "mystiques," referred to in the voice-over as: "Marxist" (Soviet Union), "Racial" (Germany), "Fascist" (Italy), and "Proletarian" (France). The film's power comes from the eerie resonance between the celebrated industrial innovations that lead to World War I in the first half, and the rearmament by Germany (associated with a "racial" or racially driven ideology of the sort Dulac warns against) in the second. Like the reality it seeks to represent, this correlation is intensified in the film, by the fact that the future remains undetermined.

By setting up parallels between the prewar period and the postwar period, as well as among the emergent nationalisms and ideological tendencies (without promoting any particular partisan discourse), the film creates an open text, one that, like her earlier films, impels the spectator to engage in the process of historical analysis, and to arrive at his or her own conclusions regarding the developments of the period.

Dulac's open approach may be considered problematic in this documentary, since it does not declare any specific partisan engagement in her representation of the different dictatorial leaders, but it is coherent when considered in context. For example, potentially objectionable early 1930s footage, presenting Mussolini as a French ally and "savior of the Italian people," acquires new meaning when a newer passage on Italy's May 1935 invasion of Ethiopia is added, creating a visual rhyme with Germany's massive military parades. By juxtaposing the ominous developments of the time with the disaster of World War I, the film's discourse, which appears neutral or open, becomes clear. In keeping with her earlier rhetorically open pure cinema aesthetic, its position is one of humanism, internationalism, and pacifism above all.[111] Seen in this light, *Le Cinéma au service de l'histoire* is also a precursor of sorts to the pacifist World War I film *La Grande Illusion* (1937), by Jean Renoir, with whom Dulac would soon collaborate (1936–38).

The final image of Dulac's *Le Cinéma au service de l'histoire* is of a map of Europe punctuated with a large superimposed question mark. Dulac's second, more outspoken yet still open variation on the film's ending, while unreleased, asks the foreboding question, "And the Cinema continues to record. What will it record in the coming years?"[112]

Chapter 6

Popular Front Activism and Vichy

Cultural and Political Activities under the Popular Front

During the Popular Front era, from 1936 to 1938, Dulac's activism for the cinema and by way of the cinema blossomed. She undertook several Socialist film projects, and through her involvement in numerous local and international organizations, played a major role in restructuring the French film industry and in cultivating a propitious environment for the future of the medium. Her role was central on several fronts, from the nationalization of the industry to the creation of a French cinematheque and a film directors' union.

In May and June 1936, a turbulent period marked by a rising fascist threat, an unprecedented economic crisis, and mass strikes, the coming to power of the Popular Front government (a brief but fruitful left-wing union under France's first Socialist prime minister, Léon Blum), created a unique national climate of widespread hope and euphoria, in which Dulac's cultural and sociopolitical activism flourished. The February 1934 right-wing riots and the July 14, 1935, counterdemonstrations of the major Communist and Socialist-led trade unions had led to the unification of the working class and certain sectors of the middle class under the Confédération générale du travail (CGT, France's largest association of trade unions). The Popular Front, in turn, garnered widespread approval by adopting the CGT's pledge to bring "bread, peace, and liberty" (rather than "bread and circuses") to all.[1]

For many French citizens, the election of this new administration not only appeared as a sure sign that there would be no war, it also brought unprecedented support for a number of long-standing Socialist projects, in which Dulac participated. Aside from creating fairer labor practices and more enriching leisure time (a forty-hour workweek, minimum wage, social security, and paid vacations), the new administration, with the help of the young and newly appointed minister of national education and fine arts, Jean Zay, instituted broad cultural reforms. These included a comprehensive popular culture program designed to ensure equal access to art, culture, and education via government subsidies for the arts, improved equipment for public schools, and state-run summer camps.[2]

This landmark cultural policy, which echoed the call of the revered Socialist leader Marcel Sembat (1862–1922) "to bring art to the masses," also corresponded to Dulac's long-held social and pedagogical aspirations and efforts in the name of cinema. In the broad Popular Front government–backed effort to support the development of art and culture, to make it more accessible to the people, and to give it a social purpose, she saw an unparalleled opportunity to put her ideas into wider practice.

Like many of her colleagues, Dulac believed that the professional members themselves should carry out the reorganization of the cinema. As such, she became involved in a number of representative structures (associations, cooperatives, and labor unions) intended to reform and, in effect, free the cinema on almost every level—economically, socially, and politically—through various means. These included diminishing commercial influence on it (via nationalization), creating new production modes and preservation institutions (collectives, archives), tackling subjects more pertinent to its social role (local action, pacifist ideals), and improving the status of its employees (via unions for filmmakers and technicians alike). Owing to the brevity and instability of this political period, not all the projects in which Dulac was involved met with success, but many left their mark and had a considerable long-term impact on the cinema and what has now come to be known as the "cultural exception," treating cultural goods differently from other commercial products, proposed by France at the General Agreement on Tariffs and Trade (GATT) negotiations in 1993.[3]

Mai '36, a Popular Movement of Art and Culture

Dulac was at the forefront of this broad reform effort, notably through her role in Mai '36, "a popular [or people's] movement of art and culture," named in reference to the Popular Front victory in May 1936.[4] This government-backed association, directed by François Moch (longtime SFIO member, economist, and

Blum cabinet administrator) and administered by a large number of women (including the Communist novelist Magdeleine Paz), in many ways reunified the Socialist and women's progress movements, in its attempt to democratize culture. In keeping with Dulac's own efforts to fight against the constraints of the commercial film industry, the Mai '36 movement sought to renovate and liberate or render public the plastic arts, literature, theater, cinema, radio, sports, and indeed almost every artistic and cultural domain.[5]

Dulac served as the director of the Section cinématographique de Mai '36, one of the movement's largest divisions created by Socialist militant François Moch. The section boasted hundreds of members from every sector of the profession, including engineers, architects, and decorators, as well as educators, activists, journalists, and union leaders. Also affiliated were major figures from several generations of filmmaking, including director Jean Renoir (*La Grande Illusion*, *La Règle du jeu*), veteran director and producer Henri Diamant-Berger, and Jacqueline Audry, an exceptional 1940s–50s female "cinema of quality" filmmaker.[6] For Dulac, and many of her colleagues, reforming the cinema so that it could achieve true freedom of expression meant first and foremost liberating French film production from its capitalist yoke, or its heavy financial constraints.

In her role as director of the Section cinématographique de Mai '36, and no doubt owing to her close ties to Gaumont, which had just declared bankruptcy in 1935, Dulac made nationalizing the film industry a priority.[7] The project of rendering certain companies and economic sectors public, which was an important part of Popular Front policy, coincided with Dulac's career-long efforts to promote and defend a *cinéma sans entraves* (i.e., unfettered by commercial considerations).[8]

In the autumn of 1936, under the auspices of Mai '36, and drawing on her administrative and production experience at Gaumont, Dulac spearheaded the project to nationalize that company, a project that would lead to several national productions, including Jean Renoir's *La Marseillaise* (1938).[9] In these efforts, Dulac worked with the CGT-based Syndicat général des travailleurs de l'industrie du film (SGTIF, General Union of Film Industry Workers) directed by Robert Jarville (a longtime friend, with whom she had cofounded the Fédération française des ciné-clubs, FFCC, in 1929) to improve the production climate. One of the principal short-term goals of this initiative was to convert the Gaumont studios into a facility for the production of films, namely, newsreels and documentaries corresponding to the social concerns of the period. To this end, Dulac formed a subcommittee of artists and technicians to establish the technical changes necessary to convert the studios into a vast state-of-the-art facility.[10] One of Dulac's broader aims, over the medium term, was to create a system of subsidies, in which taxes on movie tickets would be reinjected into the production system, a project that would be achieved in 1939 and that is still in effect in France today.

Popular Front Films

As director of the Cinema Section of Mai '36, Dulac also piloted the effort to develop new film projects, which specifically reflected the ideas of the Popular Front. In this context, after an initial short film project with Jean Renoir titled "Anna la bonne" (Anna the maid, 1936), Dulac participated with Renoir and her FFCC cofounder Robert Jarville on the elaboration of one of the quintessential productions of the Popular Front era: *La Marseillaise* (1938), a fiction film on the French Revolution.[11]

The French Revolution project began in December 1936 as a collaborative effort between Jarville's SGTIF, Renoir's leftist cinema group Ciné-Liberté, and Dulac's Cinema Section of Mai '36 (shortly before the production of Renoir's own *La Grand Illusion*). A letter from the coordinating committee, signed by Jarville, Renoir, and Dulac, and addressed to the minister of national education, Jean Zay, notes the principal goals of the project: to help the large number of film workers facing unemployment and to "restore the cinema's true cultural role."[12]

The film, whose working title was "De la Révolution française de 1789 à la victoire de Valmy" was to be a national project of, by, and for the people. It was to be financed by "public subscription," through the advance purchase of tickets (it was eventually completed by private investments). The subject matter—a call for a people's revolution—was addressed to its spectators, and the production would employ nonprofessional actors, unionized film technicians, and laborers (e.g., coopers, blacksmiths).[13]

In the early stages of the production, the film's script was overseen by a "committee of historians, authors, and directors" supervised by Dulac, Renoir, and educational filmmaker Jean Brérault (director of the Mai '36 Documentary and Educational Film subdivision, under Dulac).[14] However, Dulac, who in the early 1930s had proposed her own episodic film on the revolution, and who favored a more direct pure cinema representation of the past via a series of ten actualité-style shorts, did not entirely share Renoir's belief in the occasional need to fictionalize or "make history live" by drawing on the political events and attitudes of the 1930s. Dulac remained on the coordination committee for the film, although in April 1937 she withdrew her participation as one of the directors of the production. Since Dulac's and Renoir's archives are spotty on this collaboration, one cannot be sure what prompted this withdrawal, but the increased fictionalization and overt if inherent nationalism of *La Marseillaise*, may have contributed to her decision.[15]

Also during this period (mid- to late-1936), Dulac teamed up with Jean Brérault (1898–1973) and Mai '36 director François Moch, who headed the Union des techniciens socialistes, to supervise the social propaganda documentary *Le Retour à la vie* (The return to life, 1936). Drawing on Moch's background as an economist, this collaboration promoted Blum's popular-front fiscal policies by encouraging farmers to increase their spending and invest in production, and by denouncing the "sterile savings" or frugality of the provinces that threatened France's economy at the time.[16]

While the film was shot, in a very simple style with a fixed camera, and a rather didactic narration, Dulac's influence is evident in several respects. In keeping with her socialist and feminist ideals, in its central narrative sequence, the film uses a young spokeswoman to persuade her parents to purchase needed farm equipment as part of a collective effort to improve the national economy. In terms of visual style, it also includes numerous exterior shots of nature (water, foliage, clouds) in movement, an aspect characteristic of her earlier "integral" and "pure cinema" work, as well as of that of her mentee Brérault.[17] The film's pedagogical approach (its use of economic statistics and explanatory graphs notwithstanding) is also consistent with her broader newsreel and educational filmmaking efforts, as well as with those of Marie-Anne Colson-Malleville, who like Brérault had worked closely with educational film promoter Edmond Benoit-Lévy, and who would devote herself to documentary filmmaking in the coming years. *Le Retour à la vie* was distributed as part of a larger series of social issue films and *actualités sociales* (social newsreels) by the Service cinématographique de la Fédération de la Seine, led by Blum's director of Radio, Film, and Press and Guesdiste Marceau Pivert (1895–1958), with whom Dulac would undertake her next production efforts.[18]

From 1937 to 1939, Dulac worked with Marceau Pivert (founder in 1935 of la Gauche révolutionnaire, which regrouped the extreme left members of the

SFIO), and with Robert Talpain (the husband of Marcelle Brochet, her editor for *France-Actualités*), both active members of Mai '36, to establish L'Équipe (The team). The projects of this small independent cooperative, led by Pivert, were also integrally linked to the political, economic, and cultural policies of the Popular Front. While its efforts were cut short by the decline of the Popular Front administration in late 1937, archival documents show that one of the projects Dulac pursued was the production of films documenting the sports activities and summer camps organized by socialist and communist municipalities under Blum's minister of education, Jean Zay. Dulac also elaborated a project with Talpain titled "Le Barrage" (1939), a politically charged documentary on the history of electric power in France, in relation to the project of nationalizing that industry.[19] While these projects were never realized, their subject matter, which involved nature, sports, and light, testify to Dulac's ceaseless devotion to a visual cinema within a distinctively political context.

Labor Union Activities

In October 1937, as the Popular Front declined, and as the French economy worsened under the collective anxiety wrought by an impending war with Germany, Dulac became more involved in the unions and more steadfast in defending the rights of filmmakers, even as production opportunities became scarce. That year, the Syndicat des techniciens de la production cinématographique (STPC, Union of Film Production Technicians), a new and smaller centrist labor union devoted to the rights of the creative personnel of the film industry was established.[20] In early 1938, Dulac became president of the Section des réalisateurs of the STPC, which, despite the presence of leftist filmmakers Jean Renoir and Jean Benoît-Lévy (as treasurer), was also influenced by more right-leaning *cinéastes*, such as Léon Poirier and Marcel L'Herbier. In her role as president of the directors' section, Dulac demanded the reinforcement of internal measures, such as tax relief for French films and quotas for theaters and distributors.[21] Yet certain of the organization's efforts is somewhat perplexing.

Although the STPC claimed in its founding statutes "not to adhere to any political organization," certain of its labor protection efforts in the period leading up to and including the Vichy occupation, notably its endeavors to restrict the recruitment of foreign personnel, do not seem entirely compatible with the founding principles of the organization and its members.[22] Yet, the STPC's efforts can be understood as part of a long history of demands, like contingency quotas, and the nationalization of the industry, often linked in the fight against foreign competition. During this period (1938 to early 1942), Dulac fought to safeguard and ensure the continuation of the STPC, while speaking out against the "absolute paternalism" of Vichy's regulatory and censorship organization, the Comité d'organisation de l'industrie cinématographique (COIC, Organizational Committee for the Film Industry), which threatened to dissolve it.[23]

During this same period, in her indefatigable devotion to cinema and her efforts alongside Henri Langlois and Georges Franju for the 1936 creation of the Cinémathèque française, Dulac would also go to great ends, using her skillful diplomacy for political leverage to save for posterity the films and the cultural memory they represented, and which she had spent her life developing and defending.[24] During the first two years of the Occupation (1940–44), Dulac, Langlois, and Franju, who could have refused contact with the Vichy representative Major Hensel who oversaw the Cinémathèque française, would opt "in good faith" to remain diplomatic in order to recuperate, conserve, conceal and even grow (in the pretended name of the Vichy archive) a collection of tens of thousands of films. Among these were twenty thousand films deemed to be of public utility, the banned Alexander Kamenka collection, twenty or so films of Jean Epstein, and vast deposits of American films, which the Nazi occupiers had otherwise tapped to raid or destroy.[25] In the spring of 1941, after gaining permission to meet in the Fédération internationale des archives du film locales (Palais de Chaillot) to discuss the fiscal situation of the Cinémathèque française, and to elect a new board of directors (with L'Herbier as president, Dulac as vice president, and Langlois as general secretary), the organization succeeded in its efforts to both augment and shelter its film collections, before the invasion of France's *zone libre* (free zone) at the end of 1942.[26] Mannoni, in his *Histoire de la Cinémathèque française*, provides a glimpse into this complicated arena of institutional "double games," which, during the Occupation, led directors Dulac, Langlois, and others to wear masks of cooperation in exchange for political leverage, in this case in the service of saving French cinematic heritage.[27]

World War Two: Vichy and Occupied France

Confronted with an increasingly unstable political context and the ominous proximity of a second world war, Dulac's lifelong progressive values, her feminism, her socialist humanism, her unremitting pacifism, as well as her devotion to France's cinematic and cultural heritage, would lead her to employ her creative energy, her political caché, and her diplomatic skills in ways, that can appear both complex and disconcerting. It is difficult to comprehend why, between mid-1938 and August 1941 (the date of her last film project), the lifelong feminist and film activist—whose fundamental views clashed with those of the Vichy regime—proposed a number of short fiction and nonfiction film projects that can be seen to coincide with certain ideas promulgated by Vichy propaganda. The limited documentary evidence concerning Dulac's personal life during this period makes it difficult to pin down her precise objectives and thoughts. Notwithstanding, her political stance and project proposals (while none were produced) may be best understood within the context of the first year of the Nazi occupation of France, which began in the summer of 1940.

On June 22, 1940, after a hesitant declaration of war on Germany (September 1939), later followed by six weeks of military defeats (May 10–June 21, 1940), France signed an armistice with its invaders, ostensibly ending "the war that nobody wanted" and giving in to a four-year-long occupation, marked by mounting complicity and collaboration.[28] When it was proclaimed, an unmistakable majority of French citizens, and the last government of France's Third Republic—a *union nationale* (recalling *l'union sacrée*) of conservatives and socialists—supported the armistice (and the promised peace talks, which somewhat paradoxically answered the Popular Front pledge).[29] Widespread "joy and relief" followed the announcement of the armistice by France's greatest living World War I hero, Marshal Philippe Pétain, known as the Victor of Verdun, but "Pétain's regime had not yet revealed its exclusive, vindictive side that would by 1942 drive half of France . . . out of the spontaneous unity of 1940," as Robert Paxton notes in his book on Vichy France.[30] Since Dulac's last written film projects extend to the summer of 1941, her position may be best understood when resituated within this time-sensitive context.

Dulac's fiction and nonfiction film projects of 1938–41 may be seen as both a continuation and a departure from her earlier formal and ideological projects as an activist and pioneer filmmaker. Leading up to and during the first year of the Occupation, Dulac proposed at least twelve documentary efforts (averaging a page in length). Among these projects submitted to the COIC regulatory and censorship board between 1938 and mid-1941, several evoked a lyrical quality comparable to her avant-garde films of the mid- to late-1920s, and might be seen as an extension of her efforts as a humanist and abstract filmmaker. For example, Dulac described a project for a color film provocatively titled "Le Cycle des saisons" (The cycle of seasons), as a "visual symphony on man and nature," (one that echoes early Bergsonian and vitalist influences on the integral relationship between the animate and inanimate). Similarly, she proposed a film titled "Le Petit Monde des étangs" (The little world of ponds, which Colson-Malleville would direct a decade later: Productions Markab, 1952).[31] Another proposed project, "L'Eau à Paris," recalls Dulac's three abstract or "pure" films, and her "illustrated records" (1929–30). It proposes an exploration of diverse manifestations of water in Paris—from canals, barges, and homeless people under the bridges to rain, streams, and fountains—before ending with a shot of a dancer, and an "analysis of her dance."[32] In a November 1941 letter from the COIC, both of these projects were listed as *à l'étude* (under consideration), but they do not appear to have been approved.[33]

In the context of this censorship (which she outwardly condemned), Dulac also penned several projects of a more conventional character. While they are in keeping with her 1930s penchant for filming the daily lives of ordinary people in outdoor settings, they stand in contrast to her earlier more modernist and socially critical themes. Some of the subjects, while seemingly innocuous, share certain elements that can be linked to Vichyiste policies, founded on anti-intellectual, traditional, and conservative values, and in particular, with the *retour à la terre* (return to the land) themes of the late 1930s and early 1940s. This ideology, considered an "article of faith" among social conservatives of the era, held that France should return to a rural economy, as opposed to seeking economic development through modernization and industrialization.[34] Projects that might be seen as exhibiting or appealing to this theme include "France terre de légendes ou l'histoire apocryphe des provinces françaises" (France land of legends or the apocryphal history of the French provinces, 1941) and "La Paysannerie française" (The French peasantry, n.d.), the latter of which was a trilogy on French farm life.[35] One of Dulac's final projects, a lyrical essay on church towers titled "Les Clochers du beau pays de France" (The bell towers of the beautiful country of France, 1941), resonates with France's widespread return to religion during this period.[36] Despite the traditionalist and relatively conciliatory subject matter of these projects submitted to the Société des auteurs between March 22 and August 30, 1941 (the date of Dulac's final deposit), each was either refused or classified as "subject to approval" by the COIC censorship board.[37]

More confounding, however, are Dulac's projects that announce and support the myth of Pétain as a great leader, able to save the French from a new war. Still, dated early on, these included the pre-armistice film "Le Timbre" (The stamp, 1939), a history of the postage stamp as cultural patrimony, which in its final version concluded with the shot of a machine mass-producing the effigy of the World War I hero.[38] Later, a one-paragraph proposal, "Quelques causes de la défaite de la France" (A few reasons for the French defeat, 1940–41), while marking defeat, appears to align with the rather broadly supported notions of national unity and collectivity over individualism in the face of war.[39]

Another yet more perplexing proposal stands out. An early project, apparently submitted close to the time of the armistice, is Dulac's one-page synopsis for a biographical short to be titled "Le Maréchal Pétain" (Marshal Pétain), whose wife Dulac knew, perhaps through her long-held political ties, and her 1930s feminist activities. While the subject of the film is retroactively disconcerting, the project begs for yet defies interpretation when one takes into account both its probable date, which can be deduced from the synopsis (1940–41), and the multivalency of Dulac's prior films.[40] First, its opening description of a (newly) occupied France that "closes its eyes on the outside world, and opens its ears to the topics of [national] propaganda" resounds with criticism when one considers her long-standing internationalism.[41] In this regard, it can be seen to convey a certain melancholy reflected in Dulac's correspondence during the Vichy period lamenting the "absolute paternalism" or dictatorial character of the regime, as well as its impact on the industry and heritage of cinema, which she would fight tirelessly to protect through her work for the unions, as well as for the Cinémathèque française.[42] Significantly, her *cartes interzone* (correspondence between the northern *zone occupée* and the southern *zone libre*) to Jewish filmmaker Jean Benoît-Lévy (1940–41), who was staying in the southern *zone libre*, complain similarly of the regime's strict censorship, the lack of work and provisions, as well as of her own poor health.[43] In a *carte interzone* to Benoît-Lévy (December 18, 1940), Dulac writes telegraphically: "wishing you good moral and physical health. The family Ichac, Marcel, Lafond, Dulac is not well, will need provision of understanding. Very strict censorship sent back to me 2 cards. This is just a simple and profound souvenir of affection and union from the heart at the dawn of 1941."[44] In this context, and that of Dulac's long list of rejected proposals, the subject and tone of this project also appear to be tailored or couched in a way that could elude COIC censors.

Yet, its sardonic prologue notwithstanding, the proposal ends on a contradictory and disturbingly laudatory note regarding the former war hero. The closing lines of her abstract for "Le Maréchal Pétain" read as follows: "The Maréchal deplores the war of 1939. As an Ambassador, he serves France's cause in Spain. Called to the Government, he, who was never involved in politics, still knows that a new battle will be waged. He will save France, and at the lowest point of the defeat, create a new France. France is reborn, PETAIN, Maréchal de France, commands her."[45]

A clear interpretation of this project on Pétain is limited first by its unknown date, but also by its unspecified visual treatment, and the lack of supporting documents (e.g., personal or private correspondence, closely monitored by Vichy during the war). However, as it stands, the film's subject and closing description, coupled with the aforementioned projects, raise serious questions about Dulac's position as a progressive figure, and more specifically her relation to Vichy.

These projects invite us to more closely examine the dominant opinions circulating in France during the first year and the earliest stages of the Occupation, as well as their implications. First, according to the French historian Pierre Laborie, author of *L'Opinion française sous Vichy* (French opinion under Vichy, 1990), a crucial distinction must be made between Pétainism (support for the World War I victor) and Vichyisme (support for the Vichy regime itself).[46] In this regard, and in the context of Dulac's correspondence bemoaning the character of the new regime, the focus of this last proposal, which in its epilogue promotes Pétain as the future "savior" of France, is distinctly Pétainist, even with its reference to a "new France." If we consider Laborie's keen distinction, there is, in fact, no evidence that Dulac was Vichyiste.[47]

That said, what are the implications of Dulac's support for Pétain, as expressed in her nonfiction projects? First, it is important to note that in late 1940 through mid-1941, support for Pétain did not imply a pro-Nazi position—in December 1940, Pétain himself had attempted to remove Prime Minister Pierre Laval specifically because he was getting too close to the Nazis.[48] (Dulac's reported role in directing *Ce qu'il a dit. [Ce qu'il a fait.]* [What he said. (What he did.)], a surviving Gaumont newsreel-based compilation film made in 1939 severely criticizing Hitler, lends further weight to this thesis.)[49] Nor did support for Pétain, at least in 1940, imply a racist or anti-Semitic position.[50] While Dulac did have contact with Vichy officials, together with Cinémathèque française founder Henri Langlois, for the precise purpose of saving films, there is no evidence that suggests she was anti-Semitic, quite the contrary. Among these are her close and long-held relationships (as well as interzone correspondence) with Jewish filmmakers Jean Benoît-Lévy, whose family she helped to escape during the war, and Hans Richter, for whom she obtained a false passport for travel to the United States, as well as a personal meeting with Irène Hillel-Erlanger's son Philippe Erlanger.[51] (Richter's departure for New York, with several avant-garde films, and his contact with dancer and filmmaker Maya Deren, would provide a crucial link between the European avant-garde of the interwar period and the launching of the U.S. avant-garde and New York underground film movement in the mid- to late-1940s.) Perhaps most crucial in considering Dulac's legacy cut short by her death in 1942, is that her universalist discourse had always been one that denounced racism.[52]

Yet, in the context of her long-standing feminism, her homosexuality, and her internationalist humanist activism and writings, Dulac's project on Pétain still seems difficult to comprehend. How can one interpret the compromising epilogue of her project on Pétain? Did it constitute a "false ending" of the type that Dulac had cautioned the public about with respect to her 1920s films, only this time aimed at the COIC censors? Did it reflect a sense of desperation, despondency, or fear—also of her own persecution as a homosexual, after having been investigated as a communist—at a time of political oppression? Had Dulac become despondent, or had she completely renounced her progressive values in the face of war?[53] As Paxton has noted, shortly after its defeat, France was dominated by a sentiment of guilt, and a perception that modern values and an interwar emphasis on artistic creativity and leisure had "softened the nation."[54]

If Dulac's aforementioned projects (1938–41) appear incongruous and paradoxical, they are less so when considered in relation to the pervasive uncertainty of the late 1930s and the first year of the occupation (1940–41), as described by Laborie. This context warns against an overly simplistic explanation of Dulac's Pétainism and apparent adherence to Vichy ideas, with its extreme conservatism and racism that negated the progressive values of feminism and internationalism to which she had always been attached. It would be hasty, if not inaccurate, to conclude that she made a sudden about-face. "The elucidation of phenomena of opinion and, above all, the comprehension of collective behavior is achieved less by relating them logically with real facts . . . than by an analysis of the mental representations across which these ideas and facts are perceived, lived, commented and judged by their contemporaries," Pierre Laborie observes. "The truth that determines the attitudes of the social actors is not the truth that historians retroactively and occasionally succeed in reconstructing. It is, exclusively, that which imposes itself on them at that moment in which it is imposed."[55]

For Dulac and her generation, who had witnessed the devastation of the Great War "to end all wars," and who had heard the stories of the brutalities committed against their Belgian neighbors, the fears raised by another armed conflict with Germany were very real. Did Dulac, like many of her French contemporaries, see an armistice with Germany and Pétain's rule as a lesser evil when contrasted with the ravages that a new confrontation could bring? This desire to avoid war at any cost can be seen in the work of other French directors of the period, irrespective of their positions on the political spectrum: in particular that of the left-leaning Jewish filmmaker Jean Benoît-Lévy, with whom she corresponded regularly during this period, as well as that of her early contemporary Abel Gance, who took a clear turn to the right, dedicating his film *Vénus aveugle* (Blind Venus) to Pétain in September 1941. Gance was so profoundly affected by the Great War that his persona and his work can be fully understood only in its context. He had expressed his unwavering pacifism throughout the 1920s and 1930s.[56] Was Dulac, a lifelong socialist, humanist, and pacifist, a product of this same ethos?

Between 1938 and 1941, Dulac wrote several fiction projects, which add another dimension to her position. Most notable of these is a two-hundred-page treatment for a film about the well-known theater actress Ève Lavallière (née Eugénie Fénoglio, 1866–1929). Dulac poured a great deal of energy into this project, which she notes was based on "authentic documents."[57] Lavallière's story is almost the mirror opposite of a semiautobiographical project Dulac had written in the years leading up to World War I, "Denise Serpe," about a girl who leaves a convent to become an actress. Dulac's proposed biopic, provocatively titled "Ève Lavallière, éternelle fugitive," tells the real-life story of the modern theater actress and icon of modernity, who made famous the bobbed Joan of Arc hairstyle in France in 1909, and whose ephebic, Adonis-like airs lent credibility to her playing gender-crossing roles, although she eventually traded in her vivacity as a *garçonne* to live a religious life.[58] Given the time period, Dulac's choice of subject matter could be seen to mark a return to religion and a questioning of her earlier progressive stance as an avant-gardist and feminist. It might also be read as the product of a nation terrified at the prospect of another devastating war. Indeed, newsreels of the period show workers, artists, and politicians flocking to Notre Dame to pray for the aversion of another cataclysm.

"Ève Lavallière, éternelle fugitive"—a project that recalls her spiritual relationship with her mentor Sister Saignol at the turn of the century—could reflect the emotional turmoil that Dulac herself, as a lesbian and a feminist, had to face in addressing her religious beliefs during a troubling time. Yet, when one considers Lavallière's status as an icon of modernity during the early 1900s, it is difficult not to interpret Dulac's project as an expression of despondency, inner sadness, or mourning over the death of an age, if not a recognition that her long-held faith in progress, which had driven her aesthetic and feminist ideals, was ill-fated.

Germaine Dulac, who had long been in ill health, died on July 20, 1942, just days after the July 16 Rafle de Vel d'Hiv (the police roundup of Jews in Occupied Paris), a day that triggered a seismic shift in French public opinion and, as Laborie suggests, a "national identity crisis."[59] The apparent cause of Dulac's death was heart failure.

One can only speculate about Dulac's path had she lived beyond July of 1942. However, consistent with her lifelong humanist activism and idealism—as expressed through her films, writings and lectures; her lamentation over the reactionary and profoundly patriarchal character of Vichy; and after certain events irrefutably proved the end of democracy, provoking national outrage and a renewal of French identity, one can only imagine that, like her partner Marie-Anne Colson-Malleville and those persons closest to her, Dulac would have played a part in that renewal.

Conclusion

Once used to write her out of history, Dulac's cinema, in its aesthetic and sociopolitical complexity, is only beginning to be recognized and understood.[1] Due to the belated release of her personal archives to the public in 1996, and limited access to her extensive body of films, Dulac studies until recent years had been limited to a few films, and predominantly to a feminist theoretical approach that launched a heroic recovery of this great filmmaker in the Anglophone context. In contrast, in the French context, Dulac's work has long been subject to a depoliticized formalism, where identity politics and gender considerations have only slowly been making their way into film studies.

An archive-based history that exposes Dulac's sociopolitical and aesthetic influences, such as her engagement in the Women's Progress movement, is another step in this process of recovery. As Joan Wallach Scott has demonstrated, gender is *more than* "a useful category of historical analysis," a category that, beyond history's positivist acceptance of pluralism and inclusion, implies not just "an analysis of discrimination," but more radically, calls for a consideration of several factors: *how* hierarchies such as gender, like class (always unstable and interdependent) are constructed or legitimized; *how* processes, multiple causes, rhetoric or discourse, and organizations or structures function (often in silent and hidden ways); and finally by those *whose* interests control or contest meanings are served (as well as how these are produced).[2]

In this venture, an archival approach is not sacred. As Valérie Vignaux has noted, as with any study, an archival approach reveals a desire for an "author" and the reality beyond it, a process of selection, and the pursuit of a semblance of narrative coherence, not as preconceived, homogenous, immediate or certain, but as a product of chance or contingency.[3] As Arlette Farge reminds us in *Le Goût de l'archive*, one of the pleasures of the archive is that, disconcerting and colossal, its fragments do not sit neatly arranged and structured, waiting for someone to speak its contents.[4] Each archive is full of incongruities and discontinuous traces (events, instances, tales, and details) that splash, splatter, and rub up against each other, requiring interpretation, and of course containing gaps and absences that are equally discursive and ideologically charged. Still, in the case of Dulac, her personal papers, in concert with related archives and sources, do help give us a sense of the filmmaker, her challenges, her convictions, her perception of an audience, and her experience within a system. In addition to providing answers, her papers open up new terrain for exploration and raise a multitude of new questions about a woman director who, through her films and activism, had such a tremendous impact on cinema in an era in which women were largely excluded from the field.

Based on a range of archival materials (manuscripts, printed, filmic) as well as secondary sources, this book retraces and recontextualizes Dulac's life and films across a rapidly shifting environment over four decades and two world wars, from the Belle Époque to an occupied France under the Vichy regime. In consideration of this dynamic sociopolitical context, and through a discovery of her intellectual, personal, political, and artistic influences, my analysis has sought to shed light on her films, and her filmic ontology of a "pure cinema," a cinema of suggestion and potentiality, as it developed from symbolist figuration and contemplative abstraction in the 1910s and '20s to a conception of the newsreel (and archival documentary) as proto-direct cinema in the 1930s. Moreover, it reveals how her unwavering defense of the medium on all fronts (as art, industry, and social tool) was part and parcel of her broad-based and integral approach as a filmmaker and activist (feminist, ciné-club, corporative, syndicalist) to the new, modern art form as an instrument for international understanding, and as a carrier of history.

Yet, not just Dulac's story, this account also tells us about an era in which many women went against the tides, as Dulac noted in her 1907 lecture on the international task of women, to create things anew and "according to

Figure 32. Germaine Dulac, undated. © 1935 Gaumont Pathé Archives, collection Gaumont. Rights reserved. Collection Cinémathèque française.

their own spirit."[5] As such, this book hopes to contribute, along with those of other scholars (particularly of the Women Film Pioneers project and the Women and Film History International series), to reconstructing the lost histories of early women filmmakers, in order to better understand their important contributions, and in turn, this rich and complex period.

Chronology

This select chronology, organized by year, lists some of the major events in Dulac's life and career. Data are assembled from archival records. Film titles are arranged by date of production, with date of public premiere in parentheses (p.p.).

1882	Born Charlotte Élisabeth Germaine Saisset-Schneider on November 17 in Amiens, France.
1898–1902	Studies at the Visitandines convent or Pensionnat de la Visitation Ste. Marie de Bel-Air.
1905	Marries Albert Dulac (April 6).
1906–8	Journalist and author of "women's portraits" for the feminist and reformist weekly, *La Française* (Dec. 23, 1906–Oct. 4, 1908).
1907	Associates with the Alliance universelle des femmes pour la paix et l'éducation.
	Presents her first theater play, *L'Emprise*, at the Alliance française (Apr. 20, Paris).
1908	Travels by train from Bergen to the Cap du Nord (northern cape of Norway), which she refers to as "Ibsen's country" (Jul.–Aug.).
1908–13	Theater critic for *La Française*. Develops various theatrical and literary projects including draft of a novel, "Denise Serpe" (1908–15).
1912	Meets actress-dancer Stasia de Napierkowska (Apr. 17).
1914	Frequents Film d'arte-Italiana (FAI-Pathé) studios in Rome (Feb.–Dec.), where actress Stasia de Napierkowska is under contract.
1914	Outbreak of First World War (July 28).
	Secretary of the Croisade des femmes françaises, wartime propaganda and service organized by Mme Daniel Lesueur (pseudonym of Mme Henry Lapauze). Assists Belgian war refugees through the program Aide aux femmes des combattants (fall 1914–spring 1915).
1915	Meets Irène Hillel-Erlanger (Mar.–Apr.).

1916 Creates, with Hillel-Erlanger, a film production company named as follows: Krishna Films (June), Films Psyché (Aug.), DELIA Films (Oct.), and finally Les Films DH (Mar. 1917).
Produces Edmond Van Daele's *La Lumière du cœur* (July–Oct.; p.p. Oct. 2).
Directs *Les Sœurs ennemies* (Sept.; p.p. Mar. 23, 1917). Starring Suzanne Desprès.

1917 Joins the Société des auteurs de films (SAF).
Serves as treasurer of SAF 1919–1942.
Directs *Géo le mystérieux* (or "La Vraie Richesse") (May; p.p. Oct. 1).
Attends Diaghilev's *Ballets russes* (May).
Directs *Dans l'Ouragan de la vie* (or *Vénus Victrix*) (July; p.p. Sept. 14).
Publishes her first known article on the cinema, "Mise-en-scène," *Le Film*, no. 87 (Nov. 12).
Directs *Âmes de fous* starring Ève Francis (winter 1917–18, p.p. Oct. 26, 1918).
Meets film critic Louis Delluc, Francis's fiancé.

1918 Directs *Trois Pantins pour une poupée* (short cinematic divertissements).
Publishes second known cinema article, "Où sont les interprètes?" (Where are the actors?), *Le Film*, no. 133–34 (Oct. 14).
Armistice; war ends (Nov. 11).
Directs *Le Bonheur des autres* (U.S. p.p. March; France p.p. Oct. 31).

1919 Sets up distribution office in New York.
Directs *La Cigarette* (Mar.–July, p.p. Oct. 10).
Directs *La Fête espagnole* (Aug.–Sept. 1919; p.p. May 4, 1920).
Directs *Malencontre* (Dec. 1919–Feb. 1920, p.p. Nov. 26, 1920).

1920 Travels to New York "to study the working methods" of U.S. directors.
Meets with D. W. Griffith (Oct.).
Directs *La Belle Dame sans merci* (April; p.p. Apr. 22, 1921).

1921 Assists in establishing Club des amis du septième art (CASA) with Ricciotto Canudo (Apr. 18).
Meets Marie-Anne Colson-Malleville.
La Mort du soleil (p.p. Feb. 17, 1922).

1922 Cofounds and serves as secretary of the Club français du cinéma (CFC).
Legal separation or divorce from Albert Dulac (Feb. 9).
Directs *Werther* (unfinished).
Directs six-part newsreel series *La Femme au travail* or *Jenny l'ouvrière* for "Le Concours de la jeune fille la plus méritante" (p.p. June 7).
Attends 1st Congrès du cinéma-éducateur (one of many attended through the 1930s).
Lectures regularly on cinema in France and abroad (Belgium, Scotland, Spain, Switzerland, 1922–38).
La Souriante Madame Beudet (p.p. June 1923).

1923 *Gossette* (six-episode *ciné-roman*, p.p. Dec. 28).

Adapts script for René Le Somptier's *La Porteuse de pain* (1923), based on Xavier de Montépin and Jules Dornay's play of same title (1889).

1924 Cofounds and serves as treasurer for the Ciné Club de France (CCF, union of CASA and CFC).

Le Diable dans la ville (Mar.–Apr.; p.p. Jan. 30, 1925).

Exhibits scripts, photos, set décor, and optical innovations, such as leses and prisms, at the l'exposition "l'art dans le cinéma français," at the Musée Galliera.

Lecture "Les Procédés expressifs du cinéma" at Musée Galliera (June 17, Cinéma du Colisée).

Publishes "Les Procédés expressifs du cinématographe," *Cinémagazine*, nos. 27–29 (July).

1925 Joins the Section française de l'internationale ouvrière (SFIO).

Âme d'artiste (Oct.–Feb. p.p. Nov. 6, 1925).

Lecture "Arts contre le Cinéma" at Club du Faubourg (Apr. 2–4).

Publishes "L'Essence du cinéma, l'idée visuelle," *Cahiers du Mois*, no. 16/17 (1925).

La Folie des vaillants (Jun.–Aug., p.p. Apr. 2, 1926).

Presents *La Folie des vaillants* at L'Exposition internationale des Arts Décoratifs (Oct.).

1926 Lecture "Les esthétique et entraves du cinéma" at Théâtre du Vieux Colombier (Feb. 6).

Lecture "Rythmes, esthétiques, entraves" at Robert de Jarville's Tréteau Latin (Mar. 12).

Works as film critic and runs film column "Le Cinéma est un art nouveau" for Marguerite Durand's feminist journal, *La Fronde*. Projects the idea of creating a film museum with Durand.

Antoinette Sabrier (Jul.–Oct. 1926; p.p. Jan. 20, 1928).

1927 Publishes first and sole issue of the journal *Schémas*, a forum for the defense of a "pure cinema" (Feb.).

Publishes "Du Sentiment à la ligne," *Schémas*, no. 1 (Feb.).

Publishes articles for *La Fronde*, "Quelques réflexions sur le Congrès international du cinématographe" (June 3).

Directs *L'Invitation au voyage* (Oct.; p.p. Nov. 29, 1927).

Publishes "Les Esthétiques, les entraves, la cinégraphie intégrale," *L'Art cinématographique*, vol. 2 (Paris: Librairie Félix Alcan).

Supervises *Mon Paris* (July).

Directs *La Coquille et le clergyman* (Jul.–Sept.; p.p. Feb. 9, 1928).

1928 Riot sparked by members of Surrealist group at the outset of film's public premiere at the Studio des Ursulines (Feb. 9).

Lecture at ciné-club of Geneva on *La Coquille* (*Close-Up*, June).

Creates filmic decor for Sylio Lazzari's opera *La Tour de feu* (Jan. 6).

La Princesse Mandane (based on Pierre Benoit's *L'Oublié*) (p.p. Nov. 23).

Publishes "Films visuels et anti-visuels," *Le Rouge et le Noir* (July).

1929 Directs 3 "abstract'" films (premiere: *L'Œil de Paris*):
Étude cinégraphique sur une arabesque or *Arabesque* (p.p. April 12).
Disque 957 (p.p. May 19).
Thèmes et variations (p.p. Dec. 9).
Writes novelization of Kurt Bernhardt's film *Les Bêtes humaines* (1929) which premiered with *Arabesque*.
Named Chevalier de la Legion d'Honneur (Knight of the Legion of Honor); promoted to officer (1937).
"Technical advisor" of the *Ligue de Noir et Blanc* (April) alongside Jarville. Meeting dedicated to presentation of Vertov's "kino-eye" theories.
Cofounds with Robert de Jarville the Fédération des ciné-clubs de la langue Française (Oct.–Nov.) and presides over the subsequently named Fédération française des ciné-clubs (1930).

1930 Directs six short musical films or "disques illustrées" for Columbia: *Autrefois . . . aujourd'hui*, *Celles qui s'en font*, *Ceux qui ne s'en font pas*, *Danses espagnoles*, *Jour de fête*, and *Un Peu de Rêve sur le Faubourg* (Isis Films).
Launches independent production company L'Essor cinématographique français with Robert Boudrioz (ca. Oct.).
Hired as artistic director at Gaumont-Franco-Films-Aubert (August 1930), where she supervises numerous films in France and Germany, including *Le Valse d'amour* (1930), *Bombance* (1931), *Le Picador* (1932).
Directs *Les 24 Heures du Mans* (1930), the first of several newsreels and documentaries, including *La Fée du logis* (1931), *Le Tour de France* (1932), *Le Port de Strasbourg* (1934).
Participates in the Congrès international du cinéma indépendant (CICI) on documentary in Brussels.

1931 Writes and directs documentary on Gaumont Palace *La Fée du Logis* (May, p.p. July).
Director of "script service" at Gaumont (June).
Responsible for directing *La Rue des Clarisses* (June–July).
Plans of a film company for the production of a "newsreel-style" film on the French Revolution.
Attends the Congrès national du cinématographe éducatif de Paris (Sept. 26–30) at the Institut international du cinéma éducateur (IICE).
Participates in the Congrès de Rome, Conseil international des femmes (CIF) (5–9 Oct.). Conférence du cinématographe et de la radiodiffusion. Conférence internationale de Rome at the Institut international du cinéma éducatif (IICE).
Publishes "Le Sens du cinéma," *Revue Internationale du Cinéma Éducateur* (Dec.).

1932 President of the cinema section of the Conseil national des femmes françaises (CNFF).
Participates in the Congrès de Rome, CIF.

Publishes "Le Cinéma d'avant-garde," in *Le Cinéma des origines à nos jours*, ed. Henri Fescourt (Paris: Cygne, 1932).
Directs theatrical comedy *Les Loups* for women's art group at Le Studio féminin (Oct. 9–15).
Member of Le Club de la belle perdrix for women gastronomists. Members include Marion Gilbert and Aurore Sand. Guest speaker Lucie Delarue-Mardrus. Soroptomist club, Club Lucie Derain.

1932–35 Founds and directs Gaumont newsreel company France-Actualités.

1934 Lecture on the international role of newsreels at the Congrès de Rome, CIF. (Congrès international du cinéma d'enseignement et d'éducation, IICE-SDN) (Apr. 19–25; source: B.F., "Le Cinéma éducatif au Congrès de Rome," *Excelsior*, May 3).
Publishes "La Portée éducative et sociale des actualités," *Revue Internationale du Cinéma Éducateur* (Aug.).

1935 Participates in the Congrès de Bruxelles, CIF.
Directs montage documentary *Le Cinéma au service de l'histoire* for the opening of the all-newsreel cinema *Actual*, rue du Faubourg Saint-Antoine (Oct. 30).
"Abandons all work" as a filmmaker/director for five months (Sept. 1935–Feb. 1936) due to ongoing health concerns.
Serves as artistic and technical advisor at Gaumont (1935–1942). Artistic advisor (Sept. 1935–Feb. 1936). Technical advisor (Mar. 1936–Aug. 1939). Technical director (Sept. 1939–Jun. 1940). Technical advisor (July 1940–42).

1936 President of the cinema committee, CIF.
Conceives of film project on "L'Effort de la femme dans le monde" (Women's effort in the world) under CIF and the League of Nations (Jan. 1936; source: Laura C. Dreyfus-Barney to GD, letter Jan. 8, 1936, FGD 983).
Founding board member of the Cinémathèque française.
Director of the cinema section of Mai '36 cultural movement.
Collaborates with Robert Talpain and Marceau Pivert at the Service cinématographique de la Fédération de la Seine et les actualités prolétariennes.
Codirects with François Moch and Jean Brérault Mai '36 documentary, *Le Retour à la vie*.
Participates in elaboration of project that becomes Jean Renoir's *La Marseillaise* (1938), under the patronage of La Comité de coordination composed of Mai '36, Ciné liberté and the CGT.

1937 Promoted to officer of the Legion of Honor.
Works with Robert Talpain at L'Equipe: Société Coopérative de production de films (1937–39).
Writes for the journals *Le Populaire*, *L'Almanach Populaire*, and *Le Travailleur du film* (1937–38).

French assessor on Comité consultatif pour l'enseignement de la Société des nations (July).

1938 Participates in Congrès d'Edimbourg, CIF.

President of the directors section of the Syndicat des techniciens de la production cinématographique (Feb. 1938–42).

Project with Jean Benoît-Lévy, "Les Femmes et le cinéma."

1938–39 Film critic for various newspapers, including *Les Heures de Paris* (1931; 1937–39) and *Le Pays socialiste* (May–June 1939; source FGD 4359 press review).

1938–41 Elaborates several documentary projects and scripts for fiction films, including feature-length screenplay about Ève Lavallière.

Fiction film projects: "Bat d'af" (Morocco), and "Bimbecco" (Corsica), based on the novella *Colomba* by Prosper Merimée.

Drafts plan and questionnaire for CIF (ca. March 1938). Topics: (1) Facilitating the free circulation of educational films. (2) Raising the artistic and moral standard of spectacular productions. (3) Increasing the use of cinema in schools. (4) Creating special course of instruction. (5) List of films.

Lectures on the cinema on Radio Colonial Paris Mondial (1939), addressing cinema in Europe and amateur cinema.

1941 Vice president of film cooperative Les Artisans d'art du cinéma. Artistic director of production company Les Diffusions modernes with Jean Jay.

1942 Dies in Paris at age fifty-nine (July 20).

Service at the Église Saint François-de-Sales (Thursday, July 23, 9 a.m.).

Filmography

"Source" indicates the location of the best available print consulted. Data are assembled from film credits, archival records, and Dulac's own production files. Film lengths and release dates are from extant prints, and production files, supplemented by trade press listings and the following catalog sources: Henri Bousquet, *Catalogue Pathé des années 1896 à 1914* (Paris: Édition Henri Bousquet, 1993); Raymond Chirat, *Catalogue des films français de fiction de 1908 à 1918* (Paris: Cinémathèque française, Musée du cinéma, 1995); Raymond Chirat, with Roger Icart, *Catalogue des films français de long métrage. Films de fiction, 1919–1929* (Toulouse: Cinémathèque de Toulouse, 1984); and Henri Bousquet, *De Pathé frères à Pathé cinéma. Catalogue* (Paris: Édition Henri Bousquet, 1999).

All films were produced in France, unless otherwise noted. Films are organized by date of production; press screening and public premiere dates follow.

In certain cases, "working title" indicates a preliminary title. In a few cases, "alternate title" specifies an additional title under which the film appears to have been released. Similarly, "original length" refers to trade press listings; "alternate length" is used in a few cases where the film length listed in a report by Dulac differs significantly. Due to varying projection speeds, running time are approximate.

This filmography also includes a sample of Dulac's newsreels produced as director of France-Actualités (Gaumont), and programmed at the Musée d'Orsay (2005). Not included are films by other directors, but which Dulac produced (*La Lumière du cœur*, Van Daele, 1916); adapted for the screen (*La Porteuse du pain*, René Le Somptier, 1923); or supervised (e.g., *Mon Paris*, Albert Guyot, 1927; *Valse d'amour*, Wilhelm Thiele, 1930; *Bombance*, Pierre Billon, 1931; and *Le Picador*, Lucien Jacquelux, 1932).

Fiction Films

1916

Les Sœurs ennemies (The enemy sisters).
35mm, black and white. 765m, 38 min., 18 f/s.
Status: Lost.
Scriptwriter: Irène Hillel-Erlanger. Camera operator: Maurice Forster.
Découpage: Germaine Dulac and Irène Hillel-Erlanger.
Producer: DELIA Films. Distributor: Pathé Frères.
Starring Suzanne Desprès, Jacques Grétillat, Marguerite Véry, Renée Bartout, Laurette Caïra.
Premiere March 23, 1917.

1917

Géo le mystérieux (Géo the mysterious). Working title: *La Vraie Richesse* (True wealth).
35mm, black and white. 1242m, 61 min., 18 f/s.
Status: Lost.
Scriptwriter: Irène Hillel-Erlanger. Camera operator: Maurice Forster.
Producer: Les Films DH. Distributor: Cinématographes Harry.
Starring Jacques Grétillat, Jane Marken, Jacques Volnys, Rastrelli, Fred Jansene, Amaury, Tchan.
Press screening September 1, 1917. Premiere October 1, 1917.

Dans l'Ouragan de la vie (In the hurricane of life). Alternate title *Vénus Victrix*.
35mm, black and white. 1510m, 74 min., 18 f/s.
Status: Lost.
Adaptation: Germaine and Albert Dulac based on a poem, "Vénus Victrix," by Irène Hillel-Erlanger. Camera operator: Maurice Forster.
Producer: Les Films DH. Distributor: Cinématographes Harry.
Starring Stacia Napierkowska (Djali), Jacques Volnys (San Silvio), Yvonne de Villeroy (Régine Frény), Marcel Verdier (Bernard Belmont).
Press screening July 1917. Premiere September 14, 1917.

1918

Âmes de fous (Mad souls; ciné-roman in six episodes). Working titles: "Traqueurs de joie" (Pleasure seekers) and "Le Mystère du château maudit" (The mystery of the cursed castle).
35mm, black and white. 3874m, 190 min., 18 f/s. Alternate length 3775m, FGD 4339.
Status: Lost.
Scriptwriter: Germaine Dulac. Ciné-roman adapted by Guy de Téramond, published simultaneously in *Le Petit Journal*. Camera operator: Maurice Forster.
Producer: Les Films DH. Distributor: Cinématographes Harry.
Starring Ève Francis, Sylvio de Pedrelli, Jacques Volnys, Suzanne Parisys, André Séchan, Gastao Roxo/Polonio, Djemil Anik.
Press screening August 1918. Premiere October 26, 1918.

Trois Pantins pour une poupée (Three puppets for a doll). "Divertissements cinématographiques" (cinematic amusements used as entr'actes).
35mm, black and white. Unknown length and duration.
Status: Lost.
Scriptwriter: Germaine Dulac.

Le Bonheur des autres (The happiness of others).
35mm, black and white. Unknown length and duration.
Status: Lost.
Scriptwriter: Germaine Dulac. Camera operator: J.-A. Creuzy.
Producer: Les Films DH. Distributor: World Made Brady/Cinématographes Harry.
Starring Ève Francis (France Doré), Ginette Darnys (Ginette Millery), Viviane Vogg (Guy Middleton), Louis Bourny (Maître Beauchastel), Teddy (Teddy Beauchastel).
Premiere March 1919 (New York); October 31 (France).

1919

La Cigarette.
35mm, black and white. 1156m, 56 min. (original 1400m, 69 min.), 18 f/s. Alternate length 1900m, FGD 4340.
Source: Cinémathèque royale de Belgique.
Scriptwriters: Jacques de Javon (Jacques de Baroncelli) and Germaine Dulac. Camera operator: Louis Chaix.
Producer: Film d'art. Distributor: Agence générale cinématographique.
Starring Gabriel Signoret (Pierre Guérande), Andrée Brabant (Denise Guérande), Jules Raucourt (Maurice).
Press screening September 8, 1919. Premiere October 10, 1919 (Salle-Marivaux).

La Fête espagnole (The Spanish fiesta).
35mm, black and white, tinting and toning. 170m (fragment), 8 min. (original 1671m, 82 min.), 18 f/s. Alternate length 710m, FGD 4340.
Source: Cinémathèque française.
Scriptwriter: Louis Delluc. Camera operator: Paul Parguel.
Producer: Louis Nalpas. Distributor: Union Eclair.
Starring Ève Francis (Soledad), Gaston Modot (Réal), Jean Toulout (Miguelan), Anna Gray (old Paguien).
Press screening March 31, 1920. Premiere May 4, 1920.

1920

Malencontre (Misfortune).
35mm, black and white. 1588m, 78 min. (18 f/s).
Status: Lost.
Scriptwriter: Germaine Dulac, based on the 1910 novel by Guy Chantepleure (pseudonym for Jeanne Dussap). Camera operator: Georges Asselin.
Producer: Les Films DH. Distributor: Établissements Louis Aubert.

Starring Jacques Roussel (Patrice de Malencontre), Djemil Anik (Brinda Savage), Jeanne Brindeau (Marquise de Malencontre), France Dhélia (Flavie Clairande), Seigneur (Gladys Savage).
Press screening October 12, 1920. Premiere November 26, 1920.

La Belle Dame sans merci (The beautiful woman without mercy).
35mm, black and white, tinting and toning. 1781m, 80 min. (original 1935m, 95 min.), 18 f/s. Alternately listed as 2200m, FGD 4340.
Source: EYE Film Instituut Nederland (formerly Nederlands filmmuseum).
Adaptation: Germaine Dulac, based on an argument (premise) by Irène Hillel-Erlanger (April–May 1917). Camera operator: Jacques Oliver.
Producer: Les Films DH. Distributor: Agence générale cinématographique.
Starring Yolande Hillé, Tania Daleyme (Lola de Sandoval), Jean Toulout (Count Guy d'Amaury), Denise Lorys (Countess d'Amaury), Jean Tarride, Pierre Mareg, Lucien Glen, Louis Monfils.
Press screening March 8, 1921. Premiere April 22, 1921 (Salle Marivaux).

1921

La Mort du soleil (The death of the sun). Working title: "Le Fléau" (The scourge).
35mm, black and white. 1684m, 83 min. (original 1925m, 95 min.), 18 f/s. Alternate length 1700m, FGD 4339.
Source: Centre national de la cinématographie, Bois d'Arcy. Restored 1985.
Scriptwriter: André Legrand. Camera operator: Paul Parguel, Belval.
Producer: Les Films Legrand (with funding from the American Committee against Tuberculosis.) Distributor: Pathé/Agence Générale Cinématographique.
Starring André Nox (Lucien Faivre), Denise Lorys (Marthe Voisin), Louis Vonelly (Daniel Voisin), Régine Dumien (Jacqueline), Jeanne Bérangère, Jeanne Brindeau.
Press screening December 13, 1921. Premiere February 17, 1922 (Salle Marivaux).

1922

Werther (unfinished).
35mm, black and white. Unknown length and duration.
Status: Lost.
Scriptwriter: Germaine Dulac adapted from the novel *Die Leiden des jungen Werthers* (*The Sorrows of Young Werther*) by J. W. von Goethe. Camera operator: Belval.
Producer: Les Films DH.
Starring Gabriel de Gravonne (Werther), Denise Lorys (Charlotte), J.-David Evremond (Albert).
Unreleased.

La Femme au travail (Women at work). Alternate title *Jenny l'ouvrière* (Jenny the worker).
35mm, black and white. Five of six completed newsreel shorts. Each approx. 120m, 5 min., 18 f/s. Total 600m, 30 min.

Status: Lost.
Scriptwriter: Germaine Dulac.
Producer: Triomphe Films.
Starring Musidora, Suzanne Bianchetti, France Dhélia, Denise Lorys, Marthe Régnier, Yvette Andréyor.
Premiere June 7, 1922 (Palais de la mutualité).

La Souriante Madame Beudet (*The Smiling Madame Beudet*).
35mm, black and white. 773m, 38 min., 18 f/s. Alternate length 814m, FGD 4326.
Source: EYE Film Instituut Nederland (Swiss print: French/German intertitles).
Scriptwriter: André Obey, based on the play by Denys Amiel and André Obey. Camera operator: A. Merrin. Set designer: M. Delattre.
Producer: Charles Delac and Marcel Vandal (Film d'art). Distributor: Aubert.
Starring Germaine Dermoz (Madame Beudet), Alexandre Arquillère (Monsieur Beudet), Jean d'Yd (Monsieur Lebas), Madeleine Guitty (Madame Lebas), Yvette Grisier (maidservant), Raoul Paoli (tennis player), Thirard (auditor).
Press screening January/February 1923. Premiere June 19, 1923.

1923

Gossette (ciné-roman in six episodes).
35mm, black and white, tinted. 5477m, 268 min. (original 8200m, 403 min.), 18 f/s. Alternate length 7200m, FGD 4340.
Source: Cinémathèque française. Restored 1987 (Renée Lichtig).
Scriptwriter: Germaine Dulac, based on the novel by Charles Vayre. Published in *L'Écho de Paris* (1923). Camera operator: Henri Stuckert, Albert Cohendy. Set designer: Jean Perrier.
Assistant Director: Marie-Anne Malleville.
Producer: Société des cinéromans. Distributor: Pathé-Consortium.
Starring Régine Bouet (Gossette), Jean-David Evremond (Robert de Tayrac), Monique Chrysès (Lucienne Dornay), Jeanne Brindeau (Mme de Savières), Maurice Schutz (M. de Savières), Georges Charlia (Phillipe de Savières), Jean d'Yd (Master Varadès, the notary), Mario Nathasio (Andriano), Paul Menant (the chauffeur), Bernard (father Bonnefoy), Vialar (son Bonnefoy), Madeleine Guitty (Mme Bonnefoy).
Six episodes (1000–1200m each): 1. *La Nuit tragique* (55 min.), 2. *Le Revenant* (43 min.), 3. *Face à face* (50 min.), 4. *L'Embûche* (45 min.), 5. *Les lettres volées* (41 min.), 6. *La Vengeance du mort* (34 min.).
Press screening November 21, 1923. Premiere December 28, 1923 (Salle Marivaux).

1924

Le Diable dans la ville (The devil in the city).
35mm, black and white. 1629m, 80 min., 20 f/s. Alternate length 1800m, FGD 4339.
Source: Cinémathèque française.
Scriptwriter: Jean-Louis Bouquet. Artistic Director: Louis Nalpas. Camera operator: Henri J. Stuckert. Set designer: Marco de Gastyne.

Assistant: Marie-Anne Malleville.

Producer: Société des cinéromans. Distributor: Pathé-Consortium.

Starring Jacqueline Blanc (Blanche), Michèle Clairfont (Rose), Léon Mathot (Marc Herner, philosopher), René Donnio (the illuminated one), Albert Mayer (Alchemist Master Ludivigo), R. Vetty (Mr. Pattaus, the Mayor), Pierre de Ramey (Captain of the Guard), Emile Saint-Ober (a crazy person), Mario Nasthasio (a crazy person), Jean-François Martial, Jacques Vandenne, Canelas, Bernard, Lucien Bataille, Emilien Richaud (a crazy person).

Press screening October 29, 1924. Premiere January 30, 1925.

1925

Âme d'artiste (An artist's soul; UK release title: *The Heart of an Actress*).

35mm, black and white. 2032m, 100 min., 18 f/s. Alternate length 2300m, FGD 4339.

Source: Cinémathèque française.

Scriptwriter: Germaine Dulac and Alexander Volkoff based on the play "Opad" by Christian Molbech. Camera operator: Jules Kruger, Nicolas Toporkov. Set designer: Alexander Lochakoff.

Assistant Director: Marie-Anne Malleville.

Producer: Ciné-France-Film (Consortium Westi). Distributor: Pathé-Consortium.

Starring Ivan Pétrovich (Herbert Campbell, poet), Nicolas Koline (Morris, Helen's adoptive father), Mabel Poulton (Helen Taylor), Yvette Andréyor (Edith Campbell, poet's wife), Henry Houry (Lord Stamford, Mylord), Jeanne Bérangère (Edith's mother), Félix Barré (Phillips, theater director), Gina Manès (actress), Charles Vanel (actor).

Press screening June 23, 1925. (Salle Marivaux) Premiere November 6, 1925.

La Folie des vaillants (The folly of the brave).

35mm, black and white, tinted. 844m, 46 min. (original 1250m, 61 min.), 18 f/s.

Source: Centre national de la cinématographie, Bois d'Arcy. Restored 1989.

Scriptwriter: Germaine Dulac, based on the novella "Makar Chudra" (Radda) by Maxim Gorky. Camera operator: Paul Parguel and Maurice Forster.

Producer: Cinégraphistes français. Distributor: Mappemonde Film.

Starring Raphaël Liévin (Loïko Sodar), Lia Loo (Radda), Castelluci (Lenka).

Press screening December 17, 1925. Premiere April 2, 1926 (Salle du Colisée).

1926

Antoinette Sabrier.

35mm, black and white, tinted. 1712m, 73 min., 20 f/s (original 2300m, 98 min., 18 f/s).

Source: Cinémathèque française. Restored 1998.

Script and adaptation: Germaine Dulac, based on the play by Romain Coolus. Ciné-roman published by René Jeanne (1928). Camera operator: Henri Stuckert, Georges Daret. Set designer: G. Silvagni and Georges Quenu.

Assistant: Marie-Anne Malleville.

Artistic director: Louis Nalpas.
Producer: Société des cinéromans. Distributor: Pathé-Consortium.
Starring Ève Francis (Antoinette Sabrier), Gabriel Gabrio (Germain Sabrier), Jean Toulout (Jamagne), Yvette Armell (Hélène Doreuil), Paul Guidé (René Dangenne), Paul Menant (Chartrain), Maurice Cervières (Gaston Doreuil, Mr. Sabrier's advisor), Ashida (the dancer), Lou Davy.
Press screening April 13, 1927. Premiere January 20, 1928.

1927

L'Invitation au voyage (Invitation to a voyage).
35mm, black and white, tinted. 797m, 39 min., 18 f/s.
Source: EYE Film Instituut Nederland. Restored 1999.
Scriptwriter: Germaine Dulac, inspired by the poem of Charles Baudelaire. Camera operator: Paul Guichard. Set designer: Cesaré Silvagni, Hugo Squarciafico.
Assistants: Marie-Anne Malleville, Louis Ronjat.
Producer: Germaine Dulac. Distributor: Productions Natan.
Starring Emma Gynt (woman), Raymond Dubreuil (marine), Robert Mirfeuil (partier), Paul Lorbert (sailor), Tania Daleyme (girl), Djemil Anik (dancer), Lucien Bataille (drummer).
Premiere November 1927.

La Coquille et le clergyman (*The Seashell and the Clergyman*).
35mm, black and white. 812m, 39 min., 30 sec., 18 f/s.
Source: Light Cone Film and EYE Film Instituut Nederland. Restored 2004.
Scriptwriter: Antonin Artaud. Camera operator: Paul Guichard.
Producer/Assistant director: Louis Ronjat.
Starring Alexander Allin (the clergyman), Génica Athanasiou (the woman), Lucien Bataille (the officer).
Pre-screening October 25 and December 10, 1927 (CCF). Premiere February 9, 1928 (Studio des Ursulines).

1928

La Princesse Mandane. Working title: *L'Oublié* (The forgotten one).
35 mm, black and white. 1775m, 74 min., 20 f/s. Original length 2400m, FGD 4339.
Source: Centre national de la cinématographie, Bois d'Arcy.
Scriptwriter: Germaine Dulac, based on the novel *L'Oublié* (The forgotten one) by Pierre Benoît. Camera operator: Paul Guichard, Lucien Bellavoine. Set designer: Silvagni.
Producer: Alex Nalpas. Distributor: Films Louis Aubert.
Starring Edmonde Guy (Mandane), Mona Goya (Simoun), Groza Wesco (Lily de Thorigny), Ernest Van Duren (Étienne Pindère), Jacques Arnne (Gerys-Kahn), Paul Lorbert, Yvonne Legeay, Valenti Colino (Azyme Electropoulos), Sylvie Mai (Anna), Gérard de Wibo (Michel Voraguine), Geneviève Cargèse, Christian Gérard.
Press screening March 15, 1928. Premiere November 23, 1928.

Abstract Films or "Technical Studies"

1929

Disque 957 (Record 957).
35mm, black and white, silent. 97m, 6 min., 18 f/s (original 16 f/s).
Source: EYE Film Instituut Nederland.
Scriptwriter: Germaine Dulac (based on Preludes 5 and 6 of Frédéric Chopin). Camera operator: Alfred Guichard. Producer: Germaine Dulac.
Premiere May 19, 1929 (l'Œil de Paris).

Étude cinégraphique sur une arabesque (Cinegraphic study of an arabesque). Alternate title *Arabesque*.
35mm, black and white, silent. 140m, 7 min., 18 f/s (original 16 f/s).
Source: Cinémathèque française, Light Cone Film.
Scriptwriter: Germaine Dulac, based on *Deux arabesques* (Two arabesques, 1888–91) of Claude Debussy.
Starring Marie-Anne Malleville.
Producer: Germaine Dulac.
Premiere April 12, 1929 (l'Œil de Paris).

Thèmes et variations. Alternate title *Thème et variation*. Working title: "Thème visual et variation cinématographique."
35mm, black and white, silent. 190m, 9 min., 18 f/s (original 16 f/s).
Source: Cinémathèque française, Light Cone Film.
Scriptwriter: Germaine Dulac (based on "classical melodies" incl. Maurice Ravel).
Producer: Germaine Dulac.
Starring Lilian Constantini (dancer).
Premiere December 9, 1929 (l'Œil de Paris).

"Films musicaux" (musical films) or "Disques illustrées" (record illustrations)

1930

Autrefois . . . aujourd'hui (In the old days . . . nowadays).
35mm, black and white, sound. 177m, 7 min., 20 f/s (original 192m, 8 min.).
Source: Centre national de la cinématographie, Bois d'Arcy.
Scriptwriter: Germaine Dulac. Camera operator: Paul Guichard. Assistant: Marie-Anne Malleville.
Producer: Isis Films.
Starring Lilian Constantini, Reix Darcourt (dancers).
Records:
"Dis-moi tu, dis-moi toi" (4 min.), Columbia 1929 (author: Johann Strauss).
"Smiles, then, kisses" or "Facilita" (4 min.), Columbia 1929 (author: John Hartmann and Jack Mackintosh).

"Quatre et Trois" (4 min.), Columbia 1929 (author: Marius Brun).
Source: Special thanks to Alain Carou (BNF) for locating the original gramophone records.

Celles qui s'en font (Those [women] who worry).
35mm, black and white, sound. 130m, 6 min. (variable speed: 18 f/s for "Toute seule," 20 f/s for "À la dérive.") Original length: 146m.
Source: Lobster Films, Paris.
Scriptwriter: Germaine Dulac. Camera operator: Jean Jouannetaud.
Producer: Isis Films.
Starring Lilian Constantini, Georges Vallée.
Records:
"Toute seule" (4 min.), Parlophone 1928 (author unknown; singer Fréhel).
"À la dérive" (4 min.), Pathé 1927 (Daniderff; singer Georgette Kerlor).
Source: Bibliothèque nationale de France.

Ceux qui ne s'en font pas (Those who don't worry).
35mm, black and white, sound. 145m, 6 min., 20, then 17 f/s.
Source: Centre national de la cinématographie, Bois d'Arcy.
Scriptwriter: Germaine Dulac.
Producer: Isis Films.
Records:
"Si j'étais chef de gare" (4 min.), Columbia 1928 (from the operetta Kadubec by Maurice Yvain and André Barde; singer Georges Milton).
"Sur le Pont d'Avignon" (4 min.), Columbia 1928 (author unknown).
Source: Bibliothèque nationale de France.

Danses espagnoles (Spanish dances).
35mm, black and white, sound. 160m, 7 min. (original 146m, 6 min.), 20, then 21 f/s.
Source: Lobster Films.
Scriptwriter: Germaine Dulac. Camera operator: Jean Jouannetaud.
Producer: Isis Films.
Starring Carmencita Garcia (dancer), Marie-Anne Malleville (spectator).
Records:
"Cordoba" (4 min.), Gramophone 1926 (author: Isaac Albéniz).
"Sévillanas" (4 min.), Columbia 1928 (author: Isaac Albéniz).
Source: Bibliothèque nationale de France.

Jour de fête (Holiday).
35mm, black and white, sound. 167m, 7 min., 22 f/s.
Status: Lost.
Scriptwriter: Germaine Dulac.
Producer: Isis Films.

Records:
"Cherbourg"; "Le Caïd" (authors unknown).

Un Peu de rêve sur le faubourg (A little dreaming in the boroughs).
35mm, black and white, sound. 229m, 11 min., 22 f/s.
Source: Centre national de la cinématographie, Bois d'Arcy.
Scriptwriter: Germaine Dulac. Camera operator: Paul and Alfred Guichard.
Producer: Isis Films.
Records:
"Louise" (4 min.), Columbia 1927 (author: Gustave Charpentier).
"Paysage" (4 min.), Columbia 1928 (author: Reynaldo Hahn; singer Damia).
"Heure exquise" (4 min.), Columbia 1928 (author: Reynaldo Hahn; singer Damia).
Source: Bibliothèque nationale de France.

Documentaries

1935

Le Cinéma au service de l'histoire (Cinema in the service of history).
35mm, black and white, synchronized sound. 1500m, 51 min., 24 f/s.
Source: Pathé Archives Gaumont.
Script/Montage: Germaine Dulac. Voice-over commentary: René Celier.
Producer: Georges Macé, Albert Thierry (Cinéma Actual).
Newsreel footage from Éclair Journal, France-Actualités, Musée d'art et d'histoire, Pathé Journal.
Premiere October 30, 1935.

1936

Le Retour à la vie (The return to life).
35mm, black and white, synchronized sound. 305m, 11 min., 24 f/s.
Source: Centre national de la cinématographie, Bois d'Arcy.
Codirectors: Jean Brérault, François Moch.
Producer: Union des techniciens socialistes (UTS).

Newsreels

1932–34

Hundreds of short subjects.
35mm, black and white, synchronized sound.
Source: Gaumont Pathé Archives. Producer: France-Actualités-Gaumont

Selected titles (screened at "Germaine Dulac, au-delà des impressions," Musée d'Orsay, Paris, June 2005, courtesy of Gaumont Pathé Archives):
"France. Chronique parisienne. La nouvelle mode" (France. Parisian chronicle: the new fashion), October 5, 1932, 2 min., 24 sec.

"Paris. La fête des Catherinettes" (Paris. Catherinettes Day) December 5, 1932, 1 min., 32 sec.
"Paris. Les femmes manifestent aussi" (Paris. The women protest too), February 24, 1933, 3 min., 59 sec.
"Dijon. Enquêtes et contre enquêtes" (Dijon. Investigations and counterinvestigations), April 13, 1934, 1 min., 39 sec.
"Semaine du 6 février (obsèques)" (Week of February 6, funerals), February 23, 1934, 1 min., 13 sec.
"Cinéma d'animation et histoire. À propos des émeutes du 6 février 1934" (Animated and historical films. On the February 6, 1934 protests), April 13, 1934, 2 min., 39 sec.
"Paris. M. Roger Vercel . . . Goncourt," December 14, 1934, 1 min., 11 sec.
"Paris. Les mutilés de guerre" (Paris. War mutilees), December 14, 1934, 41 sec.

See also Éclair newsreel: "Charles Delac sur la liberté de la presse filmée." May 17, 1935. 1 min., 25 sec. (subject: Germaine Dulac and France-Actualités).

Notes

Abbreviations

2°	Folio size
4°	Quarto size
8°	Octavo size
BiFi	Bibliothèque du film, La Cinémathèque française, Paris
BNF	Bibliothèque nationale de France, Paris
BNF-ASP	Bibliothèque nationale de France, Département des arts du spectacle
CRH	Fonds de la Commission de Recherche Historique de la Cinémathèque française, BiFi
Écrits	Germaine Dulac, *Écrits sur le cinéma (1919–1937)*, preface by Prosper Hillairet (Paris: Paris expérimental, 1994)
FGD	Fonds Germaine Dulac, Bibliothèque du film
OURS	L'Office universitaire de recherche socialiste, Paris

Notes to Introduction

1. Sandy Flitterman-Lewis's insightful dissertation and resulting book, *To Desire Differently*, addresses the work of French filmmakers Germaine Dulac, Marie Epstein, and Agnès Varda. Her book played a crucial role in introducing Dulac in the United States. See also T. Williams, "Entretien avec Sandy Flitterman-Lewis."

2. The undated sixty-page manuscript, compiled from Dulac's lectures and articles by Marie-Anne Colson-Malleville and personal assistant Anita Estève, treats different phases and preoccupations of the filmmaker's work. GD, "Projet de livre sur le cinema," FGD 1371.

3. T. Williams, ed., "Germaine Dulac, au-delà des impressions."

4. Ford, "Germaine Dulac." Flitterman-Lewis, "Heart of the Avant-Garde." See also Flitterman-Lewis, *To Desire Differently*, 47–97. Exceptions include my essay on Dulac's prewar journalism, "La Naissance d'une avant-gardiste, 1906–1913," and Valérie Vignaux's article on the archive as object, "Les Papiers intimes de Germaine Dulac ou le corps de l'archive."

5. GD, "Les Arts contre le cinéma." See also "Coupures de presse," 1923–26, FGD 4343.

Chapter 1. "How I Became a Film Director"

1. Pierre de Coulevain is a pseudonym of Jeanne Philomène Laperche, author of the theosophical novel *Le Roman* Merveilleux (1913). GD, "Comment je suis," 44.

2. Ford, "Germaine Dulac,"4.

3. Madeleine Claire Waymel Saisset-Schneider (GD's mother) to Maggie Vanves. December 18, [1900], FGD 4534; Notes of Madeleine Saisset-Schneider, n.d., FGD 4536; "Faire-part du décès de Madeleine Saisset-Schneider," May 14, 1918, FGD 4537; Sister Marie-Lucie Saignol to GD, October 14, 1900, FGD 4528. Flitterman-Lewis, *To Desire Differently*, 48.

4. See Desclaux, "Nos Metteurs en scène."

5. The Schneider legacy was so significant that Dulac's paternal grandfather, Julien Aristide Adelaïde Saisset-Schneider (née Saisset, d. 1892), added his wife's last name to his own, making Dulac's father the firstborn Saisset-Schneider. Dulac's relationship to her family heritage was not one of simple awareness but rather one of long-held fascination, reflection, and deliberation. Despite her political views, she was sensitive to this background, drawing up an elaborate family tree going back to the thirteenth century. "Généalogie en ligne directe de Charlotte, Elisabeth, Germaine Saisset-Schneider [ca. 1922]," FGD 4542.

6. Winock, *La Belle Époque*, 111–13.

7. "Papiers du lieutenant-général Antoine-Virgile Saisset-Schneider (pseud.), homme politique dont *Le National* [de 1834], 28 juillet 1847," FGD 4544.

8. For more on the life of Charles Schneider, see Dominique Schneidre, *Fortune de mère*.

9. Winock, *La Belle Époque*, 111.

10. These handwritten documents are cataloged in FGD. See "Poèmes," FGD 4436; "Projets, notes et pensées," FGD 4493; and "Compositions littéraires scolaires, 1901–1902," FGD 4497.

11. Madeleine Saisset-Schneider to GD, July 14, 1904, FGD 4519. See also *Exposition des primitifs français au palais du Louvre*. The exhibit included works of the French primitifs, among them Nicolas Froment, Jean Clouet, and Jean d'Orléans.

12. Albert Dulac to GD, January 4, 1915, FGD 2350.

13. See chapter 2. GD, "Trois Rencontres avec Loïe Fuller."

14. GD, "La Musique du silence," *Écrits*, 106–8. This "crisis of the word" and penchant for "silence" and anti-ventriloquist "wordlessness" can be seen in numerous arts including modern pantomime and symbolist theater of the Belle Époque. (See T. Williams, "The 'Silent' Arts.")

15. GD, "Comment je suis," 43.

16. Interview with Mme Djemil Anik, CRH 030, 1. In turn-of-the-century France, music remained very much a live activity. During this period (phonographic recordings were limited to brief extracts, generally of less than three minutes), the pastimes

of the well-to-do classes usually entailed attending concerts in the grand concert halls of Paris or of playing and composing airs oneself.

17. Interview with Mme Djemil Anik, CRH 030, 1.

18. See also Tambling, "Power of Emotion."

19. Fescourt, *La Foi et les montagnes*, 295–96.

20. See Dauer, *Richard Wagner's Art in Its Relation to Buddhist Thought*.

21. For a more in-depth analysis of the Chopin and Georges Sand–inspired *Disque 957*, see T. Williams, "Germaine Dulac."

22. In 1915, writing from the battlefront, her husband Albert expressed his nostalgia for her piano rendition of "Claire de Lune," a piece that figures later in *La Souriante Madame Beudet* (1923). Albert Dulac to GD, January 4, 1915, FGD 2350.

23. GD, "Comment je suis," 42.

24. Desclaux, "Nos Metteurs en scène," 7.

25. GD, "Comment je suis," 42.

26. "Biofilmographie," FGD 4327, 1. The document contains annotations handwritten by Dulac.

27. Jeanne, *Cinéma 1900*, 120. According to Jeanne, the former location of Méliès's theater, which he purchased from Houdini's widow in 1888, was stamped out by the extension of boulevard Haussmann in 1923. He notes "Now there is no number 8 boulevard des Italiens, which begins with number 16 on the even side since in 1923 the buildings, numbered from 2 to 14, were leveled when boulevard Haussmann was pierced just below rue Taitbout in the direction of boulevard Montmartre, substituting what was one of the liveliest areas of the neighborhood with a great soulless void" (119).

28. GD, "L'Essence du cinéma," 64. GD, "Le Cinéma d'avant-garde, 358.

29. Lazareff, "Madame Germaine Dulac n'aimait pas le cinéma!"

30. Ibid.

31. GD to Madeleine Saisset-Schneider, July 14, 1904, FGD 4520. While the L'Opéra de Paris entertained an aristocratic and *nouveau riche* audience, the more middle-class Opéra comique gradually drew its audience from "more common" social strata. Barbier, *La Vie quotidienne*, 142–45.

32. Dauphin, "Les Femmes seules," 526. In "Sortir," Michelle Perrot, on the other hand, points to some of the opposing pressures that help explain the institution's early hold on women like Dulac: "Due to the complex ties between discipline and duty, sociability and rights, practices and language, religions pressed like a lead weight on the shoulders of women, although they also brought consolation and aid" (567).

33. Sister Saignol to GD, September 3, 1901, FGD 4258; Sister Saignol to GD, April 19, 1903, FGD 4528.

34. See Sister Saignol to GD, 1901–4, FGD 4528.

35. Winock, *La Belle Époque*, 166.

36. Mayeur, "L'Éducation des filles," 295. See also Winock, *La Belle Époque*, 166. (Cf. Molière's *Femmes savantes* [1672], a ubiquitous nineteenth-century reference exemplifying the inutility and dangers of educating women.)

37. De Giorgio, "La Bonne Catholique," 217.

38. Sister Saignol to GD, April 8, 1901, FGD 4528.

39. Ibid., April 8, 1901; October 21, 1902, and December 16, 1902; January 2, 1903; January 29, 1903.

40. Ibid., August 1, 1903.

41. Ibid., June 29, 1904.

42. Ibid.

43. In a CRH interview in 1946, Marie-Anne Colson-Malleville, responding alongside Dulac's actress Djemil Anik to a question from Musidora on *La Coquille et le Clergyman*, while denying any anticlerical message in the film, affirmed the director's anticlerical position. Interview with Mme Djemil Anik, CRH 030, 11.

44. Jean Lheureux (chiromancer) to GD, n.d. [ca. 1938], FGD 3984.

45. Winock, *La Belle Époque*, 113; General Manager (Elysée Palace Hotel) to General Saisset-Schneider, March 8, 1905, FGD 4542. Their April 6, 1905, wedding took place at the Église de la Trinité, preceded by a dinner of seventy to eighty persons (April 4, 1905) at the Elysée Palace Hotel (103, avenue des Champs Elysées). The late date was chosen to allow time for the appraisal of Albert's property (valued at 220,000 French francs in 1905), a fifteen-room Louis XV–style castle known as the Château de Bosc (Bayeux, Calvados), complete with flower and vegetable gardens and an animal farm.

46. Gustave Vapereau, *Dictionnaire universel des contemporains* 18 (1893), BNF. Michelis di Rienzi, *Panthéon des lettres, des sciences et des arts* (1893), BNF, I. 319, 419–27.

47. Among the titles by Henri Didon are *L'Enseignement supérieur et les universités catholiques* (1876), *L'Homme selon la science et la foi* (1876), *L'Homme d'action* (1895) and *Influence morale des sports athlétiques* (1897).

48. GD to Madeleine Saisset-Schneider, July 5, 1904, FGD 4507. On "man of action," see Didon's *L'Homme d'action* (1895).

49. During the war, with the help of Raymond Saisset-Schneider, Albert was named deputy chief of the Department of Commerce and Industry in the area of "Stocks Nationaux et Réquisitions Civiles" (National Supplies and Civilian Requisitions). Albert Dulac to, September 28, 1917, FGD 3621, and May 21, 1918, FGD 3633.

50. GD to Madeleine Saisset-Schneider, [July 20], 1904, FGD 4521.

51. Philosophy was not entirely foreign to Dulac's heritage, as her great-uncle Émile Saisset, a member of the renowned Institut de France, had published widely on philosophers of religion, politics, and aesthetics, including Descartes, Bacon, Pascal, and Kant. He also published the first French translation of Spinoza.

52. Albert Dulac to GD, September 20, 1904, FGD 1908.

53. Albert's assertion reads, "I try not to think any more, because thoughts get lost. I live sensations, imprecise mysterious sensations, which enter without my knowing, and which have invaded me little by little . . . it's a communion with infinity . . . Yes, sensation is indeed the source of emotional life. It is the very foundation of the harmony of things." Albert Dulac to GD, September 14, 1904, FGD 1898.

54. Albert Dulac to GD, September 14, 1904, FGD 1898.

55. Ibid., September 15, 1904, FGD 1900; ibid., May 24, 1915, FGD 2574.

56. Ibid., August 23, 1904, FGD 1881.

57. See, for example, Albert Dulac's works, *Agriculture et libre-échange*, *Manuel de la vente coopérative*, *Les Fédérations d'associations rurales*, and *La Formation des prix des denrées alimentaires*.

58. The city is home to the famed eleventh-century, proto-cinematic, Norman Romanesque Bayeux tapestry commissioned by Queen Mathilde in the year 1006.

59. GD, "L'Industrie au foyer. Les Dentellières," in "'Le Théâtre ou les théâtres' Coupures de presse, Album paginé 1–200," FGD 4402, 3.

60. Misme, "La Création de la française."

61. See notably Karl Marx and Friedrich Engels's *Communist Manifesto* (1848), August Bebel's *La Femme et le socialisme* (1879, French trans. 1883), and Engels's *L'Origine de la famille, de la propriété privée et de l'état* (1884); GD (with annotations by Albert Dulac), "La Tâche internationale de la femme française," July 15, 1907, FGD 4489; Käppeli, "Scènes féministes."

62. "La Question féminine"; "L'Utilité sociale de l'émancipation féminine." Käppeli, "Scènes féministes," 575.

63. Käppeli, "Scènes féministes," 577–78. According to Serge Bernstein, the Republican political culture is based on five principals: (1) The primacy of the individual in society. (2) The predominance of the Parliament in the institutions. (3) A secular education. (4) The promise of gradual social progress. (5) Pacifism and national defense. S. Bernstein, "La Culture républicain dans la première moitié du XXe siècle," in Serge Bernstein and Odile Rudelle, eds., *Le Modèle républicain* (Paris: PUF, 1992). Cited in Winock, *La Belle Époque*, 243.

64. The journal was subtitled "Œuvre et journal de progrès féminin" (Organization and journal of women's progress). The history of the emergence of women's associations and that of women's journals were indissociable during this period. Often, the creation of a journal coincided with the creation of an association. As Misme wrote in the first issue of the feminist weekly, "When I say 'our oeuvre,' I'm speaking not only of this paper here present: many know it, but no one should be left unaware of it, *La Française* is not only a journal. The society that this title designates is subtitled 'Œuvre et journal de progrès féminin.'" Misme, "La Création de la française."

65. The Alliance française was created in 1883 by a preeminent group of scientists and intellectuals (e.g., Louis Pasteur, Armand Colin, Jules Verne), for the purpose of promoting French language and culture.

66. GD, "L'Influence des femmes dans l'évolution de la langue française," March 25, 1907, FGD 4469, 1.

67. Ibid., 11.

68. GD (with Albert Dulac's handwritten annotations), "La Tâche internationale de la femme française," July 15, 1907, FGD 4489.

69. Winock, *La Belle Époque*, 391.

70. GD, "La Tâche internationale," 4.

71. Ibid., 2–3.

72. Ibid.

73. Ibid., 9. The term *civilized* referred no doubt to the Western countries involved in the network of associations linked to the International Council of Women. The exclusion of predominantly non-Western and developing countries from this network merits further research. Many would later be integrated in the 1930s, although largely through the colonizing nations.

74. GD, "La Tâche internationale," 6–8.

75. Ibid., 9–10.

76. Ibid., 11.

77. Ibid., 18.

78. Attendees included distinguished members of the theater and arts community, such as Madame Tristan Bernard, wife of the preeminent actor-playwright of the same name, Suzanne Desprès, and her husband Lugné-Poë, and Ms. René Lalique (wife of the famous art-nouveau glass sculptor and jewelry designer). "Salon international de la française." In addition to its artistic matinees the salon provided a forum in which women "of different backgrounds, but of similar education" could meet, for their "mutual perfection," as well as for "the general amelioration of women's intellect and condition, and thus that of society and humanity." Open daily, it also contained a lounge, tearoom, and cultural center where they could access information on issues related to women and careers, family, education, financial administration, or take courses on art, music, fashion, sewing, and cooking. GD, "Matinée italienne du Salon international" (January 1907).

79. GD, "Carlotta Zambelli"; GD, "Anne Vila"; GD, "Juliette Toutain-Grün"; GD, "Matinée italienne du Salon international" (June 1907).

80. GD, "La Tâche internationale," 16.

81. The journal's ardent defense of Dreyfus (and of Émile Zola, following his famous letter to the president titled "J'accuse . . .") produced a rupture between republican feminists and Christian feminists, the latter of which supported the nationalist anti-Dreyfusard position. Dizier-Metz, *La Bibliothèque Marguerite Durand*, 22. The journal appeared daily from December 9, 1897, through September 1, 1903, and monthly from October 1903 through March 1905 as a supplement to the "anti-clerical" and "socialist" journal *L'Action quotidienne*, where Albert Dulac also published. *La Fronde* made a brief appearance first as a weekly during the summer of 1914 (spurred by the growing suffragette movement, but ceased after the August 3 declaration of war), and finally as a daily from May 1926 through July 1928, when Dulac wrote for it. See Sullerot, *La Presse féminine*, 9. According to the French National Library, the journal's final issue appeared in "March–May 1929." *Catalogue collectif des périodiques*, 667.

82. Khanine, "Marguerite Durand."

83. The first issue of *La Fronde* appeared on December 9, 1897. According to Évelyne Sullerot, the journal sold all 200,000 copies of its first issue. Sullerot, *La Presse féminine*, 9; Dizier-Metz, *La Bibliothèque Marguerite Durand*, 10.

84. Ford, "Germaine Dulac," 5; Flitterman-Lewis, *To Desire Differently*, 48; and Dozoretz, "Germaine Dulac," 24 n58. GD, "Le Cinéma est un art nouveau."

85. When *La Fronde* went out of print, Marguerite Durand joined forces with the self-proclaimed "radical" and "anti-clerical" socialist daily *L'Action*, which she codirected with former priest Victor Charbonnel, and deputy and future senator Henry Bérenger. Bellanger et al., eds., *Histoire générale de la presse française*, 366.

86. Li, *La Presse féministe en France*, 223.

87. Misme, "La Création de la française," 1. See also Misme, "Journal 'La Française.'"

88. Misme, "Journal 'La Française,'" 4. Some critics of the period argued that the strong Republican and Dreyfusard stance of *La Fronde* (glibly nicknamed "*Le Temps* en jupons"—the *Times* in a petticoat) was pursued at the expense of more specific feminist concerns. Roberts, "Copie subversive."

89. GD, "Réjane!" Dulac signed this first article "G. De l'Estang," a pseudonym that she would use principally for her theater reviews as of October 11, 1908.

90. If the nonextant issues are considered, the total number of texts can be estimated at fifty or sixty (1906–8).

91. See Maugue, *L'Identité masculine*.

92. Roberts, "Copie subversive," 233.

93. Dulac's journalistic occupation was already subversive. While women, in their domestic confinement, had already begun to affirm their intellectualism, and imagination in the domain of literature (although often under pseudonyms), women's journalism, which required women to venture out to confront the reality of the world, represented something entirely new.

94. See Higonnet, "Femmes, images et représentations," 457; Higonnet, "Apparences, loisirs, subsistance," 311.

95. Dozoretz, "Germaine Dulac," 25.

96. T. Ferenczi, *L'Invention du journalisme en France. Naissance de la presse moderne à la fin du XIXe siècle* (Paris: Plon, 1993). Cited by Roberts, "Copie subversive," 235.

97. A few exceptions were *L'Illustration*, *L'Excelsior*, and *L'Assiette au Beurre*.

98. Mary Louise Roberts's argument with respect to the journalists of *La Fronde* puts in perspective Dulac's flowery writing style. Roberts asserts, "In addressing objective reality, the woman reporter [. . .] called into question the widespread nineteenth century notion that women were creatures of fantasy instead of reason." Roberts, "Copie subversive," 238–39.

99. Among other titles by the Countess Mathieu de Noailles are *L'Ombre des jours*, *La Nouvelle Espérance*, *Le Visage émerveillé*, *La Domination*, and *Les Éblouissements*.

100. GD, "Comtesse Mathieu de Noailles." GD, "Le Théâtre ou les théâtres," 17.

101. GD, "Mme Marguerite Rolland."

102. See Misme, "Journal 'La Française," 4.

103. GD, "Colette Yver."

104. Jane Misme, "La Femme dans le théâtre nouveau," *La Revue d'Art Dramatique*, October 1901, 608. Cited by Roberts, "Copie subversive," 244.

105. Roberts, "Copie subversive," 244.

106. Ibid., 243–44.

107. GD, "Madame Poilpot."

108. For example, Dulac detailed the musical flourishes of Toutain-Grün, such as her use of a "presto" and a "scarlatti" (named for the Italian composer regarded as the founder of modern opera). GD, "Juliette Toutain-Grün." GD, "Carlotta Zambelli." See also GD, "Matinée italienne" (January 1907).

109. See Winock, *La Belle Époque*, as well as Studlar, "'Out-Salomeing Salome.'"

110. Lugné-Poë, who had added the surname Poe to his own in honor of the U.S. poet Edgar Allan Poe, was responsible for bringing many international works (e.g., by Strinberg, Maeterlinck, and Ibsen) to the French theater scene. GD, "Matinée italienne" (January 1907).

111. GD, "Madame Suzanne Desprès."

112. According to a small green diary kept during her travels in "Ibsen's country," during the months of July and August 1908 Dulac traveled on foot from Bergen to Trondheim, and by boat from Trondheim to the Cap du Nord. GD, "Carnet de voyages," FGD 4496; GD, "Solness le constructeur. D'après la célèbre pièce d'Henrich Ibsen. Tryptique en trois périodes. Projet de film," FGD 808. While the nineteen-page film project was never produced, Dulac had planned to feature Germaine Dermoz as Mme Solness, Conrad Veidt as Master Solness, and Huguette Duflos as Hilde.

113. GD, "Le Bonheur est chose légère," FGD 4444; GD, "Le Fantôme," FGD 4449; GD, "Les Pieuvres," FGD 4454.

114. GD, "Le Jardin magnifique," FGD 4451. While the aforementioned theater projects are undated, her correspondence with Albert Dulac allows us to situate this last work in late 1914 or early 1915, just prior to her first film production. Albert Dulac to GD, September 9, 1914, FGD 2207.

115. The title of *L'Emprise* contains a double meaning. In modern French it signifies "to control," "to constrain," or "to have a hold on," but in Middle English and Anglo-French it implies an adventurous "undertaking." GD and Mlle V. Dutrey, "L'Emprise," FGD 4447; the program lists Mlle V. Dutrey as coauthor for the play's unique April 20, 1907, performance. See also GD and Mlle V. Dutrey, "'L'Emprise.' Programme, *La Française*," April 20, 1907, FGD 4447.

In 1932, when the coming of sound curbed her fiction film work, Dulac, in her continued dedication to women's progress, directed a production of Donata Vannutelli's three-act comedy *Les Loups* at the Comédie des Champs-Elysées theater. The production was organized by Magda Contino and the women's art cooperative Studio féminin (Women's studio). "Loups," *L'Effort Clartiste*, December [8], 1932, FGD 4360.

116. The event program, and the fact that no further references to it appear in *La Française*, lead one to believe that this was a single performance. See "'L'Emprise.' Programme."

117. The play was performed by Paris's Theater for the Deaf and Hard-of-Hearing on June 5, 2005, alongside a screening of Dulac's *La Souriante Madame Beudet* at the 2005 Dulac Retrospective at the Musée d'Orsay.

118. GD and Dutrey, "L'Emprise," 11.

119. Ibid., 9.

120. GD, review of *4 fois 7:28*, directed by Romain Coolus, 1908, in GD, "Le Théâtre ou les théâtres," 61. See also Winock, *La Belle Époque*, 168.

121. "L'Emprise," FGD 4447, 16–18.

122. Dulac first used the pseudonym De l'Estang for her portrait of popular theater actress "Réjane" in December 1906. The handwritten annotation "(G. Dulac)" next to G. De l'Estang in her album confirms this pseudonym. The use of pseudonyms was common among women writers during this period. Not unlike her future screenwriter Irène Hillel-Erlanger, whose nom de plume was Claude Lorrey, Dulac would use pseudonyms, such as Germaine de Sessey and Dominique Dix, to sign her early film scripts. See chapter 2.

123. GD, "Le Théâtre ou les théâtres," See also Viala, ed., *Le Théâtre en France*.

124. Ibid., 83–85.

125. Ibid., 73–75.

126. Ibid., 75.

127. Ibid., 73, 75.

128. Ibid., 73.

129. Ibid.

130. As Dulac noted in her review of Coolus's *4 fois 7:28*, and in line with her idea of expanding the arena of women's representation, Léon Blum's controversial pamphlet *Du mariage* (1907) argued that women should be given the same consideration as men with regard to premarital or extramarital sexual relations. Dulac explored the subject of extramarital relations in several films including *La Belle Dame sans merci* (1921) and her 1927 Coolus adaptation *Antoinette Sabrier*. GD, review of *4 fois 7:28*. GD, "Le Théâtre ou les théâtres," 61.

131. See Viala, *Le Théâtre en France*, 393.

132. Ibid., 396.

133. Nicknamed the "clergyman somnambule" (sleepwalking clergyman), Lugné-Poë also experimented with narrative recitatives (or a monotone offstage narration described as a "litany") in place of action, a technique Dulac used via a lengthy intertitle of a poetic recitation in *La Belle Dame sans merci* (1921). Inspired by Belgian author Maurice Maeterlinck's lyrical *Pelléas et Mélisande*, which he brought to the Parisian scene in 1893, Lugné-Poë affirmed his avant-gardism, carrying his conceptions to the extreme in his controversial production of Alfred Jarry's *Ubu Roi* (1896). Viala, *Le Théâtre en France*, 396–97.

134. For instance, while championing the psychological individualism of Dostoevsky's *Brothers Karamazov* (Théâtre des arts), Dulac also praised the sociological realism of Shaw's *Mrs. Warren's Profession* (1913).

135. GD, "Le Théâtre ou les théâtres," 44–46, 61. See also Mantzius, *Molière*.

136. Of Romain Coolus and Sam Benelli, Dulac wrote, "They write based upon life and not according to life. They see by refraction and not directly." GD, "Le Théâtre ou les théâtres," 98.

137. GD, "Le Théâtre ou les théâtres," 122–23.

Chapter 2. The Great War and Dulac's First Films

1. Ferro, "Cultural Life in France," 295. See also Eksteins, *Rites of Spring*.

2. Becker et al., *Guerres et cultures*; Winter, *La Première Guerre mondiale*.

3. Albert was a corporal in the 6th infantry division. *Le Bulletin des Écrivains*, March 1915. For more on this source and on writers in the army, see Nicolas Beaupré, "Bulletin des Écrivains de 1914 à l'Association des Ecrivains Combattants (AEC)."

4. See Audoin-Rouzeau and Becker, "Vers une histoire culturelle."

5. With few exceptions, politicians, intellectuals, and feminists all set aside their differences and their struggles, and rallied to the cry of the "union sacrée" to serve the nation. Members of the radical left, like Socialist ministers Marcel Sembat and Jules Guesde, joined the conservative right and its cabinet under President Raymond Poincaré and Prime Minister René Viviani in the common goal of defending the nation. French intellectuals, who saw themselves as the international guardians of universalism, also rallied to the national cause. Prochasson and Rasmussen, *Au Nom de la patrie*, 9.

6. Albert Dulac to GD, August 16, 1914, FGD 2164; ibid., April 6, 1915, FGD 2500. See also "Marcel Sembat 'Les Cahiers noirs' 4éme partie," 12.

7. Albert Dulac to GD, September 9, 1914, FGD 2507.

8. See Léon Jouhaux's speech for the Conféderation générale du travail (CGT, general workers union): "Cérémonie [1922]. 'A la mémoire de Marcel et Georgette Sembat' (Gaumont Palace), Fonds André Lebey, OURS." Marcel Sembat, 14 lettres et 'cérémonie,'" 50 APO 21, Fonds André Lebey, OURS. See also Braud, "Le Mouvement ouvrier et socialiste, et les arts."

9. Sembat notes several encounters and dinners with Germaine. "Marcel Sembat 'Les Cahiers noirs' 4éme partie." Journal entries dated November 26, 1912, 27, and September 22, 1913, 31. In November 1913, having given a lecture on symbolist poetry *chez Antoine* (or at the Théâtre Antoine), Sembat noted in his diary the presence of "a few friends," who included "[Albert] Dulac, [Gustav] Kahn, [Henri] Matisse." "Marcel Sembat 'Les Cahiers noirs' 4éme partie," 38, 220. Francis Jourdain (1876–1958), the son of architect Franz Jourdain, and a pioneer of the *mouvement moderne* of functionalist design also active in the Salon d'automne, would supply furniture for the films of Dulac and many of her contemporaries of the 1920s avant-garde.

10. See Albert Dulac to André Lebey, 50 APO 47 (1910, 1934), and GD to André Lebey, 50 APO 13 (1914, ca. 1925), Fonds André Lebey, OURS.

11. The dedication reads "À Yvon Delbos, ami du cinéma." GD, "Les Esthétiques," 29. See B. Lachaise, *Yvon Delbos* (Périgueux: Éditions Fanlac, 1993). Cited by G. Delluc, *Louis Delluc*, 334.

12. Several documents, including a 1934 letter from Albert Dulac to André Lebey, using masonic coding, and held at OURS, suggest that, like André Lebey, Anatole France, Yvon Delbos, and Henri Lapauze, Albert was also a Freemason. The Dulacs' association with this secret society merits further research with the lifting of privacy restrictions following the seventieth anniversary of Germaine Dulac's death. See the

masonic coding in the letter from Albert Dulac to André Lebey, 50 APO 1-52, Fonds André Lebey, OURS.

13. Henry Lapauze to GD, April 26, 1916, FGD 3981. See "Notre Avant-Garde aux arts décoratifs." Dulac exhibited a model studio and a boat containing prisms.

14. Albert Dulac to GD, October 1, 1914, FGD 2244; "Office d'utilisation des femmes," *Le Petit Comtois*, February 17, 1915. The Offices d'utilisation des femmes launched its rescue efforts on the fourth day of the war with the opening of an *atélier-cantine*, which provided food, clothing, first aid, and financial assistance to war victims. Thébaud, *La Femme au temps de la guerre de 14*, 115; Thébaud, "La Grande Guerre," 91.

15. The Offices d'utilisation des femmes, created by l'Union française pour le suffrage des femmes and l'Association des étudiantes de Paris, was just one of many moderate feminist organizations that set aside its struggle (at the height of the Frenchwomen's suffrage movement in early 1914) in order to contribute to the war effort. Jane Misme, director of *La Française*, wrote, "As long as the adversity our country suffers endures, no one is permitted to speak of his or her rights; towards it, we only have responsibilities." Cited by Thébaud, "La Grande Guerre," 91. Similarly, Marguerite Durand wrote in the brief reappearance of *La Fronde* in August 1914, "Women, your country needs you, be worthy citizens, whether our goal [the right to vote] is recognized or not." Cited by Bard, *Les Filles de Marianne*, 53.

16. A.J., "Lettre de Paris."

17. Ibid.

18. Ibid. The prestigious members of its organizational committee, which vowed to disregard "all political and religious divisions," included Ms. Raymond Poincaré and Ms. René Viviani (wives of the conservative French president and Socialist Republican prime minister, respectively), literary figures Juliette Adam, Ms. Alphonse Daudet, and Ms. Camille Flammarion, as well as aristocrats Les Duchesses d'Uzès and de Rohan.

19. GD, "Madame Serao germanophile." See also "Mme Matilde Serao est germanophile." Her script *La Mia vita per la tua* starred and was directed by Emilio Ghione in 1914. Special thanks to Luigia Annunziata (Istituto Italiano di Scienze Umane–University of Siena) for sharing her biographical findings on Matilde Serao.

20. Germaine Albert-Dulac, "L'Opinion féminine en Italie."

21. Ibid.

22. Dulac transmitted two letters to *La Française* illustrating the opposing positions of British and moderate French feminists. The first letter from British feminist Ellinor Fell incited the French to send a delegate representing the French position. The second, from Juliette Adam of *La Croisade*'s Comité pour la propagande à l'étranger (Committee for propaganda abroad), explained the organization's position in support of the French boycott. "Nouvelles Protestations contre le Congrès pacifiste de la Haye," *La Française*, May 1, 1915.

23. Jane Misme, in *La Française*, November 19, 1914. Cited by Thébaud, "La Grande Guerre," 125.

24. See Audoin-Rouzeau and Becker, "Vers une Histoire culturelle," 5–8.

25. Bard, *Les Femmes dans la société française*.

26. Thébaud, "La Grande Guerre," 125.

27. Albert Dulac to GD, September 24, 1912, FGD 2108; ibid., March 29, 1915, FGD 2490. For more on the actress, see also Napierkowska, "Mes Souvenirs"; Henry, "Les Étoiles d'aujourd'hui."

28. "Paris Dancer Dislikes U.S." Stasia Napierkowska to GD, "41 lettres" and "Croquis au crayon et à l'encre," FGD 4142–50.

29. Albert Dulac to GD, September 4, 1912, FGD 2110. "Projet de décor pour *Salomé*, pré Catalan," July 6, 1913, FGD 4456, 1. Stasia Napierkowska to GD, October 11, 1912, FGD 4096. See also Bousquet and Martinelli, "La Bella Stasia." Also in 1912, a Parisian production of *Salomé* starred modern pantomime artist Georges Wague and dancer Ida Rubinstein, likewise important for Dulac. For more on the influence of Wague and Rubinstein, see T. Williams, "The 'Silent' Arts."

30. While Dulac claimed to accompany Napierkowska to the shooting of Ugo Falena's 1917 film, *La Tragica Fine di Caligola* (alternative title: *Caligula*), her accounts of this experience are somewhat incongruous. In a 1922 interview, she noted: "When in 1914, Napierkowska—who was acting for *Film d'Art*, and with whom I'd become amicably linked—offered to take me to Italy, to have me attend the making of *Caligula* in Rome, I seized the opportunity enthusiastically." Bencey, "Une Femme 'Compositeur cinégraphique,'" 233. In another interview, conducted by modern dancer Jeanne Ronsay (a student of Djemil Anik), Dulac emphasized her initially adverse reaction when first visiting a film set on which the "distressed director, running notes in hand, curses at his entourage: 'What a trade! It is certainly not one I'd choose to do for a living!'" Ronsay, "Germaine Dulac." Considering the multiple films of this genre featuring Napierkowska (1915–17), the late date of the film's release raises questions about whether or not this was the same film shoot that Dulac attended.

31. Albert Dulac to GD, May 9, 1914, FGD 2132. Stasia Napierkowska to GD, January 15, 1915, FGD 4140.

32. Albert Dulac to GD, March–September 1914, FGD 2121–207.

33. Ibid., February 20, 1915, FGD 2427; ibid., March 7, 1915, FGD 2441; ibid., March 27, 1915, FGD 2794.

34. Ibid., May 22, 1915, FGD 2570; ibid., June 3, 1915, FGD 2592. Napierkowska would direct at least one film: *L'Héritière de la manade* (1917).

35. Bencey, "Une Femme 'Compositeur cinégraphique,'" 233.

36. Multiple letters, including one referring to their initial 1912 meeting, suggest that the actress is referring to their first romantic encounter. Stasia Napierkowska to GD, April 1914, FGD 4127. Napierkowska's letters to Dulac date from July 1912 through December 1914 (FGD 4090–139).

37. "Marcel Sembat 'Les Cahiers noirs' 4éme partie."

38. Albert Dulac to GD, June 8, 1913, FGD 2114.

39. Ibid.; ibid., May 9, 1914, FGD 2132; ibid., March 29, 1915, FGD 2490; ibid., August 28, 1915, FGD 2719.

40. Of these women, Albert quips: "A great agility of mind, no doubt, a marvelous ability to adapt to new conditions after a tough existence, with brilliant wit and spirit." Albert Dulac to GD, April 3, 1915, FGD 2498.

41. See "Marie-Anne Malleville," FGD 4012.

42. From their first meeting to the poet's illness and their separation in 1918–20, Hillel-Erlanger wrote numerous letters, dating from August 1915 to September 1918 (FGD 3881–921), and ranging in tone from romantic affection and passion to a desperate, almost suicidal love.

43. Bergson, *L'Evolution créatrice*, 306; Bergson notes, "In this sense we may say, if we are not abusing this kind of illustration, that the cinematographical character of our knowledge of things is due to the kaleidoscopic character of our adaptation to them" (306).

44. Hillel-Erlanger, *Voyages en kaléidoscope*, 77. For Hillel-Erlanger, like the letters of symbolist poetry, the elements of language, font, and type take the form of human bodies lent to them by what she calls the "Kaléido-machine." On Hillel-Erlanger's symbolist poetry, see Christophe Wall-Romana, *Cinepoetry: Imaginary Cinemas in French Poetry*.

45. I am indebted to Richard Armin, an inspiring and generous interlocutor on the life and work of Hillel-Erlanger, who is working on an English translation of her novel. As Armin has pointed out in our correspondence, the cover for the original edition resembles the visual style of the "rebellious and raucous Dadaists" (cf. Picabia), appropriating "artless mechanical diagrams as dynamic metaphors spawning generations of critical art, literature and film that dislodged bourgeois sensibilities" (Armin to author, February 2013). After the artist's untimely death on March 20, 1920, the original edition of this fascinating esoteric novel was withdrawn from publication, and according to her friend Eugene Canseliet, also removed from bookstores by her immediate family (her uncle Salomon Hillel-Manoach and her brother Robert Halfon/Camondo), possibly in an effort to protect the aristocratic family's sensibilities and reputation. Moreover, as Armin, has noted, her manuscripts and personal papers, which must have been voluminous, remain tragically undiscovered, if not destroyed.

46. See Paula Amad, *Counter-Archive*. Amad incisively explores the links between Bergson's ontology of duration, scientific filmmaking, and early French film theory and criticism in the work of Colette, Epstein, as well as Dulac.

47. Hillel-Erlanger, *Voyages en kaléidoscope*, 17.

48. The journal features Hillel-Erlanger's poem "Par Amour." *Littérature* (Paris), no. 1 (March 1919).

49. Albert Dulac to GD, October 17, 1915, FGD 2802.

50. Ibid., October 22, 1915, FGD 2812.

51. On April 8, 1916, Albert wrote, "It's with pleasure that I watch this film effort take form and create a clear goal for your activities. But are you sure this is the appropriate moment to create a business of this type? Once you've begun, you must maintain it. And will the first elements keep their passion? How I regret not being able to do these interesting things with you!" Albert Dulac to GD, April 8,

1916, FGD 3071; Albert Dulac's business card (Président du conseil d'administration et Directeur Général. Les Films DH. 188, boulevard Haussman [company address as of 1919]), FGD 3781.

52. Henri Barbusse, *Le Feu, journal d'une escouade* (Paris: E. Flammarion, 1916). Cited by Thébaud, *La Femme*, 104. See also the English translation, *Under Fire: the Story of a Squad*, transl. Fitzwater Wray (New York: E. P. Dutton, 1917). Barbusse's popular indictment of the war, initially understood as a "naturalist reportage of a combatant familiar with death," would later be seen as a proto-pacifist work. Ferro, "Cultural Life in France," 298.

53. Albert Dulac to GD, April 18, 1916, FGD 3092.

54. Ibid.

55. Bernard, *L'Effort de la femme française pendant la guerre*.

56. While, as Richard Abel argues, this crisis was already under way prior to 1914, following the departure of the French production giant, Pathé Films, from the Motion Pictures Patents Company or Trust, the war compounded this situation. Abel, *French Cinema*, 9.

57. Albert Dulac to GD, April 19, 1916, FGD 3095; ibid., April 23, 1916, FGD 3098.

58. Ibid., April 13, 1916, FGD 3082.

59. Ibid., April 27, 1916, FGD 3102.

60. Ibid.

61. Ibid., April 27, 1916, FGD 3102; ibid., May 9, 1916, FGD 3119. Henry Lapauze to GD, April 26, 1916, FGD 3981.

62. Établissements Henry Lapauze to GD, April 26, 1916, FGD 3981; Albert Dulac to GD, June 8, 1916, FGD 3151. While Dulac retained neither the name, "La Parisienne," nor the "art nouveau" design, the letter suggests that Van Dongen may have designed the final title (so that it was less "éternel féminin"). The final design connected the two letters DH with a more simple swirling form, associated with the Taoist symbol for the yin and the yang, and the masculine and feminine. However, unlike the Taoist symbol, its design remained open. Dulac illustrated the company's early name Krishna Film (under which *Les Sœurs enemies* [1917] was released), with a Hindu cross, also known as an Indian cross. Handwritten notes for *Vénus Victrix* (Les Films DH [letterhead "Films Krishna"]), 1916, FGD 355. Van Dongen later designed the modernist cover of Hillel-Erlanger's esoteric novel, *Voyages en kaléidoscope* (1920). The name DH is also the name of one of the first mixed-gender masonic lodges, Droit humain (Human Rights), founded in Belle Époque Paris.

63. Edmond Van Daële would appear in several impressionist films, including Louis Delluc's *La Fièvre* (1921), Epstein's *Coeur fidèle* (1923) and *Six et demi onze* (1927), and Abel Gance's *Napoléon* (1927).

64. Abel, *French Cinema*, 10.

65. "Notices explicatives. *La Lumière du cœur* [1916]," BNF-ASP, Coll. Auguste Rondel, RK 5873.

66. Ibid.

67. See Véray, *Les Films d'actualité pendant la guerre de 14–18*.

68. Véray, "Abel Gance," 44.

69. Véray, "Les Films patriotiques de Léonce Perret."

70. From a feminist standpoint, the choice to have the hero choose blindness so as not to see the heroine's damaged physical appearance is quite complex, and could be read as both progressive in its disregard and reactionary in its avoidance. However, broadly speaking, the man's refusal of the power linked to vision could be read positively.

71. GD, "Coup de Feu," n.d., FGD 4463.

72. See Abel, *French Cinema*, 10. Cited by Véray, "La mise en spectacle de la guerre."

73. See Véray, "La mise en spectacle de la guerre."

74. See Maugue, *L'Identité masculine*. Cited by Roberts, "Copie subversive," 233.

75. Hillel-Erlanger and Dulac originally signed these scripts with the pseudonyms "Claude Lorrey et Dominique Dix" (August 1916, Psyché Films) and "Irène Hillel et Germaine de Sessey," respectively. However, the final versions of the script and film were signed with their married names. Germaine Albert-Dulac and Irène Hillel-Erlanger, *Les Sœurs ennemies*, August 1916, FGD 302.

76. Albert Dulac to GD, June 28, 1916, FGD 3181; ibid., September 13, 1916, FGD 3220.

77. *Géo le mystérieux* was released after *Vénus Victrix*, owing to distribution problems.

78. Arlecchino, "Madame Germaine Albert-Dulac."

79. This film, distributed in France by Cinématographes Harry, was released in the United States by World Made Brady (Dulac's New York distributor). See chapter 3.

80. The film was originally titled *Les Mystères du château maudit* (The mysteries of the cursed castle). A *roman-cinéma* (film-novel), or novelization of the film written by Guy de Téramond, was published simultaneously in *Le Petit Journal*: "*Âmes de fous*, Scénario et mise-en-scène de Germaine Dulac, Adapté de Guy de Téramond," special issue of *Le Petit Journal* (Paris: Cinématographes Harry, 1918), FGD 17. See also de Téramond, "Comment on écrit un roman-cinéma."

81. GD, *Trois Pantins pour une poupée* (1918), shooting script, FGD 349, 17. See T. Williams, "'Silent' Arts."

82. Albert Dulac to GD, June 12, 1915, FGD 2609.

83. The couple's son, Philippe Erlanger (1903–1987), was a prominent twentieth-century historian, art critic, journalist, and cofounder of the Cannes International Film Festival. One of his most renowned works is *La France sans étoile*. In 1918, Irène sent a 1910 photo of herself and Philippe to Dulac and, using the symbol of a heart, signs it "with affectionate love."

84. See Simonelli, "´À la Lueur de l'ourse."

85. While not a Dulac-Hillel-Erlanger collaboration, *La Mort du soleil* (1921), made just after the latter's death from tuberculosis, is remarkable in its focus on the choice between motherhood and a career battling this disease. The film, produced by André Legrand, was financed in part by the American Society against Tuberculosis. It should

be noted that while motherhood is present in these early collaborations (from *Les Sœurs ennemies* to *La Belle Dame sans merci*, 1916–21), it disappears entirely after the latter.

86. Germaine Albert-Dulac and Hillel-Erlanger, *Les Sœurs ennemies*, Découpage, August 1916, FGD 302.

87. GD, "Projet de décor," July 6, 1913, FGD 4456. Perhaps inspired by Napierkowska's 1912 portrayal of Salomé, this appears to be a conceptual sketch for a future project.

88. Albert Dulac to GD, June 12, 1915, FGD 2609; ibid., June 1, 1915, FGD 2617.

89. See *Exposition de l'art dans le cinéma française*. Section rétrospective de l'enseignement. Paris: Prieur et Dubois imprimeurs, 1924, BNF-ASP, BNF-ASP, fonds Auguste Rondel, RK 585. See also "Notre Avant-Garde aux Arts Décoratifs." For more on the exposition, see also "L'Art dans le cinéma français" (1924), VR 247, Expositions au Musée Galliera, Beaux-Arts de la Ville de Paris, Archives de Paris; and H. Clouzot, "Paris aura-t-il un musée du geste?," *L'Europe Nouvelle*, August 9, 1924, BiFi, fonds Victor Perrot, VP 046, cited by Christophe Gauthier. See also Gauthier, *La Passion du cinéma*, 74–79 and 313. See also Laurent Mannoni, *Histoire de la cinémathèque française*.

90. Albert compared the image of the troops in the sun to a painting of Fromentin, and associated his "funambulist impression" of the nearby June 17–18 attack resulting in thousands of deaths, to an Edgar Allan Poe tale. Albert Dulac to GD, June 21, 1915, FGD 2621.

91. Albert Dulac to GD, June 21, 1915, FGD 2621. In this letter, Albert also referred to an illustrated account of this attack, appearing in the June 19, 1915, issue of *L'Ilustration*, which he asked Dulac to keep for them.

92. *Dans l'Ouragan de la vie* (Vénus Victrix), publicity brochure, BNF-ASP, Coll. Auguste Rondel, 4°RK 3406, 1.

93. *Ciné-Journal*, January 25, 1919, FGD 4342, 56.

94. See Grétillat, "Le cinéma français."

95. Dulac employed concise shots to represent exteriors: "Facade of the Ritz, Facade of an important maison de couture: Facade of the Palais de Justice. An avenue. Hotel Garden. Grand terrace." Germaine Albert-Dulac and Hillel-Erlanger, *Les Sœurs ennemies*, 1. All of the floor plans and decor for the film were designed and hand drawn by Dulac. GD, "Facade of the Ritz," 2–4.

96. GD, "Où sont les interprètes?"

97. Louis Delluc, *Le Film*, 1918. Cited by G. Delluc, *Louis Delluc*, 331.

98. See Bazin, *What Is Cinema*?

99. Germaine Albert-Dulac and Hillel-Erlanger, *Les Sœurs ennemies*, August 1916, FGD 302, 2. Dulac detailed the lighting in the script: "Head bottom lit; light encompassing the head and clock face. Light effect expanding while lamp is being lit [. . .] She turns toward the window holding the lamp in hand. Silhouette, shadow, lit head. [. . .] Increased anxiety [. . .] She puts the lamp down [. . .] face lit from below."

100. For example, the script reads: "Paulette jumps on her father's lap, affectionately placing her little head on his shoulder. Both think of Jeannine . . . Dissolve

head of Jeannine giving lessons." Germaine Albert-Dulac and Hillel-Erlanger, *Les Sœurs ennemies*, 6.

101. François Crucy, "Suzanne Desprès," *La Rampe*, no. 94 (1908), BNF-ASP, Coll. Auguste Rondel, Rt. 7052, 1.

102. Claude Briault, "Suzanne Desprès et le Théâtre d'Idées," *La Rampe*, no. 94 (1908), BNF-ASP, Coll. Auguste Rondel, Rt. 7052, 6.

103. Albert Dulac to GD, June 12, 1915, FGD 2609.

104. Ibid.

105. Ibid., June 29, 1917, FGD 3534.

106. Ibid.

107. Publicity brochure, *Dans l'Ouragan de la vie* [*Vénus Victrix*], 1916, BNF-ASP, Coll. Auguste Rondel, 4°RK 3406.

108. Studlar, "'Out-Salomeing Salome.'"

109. Albert Dulac to GD, March 28, 1917, FGD 3428.

110. One of Djemil Anik's earliest appearances was in Henri Fescourt's *Fleur d'exil* (1914). She later appeared in Fescourt's *Mathias Pascal* (1921).

111. See GD, "Où sont les interprètes?"

112. GD, "Mise-en-scène."

113. Ibid., 7.

114. Ibid., 7–8.

115. *Midinette* is now a pejorative term meaning "starry-eyed girl." *Larousse Unabridged: French-English English-French Dictionary*, vers. 1.01 (Paris: Larousse/Inso Corporation, 1996).

116. See also Laurent Mannoni, *Histoire de la Cinémathèque française*.

117. Bard, *Les Filles de Marianne*, 167.

118. Thébaud, "La Grande Guerre," 142.

119. L. Delluc, "Notes pour moi."

Chapter 3. Negotiating Art and Industry in the Postwar Context

1. Dulac uses the term "suggestion" on numerous occasions. (For example, in a 1926 interview she states, "The cinema should be a visual symphony, a succession of notes sensed by the eye, and rhythms of movements that impose a suggestion." Zahar and Burret, "Une Heure chez Mme. Germaine Dulac," 13.) In her 1924 "Aux Amis du cinema" session at the Salle du Colisée, she distinguishes this as movement "not concentrated on a story, but . . . on a sensation." Similarly, in her 1927 article "Les Esthétiques, les entraves, la cinégraphie intégrale," she writes retrospectively of this period: "the era of impressionism began. Suggestion extended action to create a more vast domain of emotion, since it was no longer trapped behind the barrier of precise facts" (42).

2. While Albert and Germaine Dulac never truly reunited after the war, letters attest to his amicable encouragement of her late 1919 to early 1920s cinema-related activities in London, Paris, and Nice. Letters from Albert Dulac to GD (June 10, 1919, to August 30 1921), FGD 3643–766. Correspondence drops off after their February 9,

1922, legal separation, with the exception of a few administrative letters through the late 1920s, often concerning Albert's apparent financial liabilities. See Albert Dulac to GD, FGD 3767–72.

3. These initiatives were carried out under her leadership at the Société des auteurs de film, the Fédération française des ciné-clubs, the Institut international du cinéma éducateur, and the Film Section of the International Council of Women, among other organizations.

4. R. Lapeyronnie, "Les Impressions de Mme Germaine Dulac. Metteur en scène cinématographiste chevalier de la Légion d'honneur," *Journal*, August 14, 1929, BNF-ASP, Coll. Auguste Rondel, RK 391.

5. GD, "Le Cinéma d'avant-garde."

6. A March 1922 letter from Albert to Germaine Dulac establishes the date of their "legal separation" as February 9, 1922. Albert to GD, March 25, 1922, FGD 3767. A letter from Albert's lawyer, Maître Bertin, sent to Germaine Dulac, as well as a statement absolving Albert's financial debt to her, refers to their parting of ways as a "separation de corps et des biens" (separation of body and belongings), a juridical status that ends any obligation of cohabitation. GD, January 28, 1928, FGD 3787. While the statement employs Dulac's maiden name, it uses the precise term "legal separation" as opposed to "divorce," which was a viable juridical option at the time: "Elisabeth, G. Saisset-Schneider, spouse legally separated both in body and belongings from Marie-Louis-Albert Dulac, a judgement pronounced by the fourth chamber of the Tribunal de la Seine on February 9, 1922, declares that all accounts dating from today between M. Albert Dulac and myself have been definitively settled." She refers to the legal separation as a divorce in her family tree. FGD 4542. There is no archival correspondence between Albert and Germaine Dulac after this date.

7. Edmond Benoît-Lévy (1858–1929) opened Paris's first non-fairground movie theater, L'Omnia, on the Grand Boulevard in 1905, and was an early writer on film authorship. His nephew, educational and fiction filmmaker Jean Benoît-Lévy (1888–1959), who worked with Dulac at the *Comité* internationale de coopération intellectuelle of the Société des nations, remained a faithful friend of Dulac and Colson-Malleville through World War II. See, for example, Edmond Benoît-Lévy, "Le Droit d'auteur cinématographique," and Valérie Vignaux, *Jean Benoît-Lévy*.

8. See "Marie-Anne Malleville," FGD 4012. I am grateful to her nephew Jean-Michel Mareau for providing me with information on these documentaries, several of which were screened at the 2005 Musée d'Orsay retrospective.

9. Germaine Albert-Dulac, "Mise-en-scène," 7. For an example of her activism regarding film authors' rights, see, "Les Auteurs des films et la censure."

10. "Société des auteurs de films," *Ciné-Club*, January 7, 1921, FGD 4342, 57.

11. Abel Gance claimed that the organization had been established in 1917/1918, although it was not registered as an association until April 18, 1921. Gauthier, *La Passion du cinéma*, 60.

12. Canudo, "L'Art pour le septième art."

13. Aladin, "La Lampe merveilleuse."

14. "Au C.A.S.A."

15. Gauthier, *La Passion du cinéma*, 63.

16. GD to Louis Moussinac, n.d., BNF-ASP, Coll. Léon Moussinac, 4°-COL-10/28. Cited by Gauthier, *La Passion du cinéma*, 64.

17. See Nourredine Ghali's excellent historicization of the term *avant-garde*, as it applies to 1920s cinema, *L'Avant-Garde Cinématographique en France*. Presentation prospectus of the Club français du cinéma (CFC), BNF-ASP, fonds Moussinac, 4°-COL-10/28. Cited by Gauthier, *La Passion du cinéma*, 64–65.

18. Gauthier, *La Passion du cinéma*, 111. See also "Ciné-Club de France."

19. De Baecque, "Les Mots de l'histoire du cinéma." See also Rancière, *Les Mots de l'histoire*.

20. Presentation brochure of the Ciné-Club de France (CCF) [1924], BNF-ASP, fonds Moussinac, 4°-COL-10/30. Cited by Gauthier, *La Passion du cinéma*, 113.

21. Gauthier, *La Passion du cinéma*, 202–3; "Statuts de la FFCC," FGD 932.

22. Gauthier, *La Passion du cinéma*, 202.

23. Ibid., 183–85.

24. GD, "Allocution inaugurale du premier congrès des ciné-clubs de langue française," November 13–14, 1929, FGD 1171.

25. As Laurent Mannoni has noted, two strong personalities of the early ciné-club movement, Dulac along with Jean Tedesco, would serve on the executive board for the creation of the Cinémathèque française as of 1936. Mannoni, *Histoire de la Cinémathèque française*, 20.

26. Mannoni, *Histoire de la Cinémathèque française*, 47, 78.

27. According to the late film and surrealism scholar Alain Virmaux, who met with Colson-Malleville in the 1960s, and whom I had the pleasure to interview on several occasions, Dulac used her Schneider family connections to gain access to the military vaults. Whether or not these efforts were in relation to the CF, or to Gaumont, where she maintained some responsibilities through the late 1930s and early 1940s, is not entirely clear. Interview with Alain Virmaux, Paris, March 21, 2001.

28. Lois Weber, seen as Dulac's U.S. counterpart at the time, was one of many women directors who, finding themselves pushed out of an increasingly "masculinized" and vertically integrated U.S. industry in the early 1920s, actively resisted emerging forms of corporate control. See "Lois Weber's Rival"; and Shelley Stamp, "'Exit Flapper, Enter Woman,' or Lois Weber in Jazz Age Hollywood." See also Kay Armatage, *The Girl from God's Country*.

29. GD, "Ayons la Foi," in *Écrits*, 21.

30. The company letterhead read Albert Dulac of Paris Films—Les Films DH, Director René Silz, 1265–69 Broadway, N.Y. GD to Louis Nalpas, November 24, 1919, BNF-ASP, Sandberg Papers, 4-Col-59/.2, Victorine 1913–1919 (1).

31. Gaumont, "Sur la crise du cinématographe en France."

32. "Communiqué du WID's Daily, New York," *Ciné pour Tous* (later retitled *Cinéa-Ciné pour Tous*), November 15, 1919, FGD 4342, 76; GD to Louis Nalpas, November 25, 1919, BNF-ASP, Sandberg Papers, 4-Col-59/.2, Victorine 1913–1919 (1).

33. Albert Dulac to GD, October 22, 1920, FGD 3709; ibid., n.d. [1921], FGD 3705.

34. Alice Guy to Ciné-Studio, September 8, 1922, BNF-ASP, Sandberg Papers, 4°-Col-59/2, Victorine 1920–1926 (2); Albert Dulac to GD, March 8, 1921, FGD 3740. The British Film Institute holds copies of both *La Souriante Madame Beudet* (1923) and *Âme d'artiste* (1925).

35. "'Le Courrier' en Allemagne." For a synopsis of the incomplete film *Werther*, see Harry Waldman, *Scenes Unseen*, 249–50.

36. Guy to Ciné-Studio.

37. Bastide, "Jacques de Baroncelli."

38. "Los Angeles à Nice. Napoléon et le Maréchal Pétain," and "Los Angeles à Nice."

39. Studio owner Louis Nalpas noted his desire to limit production to adopt the U.S. technique of focusing the action on two or three main characters, while presenting them in an original and uniquely French milieu: "The Americans know how to interest just us much with comedies or dramas set in the country or on their ranches, as through the sentimental or matrimonial adventures of young townsmen. France offers us extraordinary and unexploited resources in this regard." Louis Nalpas to Serge Sandberg, December 13, 1918, BNF-ASP, Sandberg Papers, 4°-Col-59/.2, Victorine 1913–1919 (1).

40. For more on the directors at Studios de la Victorine, see Anne-Elizabeth Dutheil de la Rochère, *Les Studios de la Victorine*.

41. Auguste Nardy, "L'Union cinématographique française. Les projets de Germaine Dulac, René le Somptier et Henri Fescourt," *Bonsoir*, November 13, 1921, BNF-ASP, Coll. Auguste Rondel, RK 391.

42. In the mid-1930s, as director of the Film Section of the cultural organization Mai '36 under the Popular Front, Dulac would play a central role in launching one of France's largest cooperative efforts, the production of Jean Renoir's *La Marseillaise* (1938). She would subsequently go on to direct the documentary *Le Retour à la vie* (1936) for the film cooperative l'Union des techniciens socialistes (Union of Socialist Technicians). This cooperative method was later adopted by New Wave directors in the 1960s, one of the most striking examples being that of the SLON cooperative, which produced the 1967 militant film *Loin du Vietnam* (Far from Vietnam). Directors included Jean-Luc Godard, Joris Ivens, William Klein, Claude Lelouch, Chris Marker, and Alain Resnais.

43. Bastide, "Jacques de Baroncelli," 31.

44. GD, "Chez D. W. Griffith"; *C. Spectacles*, December 11, 1922, FGD 4342, 74.

45. GD, "Chez D. W. Griffith."

46. Albert Dulac to GD, March 8, 1921, FGD 3740.

47. See Bard, *Les Garçonnes*, 142–43.

48. Sohn, "Entre Deux Guerres," 140. As Sohn notes, this liberation of morals stops at the "threshold" of female homosexuality, which, far from the "liberating saphism" of the turn-of-the-century, is, for the most part, condemned to secrecy (140).

49. Thébaud, "La Grande Guerre," 85–87. See also Bard, *Les Garçonnes*.

50. *Flapper* was initially a derogatory term, denoting a young wild duck. Among the other examples of usage in the *OED* are these: A. Barrère and C. G. Leland, *Dict. Slang* (1889), *Flippers, flappers*, very young girls trained to vice; J. S. Farmer *Slang* (1893), *Flapper*, a very young prostitute; J. R. Ware *Passing Eng.* (1909), *Flapper*, a very immoral young girl in her early "teens."

51. Sohn, "Entre Deux Guerres," 165.

52. Thébaud also invoked novelist Colette Yver, the author of *Princesses de science* (1907) and *Les Jardins du féminisme* (1920), who Dulac interviewed for *La Française* in 1908: "French novelist Colette Yver repeats that woman could not be 'an autonomous being,' without impunity [or negative consequences], for herself and society." Thébaud, "La Grande Guerre," 137.

53. In addition, when compared to her articles for *La Française*, Dulac's feminism was dramatically suppressed in her 1920s lectures, writings, and interviews on cinema, to the point that, when asked in an interview for the women's journal *Ève*, if her occupation was "feminine," or "if it offer[ed] a new career for her sisters," Dulac responded in the negative. GD, "Comment je suis," 44.

54. At times, and even more so as she moved towards her ideal of a "pure cinema" in her abstract films, Dulac would employ quasi-scientific film techniques of extreme close-ups and slow motion (or what Paula Amad refers to as a "radical type of naturalism") that penetrate and extract "the hidden underside to film's otherwise familiar reality." Amad, *Counter-Archive*, 212.

55. GD, presentation of *La Belle Dame sans merci* (1921), FGD 29, 2.

56. See Bordwell, "French Impressionist Cinema."

57. Dulac distributed her most recent Les Films DH, *Le Bonheur des autres* (1918), as well as her future productions, *Malencontre* (1920) and *La Belle Dame sans merci* (1921), through this office.

58. GD, *La Cigarette*, FGD 45.

59. Ibid. Other locations include various Parisian streets (rue St. Augustin, rue Royale, and rue Denfert-Rochereau).

60. Dulac used the term "artist-creator" in her article "Mise-en-scène." GD, "Où sont les interprètes?"

61. See Bastide, "Jacques de Baroncelli," 31. In this same year, Baroncelli shot *Le retour aux champs* (1918) in outdoor decors. Delluc, who praised this film for its "vivid sense of impressionism," its "illusion of the real," and its "sensation of life," situated Baroncelli alongside naturalistic filmmakers André Antoine, Léon Poirier, and Jacques Feyder. His film *Ramuncho* of the same year, set in Basque country, also employed location shooting and nonprofessional actors.

Chaix, who served as cinematographer on the wartime patriotic films of Henri Pouctal (1915–18), would become Baroncelli's regular cinematographer (1923–33). Chaix would also shoot Louis Delluc's *Le Silence* (1920) and René Clair's *Le Fantôme de Moulin Rouge* (1924). Bastide, "Jacques de Baroncelli," 31.

62. GD, "Où sont les interprètes?"

63. Ibid., 70.

64. *La Souriante Madame Beudet*, film de GD, France, 1923, BNF-ASP, fonds Moussinac, 4°-col-10/10 (16).

65. Drawing on Edward Said's foundational text, *Orientalism*, Gaylyn Studlar has addressed the use of orientalism (a colonialist hybridized depiction or imitation of Eastern cultures) as a vehicle to express women's desires for new liberties and identities in 1920s Hollywood cinema. Studlar links the use of dance and orientalism to women's desire to escape the constraints of bourgeois domesticity and to create new transformative identities "convergent with those qualities of the New Woman" that troubled social conservatives. According to Studlar, dance drew on the symbolic value of the Orient as a place of liminal identities, in an era in which women's newfound possibilities for social and sexual freedom were under question. Studlar, "'Out-Salomeing Salome,'" 105–6.

66. See Bard, *Les Garçonnes*, and Guido and Haver, *La Mise en scène*, 22.

67. Rose-Nicole, *La Vie au grand air*, September 1918, BNF JO 59058. Rose-Nicole also authored *Les Secrets de beauté de la parisienne en cent confidences* (The beauty secrets of the Parisienne in one hundred confidances).

68. Suzanne Grinberg, *L'Education physique. Revue scientifique et critique*, May 15, 1922. Reprinted in Simonet, ed., *Impressions du sport*, 56.

69. See Véray, "Entre Héroïsation et féminisme," 39–61.

70. Rose-Nicole, *La Vie au grand air; La Culture Physique*, March 1930. Cited in Simonet, *Impressions du Sport*, 59.

71. See announcement, *Cinéa-Ciné pour Tous*, no. 4 (August 1, 1919), 2.

72. Louis Delluc to Louis Nalpas, [April 29, 1919], BNF-ASP, Sandberg Papers, 4°-Col-59/.2, Victorine 1913–1919 (1), 1. In another letter to Nalpas, Delluc described Dulac as a "flexible and understanding director who reviewed the script with remarkable tact." Delluc to Nalpas, [May 6, 1919], BNF-ASP, Sandberg Papers, 4°-Col-59/.2, Victorine 1913–1919 (1).

73. Delluc to Nalpas, [May 6, 1919].

74. GD, "Le Mouvement créateur d'action."

75. Henri Barbusse, *Le Feu, journal d'une escouade* (Paris: E. Flammarion, 1916). Cited in Thébaud, *La Femme*, 104.

76. For instance, as Richard Abel has noted, Delluc described the intercutting of the film's fight to the death scene with a scene marking the heroine's indifference, or the juxtaposition of "passion and pleasure" with "blood and death," as a strikingly successful example of the relative synchronism offered by the medium. Louis Delluc, "*La Fête espagnole*." For an extensive study of Delluc's films, see also Richard Abel, "Louis Delluc."

77. Mannoni, *Histoire de la Cinémathèque française*, 61.

78. Abel, *French Cinema*, 314.

79. Fescourt, *La Foi et les montagnes*, 158. Cited by Abel, *French Cinema*, 314.

80. These include Stasia Napierkowska (1917); one of Isadora Duncan's disciples, Djemil Anik (1920, 1927); music hall dancer Edmonde Guy (1928); and ballerina Lilian Constantini (1929–30). She also employed several male sportsmen, such as

professional and amateur athletes Raoul Paoli (1923) and Georges Charlia, respectively, as well as dancer Ernest Van Duren (1928).

81. Interestingly, in preparation for an unspecified collection on surrealism and cinema, as well as for his 1965 book on Delluc, Marcel Tariol asked Colson-Malleville if he could visit Dulac's apartment to look at documents on these two collaborations. Marcel Tariol to Marie-Anne Colson-Malleville, February 13, 1964, FGD 4237.

82. Soupault, "'La Fête espagnole.'"

83. Dulac was disconcerted by what she referred to as the "Crapouillot affair," and wrote several letters of protest.

84. René Bizet, "Louis Delluc," *Le Crapouillot*, special issue on Cinema, February 16, 1921:16, BiFi, fonds Louis Delluc, LD 55.

85. According to a letter from Dulac to Moussinac, who had requested copies of all shooting scripts for his film library, the script for *La Fête espagnole* was lost. GD to Léon Moussinac, [1929], BNF-ASP, Coll. Léon Moussinac, 4°-COL-10/28. Several synopses exist. See "*La Fête espagnole*. Sentimental film by Louis Delluc. Directed by Germaine Dulac. Resumé," handwritten by Louis Delluc, FGD 245; and *La Fête espagnole*: Synopsis (made aposteriori for distributors): "Cinegraphic composition of Louis Delluc filmed by Madame Germaine Dulac for Louis Nalpas Films," FGD 246.

86. See Sadoul, *Le Cinéma français*, 23–34; and *Histoire du cinéma mondial*, 163–77. Cited in Bordwell, "French Impressionist Cinema," 7.

87. While Delluc was the most venerated critic of the period, the eloquent and neglected film critic and musicologist Émile Vuillermoz had written a regular film column for *Le Temps* since 1915. Heu, *"Le Temps" du cinéma*.

88. Delluc, "Le Point de vue," 27. At the time of the film's release in Belgium and then in France, Dulac's husband, who was managing her business affairs in Paris, wrote "Delluc called me to say that la Fête is a great success in Belgium. Continue, my dear. Great success awaits." Albert Dulac to GD, [May] 1920, FGD 3684.

89. A photo of Ève Francis wearing one of these dresses appears in *Art et Décoration*. The photo is accompanied by a caption that also shifts the credit for the film to its screenwriter: "Costume by Ève Francis in Louis Delluc's *La Fête espagnole*, directed by Germaine Dulac (1920)," *Art et Décoration*, no. 74 (November [1920]), BiFi, fonds Louis Delluc, LD 80 (2). See also Léon Moussinac, "La Mode et le costume des femmes au cinéma."

90. Fescourt, *La Foi et les montagnes*. Cited in Gilles Delluc, *Louis Delluc*, 214.

91. L. Delluc, "Le Point de vue," 27–28.

92. GD to Louis Nalpas, [1920], BNF-ASP, Sandberg Papers, 4-Col-59/.2, Victorine 1913–1919 (1).

93. L. Delluc, "Le Point de vue," 27–28.

94. Ibid., 28.

95. Epstein launched his career in the early 1920s with his first book, *Bonjour Cinema* (1921); his first film, *Pasteur* (1922); and his impressionist masterpiece, *Cœur fidele* (1923). Epstein explored this conception in alternate avant-garde and documentary modes, including in his *La Chute de la maison d'Usher* (1926) and *Finis*

Terrae (1929), the latter of which premiered alongside Dulac's films for the opening of the art house theater L'Œil de Paris. For more on Epstein, see the profusion of work by Jacques Aumont, Vincent Guigeno, Prosper Hillairet, Trond Lundemo, Laura Vichi, and the collection edited by Sarah Keller and Jason N. Paul, *Jean Epstein*.

96. Epstein, "Naissance d'un langage,"65–66.

97. Dulac employed the term *photogénie* almost exclusively when citing other writers. She invoked the notion of movement as her central concept, which she linked to the pioneers Marey, Muybridge, and the Lumière brothers, as discussed below.

98. Eric Rohmer and Michel Mardore. "Interview with Henri Langlois," *Cahiers du cinéma*, n. 135 (September 1962), cited by Mannoni, *Histoire de la Cinémathèque française*, 61.

99. Guy Chantepleure was the pseudonym of novelist Mme Edgar Dussap, née Jeanne-Caroline Violet.

100. Jean Morizot, "Un Film élégant. 'Malencontre,'" October 14, 1920, BNF-ASP, fonds Rondel, 8°RK 6061, 5.

101. While set in a château, the film contained numerous location shots from the Midi region in southern France. One critic remarked, "Throughout this film, Mme Dulac has shown so many fine views, beautiful pillows, blossoming orchards, herds grazing in the moors, haughty interiors. Brinda's room is marvelous, the living room, piano, dance are highlighted perfectly. And the exterior shots of the Midi have a nice atmosphere of heather, flowers and flowing water." Morizot, "Un Film élégant," 5–6.

102. Morizot, "Un Film élégant," 5.

103. GD to Nalpas, November 25, 1919.

104. Morizot, "Un Film élégant," 5.

105. GD to Nalpas, November 25, 1919. Alla Nazimova, née Miriam Leventon (1879–1945), had a successful theater career first in Russia, and then in the United States, before turning to film. A copy of the Capellani film is available at the Cinémathèque de la Danse.

106. "Lecture cinématique. La Belle Dame" (lecture with film clips, C.A.S.A., Paris, [May 1921]), FGD 31, 1; "Au C.A.S.A." This third presentation followed those of filmmakers Abel Gance and René Le Somptier, her colleagues at CASA.

107. Ed Friedlander suggests that Irène Hillel-Erlanger was influenced by Keats's notion of the "pleasure thermometer." According to this notion, "the pleasure of nature and music gives way to the pleasure of sexuality and romance which in turn give way to the pleasure of 'visionary dreaming'." Ed Friedlander, "Enjoying 'La Belle Dame Sans Merci,' by John Keats," 1999, http://www.pathguy.com/lbdsm.htm, accessed November 27, 2013; the pleasure thermometer is a concept in Hillel-Erlanger's esoteric novel, illustrated by Kees Van Dongen. Hillel-Erlanger, *Voyages en kaléidoscope*.

108. The title and enigmatic femme fatale character comes from a fifteenth-century French court poem by Alain Chartier.

109. "La Belle Dame," which emerged just as vampires began to gain prominence in literature, finds an heir in the 1920s figure of the "Vamp." She belongs, as Ed

Friedlander describes, to the "long tradition of supernatural beings who have charmed mortals into spiritual slavery." Friedlander, "Enjoying 'La Belle Dame Sans Merci.'"

110. Synopsis, *La Belle Dame Sans Merci* [manuscript of Irène Hillel-Erlanger, April–May 1917], FGD 21.

111. A film intertitle reads, "Numerous are the men that Lola makes suffer. At the club, laughingly, they nickname her the 'Belle Dame Sans Merci.'"

112. Reaffirming Lola's refusal, the young suitor states, "In the time it takes you to smoke a cigarette, you'll have forgotten me. How could you say such a thing?"

113. One man sketches an unattractive caricatured portrait of her, and remarks, "How she'll be tomorrow, beautiful Lola!"

114. J. L. Croze, "La Belle Dame sans merci," [ca. 1921], BNF-ASP, fonds Rondel, 8 RK 2153, 13.

115. See Desclaux, "Nos Metteurs en scène," 6; Dulac's treatment of this naturalistic setting inspired an article on this subject, further addressed in the discussion of *La Souriante Madame Beudet* (1923). See also Claude-Fayard, "Germaine Dulac et la province," FGD 4342, 77.

116. George Cukor employed a device similar to Stroheim's in *The Women* (1939), as did Fritz Lang in his early U.S. film *Fury* (1936), which Bazin mentions in "The Evolution of the Language of Cinema" (1950–55). Fittingly, Bazin's article champions those directors who "put their faith in reality" over those who "put their faith in the image," an idea that reflects Dulac's earlier calls for cinematic realism. Bazin, "The Evolution of the Language of Cinema," in *What Is Cinema?*, 1:32.

117. GD, presentation of *La Belle Dame sans merci*, 2.

118. Ibid., 3.

119. Ibid., 3–4.

120. Another important motif is the circle, which recalls the use of geometric abstraction and colored rhythm in the paintings of Robert and Sonia Delaunay, and which later becomes the basis for her films *L'Invitation au voyage* and *Disque 957*.

121. GD, presentation of *La Belle Dame sans merci*, 4.

122. According to David Bordwell, in 1927 Dulac first "identifie[d] the movement as one of 'impressionism,'" and Sadoul later "name[d] it 'Impressionism'" and suggested some points of stylistic homogeneity. Bordwell, "French Impressionist Cinema," 4–7.

123. GD, presentation of *La Belle Dame sans merci*, 3–4.

124. Ibid., 3.

125. Ibid., 2. La Duse made her sole known film, *Cenere* (Ashes), in 1917.

126. GD, presentation of *La Belle Dame sans merci*, 2.

127. Dulac's associative conception also can be seen to anticipate Bergsonian philosopher Gilles Deleuze's "rhizomatic" approach to cinematic meaning. See Gilles Deleuze, *Cinéma* (2 vols.). See also Bergson's *L'Évolution créatrice*.

128. GD, presentation of *La Belle Dame sans merci*, 4.

129. GD, "Les Procédés expressifs," 39.

130. GD, "*La Mort du soleil* et la naissance du film."

131. On the script, see the following articles: Une Cinéphile, Lyon, "Sur *La Mort du soleil*," *Ciné pour Tous*, no. 91 (May 19, 1922): 14; "La Mort du soleil," *Cinémagazine*, no. 49 (n.d.): 26; and Auguste Nardy, "La Mort du soleil," *Bonsoir*, December 17, 1921: 6. All in BNF-ASP, fonds Rondel, 4°RK 6627.

132. Landry, "La Mort du soleil." A critic for the illustrated journal *Excelsior* affirmed the originality of Dulac's conception, and emphasized the importance of the "accumulated play of synthesis and of oppositions." G., "Des Deux cotés de l'écran."

133. While these films are currently lost, a newspaper article states that a 1922 edition of this series documented the career options for young women at the time. GD, "On Tourne: Bienveillance" (We're shooting: show good will), *Excelsior*, June 16, 1922, FGD 4342, 50.

134. P.R., "Films Triomphe." Dulac announces the alternate title, *Jenny l'ouvrière*, in GD, "*La Mort du soleil* et la naissance du film," 14.

135. Gauthier, *La Passion du cinéma*, 155–56.

136. "On Tourne: Bienveillance," *Excelsior*, June 16, 1922, FGD 4342, 50. Dulac would speak out against such hindrances as a newsreel director in the 1930s. GD, "Les Difficultés du journalisme cinématographique."

137. GD, "*La Mort du soleil* et la naissance du film," 14.

Chapter 4. Dulac's Aesthetic Matures

1. Denys Amiel and André Obey's two-act tragicomedy starred Mme Greta Prozor (and later Marcelle Géniat) as Mme Beudet, and actor Jacques Baumer of symbolist director Lugné-Poë's Théâtre de l'œuvre. Despite initial difficulties, which led to the founding of the Canard sauvage, a cooperative regrouping eleven authors "each almost as poor as the other," the play was a great critical success, and had a long run at several prominent theaters. Denys Amiel, "Quelques Souvenirs doux-amers sur les malheurs et la victoire de 'la Souriante Madame Beudet.'" *Comœdia*, March 18, 1935, BNF-ASP, fonds Rondel, Rf. 50.015 (23). The play began a long run at Paris's Odéon theater and the New York's Apollo Theater in 1922, before confirming its status as a classic at the Comédie-Française in March 1935. Denys Amiel and André Obey, *La Souriante Madame Beudet. Programme officiel des tournées Ch[arles] Baret* (film script), BNF-ASP, fonds Rondel, Rf. 50.015 (4); and Denys Amiel and André Obey, *La Souriante Madame Beudet. n. 7, Supplement to La Revue Hebdomadaire, August 5, 1922. Paris: Librairie Stock, 1922* (film script).

2. André Obey to Marcel Vandal, November 8, 1922, FGD 319.

3. Dulac refers to M. Beudet as an accountant in her 1924 Musée Galliera talk. GD, "Les Procédés expressifs," 37.

4. GD, "*La Souriante Madame Beudet*, film de Germaine Dulac, France, 1923" (script), BNF-ASP, fonds Moussinac, 4-col-10/10 (16), 1.

5. Émile Vuillermoz, "La Souriante Madame Beudet," [*Le Temps*], February 2, 1923, BNF-ASP, fonds Rondel, Rf. 50.016, 1.

6. Claude-Fayard (pseudonym), "Germaine Dulac et la province," FGD 4342, 77.

7. The opposition between interior and exterior is characteristic of many of Dulac's films, from *La Belle Dame* (1921), where the confined Countess and liberated Lola are separated by the domestic threshold, to *L'Invitation au voyage* (1927), whose cabaret's fantasy provoking maritime window opens out onto a cluttered back lot, to *La Princesse Mandane* (1928), whose heroine is imprisoned in her palace.

8. Claude-Fayard, "Germaine Dulac et la province," 77.

9. GD, "Projet de livre sur le cinéma," FGD 1371.

10. The Pre-Raphaelite school, known for its portrayal of melancholic and dreamy women, lost in their interior world, and manifesting little facial expression beyond that of the eyes, coincides perfectly with Dulac's representation of Mme Beudet.

11. GD, "La Souriante Madame Beudet" (script).

12. GD, "Les Procédés expressifs," 36.

13. GD, "Le Sens du cinéma," 162; GD, "Les Procédés expressifs," 37.

14. Dulac refers to the extreme close-up as both "psychological shot," or as "the impressionist note, the passing influence of things that surround us." GD, "Les Procédés expressifs," 37.

15. GD, "Les Procédés expressifs," 36.

16. Guesde was one of those of whom Marx is reported to have said that, if they were Marxists, "what is certain is that I am not a Marxist." Guesde, *La Femme et la société bourgeoise*. Guesde's granddaughter, the dancer and actress known as Lilian Constantini, would perform in Dulac's *Thèmes et variations* (1929), as well as in what Dulac termed her "illustrated records" or "musical films" for Columbia Records (1930).

17. Sergei Eisenstein, "Methods of Montage" (1929) in *Film Form*, 82–83.

18. See Sergei Eisenstein, "The Cinematographic Principle and the Ideogram" (1929), in *Film Form*, 28–44; and Sergei Eisenstein, "A Dialectic Approach to Film Form" (1929), in *Film Form*, 45–71.

19. GD, presentation of *La Belle Dame sans merci* 1921, GDA 29, 3–4.

20. GD, "Le Cinéma, art des nuances spirituelles." 51.

21. GD, "Du Sentiment à la ligne," 28. Dulac founded and edited the journal *Schémas*.

22. Jacques Guillon, "Germaine Dulac et le cinéma actuel," 136.

23. In one shot, we see an abstract representation of a car driving through clouds. As described in the film's shooting script: "Mme Beudet imagines herself driving a car." GD, "*La Souriante Madame Beudet*" (script).

24. Dulac noted in 1924, "the poor woman, overcome by her poor noisy husband, dreams of a strong and powerful man who would deliver her from her accountant husband." GD, "Les Procédés expressifs," 37.

25. Dulac wrote: "An expression to keep its full value doesn't change shots." GD, "Films visuels et anti-visuels," 121.

26. Demenÿ was not only one of cinema's foremost pioneers, alongside U.S. photographer Eadweard Muybridge and French scientist Étienne-Jules Marey (with whom

he trained), he was also a great innovator of physical education, having developed and popularized a method of scientific and aesthetic exercise known as harmonious gymnastics. Dulac spoke highly of Demenÿ's contributions to the cinema, without which she said it could never have existed. GD, "Film" (article for an encyclopedia), FGD 1365, 5. Guido and Haver, *La Mise en scène*.

27. GD, "Du Sentiment à la ligne," 30; In her 1925 "L'Essence du cinéma, idée visuelle," Dulac writes "the external goal of cinema is to reproduce movement visually in all of its phases" (63).

28. GD, "Commentaire et transition," *Schémas*, no. 1 (February 1927), FGD 1387.

29. Obey, *L'Orgue du stade* (Paris: Gallimard, 1924).

30. GD, "La Souriante Madame Beudet" (synopsis), n.d., FGD 310.

31. GD, *La Souriante Madame Beudet* (script), FGD 309.

32. The script reads: "Above, the theater with the curtain which falls before the two reconciled puppets and which in falling reveals the word 'Theater' painted on its canvas." Ibid.

33. Dulac contrasted the modernity of the hieratic acting style of Germaine Dermoz (Mme Beudet), appropriate for the modern medium of cinema, with the traditional theatricality and exaggerated acting of Alexandre Arquillère (M. Beudet).

34. For more on the French and German subtitles of the Swiss print held at EYE, please see Charles Musser, "The Clash between Theater and Film," 123. Dulac viewed the public, and its undeveloped taste, as one of the primary obstacles in developing the art of cinema. See GD, "Le Mouvement créateur," 46; GD, "Le Veritable Esprit du septième art," 54; and GD, "Défense et attaque du cinéma."

35. We find notes for Dulac's adaptation of the Xavier de Montépin novel, *La Porteuse du pain*, on the back of her script for *La Souriante Madame Beudet* (1923). GD, *La Souriante Madame Beudet* (script). During this period, Le Somptier and Dulac worked together at the Société des auteurs as vice president and treasurer, respectively. "A la Société des auteurs de films." Always resourceful, Dulac wrote a novelized version of Kurt Bernhardt's film *Les Bêtes humaines* (1929) for the Société des cinéromans, when French film production hit an all-time low in 1929. This practice, which merits further research, was relatively widespread. Examples include Ricciotto Canudo's ciné-novel based on Abel Gance's *La Roue* (1922), and René Jeanne's novelization of Dulac's *Antoinette Sabrier* (1927).

36. GD to Henri Fescourt, July 20, 1923, FGD 3791.

37. GD, "Le Mouvement créateur d'action," 49; GD, "Le Véritable ésprit du septième art," 53.

38. One critic described *Gossette* as a film as "unconventional," but also one that would greatly aid in the "rénovation du roman-cinéma." "Gossette," *L'Avenir*, December 28, 1923, FGD 4342, 3. François Albera explores the uniqueness of Dulac's conception of "avant-garde" as it relates to her position on commercial cinema (distinct from mercantile cinema) specifically with regard to *Gossette* and *Âme d'artiste*. Albera, "Germaine Dulac et 'l'essor definitive de l'avant-garde.'"

39. Jarville, "Dans les studios." See also Fescourt, "La Technique nouvelle du cinéroman," FGD 4342, 75; and Fescourt and Bouquet, *L'Idée et l'écran*. As critic Jean

Chataigner asserted in his film review, "Mme Dulac is making the cinema progress step by step, and the public is following and applauding her." Jean Chataigner, "Le Diable dans la ville," January 30, 1925, BNF-ASP, fonds Rondel, 8°RK3623 (1), 2.

40. *Âme d'artiste*, film de Germaine Dulac, France, 1925, BNF-ASP, fonds Moussinac, 4-col-10/10 (1).

41. Other motifs of *Âme d'artiste* that recur in Dulac's work include dance, oriental decors, cross-dressing, and travel. Dulac also employed newsreels in an innovative fashion to communicate her heroine's imagined vision of distant lands.

42. Marie-Anne Colson-Malleville in "Interview Mme Djemil Anik (actress): souvenirs sur Germaine Dulac (conducted by Musidora and Malleville [*sic*])," July 5, 1946, CRH 030, 1.

43. This information comes from a meeting of the Comité de recherche historique de la Cinémathèque française, hosted by Dulac's companion, Colson-Malleville, and attended by dancer Djemil Anik, eurhythmics founder Jacques Dalcroze, and actress Musidora. "Interview Mme. Djemil Anik," 13.

44. Maxime Gorki, "Radda," *Les Annales Politiques et Littéraires*, no. 1003 (September 14, 1902): 174–76, BNF-ASP, Fol. Jo. 693.

45. Dulac also reaffirmed her commitment to the pacifist movement in this year when she took the reigns as vice president of the Comité de desarmement morale (Committee for Moral Disarmament), a feminist and pacifist organization. "Tribune libre des femmes," *L'Ère Nouvelle*, November 7, 1925, FGD 4343, 41 insert.

46. "Contrat pour la fabrication du film dont le sujet est inspiré par les œuvres de Maxime Gorky," FGD 254, 1.

47. Ibid. The case of *La Folie des vaillants* is quite particular, as Dulac was asked to take over a project initiated by Russian director A. Nikitine. With access to only a fraction of the initial budget of 78,000 francs, Dulac was asked to integrate the already existing footage. This may explain a few of the film's incongruous static shots, such as that of the palace of the wealthy magnate Tirza, who Radda also rejects. These shots are integrated alongside the more subtle and fluid shots of nature, and the more rhythmic montage sequences, characteristic of Dulac. The budget of *La Folie des vaillants* was miniscule when compared to the 2 million franc budget of Marcel L'Herbier's *Resurrection*, or the 20 million franc budget of a Universal production, made that same year. See Abel, *French Cinema*, 28.

48. Untitled clipping accompanying letter from René Ginet to GD, FGD 4346.

49. On the relationship between music and cinema, see "La Naissance d'un sixième art. Essai sur le cinématographe," *Les Entretiens Idéalistes* 10, no. 61 (October 25, 1911): 169–79. As Émile Vuillermoz wrote in 1927, "It is clear that in the near or distant future, we can hope to orient certain particularly talented cinégraphistés [filmmakers] toward what Germaine Dulac so aptly calls the pure visual symphony" ("La Musique des images").

50. GD, "L'Essence du cinéma," 66.

51. Canudo, *L'Usine aux images*, 92.

52. GD, "Les Esthétiques," 104.

53. See Guido, "Vers une 'Symphonie visuelle d'images rythmées.'"

54. GD, "L'Action de l'avant-garde cinématographique," 1058.

55. GD, "Le Mouvement créateur d'action," 50.

56. She wrote "the movement's 'spirit' (état d'esprit) [is] realized not only through a suite of images, but through the double movement of the image and its juxtaposition." Ibid., 49.

57. GD, "Le Mouvement créateur d'action," 47.

58. In ibid., Dulac referred to the film as "the song of the rail and the wheels" (48).

59. GD, "Le Mouvement créateur d'action," 49.

60. GD, "L'Essence du cinéma," 67.

61. GD, "Tout Film." GD, "Concessions," 70.

62. GD, "Tout Film," 68.

63. "Interview Mme Djemil Anik," 13; "Contrat pour la fabrication du film dont le sujet," 4.

64. GD, "Les Esthétiques," 48.

65. GD, "La Musique du silence," 108.

66. *Antoinette Sabrier*, the story of a woman caught between her oil-baron husband and her lover, exists in at least three distinct versions among surviving prints, including one Catholic print, in which all of the film's exotic festive scenes are cut.

67. The Dulac-Artaud project might also be read in the context of the Belle Époque, as an anticlerical piece. Its title also evokes symbolist pioneer Lugné-Poë, nicknamed the "sleepwalking clergyman." In a CRH interview in 1946 conducted by actress Musidora, Marie-Anne Colson-Malleville, while affirming Dulac's strong anticlerical position, denied any anticlerical message. More significantly, she altogether disavowed the importance of the film to Dulac: "The script is hers, but the idea is Mr. Artaud's. . . . No, I don't think she would have written *The Seashell and the Clergyman*, for it wasn't worth much." "Interview Mme. Djemil Anik," 11.

68. In her psychoanalytic study, *To Desire Differently*, Sandy Flitterman-Lewis convincingly demonstrates Dulac's privileging of the female protagonist's desire (98–136). See also *Artaud/Dulac*, Alain Virmaux's study of the brouhaha during the film's projection at the Studio des Ursulines (February 1928), which fueled the long-standing myth surrounding the Dulac-Artaud rivalry.

69. The film, brought to the United States in the late 1930s by Iris Barry, film critic and founder of the Museum of Modern Art film department, is now available on DVD in the United States, but unfortunately only in flawed form. Despite Sandy Flitterman-Lewis's scholarship on the print, U.S. DVDs, including the 2005 Kino Video release, still present the reels of the film in the incorrect order. The EYE Film Instituut's meticulously faithful restoration of the film is available through Light Cone (Paris).

70. GD, "Rythme et technique," 112–13.

71. Kuenzli, "*La Coquille et le clergyman*."

72. Virmaux, *Artaud/Dulac*.

73. Colson-Malleville, "Interview."

74. GD, "Les Esthétiques," 31.

75. Interview with Alain Virmaux, Paris, March 21, 2001.

76. As historian Gabriele Klein has noted, the classic dancer transformed the reality of her body into the image of this fantasy. She writes "The ballerina is not only a male fantasy. Rather, the realization of her body entirely reflects the male image to the extent that it presents itself as a being that is asexual, ethereal and almost devoid of flesh. [. . .] The assimilation of the male ideal does not remain external to the dancer. [. . .] Ballerinas, torn from their own body and material foundation, present beautifully on scene that which in social reality is *synonymous with the sidelining of women* [. . .] *and the domination of the female body*" (original emphasis). Gabriele Klein, "La Construction du féminin et du masculin dans la danse des modernes." In 1935, dance critic Fernand Divoire's description of Edmonde Guy, who played the role of the princess and the ballerina in *Princesse Mandane*, corresponds entirely to this image: "Edmonde Guy—Is she a dancer? Yes, if grace with that degree of sensibility is dance. . . . For Edmonde Guy is delicate and fragile grace" (*Pour la danse*, 105).

77. GD, "Les Esthétiques," 46.

78. In her critical writings, Dulac inferred that such films should be played silent. This concurs with her titles "impressions cinégraphiques," her view of cinema as "visual music," as well as the slight variations between the structures of the films and their musical sources. Nonetheless, at the time, the films were shown with accompaniment at least on some occasions, including for a late screening of *La Coquille et le clergyman* and her abstract films in 1929. Program for *La Coquille et le clergyman*, Jean Vigo papers. Courtesy of Madame Luce Vigo.

79. Duncan, "La Danse et la nature."

80. GD, "L'Action de l'avant-garde cinématographique," 1058.

81. See GD, "Du Sentiment à la ligne."

82. This juxtaposition, which elicits reflection on the cultural instrumentalization of the female body, is even more interesting when one considers Constantini's fascinating background as granddaughter of feminist and Marxist leader Jules Guesde and future wife of capitalist heir Charles Schneider (see chapter 5).

83. "4 projets de films, dont *Thème visuel et variation cinégraphique*" (synopsis), FGD 323.

84. Amad, op. cit., 252.

85. Zahar and Burret, "Une Heure chez Mme. Germaine Dulac."

86. GD, "La Nouvelle Évolution," 139.

87. Henry Miller describes a May 1930 meeting with Dulac in her admirably decorated book-lined study on the subject of hiring his paramour June Mansfield for a sound feature, which may have been the dual language musical she supervised that year, *Valse d'amour* (1930), if not *La rue de clarisses* (1931). Calling attention to the sensual, even erotic character of certain of Dulac's abstract films (a parallel reading of which might be applied to the more feminine *Arabesque*), Miller reflects on *Thèmes et Variations*, which premiered at L'Œil de Paris (Dec. 1930): "I saw one

of hers at 'The Eye of Paris'—called *Theme with Variations*. Quite a beautiful thing, with a woman dancing throughout and for variations on the dance shots sandwiched in, of machinery in motion, often very direct, obscene, scarcely symbolic at all. For instance, she is bending backward on her toes—a crazy shot, up-ended—her arms flutter ecstatically as if she held something unmentionable in her grasp. Presto! a huge piston rod, thoroughly greased, shoots insistently backward and forward, plunges into a groove, comes out again black and greasy, to plunge forward once more" (*Letters to Emil*, 32). Of Dulac, Miller exclaims: "There is a woman, one grand Lesbienne," and characterizes her work as "another realm of film magic. Thoroughly French, absolutely artistic, unsentimental, and beyond realism" (52–53). See also *Letters to Emil*, 63.

88. *Disque 957* opens with a passage from Georges Sand's novel *Winter in Mallorca*, which references a rainy stay on the island during the early stages (1838) of her relationship with Chopin (1837–47). For a more detailed study of this film in relation to her early project on Chopin and Georges Sand project, see T. Williams, "Germaine Dulac."

89. GD, "Étude romantique. Le disque," FGD 211, 1.

90. Among some typewritten notes for Dulac's 1918 project are a list of characteristics pertaining to Chopin's preludes, including nos. 5 and 6, on which *Disque 957* is based. While Dulac's notes on the 5th Prelude relate to the serene yet impassioned tone and its proliferation of abstract visual elements, those on Prelude 6 correspond to the evening of "gloomy rain that gives the soul a terrible beating" of the cited Georges Sand passage. See "Chopin. Notes biographiques et bibliographiques," FGD 639, and "Préludes de Chopin," by I. Phillip, FGD 642.

91. "Du Sentiment à la ligne," FGD 1381, 3–4.

92. GD, "La Musique du silence," 106.

93. Edouard Ganche, *La Vie de F. Chopin dans son œuvre*, Paris: Société des Auteurs, 1909, FGD 645, 9. GD, "Aphorismes," 61. Also in 1925, referring specifically to Debussy's and Chopin's classical music pieces, she writes, "Debussy's *Le Jardin sous la pluie* or Chopin's *Le Prélude de la Goutte d'Eau* [. . .] are expressions of a soul that pours out and reacts amongst things. [. . .] Similarly, the sensitivity of the cineaste can be expressed by a superimposition of light and movement, of a vision that will move the soul of the spectator [. . .] it is not the exterior fact that is of interest really, it's the inner emanation, a certain movement of things and of people, seen through his or her state of a mind." (sic.) GD, "L'Essence du cinéma," 37.

94. GD, "Disque 957," FGD 212, 3.

95. GD, "Arabesque. Ballet cinégraphique de Germaine Dulac" (annotated alternative title: Étude cinégraphique sur une arabesque), FGD 232, 1.

96. The second section of Dulac's film, or its "second arabesque," which according to Dulac corresponds to the first arabesque of Debussy's suite, differs only in that it contains slightly more concrete forms. She writes, "Like the first, this film of undulations will be a film of scintillations and movements. Nature, flowers, branches,

scarves, gossamer threads, etc." In an early draft of her project description for *Arabesque*, Dulac wrote, "Impression to give, reflections of water and crystallin objects in movement playing in the sunlight in movement. [. . .] Each movement follows the rhythm of the arabesque and can also be assimilated to the figure of a ballet, but one in which no artist plays a part, light, water and surfaces reflecting forms, playing alone." GD, "Projet d'essai cinégraphique," FGD 226, 1.

97. GD, "Trois Rencontres avec Loïe Fuller," 109.

98. Dulac's earliest reference to the figure of the "grain of wheat" appears to be that found in her short article "Aphorismes," 60. Later references include "Du Sentiment à la ligne" and "Les Esthétiques."

99. GD, "Du Sentiment à la ligne," 31.

100. GD, "Du Sentiment à la ligne" (manuscript), FGD 1381,3.

101. Higonnet, "Femmes, images et représentations," 457.

102. Isadora Duncan, *Der Tanz der Zukunft* (Dance of the future) (Leipzig: Eugen Diderichs, 1903), 43–44. Cited by Klein, "La Construction du féminin," 187.

103. Klein, "La Construction du féminin," 189.

104. GD, "Du Sentiment à la ligne," 31.

105. Moreover, certain aspects of Dulac's aesthetic closely coincide with 1930s realist tendencies. For example, Dulac privileged a material incarnation of *cinegraphic* movement and rhythm—found in the figure of the dance, as in her passionate exposés on a grain of wheat in her 1925 essay "Films visuels et anti-visuels" and in Dr. Jean Comandon's *La Germination d'un grain de blé* (Germination of a grain of wheat)—and which could be contained within the individual shot. GD, "Films visuels," 121.

106. GD, "La Formule du cinéma pur est dans le documentaire"; GD, "La Portée educative."

Chapter 5. Fiction, Newsreels, and Social Documentary in the Sound Era

1. Henri Fescourt and Charles Ford devoted no more than half a page each to her 1930s filmmaking and activism, although both praised her enduring spirit of innovation: Fescourt, *La Foi et les montagnes*, 302; Ford, "Germaine Dulac," 41. Sandy Flitterman-Lewis briefly refers to this period as one that, in light of the political context of the time and Dulac's interests in the "social and historical aspects" of cinema, put an end to the director's formal exploration: "it seems possible that the urgency of events eclipsed theoretical investigation into the specific properties of the medium." *To Desire Differently*, 71. Siân Reynolds's online introduction to three of Dulac's articles on the newsreel, along with Flitterman-Lewis's research on women artists, including Dulac and Virginia Woolf, during the Second World War, are beginning to broaden this focus (introduction to "Germaine Dulac and Newsreel," http://tlweb.latrobe.edu.au/humanities/screeningthepast/classics/cl0301/gdcl12a.htm, accessed December 17, 2013).

2. Titles of Dulac's musical films include *Autrefois . . . aujourd'hui*, *Celles qui s'en font*, *Ceux qui ne s'en font pas*, *Danses espagnoles*, *Jour de fête*, and *Un Peu de rêve*

sur le faubourg. For more on this topic, see also Kelley Conway, *Chanteuse in the City*; and Charles O'Brien, *Cinema's Conversion to Sound*. Select Colson-Malleville titles, each projected at the 2005 Dulac Rétrospective (Musée d'Orsay), include *Les Assistantes sociales en Algérie* (1948), *Du Manuel au Robot* (1953), *Les Rails sous les palmiers* (1954), codirected by Henri Volpi and Marcel Villet, *L'Idée de François Buloz* (1956), *El Oued, la ville aux milles coupoles* (1947). Colson-Malleville also directed a poetic short based on a Dulac synopsis, *Le Petit Monde des étangs* (1952).

3. I had the pleasure of visiting with Constantini and Schneider's daughter Dominique Schneidre in her home overlooking the Jardins de Luxembourg in the spring of 2005. Incidentally, her sister Catherine was once married to the 1950s–60s filmmaker Roger Vadim (Dominique Schneidre [pseud.], *Fortune de mère*). See also Augustin Habaru, *Le Creusot, terre féodale, Schneider et les marchands de canons*, and Claude Beaud, "Les Schneider marchands de canons."

4. GD, "La Portée éducative," 204–5.

5. For more on the comparison between Dulac and Vertov, see T. Williams, "Germaine Dulac and the French Film Industry between the Wars."

6. Significantly, Dulac later asserted that if she had returned to making fiction films, they would likely have taken on many of the formal and social-oriented characteristics of her nonfiction work.

7. See T. Williams, "Pour une femme moderne et un nouveau cinéma."

8. While the Vichy regime persisted until the liberation of France in 1945, the scope of this study ends in 1942 with Dulac's death.

9. From 1928 to 1929, the number of French films produced almost halved, dropping from ninety-four to fifty-two. See Choukroun, "Le Cinéma français au temps de Jean Vigo."

10. GD to Léon Moussinac, *Panoramique du cinéma* correspondence, [1929], BNF-ASP, Coll. Léon Moussinac, 4°-COL-10/17 (19).

11. Émile Vuillermoz, "La Tour du Feu," BNF-ASP, fonds Moussinac, 4-COL-10/13 (146), 2pp. GD, *Bêtes humaines*, novel by GD based on the 1929 film of Kurt Bernhardt, 1930, FGD 4462; and J. Beulet (Éditions Tallandier) to GD, Paris, June 10, 1930, FGD 4462.

12. GD, "La Responsabilité du public"; R. Lapeyronnie, "Les Impressions de Mme Germaine Dulac. Metteur en scène cinématographiste chevalier de la Légion d'honneur," *Journal* (Paris), August 14, 1929, BNF-ASP, fonds Rondel, RK 391; Guillon, "Germaine Dulac et le cinéma actuel"; GD, "Quelques Réflexions sur le contingentement"; GD, "Proportions."

13. Boudrioz had begun his career in 1908 as a journalist, novelist, and politician, close to Socialist leader Jean Jaurès. Just after the war, when Boudrioz was making his largely experimental film *Zon* (1919), which Dulac greatly appreciated, the two became friends. Like Dulac, Boudrioz was a filmmaker who constantly sought to innovate in the 1910s–20s (e.g., in his collaboration on Abel Gance's train sequence in *La Roue*, 1922). While he continued making films in the 1930s, he was never quite able to establish himself.

14. The company was launched with a capital of 200,000 French francs, and located in the opera district (60, rue de la Chaussée d'Antin, Paris). See GD and Robert Boudrioz "Statuts. L'Essor cinématographique francais," FGD 856.

15. GD and Robert Boudrioz, GD, "Contract of GD and Robert Boudrioz. L'Essor cinématographique française.," n.d., FGD 857.

16. See Gauthier, *La Passion du cinéma*.

17. Couesnon & Cie, phonos et disques de Columbia, to GD, 1930, FGD 412. Notably, the clause spells out Dulac and Boudrioz's right to make films that are shorter than 400 meters in length, above and beyond their normal operations. These films were to be personal and noncommercial in nature. Dulac's handwritten notes concerning the contract read: "Restriction for films under 400m, which are not documentary, advertising, or current commercial films exploitable by the company that could be made by one of the two filmmakers for personal benefit. In other words, films of personal research for non-commercial circuits." GD, "Contract of GD and Robert Boudrioz. L'Essor cinématographique française," handwritten annotations by GD, FGD 858.

18. The project was temporarily postponed in November 1930 and was eventually adjourned in March 1931, due to the economic depression. Robert Boudrioz to Albert Arnould, November 30, 1930, FGD 867. See A. Arnould to GD, March 7, 1931, referring to the closure of the company due to the *crise actuelle* (current crisis), FGD 869.

19. Dulac's contract, GFFA, Gaumont-Franco-Films-Aubert, August 14, 1930, FGD 874, 1. In July 1930, in response to an offer from a Mr. Guy Ferrant to direct a film for Gaumont, Dulac expressed her desire to be permanently attached to the company. GFFA Legal Department, GD/GFFA Affair Report, July 30, 1931, FGD 880, 1. While there is no documentation showing that Schneider had a role in Dulac's hire, the fact that France-Actualités-Gaumont was financed in part by the Comité des forges (French Steel commission), linked to the Schneider Empire, is only one of several elements inviting further investigation into this question.

20. Dulac's contract emphasized the ubiquitous nature of her role as assistant artistic director, providing for her collaboration in the creation of *all* films the company was to produce, as well as her participation in virtually every step of the production process (script, découpage, directing, editing, sound design). Its second clause permitted her to continue her teaching activities through private or public lectures (although it stipulated that these were to be submitted in advance to Gaumont). A third clause authorized her to direct one feature per year. For these activities, Dulac was to receive a monthly salary of 8,500 francs, as well as a bonus calculated on an annual basis of 100,000 francs pro-rata for each feature. GD contract, 1–2.

21. GD/GFFA Affair Report, 3.

22. Ibid., 2. Note concerning Dulac's contract, MS by M.-A. Malleville, ff., n.d., FGD 875.

23. GD to Paul Devinat, general secretary of GFFA, January 3, 1931, FGD 876.

24. See "Spectacles."

25. *Bombance* (Feast) was the first installment of a four-film series intended to launch two comic hopefuls. The film is a satirical depression era tale of two unemployed and rotund middle-aged men who pick up work at the docks in the hopes of affording a feast, but who, out of shape, and unable to do the work required, end up "feasting" on simple sandwiches. The later film, *Le Picador*, which replays the time-worn tale of paternal jealousy (e.g., Gance's *La Roue*, 1922), is the story of a bullfighter who falls in love with his adoptive daughter, and who becomes atrociously jealous of all men who approach her. *Le Picador*, film program, BNF-ASP, fonds Rondel, 8° RK 7421 (3).

26. In August 1931, Dulac wrote, "I only supervised 200m of a small film, and that, at the end of the shoot, because we had to save the film." GD to Georges Leveque (lawyer), [August] 1931, FGD 882, 1.

27. The script is undeveloped, the characters lack depth, and the film's narration lacks the overall rhythmic structure that Dulac sought, and that was epitomized by her own declared cinematic ideal, elaborated in the 1920s. The fact that Jim Gerald, the actor originally chosen to star in the film, refused the project suggests that it may have been flawed from the outset. In addition, the production director (a Mr. Costil) later blamed Dulac unjustly for the film's failure. "Réunions du Comité de Production. Procès Vérbaux. GFFA," February 4, 1931, FGD 892. In a letter to her lawyer, Georges Leveque, she wrote of "the little note, placed in *La Griffe* by Mr. Costil's secret envoys, which seeks to attribute the failure of the GFFA production to me. Now I was not involved in this production, since as Assistant Artistic Director, I was responsible from August 15, 1930 to June 1, 1931, solely for, if I dare say, the material preparation of the films, never having the power to choose or impose a subject, nor to supervise in studio, the two most important points relating to the quality of a production." GD to Leveque, 1.

28. Dulac was scheduled to direct a feature film, written by J. Bedouin and titled *La Rue des Clarisses*. However, owing to delays with other productions, the project was eventually abandoned. See "La Nouvelle Production française."

29. This congress followed the 1st Congrès international du cinéma indépendant, organized by surrealist Robert Aron, and held from September 2 through 7, 1929, at the Château de la Sarraz in Switzerland, which Dulac, inexplicably, did not attend. In an article devoted to the work of the first CICI, Arnold Kohler mourned the absence of several key personalities, including Dulac, Epstein, L'Herbier, Gance, and Man Ray based in France; Piscator and Lotte Reininger from Germany; and Pudovkin and Vertov of the Soviet Union. Kohler, untitled, 8. It should be noted that Dulac nonetheless persisted in realizing one of the primary missions of the 1st CICI (i.e., the establishment of a permanent link between film associations and ciné-clubs, and the improvement of independent film distribution) when she inaugurated the Fédération française des ciné-clubs (FFCC, French Federation of ciné-clubs) in November 1929. See "Présentation du Congrès international du cinéma indépendant de la Sarraz (CICI, International Congress of Independent Cinema)," [September 1929],

BNF-ASP, fonds Moussinac, 4º-COL-10/34; and GD, "Allocution inaugurale du premier congrès des ciné-clubs de langue française," November 13–14, 1929, FGD 1171. See also Christophe Gauthier, *La Passion du cinéma*, 198–202.

30. See Buache, "Le Cinéma indépendant et d'avant-garde à la fin du muet."

31. See, for example, Dulac's historical article, "Le Cinéma d'avant-garde," Dulac had long expressed her interest in nonfiction cinema in all of its manifestations, from the educational film to the documentary and the newsreel. We find evidence of her pedagogical aspirations as early as 1904. Her work in the domain of "journalisme cinématographique" (film journalism) dates back to 1918, when she collaborated on the first of a series of documentary shorts titled "France's Most Deserving Young Woman" featuring the ubiquitous actress Musidora. See GD, "On Tourne. Bienveillance," *Excelsior*, June 16, 1922, FGD 4342, 50. We can also trace Dulac's involvement in educational cinema to several conferences of the 1920s, beginning with the Congrès du cinéma éducateur organized by Adrien Bruneau, the director of the Cinémathèque de la Ville de Paris in 1926. Similarly, the basis of her theories of pure cinema, on what she terms "la matière-vie elle-même" (the material of life itself), and her inclusion of figures, such as scientific filmmaker Dr. Jean Comandon, in her 1927 journal *Schémas*, dedicated to the question of pure cinema, also attest to her long-held interest in the nonfiction form. See GD, "Du Sentiment à la ligne."

32. Cauvin, "Le IIe Congrès international du cinéma indépendant"; Borde, "À propos du 2e Congrès."

33. Borde, "À propos du 2e Congrès."

34. According to the Raymond Borde interview, Dulac commissioned debutant filmmaker Pierre Billon to make a feature titled *Route nationale no. 13*, with Storck as his assistant, although Billon's first film at Gaumont appears to be the low-budget feature *Bombance* (1930). Borde, "À propos du 2e Congrès," 146; "Réunions du Comité de production," December 22, 1930, January 19, 1931, and May 6, 1931, FGD 892; Following the Brussels congress, Dulac also arranged for Jean Grémillon to shoot the films *Attendre* and *Daïnah la métisse* at Gaumont's facilities in Nice, although his contract was later terminated by Gaumont owing to "difficulties" with the filmmaker. The idea of a super-production directed by Pabst was also raised. "Réunions du Comité de production. Ordres du jour et procès verbaux. Affaire GD/GFFA," January 19, 1931, 1, FGD 892. Dulac also organized the production and distribution of a series of "six sound documentaries by [scientific filmmaker] Jean Painlevé." See "Réunions du comité de production. Ordres du jour et procès verbaux. Affaire GD/GFFA," February 17, 1931, FGD 892.

35. Gaumont's November 1930 production program lists twenty features of 2,000 meters and twenty shorts of 900–1,200 meters in length, as well as ten shorts for the "Journal Vivant." "Troisième Comité de Production, 21 Novembre 1930, Programme de Production pour 1931–1932," FGD 892, 1. On Vigo and Grémillon, see also Salles-Gomés, *Jean Vigo*, 103.

36. Vigo, "Jean Vigo et *Les Amis du cinéma de Nice*," 43.

37. GD, "La Nouvelle Évolution,"139.

38. The question of how to complete the program of the "Journal vivant," ordinarily composed of short advertising films, was addressed at the January 19 meeting. Vigo's film, known today as *Taris, la natation*, was the first in the new series of documentary shorts on famous sports figures. A short film on tennis champion Henri Cochet was among the projects planned. "Réunions du Comité de production," January 19, 1931, FGD 892, 1; Buache, Beretta, and Vercelottim, "Hommage à Jean Vigo." See also Buache, "Le Cinéma indépendant et d'avant-garde à la fin du muet."

39. See also T. Williams, "Pour une femme moderne et un nouveau cinéma."

40. In a memo, Dulac stated her intention "to frame the technical information that should be given to the public through varied and fantastical images." According to her synopsis, when the curtains open, swirling letters appear on the screen and come together to form a phrase welcoming the public to the "New Gaumont-Palace." Next a luminous letter G detaches; a woman is seated on the transversal bar of the letter G; two rows of "boys" form a huddle; and finally one breaks away and lowers the woman, who then comes to the fore, and speaks to the public. GD to Mr. Costil, memo April 20, 1931, FGD 528. *La Fée du logis*, documentary on Gaumont Palace, synopsis, FGD 520.

41. *La Fée du logis*, documentary on Gaumont-Palace, synopsis, FGD 520.

42. Paul Kastor (Service Edition Films, GFFA) to GD, memo June 22, 1931, FGD 529.

43. Magda Contino, portraying Dulac as an indomitable and tireless film journalist, transformed the habitual term "chasseur d'image" (image-hunter) to the feminine "chasseresse d'images" (image-huntress). Magda Contino, "Germaine Dulac, metteur en scène et chasseresse d'images," December 11, 1936, BNF-ASP, Coll. Auguste Rondel, RK 391 (GD), 36.

44. "Caméréclair 300m."

45. Whether circumnavigating regulatory barriers to capture images of the notorious criminal Gorguloff, or following the Tour de France bus, for Dulac the subject matter determined the path of the films.

46. "Une Heureuse Initiative. Le cinéma journalistique."

47. "En Suivant le 'Tour de France.'" *Excelsior*, July 15, 1932, FGD 4360.

48. E.T., "A Côté de la caravane."

49. Gid, "En Suivant le 'Tour de France' cycliste."

50. GD, "Les Difficultés du journalisme cinématographique."

51. Huret, *Ciné actualités*.

52. *Le Port de Strasbourg* (1934), a documentary on the largest river port in eastern France, was appreciated for its artistic qualities, as well as for its pedagogical interest for both specialized and general audiences. "Un Film documentaire remarquable. 'Le Port de Strasbourg,'" *Derniers Nouvelles de Strasbourg*, March 24, 1934, in "Notes from GD to Georges Colson," FGD 903. See also Oberling (director of GFFA) to GD, praising Dulac's realization, March 27, 1934, "Notes from GD to Georges Colson," FGD 903. According to the press of the period, Dulac also planned to make educational

and teaching films. *Agences d'informations cinégraphiques*, September 22, 1932. "France-Actualités-Gaumont," *La Métropole* (Anvers, Belgium), October 2, 1932; *Le Cinéopse*, October 1932.

53. GD to Georges Colson (France-Actualités administrator), May 9, 1934, FGD 903, 1. Parguel shot several of Dulac's films, notably *La Fête espagnole*, *La Mort du soleil*, and *La Folie des vaillants*.

54. Huret, *Ciné actualités*. See also Huret, *Les Actualités Filmées françaises*.

55. See, for example, Vincent Pinel, *Louis Lumière inventeur et cinéaste*.

56. Vertov, *Kino-Eye*.

57. Dubouy, "Actualités."

58. Georges Blond, "Les Actualités. Rentrée" (ca. 1932), FGD 4360.

59. Contino, "Germaine Dulac," 36.

60. GD, "L'Action de l'avant-garde cinématographique."

61. GD, "Le Sens du cinéma," 162.

62. Dulac develops this idea in her "abstract" films of 1929, as well as in her articles: "Du Sentiment à la ligne," 3–4, and "L'Action de l'avant-garde cinématographique," 157.

63. GD, "Le Sens du cinéma," 161.

64. GD, "Les Procédés expressifs,"37.

65. GD, "La Nouvelle Évolution," 138.

66. In ibid., she states, "The image [. . .] is, itself, expression, stronger than the word since it is more suggestive, knowing how to penetrate beyond itself, in the domain of the unexpressed."

67. This statement also echoes Vertov's conception of "kino-glaz" (ciné-oeil or kino-eye), expressed in his article "The Birth of the Kino-Eye" (1924). In Sadoul, *Dziga Vertov*, 40–41, 160. It is difficult to imagine that Dulac was not aware of Vertov's work, particularly in her proximity to Jean Vigo, who collaborated with Vertov's brother Boris Kauffmann on *A propos de Nice* (1930). Curiously, Dulac never mentions him. She may have seen his newsreel film *Kino-Pravda*, no. 22 (originally titled "Lenin vie dans le Coeur du paysan," 1925), presented as "Histoire d'une bouchée de pain" at Exposition des arts décoratifs (1925), as well as his film *L'Onziéme Heure*, presented at the 2nd CICI (Brussels, 1930), both of which she attended. Titles listed in Sadoul, *Dziga Vertov*, 160.

68. GD, "Le Sens du cinéma," 162.

69. This ideal can also be found in Vertov's 1922 writings on "Kino-Pravda." Vertov, *Kino-Eye*, 11.

70. GD, "Nos Bonnes Volontés," 152.

71. GD, "Théorie et pratique," December 7, 1925, FGD 1312.

72. GD, "Le Cinéma d'avant-garde," 186.

73. In "Le Sens du cinéma," a study for the Committee of Arts and Letters of the League of Nations, published in the *Revue Internationale du Cinéma Éducateur* (December 1931), Dulac wrote "The Cinema, by recording a truth, demonstrates it" (164).

74. GD, "Les Actualités."

75. See "École technique de photographie et de cinématographie," FGD 1235–46. See "Notes ms de GD, dont: 'Rue de Vaugirard 1942," FGD 1246. Dulac also lectured on the need to protect them. "De l'Utilité des Écoles Cinématographique au point de vue international et national et de leur protection," FGD 1275.

76. GD, "La Portée éducative," 204.

77. GD, "Une Opinion."

78. GD to George Colson (handwritten note), [April 24, 1934], FGD 903, 3.

79. In this regard Dulac might be seen to anticipate the cinéma-vérité trend in filmmaking, and more specifically direct cinema, with its emphasis on improvisation and the minimization of authorial intervention. See T. Williams, "Germaine Dulac and the French Film Industry."

80. See "Paris. La semaine du 6 février (newsreels)," February 23, 1934, and March 2, 1934, Cinémathèque Gaumont, Actualités, 3408GJ 00004; "Chamonix. Autour de l'affaire Stavisky (newsreel)," March 30, 1934; Cinémathèque Gaumont, 3413GJ 00009; "Cinéma d'animation et histoire. À propos des émeutes du 6 février 1934," April 13, 1934, Cinémathèque Gaumont, 3416GJ 00009.

81. Dulac supervised several newsreels on the assassination of Counselor Prince. Titles included "France. À propos de la mort mystérieuse du Conseilleur Prince (newsreel)," March 2, 1934, Cinémathèque Gaumont, 3409GJ 00006; "Paris-Vie Judiciaire. À propos de la mort du Conseilleur Prince, les rouages d'une enquête," which may have been a variation on the first title; "Liste de bandes d'actualités de France-Actualités," March 2 and 30, 1934, FGD 925. Of the third and most incriminating newsreel projected in Dijon from April 13–20, only a brief extract remains. "Dijon. Enquêtes et contre-enquêtes," April 13, 1934, Cinémathèque Gaumont, 3416GJ 00008. See also "Minutes du procès," March 9, 1935, FGD 920, and "Notes relatives au procès," n.d., FGD 926.

82. Dulac noted having located several news articles that were not submitted to the same restrictions as the newsreel. She referred to articles from *Excelsior*, *Le Petit Parisien* and notably one from the right-wing journal *l'Action française*, which called into question Dr. Pfeiffer's character, namely his habitual gambling, and that he left Dijon the night after the assassination. GD to Mr. Demangeot (director of *Lit Tout*), April 4, 1935, FGD 922.

83. GD to Paul Guichard, March 15, 1935, FGD 922. Paul Guichard, who had begun as a newsreel cameraman during World War I, had shot the majority of Dulac's films since 1927, including *La Coquille et le clergyman* (1927), *L'Invitation au voyage* (1927), *La Princesse Mandane* (1928), and several of her "illustrated records" (1930).

84. See "Paris. Interview de M. Charles Delac. La liberté de la presse filmée menacée (newsreel)," May 17, 1935, Cinémathèque Gaumont, 3520GJ 00016. Dulac had known the president of the French film syndicate, since her first productions for Film d'art, where Delac was a producer in the late teens and early 1920s.

85. See GD, "Pour ou contre la Censure des films"; GD, "Les Actualités."

86. GD, "Une Opinion."

87. Dulac's approach to the use of footage of Hitler differs from that of her contemporary Leni Riefenstahl's notorious *Triumph of the Will* (1936). While both filmmakers

use the argument of inclusiveness, Riefenstahl's coverage of the Nazi congresses is an organized mise-en-scène that centers on and glorifies Hitler's nationalism. In contrast, Dulac offset such footage with that of other international leaders and social realities, and situated it within a structure that recalled the horrors of World War I, an approach that was linked to her international pacifist efforts.

88. GD, "Une Opinion," 213. Dulac commented on this letter, forwarded by Paz, in an article a few weeks later. GD, "Considérations sur l'actualité cinématographique."

89. GD, "La Nouvelle Évolution," 138.

90. Guillon, "Germaine Dulac et le cinéma actuel."

91. Blond, "Les Actualités."

92. GD, "La Portée éducative," 205.

93. "Pour la Paix le désarmement morale"; "Le Désarmement moral par les femmes."

94. Société des nations Comité international de cooperation intellectuelle (SDN-CICI): meeting agenda (Geneva), March 22, 1937, FGD 990; meeting invitation, Geneva, May 7, 1937, FGD 990.

95. SDN-CICI, Annex, no. 2, July 2–3, 1937, FGD 990. According to the League of Nations report, Dulac studied the question of newsreels in particular. SDN-CICI, meeting invitation.

96. GD, "La Question des actualités" (lecture), n.d., FGD 1129, 4.

97. Reynolds, introduction, 12. See also chapter 12, "Cinema in the Service of History: The Newsreel," and chapter 13, "L'Art du cinéma international et national et son rôle sociale et éducatif," in GD, "Projet de livre sur le cinéma," FGD 1371.

98. GD, "L'Action de l'avant-garde cinématographique," 58.

99. Cited by Reynolds, introduction, 12.

100. GD, "De l'Utilité des écoles cinématographiques," 197–98. A modified version of this text was presented at the Semaine du cinéma français in April 1929, and at the Journée de la Cinématographie Parlante on June 3, 1930, organized by the Société d'economie internationale.

101. GD, "Le Succès d'un film?," 150.

102. GD, "La Portée éducative," 204. This idea of a universal and intimate cinema echoes her conceptions of a "pure," "objective" and "expanded" cinema, as well as her view (shared with Vertov) that the camera could capture all life, from the "infinitely small" to the "infinitely large." Dulac's notion that the cinema could bring everything into one universal and objective plane, finds resonance in philosopher Gilles Deleuze's Bergson-inspired conception of cinema: that is, one which, through the "plan d'immanence" (immanent shot or plane) is able to bring all elements into an equal relation with the spectator. See Deleuze, *Cinéma*, 1:6.

103. GD, "La Portée éducative," 204.

104. Dulac may have suffered a stroke. The film, located and documented by Raymond Borde and Pierre Guibbert, has had increased circulation since the 2005 Dulac Retrospective in Paris. Borde and Guibert, "'Le Cinéma au service de l'histoire.'"

105. The film premiered on October 30, 1935, at the Cinéma-Actual, which was located at 100, rue du Faubourg St. Antoine in Paris (which coincidentally was until recently the location of the Bibliothèque du film, where Dulac's archives were first

made accessible to the public in 1996). René Celier (*Actual* Newsreel Cinemas) to GD, October 17, 1935, FGD 477.

106. Lucien Jacquelux to GD, September 16, 1935, FGD 507.

107. Dulac employed archival footage from Éclair-Journal, France-Actualités, and the Musée d'art et d'histoire (Trocadéro). GD to Mr. Moors, December 5, 1935, FGD 480.

108. GD, "La Question des actualités."

109. GD, "Le Cinéma au service de l'histoire. Découpage," FGD 452–55.

110. Ibid. René Celier to GD, June 25, 1935, FGD 469.

111. Despite Dulac's "inclusive" approach, it has been possible to see in this film an economically weak France in the face of a militarily strong Germany, a factor that right-wing critics of the Popular Front would later cite as the cause of France's defeat. Conversely, her positive representation of the early socialist-turned-fascist Mussolini as a "civilized" dictator in relation to Hitler could be interpreted as announcing her support of a fascist Vichy. We must remember, though, that this film was made in 1935, without the wisdom of hindsight. From a contemporary perspective, the position that Dulac took in *Le Cinéma au service de l'histoire* was not only one of historical unknowns and potentialities, but also one that was above all in line with her implacable pacifism and her efforts to use the cinema in the service of a better humanity. The film would eventually be banned under Vichy. Borde and Guibert, "'Le Cinéma au service de l'histoire,'" 19.

112. GD, "Variations et corrections" (handwritten), FGD 465, 2.

Chapter 6. Popular Front Activism and Vichy

1. Dolléans, *Histoire du mouvement ouvrier*, 105–6.

2. Ibid., 109.

3. The cultural exception was proposed by France but is not, of course, specific to France.

4. Mai '36, FGD 942–55; Mai '36, Statuts, FGD 942. The Mai '36 group (head office: 2, place de la Madeleine, Paris 8th arrondissement) was also linked to the Gauche révolutionnaire (Revolutionary left), through leading members such as "leftist socialist" Marceau Pivert and feminist and communist of Trotskyist sympathies, Magdeleine Paz.

5. For a comprehensive look at cultural renovation under the Popular Front, see Pascal Ory, *La Belle Illusion*.

6. Dulac teamed up with her collaborators at Gaumont, editors Marcelle Laville and Pivert's wife, Marcelle Brochet, to create a militant version of her former newsreel enterprise. This took the form of a weekly filmed journal known as *actualités sociales* (social newsreels). Marie-Anne Colson-Malleville, Dulac's companion and future documentary filmmaker, was also an active member of the group. See "Interview Mme Djemil Anik [actress]. Souvenirs sur Germaine Dulac [conducted by Musidora and Marie-Anne Colson-Malleville]," July 5, 1946, CRH 030.

7. "Rapport de Mai '36 sur la nationalisation de la société G.F.F.A.," (Mai '36 report on the nationalization of GFFA), FGD 945. Mai '36 Film Section to the Conseil des Ministres [Popular Front cabinet], November 9, 1936, FGD 948. This nationalization,

proposed by Dulac and her colleagues, was facilitated by the partial liquidation of Gaumont-Franco-Films-Aubert in 1935 and by the bankruptcy of Pathé-Natan in 1936, France's two largest film companies. The bankruptcy of these companies, both of which were ceded to the government, had contributed to the increased atomization of French film production during this period. See Créton, *Histoire économique du cinéma français*, 43.

8. Dulac had dedicated her 1927 article, which argued for a "cinéma sans entraves" (an unfettered cinema), to the former secretary of education (Jean Zay's predecessor): "To Yvon Delbos, friend of the cinema." GD, "Les Esthétiques."

9. In December 1936, it was upon Dulac's request that the finance minister set up a subcommittee for the purpose of nationalizing Gaumont. Fabien Albertin (Deputy of the Bouches-du-Rhone, French Parliamentary Assembly Finance Committee) to GD (Mai '36), December 5, 1936, FGD 952.

10. In fall 1936, Dulac led this committee, which included decorators, directors, electrical and sound engineers, editors, lab specialists, and cameramen, in drafting an ambitious renovation project. The proposal included the creation of two modern sets, the refitting of two existing sets with a complete and modern sound setup, several "fast, comfortable, powerful, and spacious cars with 18–20 horsepower engines," and the construction of a sizeable auditorium for orchestral and newsreel recordings. Minutes, Mai '36, Technical Research Subcommittee, September 12, 1936–April 19, 1937, FGD 943; minutes, Gregoire-Breteau meeting, October 28, 1936.

11. "Comité de coordination du film. Projet de film national [*La Marseillaise*]," FGD 937. Jean Renoir to GD, September 3, 1936, FGD 941. It is unclear what became of Dulac and Renoir's short film project "Anna la Bonne."

12. Coordination Committee to Jean Zay (minister of National Education), December 30, 1936, FGD 941.

13. "Projet de film national"; "Note sur le financement," FGD 940.

14. For more information on Brérault, see "Pathé-cinéma. Département des Films d'enseignement. 28 prospectus de présentation des films. Scénarios par Jean Brérault, Instituteur," FGD 589. See also Josette Ueberschlag, *Jean Brérault, l'instituteur cinéaste*, 264–65.

15. "Comité de Coordination. Procés-Verbal de la Séance du 19 avril 1937" (La Marseillaise), FGD 941. Tangui Perron cites disagreements between the members of Renoir's Ciné-Liberté group (associated with the Parti communiste française, the PCF), and the socialist militants (mostly Pivertistes), led by Dulac, who reproach the PCF for what he calls its "patriotic and populist opportunism," noting that the latter refused to be associated with a "project judged to be too nationalist." Perron, citing Christian Delage, also points to a rupture within the group over another unspecified project, noting what Dulac deems as the "impossibility of a fictionalized account of the life of Jean Jaurès" (French socialist leader assassinated at the outbreak of World War I). Perron, "Petit Aperçu pour une histoire de la SFIO et du cinéma," 27–28. See also Christian Delage, *Le Cinéma à l'époque du Front populaire*, and Pascal Ory, "De 'Ciné-Liberté à la Marseillaise,'" both cited by Perron, "Petit Aperçu pour une histoire de la SFIO et du cinéma," 26 and 28.

16. Service cinématographique de la Fédération de la Seine, *L'Almanach populaire*, 1937: 154 and 1938: 230–31.

17. Ueberschlag, *Jean Brérault*, 89, 264–65.

18. Service cinématographique de la Fédération de la Seine, *L'Almanach populaire*, 1937: 154 and 1938: 230–31. See also Perron, "Petit Aperçu pour une histoire de la SFIO et du cinéma," 27–28.

19. "Le Barrage. Projet de scénario par l'Équipe cinématographique de la fédération de la Seine," synopsis [1939], FGD 448.

20. "Statuts du Syndicat des artisans du film," May 7, 1937, FGD 970; GD, "Soyons unis."

21. GD (STPC) to Charles Delac (film producer of Vandal, Delac & Cie/Film d'art, and president of the Chambre syndicale française de la cinématographie), letter draft, "Notes manuscrits de Germaine Dulac, Conseil économique, STPC," handwritten notes of GD, Economic Council, STPC, n.d., FGD 969.

22. "Statuts du Syndicat des artisans du film," FGD 970. See also GD, "Soyons unis . . ."; T. Williams, "'Soyons unis,'" 65–67; and Vignaux, "Le Syndicat des techniciens de la production cinématographique," 68–86.

23. GD to Madame Léonetti, March 26, 1942, FGD 964, reprinted in *1895*, no. 40 (July 2003): 85–86. See also correspondence, "Comité d'organisation de l'industrie cinématographique," November 21, 1941, FGD 542.

24. Mannoni, *Histoire de la Cinémathèque française*.

25. Ibid., 91–92.

26. Catherine Hessling, Marcel Carné, Jean Dréville, Jean Painlevé, and Marc Allegret are among those present. Ibid., 91.

27. Mannoni, *Histoire de la Cinémathèque française*, 96–97.

28. Weber, *Hollow Years*, 23–25, 257–79.

29. See Paxton, *Vichy France*, 8–11.

30. Ibid., xv.

31. GD, "Le Cycle des saisons," film project, n.d., FGD 514.

32. GD, "L'Eau à Paris," film project, n.d., FGD 515.

33. See also correspondence, "Comité d'organisation de l'industrie cinématographique," November 21, 1941, FGD 542.

34. Paxton, *Vichy France*, 200.

35. GD, "France terre de légendes ou L'histoire apocryphe des provinces françaises," film project deposited at the SAF, March 22, 1941, FGD 535; "La Paysannerie française," FGD 543.

36. GD, "Les Clochers du beau pays de France," film project deposited at the SAF, August 30, 1941, n.d., FGD 512. August 1941 marks Dulac's final submission of projects to the SAF.

37. See also correspondence, "Comité d'organisation de l'industrie cinématographique [COIC]," November 21, 1941, FGD 542.

38. GD, "Le Timbre," film project, [1939], FGD 551–73.

39. GD, "Quelques causes de la défaite de la France," film project, n.d. FGD 549.

40. GD, "Le Maréchal Pétain," film project, n.d., FGD 539.

41. Ibid.

42. See March 26, 1942, letter denouncing COIC's "absolute paternalism." GD to Léonetti, FGD 964.

43. GD (Paris) to Jean Benoît-Lévy [zone libre, after 1942 zone sud], *cartes interzone*, November 19, 1940–February 18, 1941, Benoît-Lévy papers. Special thanks to Valérie Vignaux for sharing these documents. See also Vignaux, *Jean Benoit-Lévy*.

44. GD to Jean Benoît-Lévy, *carte interzone*, December 18, 1940, Benoît-Lévy papers.

45. GD, "Le Maréchal Pétain," n.d.

46. Laborie, *L'Opinion française sous Vichy*.

47. GD to Jean Benoît-Lévy, *cartes interzone*, November 19, 1940–February 18, 1941, Benoît-Lévy papers; GD to Mme Leonetti.

48. Paxton, *Vichy France*, 322–25.

49. "Ce qu'il a dit. [Ce qu'il a fait.] Déclarations du Chancelier Adolf Hitler" (What he said. [What he did.]), September 7, 1939, 5 min., 25 sec. In a filmed interview I conducted (March 2005), Léon Ben Danou, who assisted Dulac during this period (1932–39), cites her directorial role in this film. In keeping with her prior approach to nonfiction filmmaking, the film set up a contrast between Hitler's words and actions, letting the incongruities speak for themselves. The filmed interview, "La Femme derrière la caméra" (a quote from Danou) was shown at the 2005 Dulac Retrospective, Musée d'Orsay, Paris. See also his memoir: L. B. Danou, *Le Cinéma de ma mémoire*.

50. Paxton, *Vichy France*, 175.

51. GD to Jean Benoît-Lévy, *cartes interzone*, November 19, 1940–February 18, 1941, Benoît-Lévy papers. Special thanks to Dr. Ester Carla de Miro, University of Genoa, who graciously provided this information she obtained during an interview with Hans Richter. In the spring of 1942, Dulac made contact with Irène Hillel-Erlanger's son Philippe, who in his biography gives her credit for his cinephilia leading to his subsequent founding of the Cannes Film Festival. During this period, Dulac, upon returning from Vichy (and whom he describes as a masculine woman with short hair and lots of rings, walking with two canes after subsequent "attacks" caused partial paralysis), met with him at the Parc Monceau and advised him to flee the Occupied Zone. Erlanger, *La France sans étoile*, 165.

52. See notably GD, "La Portée éducative."

53. According to Alain Virmaux (who graciously communicated this information to me), a project bearing the title "Le Juif devant les juges" (The Jew on trial) appears on an SAF register as having been deposited by Dulac in 1937. The document has since been lost, however, according to the Société des auteurs et compositeurs dramatique, which searched for the project proposal. Since it does not appear in the SAF or the Dulac Archive, it is at present difficult to ascertain its precise subject and discourse. Based on its early date, it is possible that this Popular Front–era project was a reference to the ongoing defamation of gay Jewish-born film producer

and pioneer of vertical integration and French television, Bernard Natan (of Pathé-Natan, aka Pathé-Cinéma), victim of numerous defamation campaigns that led to his wrongful arrest and trial for fraud, if not of Popular Front leader Léon Blum, who Dulac had long supported. See André Rossel-Kirschen, *Pathé-Natan*.

54. Paxton, *Vichy France*, 22–24.

55. Laborie, *L'Opinion française sous Vichy*, 33–34.

56. Véray, "Abel Gance."

57. GD, "Ève Lavallière," film project deposited at the SAF, April 23, 1941, FGD 686–705.

58. Bard, *Les Garçonnes*, 21.

59. Laborie, *L'Opinion française sous Vichy*.

Conclusion

1. See, for example, Bellour and Brochier, *Dictionnaire du cinéma*, 8–9. In a preface to their work "reserved for great filmmakers," as Alain Virmaux has noted, the authors single out Dulac (due to her film *La Coquille*) as someone who will be excluded as a "profession of non-faith." While such provocation was popular during the period leading up to Mai '68 (the simmering sociopolitical movement ignited by May–June 1968 student revolts), the extent of the exclusion is still surprising: "Considering that we always saw her well situated [*en bonne place*], and that her films, albeit historical, are devilishly bad," they add parenthetically, "(Let us recall the famous dialogue between Artaud and Desnos, one great evening of a premiere of the aforementioned short film that cheerfully massacred a beautiful screenplay by Artaud: *Who is Mme Germaine Dulac? Mme Germaine Dulac is a cow.*) And then, the French avant-garde is already represented by Delluc, Epstein, Gance, and L'Herbier." With the postwar era's "cult of Artaud," the authors further refer the reader to Ado Kyrou's ungracious and highly contested account of the premiere in *Le Surréalism au cinéma* (Paris: Terrain vague, [1952], 1963), adding intensity to a position perhaps revised since. See also Alain Virmaux, *Artaud/Dulac*.

2. Scott, *Gender and the Politics of History*, 4. Such "contests about meaning," Scott writes, "involve the introduction of new oppositions, the reversal of hierarchies, the attempt to expose repressed terms, to challenge the natural status of seemingly dichotomous pairs, and to expose their interdependence and their internal instability" (7).

3. Vignaux, *Jean Benoît-Lévy. Ou le corps comme utopie*, 218. See also Foucault, *L'Archéologie du savoir*, 35.

4. Farge, *Le Goût de l'archive*.

5. GD, "La Tâche internationale de la femme française," July 15, 1907, FGD 4489, 2–3.

Bibliography

Archival Collections

Jean Benoît-Lévy papers. Private collection in the family's possession. Contains correspondence, November 1940 to February 1941 (*cartes interzone*).

Fonds Marie-Louise Bouglé. Bibliothèque historique de la Ville de Paris, Paris.

Fonds de la Commission de Recherche Historique de la Cinémathèque française, Bibliothèque du film, La Cinémathèque française, Paris. Date limits: 1943–66. Collection size: six boxes.

Fonds Louis Delluc, Bibliothèque du film, La Cinémathèque française, Paris.

Fonds Germaine Dulac (formerly fonds Marie-Anne Colson-Malleville), Bibliothèque du film, La Cinémathèque française, Paris. Subjects: 1. Germaine Dulac. Date limits: 1829–1964. Collection size: 40 Cauchard boxes, 16 binders. 2. French film production company L'Équipe, founded in 1937 by Germaine Dulac. Date limits: 1937–54. Collection size: 6 boxes.

Fonds Archives de Marguerite Durand, Bibliothèque Marguerite Durand, Paris. Subject: history of women and feminism.

Fonds Henri Fescourt, Bibliothèque du film, La Cinémathèque française, Paris. Date limits: 1912–49. Collection size: 2 boxes.

Fonds Abel Gance, Bibliothèque nationale de France, Département des arts du spectacle (BNF-ASP), Paris.

Fonds André Lebey, L'Office universitaire de recherche socialiste (OURS), Paris. 1877–1938.

Collection (Coll.) Léon Moussinac, Bibliothèque nationale de France, Département des arts du spectacle (BNF-ASP), Paris.

Collection (Coll.) Auguste Rondel, Bibliothèque nationale de France, Département des arts du spectacle (BNF-ASP), Paris.

Serge Sandberg. Papers. Subject: Studio des Victorines. Bibliothèque nationale de France, Département des arts du spectacle (BNF-ASP), Paris.

Marcel Sembat. Papers. L'Office universitaire de recherche socialiste (OURS), Paris.

Jean Vigo Papers. Private collection in the family's possession. Contains correspondence and programs.

Selected Published Works by Germaine Dulac, Annotated

BOOKS, JOURNALS, AND PAMPHLETS

Dulac, Germaine. *Bêtes humaines.* Dulac's novelization of the 1929 film directed by Kurt Bernhardt. Paris: Éditions Jules Tallandier, 1930.

———. *Écrits sur le cinéma (1919–1937).* Preface by Prosper Hillairet. Paris: Paris expérimental, 1994.

———, ed. *Schémas*, no. 1 (February 1927). Paris: Imprimateur Gutenberg, 1927. Copy of this first and sole volume is held in fonds Germaine Dulac, Bibliothèque du film, La Cinémathèque française, Paris.

Dulac, Germaine, and Albert Dulac. "Aperçu historique: De l'influence des femmes sur la langue française." Paris: n.s., 1907. Original manuscript in fonds Germaine Dulac, Bibliothèque du film, La Cinémathèque française, Paris.

ARTICLES BY GERMAINE DULAC

[pseud. Germaine Albert-Dulac]. "Anne Vila." *La Française*, January 20, 1907, 1.

"Aphorismes . . ." *Paris-Midi*, December 1, 1925. Reprinted in *Écrits sur le cinéma*, 60–61.

"À propos d'*Âme d'Artiste*." *Ciné-Miroir*, June 1, 1925. Reprinted in *Écrits sur le cinéma*, 57–59.

"Aux Amis du cinéma." *Cinémagazine*, December 19, 1924. Reprinted as "Le Mouvement créateur de l'action" in *Écrits sur le cinéma*, 46–50.

"The Avant-Garde Cinema." In Sitney, ed., *The Avant-Garde Film*, 43–48.

"Avec Mme Germaine Dulac (par Y[von] D[elbos])." *Comœdia*, November 18, 1927. Interview with French minister of education. Reprinted in *Écrits sur le cinéma*, 96.

"Avez-vous peur du cinéma? Réponse de Germaine Dulac." *Du Cinéma*, no. 1 (December 1928). Reprinted in *Écrits sur le cinéma*, 125.

"Ayons la Foi." *Le Film*, October 15, 1919. Reprinted in *Écrits sur le cinéma*, 21.

[pseud. Germaine Albert-Dulac]. "Carlotta Zambelli." *La Française*, no. 12 (January 6, 1907): 1.

"Chez D. W. Griffith." *Cinéa*, June 17, 1921. Reprinted in *Écrits sur le cinéma*, 22–25.

[pseud. Germaine Albert-Dulac]. "Colette Yver." *La Française* 2, no. 36 (June 23, 1907): 1.

"Comment je suis devenue 'metteur en scène' cinématographique." *Ève*, August 31, 1924. Reprinted in *Écrits sur le cinéma*, 42–44.

[pseud. Germaine Albert-Dulac]. "Comtesse Mathieu de Noailles." *La Française*, no. 30 (May 12, 1907): 1.

"Concessions." *Comœdia*, April 2, 1926. Reprinted in *Écrits sur le cinéma*, 69–70.

"Conférence de Madame Germaine Dulac. Faite à la séance des 'Amis du Cinéma' donnée le 7 décembre dans la Salla [*sic*] du Colisée." *Cinémagazine* 4, no. 1 (December 19, 1924). Reprinted in *Écrits sur le cinéma*, 516–18.

"Considérations sur l'actualité cinématographique." *Le Populaire*, December 19, 1936. Reprinted in *Écrits sur le cinéma*, 215–16.

"Conversation." *Hebdo-Film*, April 9, 1927. Reprinted in *Écrits sur le cinéma*, 90–93.

"Dans son cadre visuel le cinéma n'a point de limites." *Paris Nouvelles*, May 9, 1931. Reprinted in *Écrits sur le cinéma*, 146–47.

"Défense et attaque du cinéma." *Paris*, April 25, 1925. Reprinted in *Écrits sur le cinéma*, 55–56.

"De l'Utilité des écoles cinématographiques. Au point de vue international et national et de leur projection." *La Revue d'Économie Internationale*, 1933. Reprinted in *Écrits sur le cinéma*, 195–98.

"Difficultés." *Indépendance Belge*, May 1, 1926. Reprinted in *Écrits sur le cinéma*, 71–72.

"Du Sentiment à la ligne." *Germaine Dulac Présente. Schémas*, no. 1 (February 1927): 26–31. Reprinted in *Écrits sur le cinéma*, 87–89. Reprinted as "Du Sentiment à la ligne" [1927], trans. Felicity Sparrow and Claudine Nicholson, in *Film as Film: Formal Experiment in Film, 1910–1975*, ed. David Curtis and Richard Francis. London: Hayward Gallery, 1979, 128–29.

"Entretien de Germaine Dulac avec Paul Desclaux." *Mon Ciné*, no. 88 (October 25, 1923): 6–8. Reprinted in *Écrits sur le cinéma*, 27–30.

"Film parlant . . . film en couleur." *Paris-Midi*, August 17, 1928. Reprinted in *Écrits sur le cinéma*, 122.

"Films visuels et anti-visuels." *Le Rouge et le Noir*, July 1928, 31–41. Reprinted in Lherminier, ed., *L'art du cinéma*, 67–72. Reprinted in *Écrits sur le cinéma*, 115–21. Translated by Robert Lamberton as "From 'Visual and Anti-Visual films'" in Sitney, ed., *The Avant-Garde Film*, 31–35.

"Germaine Dulac et le cinéma actuel par Jacques Guillon." *Ma Revue*, September 1930. Reprinted in *Écrits sur le cinéma*, 134–36.

"Images et rythmes." *Jeudi*, November 13, 1924. Reprinted in *Écrits sur le cinéma*, 45.

"Indépendance." *La Critique Indépendante*, December 25, 1931. Reprinted in *Écrits sur le cinéma*, 154–55.

"Jouer avec les bruits." *Cinéa-Ciné pour Tous*, August 1–15, 1929. Reprinted in Lherminier, ed., *L'Art du cinéma*, 250. Reprinted in *Écrits sur le cinéma*, 128–29.

[pseud. Germaine Albert-Dulac]. "Juliette Toutain-Grün." *La Française*, no. 12 (January 27, 1907): 1.

"La Création d'un vocabulaire cinématographique." *L'Écho de Paris*, April 15, 1922. Reprinted in *Écrits sur le cinéma*, 26.

"L'Action de l'avant-garde cinématographique." *L'État moderne* 12 (December 1931): 1,057–60. Reprinted in *Ciné-Amateur*, no. 9 (January 1932). Reprinted in *Écrits sur le cinéma*, 156–59.

"*La Folie des vaillants* (fragments)." *Cinégraphie* 1 (September 15, 1927): 9–10.

"La Formule du cinéma pur est dans le documentaire." *L'Action nouvelle*, June 1932.

"*La Mort du soleil* et la naissance du film." *Cinéa*, no. 41 (February 17, 1922): 14.

"La Musique du silence." *Cinégraphie*, no. 5 (January 15, 1928): 77–78. Reprinted in *Écrits sur le cinéma*, 106–8.

"La Nouvelle Dramaturgie de la couleur." *Pour Vous*, April 16, 1936. Reprinted in *Écrits sur le cinéma*, 208–9.

"La Nouvelle Évolution." Lecture presented at the Salon d'Automne, December 3, 1930. Reprinted in *Cinégraph*, January 1931. Reprinted in *Écrits sur le cinéma*, 137–41.

"La Photographie et la cinématographie vues par Madame Germaine Dulac." *Photo-Ciné*, no. 2 (February 15, 1927): 18–19.

"La Portée éducative et sociale des actualités." *Revue Internationale du Cinéma Éducateur*, August 1934. Reprinted in *Écrits sur le cinéma*, 203–7. Published in English as "The Educational and Social Value of the Newsreel," *Educational Cinematography* (1934): 545–50.

"La Responsabilité du public." *Cinégraph*, August 1930. Reprinted in *Écrits sur le cinéma*, 132–33.

"L'Art des nuances spirituelles." *Cinéa-Ciné pour Tous*, January 1925. Reprinted in Lherminier, ed., *L'Art du cinéma*, 559–60. Reprinted as "Le cinéma, art des nuances spirituelles" in *Écrits sur le cinéma*, 51–52.

"La Situation du cinéma français." *Bordeaux-Ciné*, March 26, 1937. Bibliothèque Marguerite Durand, Paris.

"L'Avenir du ciné: une interview avec Germaine Dulac [par Paul Guiton]." *Le Petit Dauphinois*, January 6, 1927. Reprinted in *Écrits sur le cinéma*, 81–83.

"Le Cinéma, art des nuances spirituelles." *Cinéa-Ciné pour Tous* 28 (January 1, 1925): 18. Reprinted in *Écrits sur le cinéma*, 51–52.

"Le Cinéma d'actualité." *L'Étoile Belge*, August 29, 1934. Reprinted in *Écrits sur le cinéma*, 199–202.

"Le Cinéma d'avant-garde." In Fescourt, ed., *Le Cinéma des origines à nos jours*, 357–64. Reprinted in *Écrits sur le cinéma*, 182–90.

"Le Cinéma est un art nouveau. Mon opinion." *La Fronde*, September 17, 1926.

"Le Cinéma français vu par Mme Germaine Dulac." *Nouveau Siècle*, July 12, 1926. Reprinted in *Écrits sur le cinéma*, 75–78.

"Le Mouvement créateur d'action." (Lecture at the ciné-club Les amis du cinéma on December 7, 1924.) *Cinémagazine*, December 19, 1924: 49. Reprinted in *Le Rouge et le Noir*. July 1928. Reprinted in Lherminier, ed., *L'Art du cinéma*, 63–72. Reprinted in *Écrits sur le cinéma*, 46–50.

"Les Actualités ne sont pas toujours ce qu'elles devraient être." *L'Étoile Belge*, August 29, 1934. Reprinted in *Écrits sur le cinéma*, 201–202.

"Les Arts contre le cinéma." Lecture presented at the Club du Faubourg (Paris). *Hebdo-Film*, April 4, 1925. Reprinted in *Cinémagazine* 5, no. 16 (April 17, 1925).

"Les Difficultés du journalisme cinématographique." *Lyon Républicain*, May 18, 1933. Reprinted in *Écrits sur le cinéma*, 192–94.

"Le Sens du cinéma." *Revue Internationale du Cinéma Éducateur*, December 1931. Reprinted in *Écrits sur le cinéma*, 160–79. Translated as "The Meaning of Cinema," *International Review of Educational Cinematography*, December 1931, 1,089–109.

"L'Essence du cinéma. L'idée visuelle." *Les Cahiers du Mois*, no. 16 (October 17, 1925): 64–65. Reprinted in *Écrits sur le cinéma*, 62–67. Translated by Robert Lamberton as "The Essence of the Cinema: The Visual Idea" in Sitney, ed., *The Avant-Garde Film*, 36–42.

"Les Esthétiques, les entraves, la cinégraphie intégrale." In Henri Fescourt, ed., *L'Art cinématographique*, 2:29–50. Paris: Librairie Félix Alcan, 1927. Reprinted in *Écrits sur le cinéma*, 98–105. Translated by Stuart Liebman as "The Aesthetics, the Obstacles: Integral *Cinégraphie*," *Framework* 19 (1982): 6–9. Translated by Stuart Liebman as "Aesthetics, Obstacles, Integral *Cinégraphie*," in Abel, ed., *French Film Theory and Criticism*, 1:389–97.

"Les Œuvres d'avant-garde cinématographique. Leur destin devant le public et l'industrie du film." *Le Cinéma des origines à nos jours*, prefaced and edited by Henri Fescourt, 357–64. Paris: Éditions du Cygne, 1932. Reprinted in Marcel L'Herbier, *Intelligence du cinématographe*, 341–53. Paris: Corrêa, 1946.

"Les Procédés expressifs du cinématographe." Lecture given at the Musée Galliera on June 17, 1924. *Cinémagazine*, no. 27–29 (July 11, 1924). Reprinted in *Écrits sur le cinéma*, 31–41. Translated by Stuart Liebman as "The Expressive Techniques of the Cinema (1924)," in Abel, ed., *French Film Theory and Criticism*, 1:305–13.

"Le Succès d'un film ?" *Toute la Terre*, May 16, 1931. Reprinted in *Écrits sur le cinéma*, 148–50.

"Le Véritable Ésprit du septième art." *Le Soir*, April 16, 1925. Reprinted in *Écrits sur le cinéma*, 53–54.

"L'Évolution nécessaire." *Ciné-Club*, March 1931. Reprinted in *Écrits sur le cinéma*, 142–145.

"L'Œuvre cinématographique est terminée quand le spectacle commence." *Le Travailleur du Film*, January 26, 1937. Reprinted in *Écrits sur le cinéma*, 215–19.

[pseud. Germaine Albert-Dulac]. "L'Opinion féminine en Italie sur l'intervention italienne." *Excelsior*, April 14, 1915, 8.

[pseud. Germaine Albert-Dulac]. "Madame Poilpot." *La Française*, no. 32 (May 26, 1907): 1.

"Madame Serao germanophile." *La Renaissance Politique, Littéraire et Artistique*, February 9, 1915.

[pseud. Germaine Albert-Dulac]. "Madame Suzanne Desprès." *La Française* 2, no. 56 (November 17, 1907): 1.

[pseud. Germaine Albert-Dulac]. "Matinée italienne du Salon international." *La Française* 1, no. 14 (January 20, 1907): 1.

[pseud. Germaine Albert-Dulac]. "Matinée italienne du Salon international." *La Française*, June 30, 1907, 2.

"Mise-en-scène." *Le Film*, no. 87 (November 12, 1917): 7–9.

[pseud. Germaine Albert-Dulac]. "Mme Marguerite Rolland." *La Française* 1, no. 18 (February 17, 1907): 1.

"Nos Bonnes Volontés sont tendues vers le triomphe d'une idée." *La Vie Alpine*, November 1931. Reprinted in *Écrits sur le cinéma*, 151–53.

"Nos Enquêtes sur le 'film parlé.' Réponse de Mme Germaine Dulac." *Comœdia*, June 19, 1928. Reprinted in *Écrits sur le cinéma*, 114.

"Notes de Germaine Dulac." *Cinégraph*, November 24, 1929. Reprinted in *Écrits sur le cinéma*, 130.

"Opinions." *Cinégraphie*, 2 (October 15, 1927): 40.

"Où sont les interprètes?" *Le Film*, no. 133–34 (October 14, 1918): 69–70.
"Photographie-Cinégraphie." *Stéréo-Revue*, October 25, 1926. Reprinted in *Photo-ciné*, August 1927. Reprinted in *Écrits sur le cinéma*, 79–80.
"Pour ou contre la censure des films?" *Pour Vous*, May 11, 1933. Reprinted in *Écrits sur le cinéma*, 191.
"Proportions." *Cinéma*. January 1929. Reprinted in *Écrits sur le cinéma*, 128–29.
"Quelques Réflexions sur le 'cinéma pur." *Figaro-Cinéma*, July 2, 1926. Reprinted in *Écrits sur le cinéma*, 73–74.
"Quelques Réflexions sur le contingentement." *Ciné-Export Journal*, July 1928. Reprinted in *Écrits sur le cinéma*, 123–24.
"Que pensez-vous du film en couleurs? Réponse de Germaine Dulac." *Pour Vous*, May 22, 1930. Reprinted in *Écrits sur le cinéma*, 131.
"Qu'est-ce que le Cinéma?" *La Critique Indépendante*, February 12, 1932. Reprinted in *Écrits sur le cinéma*, 180–81.
[pseud. G. De l'Estang]. "Réjane!" *La Française*, December 23, 1906.
"Renaissance du film français." *Heures de Paris* (February 15, 1938).
"Réponse à l'enquête 'Le film sonore. Qu'en pensent nos réalisateurs?'" *Cinéa-Ciné pour Tous*, no. 138 (August 1, 1929): 12.
"Rythme et technique." *Filmliga*, April 11, 1928. Reprinted in *Écrits sur le cinéma*, 111–13.
"Soyons unis . . ." *Le Travailleur du Film*, November 18, 1936. Reprinted in *Écrits sur le cinéma*, 210–11.
"Sur les Films russes." *La Vie Économique des Soviets*, February 20, 1927. Reprinted in *Écrits sur le cinéma*, 84–86.
"Tout Film ressort d'une esthétique." *Comœdia*, January 15, 1926. Reprinted in *Écrits sur le cinéma*, 68.
"Trois Rencontres avec Loïe Fuller." *Bulletin de l'Union des Artistes*, no. 30 (February 1928). Reprinted in *Écrits sur le cinéma*, 109–10.
"Un Article ? . . ." *Le Film*, October 16, 1919.
"Une Opinion de Germaine Dulac." *La Critique Cinématographique*, December 5, 1936. Reprinted in *Écrits sur le cinéma*, 212.
"Unissons-Nous." *Photo-Ciné*, June–July 1927. Reprinted in *Écrits sur le cinéma*, 94–95.
"Visualisation." *La Rumeur*, November 29, 1927. Reprinted in *Écrits sur le cinéma*, 97.

Other Works Cited

Abel, Richard. *French Cinema: The First Wave, 1915–1929*. Princeton, N.J.: Princeton University Press, 1984.
———. "Louis Delluc: The Critic as Cineaste." *Quarterly Review of Film Studies*, May 1976, 205–44.
———, ed. *French Film Theory and Criticism: A History/Anthology*. Vol. 1, *1907–1929*, and vol. 2, *1929–1939*. Princeton, N.J.: Princeton University Press, 1988, 1993.
A.J. "Lettre de Paris, Une œuvre à signaler. La croisade française." *Gazette de Lausanne*, March 14, 1915.

Aladin, "La Lampe merveilleuse. Chronique du cinéma. Au C.A.S.A." *L'Avenir*, April 20, 1921.

"À la Société des auteurs de films." *Le Cinéopse*, February 1, 1923.

Albera, François. "Germaine Dulac et 'l'essor définitive de l'avant-garde.'" In T. Williams, ed., "Germaine Dulac, au-delà des impressions," 75–91.

Amad, Paula. *Counter-Archive: Film, the Everyday, and Albert Kahn's "Archives de la Planète."* New York: Columbia University Press, 2010.

Amiel, Denys, and André Obey. *La Souriante Madame Beudet*. Supplement to *La Revue Hebdomadaire*. Paris: Librairie Stock, [August 5,] 1922.

Amunategui, Francisco. "Les Écrans. *L'Invitation au voyage.*" *La Revue Nouvelle* 4 (December 1927).

Arlecchino. "Madame Germaine Albert-Dulac." *La Cinématographie Française*, no. 2 (November 16, 1918).

Armatage, Kay. *The Girl from God's Country: Nell Shipman and the Silent Cinema*. Toronto: University of Toronto Press, 2003.

Artaud, Antonin. "La Coquille et le clergyman [Scénario]." *Les Œuvres complètes d'Antonin Artaud*. 4th ed. Vol. 3. Paris: Éditions Gallimard, 1978, 18–25. Translated by Victor Corti as "The Shell and the Clergyman," *Tulane Drama Review* 11 (fall 1966): 173–78.

"Au C.A.S.A." *Cinéa*, no. 3 (May 20, 1921): 21.

Audoin-Rouzeau, Stéphane, and Annette Becker. "Vers une histoire culturelle de la première guerre mondiale." In "La Guerre de 14–18, essai d'histoire culturelle." Special issue, *Vingtième Siècle. Revue d'Histoire* (Paris), no. 41 (January–March 1994): 5–8.

Barbier, Patrick. *La Vie quotidienne à l'opéra au temps de Rossini et de Balzac*. Paris: Hachette, 1987.

Bard, Christine. *Les Femmes dans la société française au 20e siècle*. Paris: Armand Colin, 2001.

———. *Les Filles de Marianne. Histoire des féminismes, 1914–1940*. Paris: Fayard, 1995.

———. *Les Garçonnes. Modes et fantasmes des Années Folles*. Paris: Flammarion, 1998.

Baroncelli, Jacques de. *Écrits sur le cinéma suivi de Mémoires*. Ed. Bernard Bastide. Perpignan: L'Institut Jean Vigo, 1996.

Barthes, Roland. *Mythologies*. New York: Abraham & Strauss, 1964.

Bastide, Bernard. "Jacques de Baroncelli, entre Judet et Rocambole." In Jacques de Baroncelli, *Écrits sur le cinéma suivi de mémoires*, 31. Perpignan: L'Institut Jean Vigo, 1996.

Bazin, André. *What Is Cinema?* Vol. 1. Transl. Hugh Gray. Berkeley: University of California Press, 1967. Originally published as *Qu'est-ce que le cinéma?* 4 vols. Paris: Cerf, 1958–65.

Bean, Jennifer M., and Diane Negra, eds. *A Feminist Reader in Early Cinema*. Durham, N.C.: Duke University Press, 2002.

Beaud, Claude. "Les Schneider marchands de canons (1870–1914)." *Histoire, Économie et Société* 14, no. 1 (1995): 107–31.

Beaupré, Nicolas. "Bulletin des Écrivains de 1914 à l'Association des Écrivains Combattants (AEC)." In *La Politique et la guerre. Pour comprendre le XXe Siècle européen. Hommage à Jean-Jacques Becker*, 301–15. Paris: Éditions Agnès Viénot, Noesis, 2002.

Becker, Jean-Jacques, Jay M. Winter, Gerd Krumeich, et al. *Guerres et cultures, 1914–1918*. Paris: A. Colin, 1994.

Bellanger, Claude, Jacques Godechot, Pierre Guiral, and Fernand Terrou, eds. *Histoire générale de la presse française*. Vol. 3, *De 1871 à 1940*. Paris: Presses universitaires de France, 1972.

Bellour, Raymond, and Jean-Jacques Brochier. *Dictionnaire du cinéma*. Paris: Éditions universitaires, 1966.

Bencey, André. "Germaine Albert-Dulac." *Cinémagazine* 2 (February 24, 1922): 231–35.

———. "Une Femme 'Compositeur cinégraphique.' Germaine Albert-Dulac." *Cinémagazine*, no. 8 (February 24, 1922): 232–33.

Benoit-Lévy, Edmond. "Le Droit d'auteur cinématographique." *Phono-Cine-Gazette* 62 (October 15, 1907): 365.

Bergson, Henri. *L'Évolution créatrice*. Paris: Presses Universitaires de France, 2013.

———. *Matière et mémoire: essai sur la relation du corps à l'esprit*. Paris: Presses universitaires de France, 2012.

Bernard, Anne-Marie. *L'Effort de la femme française pendant la guerre*. Melun: Imprimerie administrative, 1919.

Bernstein, Matthew, and Gaylyn Studlar, eds. *Visions of the East: Orientalism in Film*. New Brunswick, N.J.: Rutgers University Press, 1997.

Bernstein, Serge, and Odile Rudelle, eds. *Le Modèle Républicain*. Paris: Presses universitaires de France, 1992.

Borde, Raymond. "À propos du 2e Congrès international du cinéma indépendant à Bruxelles 1930. Interview de Henri Storck." In *3e Congrès International du cinéma independent*, 144–46. Lausanne: Cinémathèque Suisse, 1963.

Borde, Raymond, and Charles Perrin. *Les Offices du cinéma éducateur et la survivance du muet, 1925–1940*. Lyon: Presses universitaires de Lyon, 1992.

Borde, Raymond, and Pierre Guibbert, eds. "'Le Cinéma au service de l'histoire' (1935). Un film retrouvé de Germaine Dulac." In Special issue, *Archives* (Perpignan), no. 44/45 (November/December 1991): 1–20. Published by L'Institut de Jean Vigo-Cinémathèque de Toulouse.

Bordwell, David. "French Impressionist Cinema: Film Culture, Film Theory, and Film Style." PhD diss., University of Iowa, 1974. Reprint New York: Arno, 1980. Reprint North Stratford, N.H.: Ayers Company Publishers, 2002.

Bousquet, Henri, and Vittorio Martinelli. "La Bella Stasia." *Immagine. Note di Storia del Cinema*, no. 8 (spring–summer 1988): 5. Associazione Italiana par le Richerche di Storia del Cinema, Rome.

Braud, Maurice. "Le Mouvement ouvrier et socialiste, et les arts. Le cas de Marcel Sembat (1862–1922)." Master's thesis, École des hautes études des sciences sociales (EHESS), September 1986. A copy is conserved at L'Office universitaire de recherche socialiste (OURS) in Paris.

Buache, Freddy. "Le Cinéma indépendant et d'avant-garde à la fin du muet." Special issue, *Travelling. Documents de la Cinémathèque Suisse* 1, no. 55 (summer 1979), and nos. 56–57 (spring 1980).

Buache, Freddy, Vinicio Beretta, and Franco Vercelottim. "Hommage à Jean Vigo." *Travelling. Documents de la Cinémathèque Suisse*, no. 4 (1962).

Burch, Noël, and Jean André Fieschi. "La Première Vague." In "De la Première Vague (L'Herbier, Epstein, Dulac, Delluc) à la nouvelle garde." Special issue, *Cahiers du Cinéma*, no. 202 (June–July 1968): 20–25.

"Caméréclair 300m." *Cinématographie Française*, September 3, 1932.

Canudo, Ricciotto. "L'Art pour le septième art." *Cinéa*, no. 2 (May 13, 1921): 21.

———. *L'Usine aux images*. Ed. Jean-Paul Morel. Paris: Séguier, 1995.

Catalogue collectif des périodiques. Paris: Bibliothèque Nationale, 1973.

Cauvin, André. "Le IIe congrès international du cinéma indépendant à Bruxelles, 1930." *Travelling. Cahiers de la Cinémathèque Suisse* (Lausanne) 1, no. 55 (summer 1979): 36–38.

Choukroun, Jacques. "Le Cinéma français au temps de Jean Vigo." In "De L'Atalante à Jean Vigo," 61. Special issue, *Archives* 90–91 (March 2002). Perpignan: l'Institut Jean Vigo.

"Ciné-Club de France." *Le Tout Cinéma* (annual), 1926.

"Cinéma pur, art multiple . . ." *Cinéa-Ciné pour Tous* 68 (September 1, 1926): 9–10.

"Cinéma pur, art naissant . . ." *Cinéa-Ciné pour Tous* 71 (October 15, 1926): 9–10.

Clair, René. "Les Bons Films. *La Fête espagnole*." *Le Crapouillot*, April 1, 1920, 16.

———. "Les Films du mois. *La Souriante Madame Beudet*." *Théâtre et Comœdia Illustré* 24 (December 1923).

Colombat, A. "*L'Invitation au voyage*." *On Tourne*, November–December 1928, 10.

Conway, Kelley. *Chanteuse in the City: The Realist Singer in French Film*. Berkeley: University of California Press, 2004.

Cornwell, Regina. "Maya Deren and Germaine Dulac: Activists of the Avant-Garde." *Film Library Quarterly* 5, no. 1 (winter 1971–72): 29–38. Reprinted in Patricia Erens, ed., *Sexual Stratagems*, 185–201 (New York: Horizon Press, 1979).

Créton, Laurent. *Histoire économique du cinéma français. Production et financement, 1940–1959*. Paris: CNRS Éditions, 2004.

Danou, L. B. *Le Cinéma de ma mémoire. En hommage personnel à Germaine Dulac telle que je l'ai connue, 1932–1939*. Paris: Danou Édition, 2005.

Dauer, Dorothy W. *Richard Wagner's Art in Its Relation to Buddhist Thought*. Scripta Humanista Kentuckiensa, supplement to the *Kentucky Foreign Language Quarterly* 7 (1964): 1–35.

Dauphin, Cécile. "Les Femmes seules." In *Histoire des femmes en occident*, 4:513–35.

De Baecque, Antoine. "Les Mots de l'histoire du cinéma. Entretien avec Jacques Rancière." *Cahiers du Cinéma*, no. 496 (November 1995): 8, 49–54.

De Giorgio, Michela. "La Bonne Catholique." In *Histoire des femmes en occident*, 4:217–35.

Delage, Christian. "Le Cinéma à l'époque du Front populaire." Master's thesis, Université de Paris I, 1977.

Deleuze, Gilles. *Cinéma 1. L'Image-Mouvement.* Paris: Éditions de Minuit, 1983.

———. *Cinéma 2. L'Image-Temps.* Paris: Éditions de Minuit, 1985.

Delluc, Gilles. *Louis Delluc, 1890–1924. L'éveilleur du cinéma français au temps des années folles.* Périgueux: Pilote 24, 2002.

Delluc, Louis. "*La Fête espagnole.*" *Le Journal du Ciné-Club*, no. 16 (April 30, 1920): 11. Reprinted in Abel, ed., *French Cinema*, 314.

———. "Le Point de vue de l'auteur." *Paris-Midi*, May 4, 1920. Reprinted in *Écrits cinématographiques*, vol. 3, *Drames de cinéma, scénarios et projets de films*, 27–28 (Paris: Cinémathèque française & Éditions de l'Etoile/Cahiers du Cinéma, 1990).

———. "Notes pour moi." *Le Film*, no. 100 (February 11, 1918). Reprinted in L. Delluc, *Écrits cinématographiques*, vol. 2, *Cinéma et cie* (Paris: Cinémathèque française, 1986), 61–62.

De Miro, Ester Carla. "Germaine qui ?" In "Le cinéma en l'an 2000," ed. Dominique Noguez. Special issue, *La Revue d'esthéthique*, no. 6 (1980): 39–50.

Desclaux, Paul. "Nos Metteurs en scène. Germaine Dulac." *Mon Ciné* 2, no. 88 (October 25, 1923): 6–8. Reprinted as "Entretien de Germaine Dulac avec Paul Desclaux," in GD, *Écrits sur le cinéma*, 27–30.

Divoire, Fernand. *Pour la Danse.* Paris: Éditions de la danse, 1935.

Dizier-Metz, Annie. *La Bibliothèque Marguerite Durand. Histoire d'une femme, mémoire des femmes.* Paris: Bibliothèque Marguerite Durand, 1992.

Dolléans, Édoaurd. *Histoire du mouvement ouvrier.* Vol. 3, *1921 à nos jours.* Paris: Armand Colin, 1953.

Dozoretz, Wendy. "Dulac versus Artaud." *Wide Angle* 3, no. 1 (1979): 46–53.

———. "Germaine Dulac: Filmmaker, Polemicist, Theoretician." PhD diss., New York University, 1982.

Dubouy, M. Y. "Actualités." *Cinématographie française*, October 1, 1932.

Dulac, Albert. *Agriculture et libre-echéange dans le Royaume-Uni, essai sur les conditions économiques de la production agricole sous un régime libre-échangiste.* Paris: L. Larose, 1903.

———. *La Formation des prix des denrées alimentaires de première nécessité.* Paris: M. Rivière, 1911.

———. *Les Fédérations d'associations rurales en Bavière.* Paris: A. Rousseau, 1907.

———. *Manuel de la vente coopérative des grains.* Versailles: Gérardin, 1906.

Duncan, Isadora. "La Danse et la nature." In *Écrits sur la danse.* Paris: Éditions du Grenier, 1927. Selections from *Der Tanz der Zukunft* (Leipzig: Eugen Diderichs, 1903).

Durand, Marguerite. "En Cinq Ans." *La Fronde*, December 15, 1902.

Dutheil de la Rochère, Anne-Elizabeth. *Les Studios de la Victorine, 1919–1929.* Paris: Association française de recherche sur l'histoire du cinéma & Cinémathèque de Nice, 1998.

Eisenstein, Sergei. *Film Form: Essays in Film Theory.* Ed. and transl. Jay Leyda. San Diego: Harcourt Brace Jovanovich, 1949.

Eksteins, Modris. *Rites of Spring: The Great War and the Birth of the Modern Age.* Boston: Mariner Books, 2000.

Epstein, Jean. *Écrits sur le cinéma. 1921–1953.* Vol. 2, *1946–1953*. Paris: Seghers, 1975.

———. "Naissance d'un langage" [1948]. In *Écrits sur le cinéma*, 2:59–70.

Erlanger, Philippe. *La France sans étoile. Souvenirs de l'avant-guerre et du temps de l'occupation.* Paris: Plon, 1974.

E.T. "À Côté de la caravane." *L'Intransigéant*, July 7, 1932.

Exposition des primitifs français au palais du Louvre (Pavillon de Marsan) et à la BN du 12 avril au 14 juillet (catalog). Paris: Palais du Louvre and Bibliothèque nationale, 1904.

Farge, Arlette. *Le Goût de l'archive.* Paris: Éditions du Seuil, 1989.

Ferenczi, T[homas]. *L'Invention du journalisme en France. Naissance de la presse moderne à la fin du XIXe siècle.* Paris: Plon, 1993.

Ferro, Marc. "Cultural Life in France, 1914–1918." In Aviel Roshwald and Richard Stites, eds., *European Culture in the Great War: The Arts, Entertainment, and Propaganda, 1914–1918*, 295–307. Cambridge: Cambridge University Press, 1999.

Fescourt, Henri. *La Foi et les montagnes, ou le septième art au passé.* Paris: Paul Montel, 1959. Reprinted Paris: Éditions d'aujourd'hui, 1979.

———. *Le Cinéma des origines à nos jours.* Paris: Éditions de Cygne, 1932.

Fescourt, Henri, and Jean-Louis Bouquet. *L'Idée et l'écran. Opinions sur le cinéma.* Vol. 1. Paris: G. Haberschill and A. Sergent, 1925.

Flitterman, Sandy. "Heart of the Avant-Garde: Some Biographical Notes on Germaine Dulac." *Women and Film* 1, no. 5–6 (1974): 58–61.

———. "Montage/Discourse: Germaine Dulac's *The Smiling Madame Beudet*." *Wide Angle* 4, no. 3 (1980): 54–59.

———. "Women, Representation and Cinematic Discourse: The Example of French Cinema." PhD diss., University of California at Berkeley, 1982.

Flitterman-Lewis, Sandy. "Entretien avec Sandy Flitterman-Lewis." In T. Williams, ed., "Germaine Dulac, au-delà des impressions," 233–38.

———. "Germaine Dulac (1882–1942)." *Anthologie du cinéma* 4, no. 42 (January 1968): 1–48. Paris: L'Avant-Scène and C.I.B., 1968.

———. "The Image and the Spark: Dulac and Artaud Reviewed." In Rudolf E. Kuenzli, ed., *Dada and Surrealist Film*, 110–27. Cambridge, Mass.: MIT Press, 1996.

———. "Poetry of the Unconscious: Circuits of Desire in Two Films by Germaine Dulac: *The Smiling Madame Beudet* (1923) and *The Seashell and the Clergyman* (1927)." In Susan Hayward and Ginette Vincendeau, eds., *French Cinema: Texts and Contexts*, 7–23. London: Methuen, 1987.

———. *To Desire Differently: Feminism and the French Cinema.* Urbana: University of Illinois Press, 1990. 2nd (exp.) ed., New York: Columbia University Press, 1996.

Ford, Charles. *Femmes Cinéastes ou le triomphe de la volonté.* Paris: Denoël, 1972.

Foucault, Michel. *L'Archéologie du savoir.* Paris: Gallimard, 1969.

Francis, Ève. *Les Temps héroïques. Théâtre, cinéma.* Paris: Denoël, 1949.

G., J.-L. "Des Deux Cotés de l'écran." *Excelsior*, February 17, 1922, 6.

Gaumont, Léon. "Sur la crise du cinématographe en France." *Le Courrier cinématographique* 7, no. 10 (March 17, 1917): 4.

Gauthier, Christophe. *La Passion du cinéma. Cinéphiles, ciné-clubs et salles spécialisées à Paris de 1920 à 1929*. Paris: Association française de recherche sur l'histoire du cinéma, 1999.

"Germaine Dulac." *Cinéa-Ciné pour Tous* 41 (July 15, 1925): 10–11.

"Germaine Dulac. Conférencière." *Cinemagazine*, no. 11 (March 15, 1929): 454.

Ghali, Noureddine. *L'Avant-Garde Cinématographique en France dans les années vingt. Idées, conceptions, théories*. Paris: Paris expérimental, 1995.

Gid, Raymond. "En Suivant le tour de France cycliste." *Le Miroir du Monde*, July 16, 1932, 102.

Grétillat, Jacques. "Le cinéma français." *Le Film* 5, no. 130 (September 9, 1918): 10.

Guesde, Jules. *La Femme et la société bourgeoise*. Paris: Librairie de l'humanité, 1923.

Guido, Laurent. *"L'Âge du rythme." Cinéma, musicalité et culture du corps dans les théories françaises des années 1910–1930*. Lausanne: Payot Lausanne, 2007.

———. "Vers Une 'Symphonie visuelle d'images rythmées.' Germaine Dulac et les théories françaises du rythme." In T. Williams, ed., "Germaine Dulac, au-delà des impressions," 107–24.

Guido, Laurent, and Gianni Haver, eds. *Images de la femme sportive aux XIXe et XXe siècles*. Lausanne: Georg éditeur, 2003.

———. *La Mise en scène du corps sportif. De la Belle Époque à l'âge des extremes/ Spotlighting the Sporting Body: From the Belle Époque to the Age of Extremes*. (Lausanne: Musée Olympique, 2003): 22. Bilingual ed.

Guillon, Jacques. "Germaine Dulac et le cinéma actuel." Interview. *Ma Revue*, September 1930. Reprinted in GD, *Écrits sur le cinéma*, 134–36.

Guiton, Paul. "L'Avenir du ciné une interview avec Germaine Dulac." *Le Petit Dauphinois*, January 6, 1927. Reprinted in GD, *Écrits sur le cinéma*, 81–83.

Gunning, Tom. "Light, Motion, Cinema!: The Heritage of Loïe Fuller and Germaine Dulac." *Framework: The Journal of Cinema and Media* 46, no. 1 (2013): 8.

Habaru, Augustin. *Le Creusot, terre féodale, schneider et les marchands de canons*. Paris: L'Eglantine, 1934.

Hayward, Susan. *French Film: Texts and Contexts*. London: Routledge, 2000.

———. *French National Cinema*. London: Routledge, [1993], 2005.

Henry, Pierre. "Les Étoiles d'aujourd'hui. Stasia Napierkowska." *Cinéa-Ciné pour Tous*, no. 49 (November 15, 1925): 19–20.

Heu, Pascal Manuel. *"Le Temps" du cinéma. Émile Vuillermoz, père de la critique cinématographique, 1910–1930*. Paris: l'Harmattan, 2003.

Higonnet, Anne. "Apparences, loisirs, subsistance." In *Histoire des femmes en occident*, 4:249–74.

———. "Femmes, images et représentations." In *Histoire des femmes en occident*, 5:457–508.

Hillel-Erlanger, Irène. *Voyages en kaléidoscope*. 1920; reprinted Paris: Allia, 1996.

Histoire des femmes en occident. Vol. 4, *Le XIXe siècle*, ed. Geneviève Fraisse and Michelle Perrot. Paris: Plon, 1991.

Histoire des femmes en occident. Vol. 5, *Le XXe siècle*, ed. Françoise Thébaud. Paris: Académique Perrin Éditions, 2002.

Huret, Marcel. *Ciné actualités. Histoire de la presse filmée, 1895–1980.* Paris: Henri Veyrier (coll. Cinéma), 1984.

———. *Les Actualités Filmées françaises.* 16th conference of the Institut Jean-Vigo, "Cinéma et histoire, histoire du cinéma," Perpignan, December 1995. *Les Cahiers de la cinémathèque*, no. 66, Institut Jean-Vigo, 1997.

Jarville, Robert de. "Dans les Studios. Comment travaille Mme Germaine Dulac." *Le Courrier Cinématographique*, January 31, 1924, 9.

———. "Les Arts contre le cinéma. Conférence par Mme Germaine Dulac." *Cinémagazine* 5 (April 17, 1925): 112–14.

Jeanne, René. *Cinéma 1900.* Paris: Flammarion, 1965.

Jeanne, René, and Charles Ford. *Histoire encyclopédique du cinéma.* Paris: Robert Laffont, 1947.

Käppeli, Anne-Marie. "Scènes féministes." In *Histoire des femmes en occident*, 4:603–6.

Keller, Sarah, and Jason N. Paul, eds. *Jean Epstein: Critical Essays and New Translations.* Amsterdam: Amsterdam University Press, 2012.

Khanine, Anne-Françoise. "Marguerite Durand. Une pionnière du féminisme et du journalisme du début du siècle." *Lunes*, no. 1 (1997): 46.

Klein, Gabriele. "La Construction du féminin et du masculin dans la danse des modernes." In *Histoires de corps, à propos de la formation du danseur*, 186–87. Paris: Cité de la musique, 1998.

Kohler, Arnold. Untitled article on the Sarraz Congress, the first international conference of independent filmmakers, CICI. *La Suisse* (Geneva). September 3, 1929. Reprinted in *Travelling. Cahiers de la Cinémathèque Suisse*, no. 55 (summer 1979): 8.

Kuenzli, Rudolf. "*La Coquille et le clergyman*. De la critique du narcissisme surréaliste au cinéma comme symphonie des rythmes." In T. Williams, ed. "Germaine Dulac, au-delà des impressions," 139–50.

Kyrou, Ado. *Le Surréalism au cinéma*, Paris: Terrain Vague, (1952), 1963.

Laborie, Pierre. *L'Opinion française sous Vichy. Les Français et la crise d'identité nationale, 1936–1944.* Paris: Éditions du Seuil, 1990.

"La Fête espagnole." *Le Journal du Ciné-Club*, no. 16 (April 30, 1920): 11.

"La Naissance d'un sixième art—essai sur le cinématographe." *Les Entretiens idéalistes* 10, no. 61 (October 25, 1911): 169–79.

Landry, Lionel. "La Mort du soleil." *Cinéa*, no. 36 (January 13, 1922): 15.

"La Nouvelle Production française." *Cinéma*, July/August 1931.

Lapierre, Marcel. *Les cent visages du cinéma.* Paris: Grasset, 1948.

Lazareff, Pierre. "Madame Germaine Dulac n'aimait pas le cinéma!" *Cinémonde*, May 30, 1929, 554.

"Le Courrier en Allemagne. Artistes français en Allemagne." *Le Courier*, June 17, 1922.

"Le Désarmement moral par les femmes." *Le Quotidien*, October 21, 1925.

"Les Auteurs des films et la censure." *Le Petit Niçois*, November 21, 1923.

Lherminier, Pierre, ed. *L'Art du cinéma.* Paris: Pierre Seghers, 1960.

Li, Dzeh-Djen. *La Presse féministe en France, 1869–1914.* Paris: Rodstein, 1934.

"Lois Weber's Rival." Photoplay, February 1921.

"Los Angeles à Nice." *Le Petit Niçois*, August 4, 1924.

"Los Angeles à Nice. Napoléon et le Maréchal Pétain." *Le Petit Niçois*, December 16, 1922.

Mannoni, Laurent. *Histoire de la Cinémathèque française*. Paris: Gallimard, 2006.

Mantzius, Karl. *Molière. Les théâtres, le public et les comédiens de son temps*. Paris: Armand Colin, 1908.

"Marcel Sembat 'Les Cahiers noirs' 4éme partie. 1911–1915." Special issue, *Cahier et revue de l'OURS* (Paris), no. 157 (January 1985). Journal conserved at L'Office universitaire de recherche socialiste (OURS) in Paris.

Maugue, Annelise. *L'Identité masculine en crise au tournant du siècle*. Paris: Rivage, 1987.

Mayeur, Françoise. "L'Éducation des filles. Le modèle laïque." In Fraisse, *Histoire des femmes*, 4:231–48.

Miller, Henry. *Letters to Emil*. Ed. George Wickes. New York: New Directions, 1989.

Misme, Jane. "Journal 'La Française.'" *La Française* 1, no. 26 (April 14, 1907): 4.

———. "La Création de la française." *La Française*, October 21, 1906, 1.

Mitry, Jean. *Histoire du cinéma*. Vol. 2, *1915–1923*. Paris: Éditions universitaires, 1969.

———. *Histoire du cinéma*. Vol. 3, *1923–1930*. Paris: Éditions universitaires, 1973.

"Mme Matilde Serao est germanophile." *La France* [review], February 15, 1915.

Moussinac, Léon. "La Mode et le costume des femmes au cinéma." *Cinémagazine*, no. 3 (February 4–10, 1921): 15–16.

———. "Le Cinéma. *La Souriante Madame Beudet*." *Le Crapouillot*, July 16, 1923, 15–16.

Musser, Charles. "The Clash between Theater and Film: Germaine Dulac, André Bazin and *La Souriante Madame Beudet*." *New Review of Film and Television Studies* 5, no. 2 (2007): 111–34.

Napierkowska, Stacia (pseud.). "Mes Souvenirs par Stacia Napierkowska." *Ciné-Miroir* 2, no. 25 (May 1, 1923): 141.

"Nos Metteurs en scène. Germaine Dulac." *Mon Ciné*, no. 88 (October 25, 1923): 6.

"Notices explicatives. *Les Sœurs ennemies*." *Pathé Journal* 9, no. 41 (1917): 2.

"Notre Avant-Garde aux arts décoratifs," *Cinéa-Ciné pour Tous* [réunis], no. 46 (October 1, 1925): 11–12.

"Nouvelles Protestations contre le Congrès pacifiste de la Haye." *La Française*, May 1, 1915.

Obey, André. *L'Orgue du Stade*. Paris: Gallimard, 1924.

O'Brien, Charles. *Cinema's Conversion to Sound: Technology and Film Style in France and the U.S.* Bloomington: Indiana University Press, 2005.

"Office d'utilisation des femmes." *Le Petit Comtois*, February 17, 1915.

Ory, Pascal. "De 'Cine-Liberté à la Marseillaise': espoirs et limites d'un cinéma libérté (1936–1938)." *Le Mouvement Social*, no. 91 (April–June 1975).

———. *La Belle Illusion. Culture et politique sous le signe du Front populaire, 1935–1938*. Paris: Plon, 1994.

Ozouf, Mona. *L'École, l'église et la République, 1871–1914*. Paris: Armand Colin, 1963.

"Paris Dancer Dislikes U.S." *New York Times* (Paris), April 27, 1917.

Paxton, Robert O. *Vichy France: Old Guard and New Order, 1940–1944*. New York: Columbia University Press, 1982.
Perron, Tangui. "Petit Aperçu pour une histoire de la SFIO et du cinéma." *Cahier et revue de l'OURS*, no. 211 (May–June 1993): 25–28.
Perrot, Michelle. "Sortir." In *Histoire des femmes en occident*, 4:539–74.
Pinel, Vincent. *Louis Lumière inventeur et cinéaste*. Paris: Nathan, 1994.
"Pour la Paix le désarmement morale." *L'Ère Nouvelle*, October 25, 1925.
Prochasson, Christophe, and Anne Rasmussen. *Au Nom de la patrie. Les intellectuels et la première guerre mondiale, 1910–1919*. Paris: Éditions de la découverte, 1996.
R., P. "Films Triomphe. Concours de la jeune fille la plus méritante de France. 600 mètres." *Hebdo Film*, June 10, 1922.
Rancière, Jacques. *Les Mots de l'histoire*. Paris: Éditions du Seuil, 1992.
Roberts, Mary Louise. "Copie subversive. Le journalisme féministe en France à la fin du siècle dernière." *CLIO*, no. 6 (1997): 230–47.
Ronsay, Jeanne. "Germaine Dulac." *Mon Film*, no. 127 (Christmas 1929).
Rose-Nicole. *Les Secrets de beauté de la parisienne en cent confidences*. Paris: Nilsson, 1921.
Rossel-Kirschen, André. *Pathé-Natan. La véritable histoire*. Paris: Pilote 24, 2004.
Sadoul, Georges. *Dziga Vertov*. Paris: Éd. Champs Libres, 1971.
———. *Histoire du cinéma mondial*. Paris: Flammarion, 1968.
———. *Histoire générale du cinéma*. Vol. 4, *Le Cinéma devient un art, 1909–1920* (Paris: Denoël, 1974). Vol. 5, *L'Art muet, 1919–1929* (Paris: Denoël, 1975).
———. *Le Cinéma français*. Paris: Flammarion, 1962.
———. "Souvenir d'un témoin." *Études cinématographiques* 38–89 (spring 1965): 9–28.
Said, Edward W. *Orientalism: Western Representations of the Orient*. New York: Vintage Books, 1978.
Salles-Gomés, Paolo-Emilio. *Jean Vigo*. Paris: Éditions du Seuil, 1957.
"Salon International de la Française." *La Française* 1, no. 8 (December 9, 1906): 1.
Schneidre, Dominique. *Fortune de mère*. Paris: Fayard, 2001. Biography of the author's parents, Lilian Constantini and Charles Schneider.
Scott, Joan Wallach. *Gender and the Politics of History*. Rev. ed. New York: Columbia University Press, 1999.
Service cinématographique de la Fédération de la Seine. *L'Almanach Populaire*. Paris: Section française de l'Internationale ouvrière (SFIO), 1937, 1938.
Simonelli, Jacques. "À la Lueur de l'ourse." In Hillel-Erlanger, *Voyages en kaléidoscope*, 148–99.
Simonet, Pierre, ed., *Impressions du sport*. Saverdun: L'Institut National du Sport, 2002.
Sitney, P. Adams, ed. *The Avant-Garde Film: A Reader of Theory and Criticism*. New York: New York University Press, 1978.
Sohn, Anne-Marie. "Entre Deux Guerres. Les rôles féminins en France et en Angleterre." In *Histoire des femmes en occident*, 5:165–95.

Soupault, Phillipe. "'La Fête espagnole,' par Louis Delluc." *Littérature*, no. 14 (June 1920): 52.
"Spectacles." *La Voix des Pyrenées* (Tarbes), September 4, 1932.
Stamp, Shelley. "'Exit Flapper, Enter Woman,' or Lois Weber in Jazz Age Hollywood." *Framework: The Journal of Cinema and Media* 51, no. 2 (2013).
Studlar, Gaylyn. "'Out-Salomeing Salome': Dance, the New Woman, and Fan Magazine Orientalism." In Bernstein and Studlar, eds., *Visions of the East*, 99–129.
Sullerot, Évelyne. *La Presse féminine*. Paris: Armand Colin, 1963.
Tambling, Jeremy. "The Power of Emotion: Wagner and Film." In Jeongwon Joe and Sander L. Gilman, eds., *Wagner and Cinema*, 273–93. Bloomington: Indiana University Press, 2010.
Téramond, Guy [de]. "Comment on écrit un Roman-Cinéma." *Cinémagazine*, no. 2 (January–February 1921): 13–16. Author of novelization of *Gossette* (Dulac, 1923).
Thébaud, Françoise. *La Femme au temps de la guerre de 14*. Paris: Stock, 1986.
———. "La Grande Guerre. La triomphe de la division sexuelle." In *Histoire des femmes en occident*, 5:85–144.
Trebuil, Christophe. *Un Cinéma aux mille visages. Le film à épisodes en France*. Paris: AFRHC, 2012.
Ueberschlag, Josette. *Jean Brérault, l'instituteur cinéaste. 1898–1973*. Saint-Étienne: Publications de l'Université de Saint-Étienne, 2007.
"Une Heureuse Initiative. Le cinéma journalistique." *La Liberté*, July 25, 1932.
Véray, Laurent. "Abel Gance, cinéaste à l'œuvre cicatricielle." In "Abel Gance. Nouveaux regards," ed. Laurent Véray. Special issue, *1895*, no. 31 (October 2000): 19–53.
———. "Entre héroïsation et féminisme. L'image de Suzanne Lenglen de 1920 à 1926." In Guido and Haver, eds., *Images de la femme sportive aux XIXe et XXe siècles*, 39–61.
———. *Les Films d'actualité pendant la guerre de 14–18*. Paris: AFRHC, 1995.
———. "Les Films patriotiques de Léonce Perret." In "Léonce Perret," ed. Bernard Bastide and Jean A. Gili. Special issue, *1895* (2003): 72–100.
———. "La Mise en spectacle de la guerre (1914–1918)." *Cinémathèque*, no. 16 (autumn 1999): 116–32.
Vertov, Dziga. "The Birth of the Kino-Eye" (1924). In Sadoul, *Dziga Vertov*, 40–41, 160.
———. *Kino-Eye: The Writings of Dziga Vertov*. Ed. Annette Michelson. Berkeley: University of California Press, 1984.
Viala, Alain, ed. *Le Théâtre en France des origines à nos jours*. Paris: Presses universitaires de France, 1997.
Vignaux, Valérie. *Jean Benoit-Lévy. Ou le corps comme utopie. Une histoire du cinéma éducateur dans l'entre-deux-guerres en France*. Paris: Association française de recherche sur l'histoire du cinéma (AFRHC), 2007.
———. "Les Papiers intimes de Germaine Dulac ou le corps de l'archive." In T. Williams, "Germaine Dulac, au-delà des impressions," 9–22.

———. "Le Syndicat des techniciens de la production cinématographique, section des réalisateurs." *1895*, no. 40 (July 2003): 68–86. Paris: Association française de recherche sur l'histoire du cinéma (AFRHC).

Vigo, Luce. "Jean Vigo et *Les Amis du cinéma de Nice*." In "De 'L'Atalante' à Jean Vigo." Special issue, *Archives* (Perpignan), no. 90/91 (March 2002): 43–45.

Virmaux, Alain. *Artaud/Dulac:* La Coquille et le clergyman, *essai d'élucidation sur une querelle mythique/*The Seashell and the Clergyman*: An Attempt to Shed Light on a Mythic Incident.* Bilingual ed. Transl. Tami Williams. Paris: Paris expérimental, 1999. 2nd rev. and augmented ed., transl. Dominique Virmaux and Tami Williams (Paris: Paris expérimental and Light Cone, 2009; available in DVD boxset).

Virmaux, Alain, and Odette Virmaux. *Les Surréalistes et le cinéma.* Paris: Éditions Seghers, 1976.

Vuillermoz, Émile. "La Musique des images." In Henri Fescourt, ed., *L'Art cinématographique*, 3:63. Paris: Librairie Félix Alcan, 1927.

———. "La Souriante Madame Beudet." *Le Temps*, February 2, 1923, 1.

Wahl, Lucien. "Les Grandes Figures disparues." *L'Ecran Français*, no. 1 (July 4, 1945): 15.

Waldman, Harry. *Scenes Unseen: Unreleased and Uncompleted Films from the World's Master Filmmakers, 1912–1990.* Jefferson, N.C.: McFarland, 1991.

Wall-Romana, Christophe. *Cinepoetry: Imaginary Cinemas in French Poetry.* New York: Fordham University Press, 2012.

Weber, Eugene. *The Hollow Years: France in the 1930s.* New York: W. W. Norton, 1994.

Williams, Alan. *Republic of Images: A History of French Filmmaking.* Cambridge, Mass.: Harvard University Press, 1992.

Williams, Tami. "Entretien avec Sandy Flitterman-Lewis." In T. Williams, ed., "Germaine Dulac, au-delà des impressions," 233–38.

———. "Germaine Dulac. Du figuratif à l'abstraction." In Nicole Brenez and Christian Lébrat, eds., *Jeune, dure et pure! Une histoire du cinéma expérimental en France*, 78–82. Paris: Cinémathèque française, 2001.

———. "Germaine Dulac and the French Film Industry between the Wars: Modernizing the 'News-Real.'" In Angela Kershaw and A. M. Kimyongur, eds., *Gender and Politics: Women in Europe between the Wars*, 171–89. Aldershot, England: Ashgate Press, 2007.

———. "La Naissance d'une avant-gardiste. Idées progressistes et strategies subversives dans la carrière pré-cinématographique de Germaine Dulac (1906–1913)." In T. Williams, "Germaine Dulac, au-delà des impressions," 25–45.

———. "Pour une femme moderne et un nouveau cinéma: la sport et la dance dans les films de Germaine Dulac." In Guido and Haver, eds., *Images de la femme sportive aux XIXe et XXe siècles*, 81–98.

———. "The 'Silent' Arts: Modern Pantomime and the Making of an Art Cinema in Belle Époque Paris, the Case of Georges Wague and Germaine Dulac." In André Gaudreault, Nicolas Dulac, and Santiago Hidalgo, eds., *The Blackwell Companion to Early Cinema, 1890–1914*, 99–118. Oxford: Blackwell Publishing, 2012.

———. "'Soyons unis.' Un aperçu des activités syndicales de Germaine Dulac." *1895*, no. 40 (July 2003): 65–67.
———, ed. "Germaine Dulac, au-delà des impressions." With the collaboration of Laurent Véray. Special issue of journal *1895*. Paris: AFRHC and Cineteca Bologna, 2006.
Winock, Michel. *La Belle Époque. La France de 1900 à 1914*. Paris: Perrin, 2002.
Winter, Jay. *La Première Guerre mondiale. L'éclatement d'un monde*. Paris: Sélection Reader's Digest, 1990.
Zahar, Marcel, and Daniel Burret. "Une Heure chez Mme Germaine Dulac." *Cinéa-Ciné pour Tous*, new series no. 63 (June 15, 1926): 13–14.

Index

Note: Page numbers in *italics* refer to illustrations.

Tami Williams is an assistant professor of English and Film Studies at the University of Wisconsin-Milwaukee.

Women and Film History International

A Great Big Girl Like Me: The Films of Marie Dressler *Victoria Sturtevant*

The Uncanny Gaze: The Drama of Early German Cinema *Heide Schlüpmann*

Universal Women: Filmmaking and Institutional Change in Early Hollywood *Mark Garrett Cooper*

Exporting Perilous Pauline: Pearl White and the Serial Film Craze *Edited by Marina Dahlquist*

Germaine Dulac: A Cinema of Sensations *Tami Williams*

The University of Illinois Press
is a founding member of the
Association of American University Presses.

Composed in 9.5/14 Officina Serif STD
with Officina Serif and Sans display
by Lisa Connery
at the University of Illinois Press
Designed by Copenhaver Cumpston
Manufactured by Sheridan Books, Inc.

University of Illinois Press
1325 South Oak Street
Champaign, IL 61820-6903
www.press.uillinois.edu